Pathways of Desire

The Sexual Migration of Mexican Gay Men

HÉCTOR CARRILLO

The University of Chicago Press   Chicago and London

The University of Chicago Press, Chicago 60637
The University of Chicago Press, Ltd., London
© 2017 by Héctor Carrillo
Published 2017
Printed in the United States of America

26 25 24 23 22 21 20 19 18 17   1 2 3 4 5

ISBN-13: 978-0-226-50817-7 (cloth)
ISBN-13: 978-0-226-51773-5 (paper)
ISBN-13: 978-0-226-51787-2 (e-book)
DOI: 10.7208/chicago/9780226517872.001.0001

Library of Congress Cataloging-in-Publication Data

Names: Carrillo, Héctor, author.
Title: Pathways of desire: the sexual migration of Mexican gay men /
    Héctor Carrillo.
Description: Chicago: The University of Chicago Press, 2017. | Includes
    bibliographical references and index.
Identifiers: LCCN 2017028627 | ISBN 9780226508177 (cloth: alk. paper) |
    ISBN 9780226517735 (pbk: alk. paper) | ISBN 9780226517872 (e-book)
Subjects: LCSH: Gay men—Mexico—Case studies. | Hispanic American
    gay men—Case studies. | Mexicans—Relocation—United States—Case
    studies. | Gay community—United States. | Mexico—Emigration and
    immigration—Social aspects.
Classification: LCC HQ76.2.M6 C37 2017 | DDC 306.76/62—dc23
LC record available at https://lccn.loc.gov/2017028627

♾ This paper meets the requirements of ANSI/NISO Z39.48-1992
(Permanence of Paper).

Contents

Introduction

In 2004, when I interviewed Máximo[1] (born 1964), a gay man from northern Mexico, he told me he had migrated from Hermosillo, Sonora,[2] to Los Angeles six years earlier because "I was tired of Hermosillo. And . . . ever since I was a child, I was always attracted to [American] life, to living here in the United States." But Máximo had not considered making his longtime dream a reality until he realized, as he approached the age of forty, that it was becoming unbearable for him to hide his same-sex desires and pretend to be a heterosexual man when apart from his gay circle of friends: "[I was] a handsome guy, a guy with a profession and with a good economic situation, and I was not married." He felt that his unmarried status invited gossip and "insinuations" among the non-gay people in his everyday life. For instance, his coworkers were constantly trying to find out "whether I was gay or not . . . and that was limiting to me. Given that I was openly [gay] . . . with my gay friends at parties . . . it was limiting to think that that information might reach my boss." Additionally, Máximo's family "was close by, so I had to see them all the time. I had to talk to them all the time. . . . It's not that I didn't like that, but then they would start pressuring me. They would constantly ask me, 'When are you getting married? You're already old enough.'"

Máximo did not feel entitled to tell his family that he did not plan to marry a woman, nor could he imagine revealing his homosexuality to his relatives and coworkers. And yet, in contrast to the rest of his gay friends, who still lived with their families, Máximo lived alone. For that reason, his home had become his gay friends' preferred gathering place and a local site for the enactment of gay solidarity.[3] "They had the freedom to come to my house at all hours," he said. "We had our little parties and gatherings. They came to drink, and to watch television." Any excuse was a good one for his friends to gather in his house. "'Tonight is the Miss Universe beauty contest, the Miss Mexico.' . . . We could get drunk if we wanted to."

Despite this gay life that he and his friends had crafted for themselves, Máximo had become very uncomfortable about his situation and wanted to alleviate the social pressure that burdened him. Therefore, in the mid-1990s he began to think about moving to a larger city (at that time, Hermosillo had a population of approximately 560,000).[4] "I had to leave Hermosillo," he remarked. "I had to find a way to get to a larger city.[5] Hermosillo had become too small a place for me." When his company announced opportunities for transferring to its branches in other parts of Mexico, Máximo applied right away. "They conducted some psychometric testing and skills tests to decide who would go to Monterrey, Cuernavaca, or Mexico City. . . . And for me, going to Mexico City was my ideal—[it was] the largest city in Mexico and not at all like Hermosillo." Unfortunately, Máximo was not selected for a transfer, so he decided his alternative was to migrate to the United States.

He quit his job and left for Los Angeles, entering the United States with his Mexican passport and US tourist visa. A trip that started as an exploratory visit became a longer stay. Living in Los Angeles was a friend from Máximo's elementary school days who welcomed him into her home. This friend, a lesbian, had moved to Los Angeles with her girlfriend when she was eighteen. Máximo initially paid for his expenses with his savings, which lasted him three months. Then he took a job at a coffee shop and later, aided by a gay man, obtained work as a janitor and security guard in a Presbyterian church. These jobs required much lower skills than the professional positions he had held in Mexico. Máximo also began to seek out gay life. He went to LA's gay dance clubs and, wanting to restart his sex life, visited a gay bathhouse for the first time. A Mexican gay friend who lived in San Diego had told him that such bathhouses existed in American cities. However, Máximo was fearful of AIDS, and he "wanted to have sex with someone safe." His friend advised him: "'OK, I already told you where you can go. Now the responsibility is yours. Be very careful with what you do.'"

While in the bathhouse, Máximo was selective about whom he sought out for sex. "I love Latinos," he said. "What I don't like about American *güeros* [literally 'blonds,' a euphemism for 'Whites'] is that they're very cold. . . . And I'm quite attracted to Latino beauty." Despite his stated preference, Máximo nonetheless was not attracted to all Latino types. When he discussed how he had also begun to participate in a gay online chat room, he recalled that he once noticed a man who, as he "entered" the room, indicated he lived in Los Angeles and was Latino. Máximo sent this man an instant message inquiring about his place of origin. The man responded that he was from Guatemala. Because this interaction took place during the rudimentary early stages of gay online dating and sexual encounters, photographs were not featured in online profiles, so Máximo had to imagine how this man might look. "So I thought, 'another *oaxaquita*'"—a term Máximo used disdainfully to refer to the "little Indians from Oaxaca; not just the Oaxacans but all men who look indigenous," to whom he was not attracted. He clarified that "when I say *oaxaquita*, I mean a short person, with very dark skin, slanted eyes, his hair sticking up. The classic Indian. . . . It's not discrimination." Máximo responded to this man's request by saying, "OK, nice to meet you, *bye, bye*."[6]

Based on his own racial assumptions about southern Mexicans and Central Americans, Máximo decided he would not find this man attractive. But the man persisted, and eventually Máximo agreed to meet him: "When I got to his house, he was waiting on the sidewalk. He got out of his car, I saw him, and I thought '*wow!*'" The man looked nothing like Máximo had imagined, and they became boyfriends.

Máximo was comfortable with his life in Los Angeles. But two years after moving there his circumstances changed, and he ended up relocating to San Diego, the site of my research, where he obtained a new job and joined the local gay community. His roommate in Los Angeles had asked him to move out, and the man he was dating—the same Guatemalan he had initially rejected—had disappointed him by not offering to house him temporarily. Moreover, his status as a Mexican tourist in California had changed abruptly. Up to that point, and despite his working in the United States without a work permit, Máximo had traveled freely back and forth between Mexico and California, using his passport and US visa to reenter the United States. In his own mind, he could still claim he was a tourist living in the United States—albeit one who was bending the rules by working without a permit. But his visa was about to expire, so Máximo went back to the American consulate in Hermosillo to renew it. Unfortunately, although he had held a visa for many years, the officer with whom he interacted this time "*se quiere poner los moños*" (was arrogant and arbitrary) and denied his renewal application. Incensed, Máximo asked to speak with the consul, who upon hearing his complaint simply grabbed his passport, which still had a valid visa, and canceled his visa on the spot.

No longer having the formal documentation to return to his life in Los Angeles, Máximo despaired. But it occurred to him to call his Mexican gay friend in San Diego to ask him for advice on what to do. This man offered to meet him in Tijuana and drive him to Mexicali (a large Mexican city at the border with the smaller Calexico, California), where he had some "contacts" among *coyotes*—the smugglers who help undocumented immigrants cross into the United States. The *coyotes* took one look at Máximo and said, "*A este lo pasamos caminando*" (We'll cross this one walking). By this they meant that Máximo's middle-class, professional looks appeared convincing enough for him to pretend he was an American citizen. So they brought him to the formal border-crossing point and instructed him to "look self-assured, get in the line that has that agent with the glasses, and tell him you have *American citizenship* [*spoken in English*]." Máximo was scared, but he did as he was told. He successfully reentered California in this manner.[7] Also, concerned about the prospect of crossing without papers at the US Customs and Border Protection checkpoint in San Clemente, located between San Diego and Los Angeles, he decided to stay put in San Diego. "I feel very comfortable living here," he said. "I like the freedoms . . . [the freedom] of expression. . . . You can say whatever you think. . . . You have opportunities to do things. . . . They give you opportunities to grow if you wish." Implicit in Máximo's comment was a sense that he finally found a place where he could be openly gay. "Ever since I arrived in the US, I've been open about that," he declared. "Since I arrived, always, always."

———

Máximo's story captures many of the themes of this book. *Pathways of Desire* is an investigation of the phenomenon that I call "sexual migration," which I have defined as international migration processes that are "motivated, fully or partially, by the sexuality of those who migrate."[8] In my earlier work on this topic, I characterized sexual migration as the kind of migration that results from "motivations connected to sexual desires and pleasures, the pursuit of romantic relations with foreign partners, the exploration of new self-definitions of sexual identity, the need to distance oneself from experiences of discrimination or oppression caused by sexual difference, or the search for greater sexual equality and rights."[9] However, my current analysis has helped me refine and expand my description of the components and varieties of sexual migration, as well as examine more thoroughly how sexual motivations for migration intertwine with economic and family-related motivations that are more typically considered in migration studies.

A first goal of this book is to examine the role of sexuality as an important catalyst of the transnational relocation of gay and bisexual men, especially when it involves movement from countries of the so-called global South, such as Mexico, to richer countries in the so-called global North, such as the United States.[10] My analysis takes this motivation seriously, but also scrutinizes a common assumption that such transnational movement is logical—that it makes sense that gay men would want to leave sexually oppressive places in the global South and go to the more sexually enlightened global North. This assumption ties the idea of sexual freedom to the process of transnational sexual migration—which, according to Eithne Luibhéid, can easily lead to "accounts of queer migration [that] tend to remain organized around a narrative of movement from repression to freedom, or a heroic journey undertaken in search of liberation."[11]

As Máximo's story exemplifies, the pursuit of sexual freedom is indeed central in many of my Mexican participants' narratives. Yet my goal is not to confirm or reify a simple narrative of sexual freedom that can be achieved through migration. Instead, I have sought to produce a nuanced account of the social, cultural, and political processes encapsulated in the concept of sexual freedom. My analysis contemplates a wide variety of questions about issues such as the ones suggested by Máximo's story: What is the constellation of motivations that come to be represented by the notion of sexual freedom, and how are those motivations socially generated? Why do men such as Máximo decide to leave Mexico, while many others stay and enact their same-sex desires there? What are the pathways that men such as Máximo follow from Mexico to the United States? What happens to them upon arrival? How do they access gay life in their new location? How do they change after migrating? Are they the only ones who change, or does their presence in any way impact those with whom they interact in the United States? And, ultimately, do they achieve the sexual freedom they sought and craved?

In the pages that follow, my answers to these questions emphasize the importance of attending to the whole arc of the migration experience, thereby seeing how immigrants' pre-migration origins shape later experiences post-migration. My answers also call attention to key aspects of sexual immigrants' processes of incorporation into US gay life, including the effect of perceived cultural differences between Mexican and American gay men, and the dynamics of cross-racial attraction, power, and vulnerability in relationships.

A second goal of *Pathways of Desire* is to demonstrate the importance of including sexuality as a topic or variable in migration studies. Even more so than gender, sexuality is typically absent as a social factor in mainstream sociological studies of transnational migration, including studies conducted with Mexican immigrants. As noted by other scholars before me who have sought to *queer* migration studies, this omission is problematic on a number of fronts.[12] Mexican migration usually is depicted as involving heterosexual men who migrate in search of economic opportunity (or as "a rite of passage" that provides them "an accepted means for demonstrating their worthiness, ambition, and manhood to others").[13] In the case of Mexican women and children, they are usually viewed as migrating to reunite with close relatives, parents, or spouses who preceded them in making the journey.[14] In other words, Mexican migration is assumed to be largely heteronormative.[15]

Left out of this dominant framework are not only Mexican immigrants who are not heterosexual but, more generally, those who relocate primarily for lifestyle reasons—reasons that may include the desire for greater self-determination, independence, and freedom from constraining social and cultural structures.[16] Indeed, some of the literature on Mexican immigrant women published over the past two decades, including the groundbreaking work by Pierrette Hondagneu-Sotelo, has shown that they often migrate seeking primarily to achieve greater independence from men, or imagining that the relocation will give them an opportunity to shift the dynamics of gender relations with male spouses, boyfriends, or men in general.[17] But in the case of heterosexual Mexican men, even when the work on Mexican migration and gender has suggested that some men indeed willingly pursue more egalitarian relations with women after relocating, very little is known about whether any of them migrate for lifestyle reasons. In this regard, as the anthropologist Matthew Gutmann has noted, the absence of "major studies focusing on Mexican migrants-*as-men*" is noteworthy.[18]

The problem in part is that studies of Mexican migration rarely ask participants questions about sexuality, sexual orientation, or sexuality-related motivations for migrating. And, surprisingly, even recent studies that explicitly account for the social mechanisms influencing Mexicans' decisions to migrate to the United States have not asked questions about sexuality.[19] This omission limits our understanding of diversity within Mexican immigrant populations. It also limits the potential for addressing how Mexicans' lifestyle-related motivations to migrate are shaped by imaginaries about the lives (including the sexual lives) they might be able to have in the United States, as well as how those imaginaries themselves are shaped.

A third, and related, goal of *Pathways of Desire* is to examine how, through their actions, Mexican immigrants such as those in my study disseminate (deliberately or otherwise) their own cultural understandings in transnational or global contexts—that is, to examine their role as innovators contributing their own ideas and practices as part of the processes of sexual globalization. The perspectives of Mexican gay immigrant men can help us reconsider common assumptions about the directionality of cultural globalization (and specifically sexual globalization, understood in terms of global exchanges that transport sexual beliefs and practices around the world)[20]—namely, the idea that the direction of influence always runs from the global North to the global South. Given the enormous resource disparities between countries such as the United States and Mexico, it is important to examine how, despite the many barriers those disparities create, Mexican gay men manage to assert themselves and exercise forms of individual and collective agency. But to understand such agency, we must also take into account the considerable and rapid changes related to sexuality and sexual rights that are taking place in countries of the global South such as Mexico—changes which may help Mexicans imagine the kinds of contributions they may make as they incorporate themselves into US gay life.

Finally, *Pathways of Desire* examines the practical implications of the various issues I have raised in terms of the well-being of immigrant populations, which I explore specifically in the context of my participants' sexual health. This goal is meant to demonstrate the importance of contextualizing public health strategies within the larger sociocultural forces affecting sexual behavior and the dynamics of sexual interaction.

My analysis for *Pathways of Desire* is based on an extensive ethnographic case study conducted with a large, qualitative sample of Mexican gay and bisexual men. These are men who, like Máximo, migrated from various locations throughout Mexico to the US-Mexico border region, specifically to San Diego, California, and its surrounding areas. This work builds on and also expands the scope of previous work on the sexual migration of Mexican and other Latin American gays and lesbians.[21] I am particularly indebted to Lionel Cantú for his visionary study of Mexican gay immigrants, a source of inspiration for my own research.[22] My work also benefits from Martin Manalansan's research on the sexual migration of Filipino gay men.[23] My own approach is generally consistent with these and other helpful studies of sexual migration, but it also differs in significant ways.

First, where other studies focused primarily or exclusively on the post-migration lives of gay and lesbian immigrants—which caused them generally to view such immigrants as a culturally and socially homogeneous group—I purposely designed my study to examine internal diversity, in terms of both my participants' pre-migration lives in Mexico and their post-migration lives in the United States. To facilitate this analysis, I recruited what qualitative researchers would consider to be a large sample, with the goal of achieving sufficient diversity of lived experience. My team and I were able to recruit Mexican men who moved to San Diego from a wide variety of places in Mexico, from large cities and less populous places throughout the country, within which their social class positions also varied considerably. Indeed, I believe this is the largest empirical qualitative study of sexual migration to date.

Second, by obtaining information about my immigrant participants' lives before and after migration, I also sought to systematically examine the effects on these men's sexuality of the often dramatic shifts in social contexts they experience as a result of their transnational relocation. As part of this analysis, I took into account how their pre-migration lived experiences influenced how they fared in their new location and how these affected their processes of gaining access to gay San Diego and becoming part of its community. In this respect my work problematizes a common approach in migration studies—particularly those that focus on sexual health—which involves asking immigrants exclusively about their post-migration lives, effectively treating as a black box the diversity of their lives before migration. In the absence of information about immigrants' pre-migration lives and sexual lives, researchers are often forced to operate with unexamined and even stereotypical assumptions about the cultural understandings with which those immigrants arrive in the United States. For instance, in relation to topics such as sexuality, studies of Mexican and Latina/o immigrants often presume the common-sensical notion that in their home countries they universally adopted "traditional," Catholic sexual values, and were exposed exclusively to a sexually repressive culture imagined as being frozen in time. But studies such as the present one challenge such assumptions.

Third, as part of my interest in analyzing whether and how Mexican gay immigrant men change after relocating, I sought to explore how their experiences are similar to or different from those of US Latino gay men—men who were socialized as members of an ethnic community in the United States. I therefore decided to recruit and interview US Latino gay men for comparison purposes. Furthermore, with an interest in examining the dynamics of the sexual and romantic relations in which Mexican gay immigrant men engage after migrating—which often involve sex partners considerably different from them in terms of race and class—I felt it would be prudent to analyze those dynamics from the viewpoints of both immigrant gay men and the American gay men who interact sexually and romantically with them. Thus, in addition to Mexican immigrants and US gay Latinos, I recruited a third group: American gay men of any ethnicity involved in recent sexual and romantic relations with Mexican or Latino men, including those having a particular attraction to, and predilection for dating and having sex with, Mexicans and Latinos. These various features make my present study unique in terms of its overall design, size, and scope.

A Synthetic Approach to the Study of Sexuality

While engaging with various academic specialty areas, including migration studies and racial and ethnic studies, *Pathways of Desire* is first and foremost in dialogue with an extensive and vibrant body of literature in sexuality studies. I approach the study of sexuality from sociological, anthropological, and historical perspectives as a crucial domain of everyday life that both shapes and is shaped by a host of other social institutions. Thus, to study sexuality is simultaneously to shed light on culture, power, social interaction, social inequality, globalization, social movements, science, health, morality, and public policy. At the same time, only a full understanding of the broader social contexts within which sexual practice unfolds is sufficient to make sense of the varied meanings, embodied experiences, power relationships, and personal and collective identities that take shape in relation to sexuality.

Although precursors of a sociological study of sexuality can be found even in the discipline's foundational texts, my approach essentially begins with the classic symbolic interactionist scholarship associated especially with the work of John Gagnon and William Simon. Writing in the 1970s, Gagnon and Simon broke with prevailing biologically determinist, Freudian, and Kinseyan accounts to characterize sexuality as "scripted," meaningful behavior that is firmly rooted in social and historical contexts.[24] Their emphasis on the intersubjective emergence of sexual meanings in moments of physical and emotional interaction has since been amplified by other scholarship that emphasizes both the structural determinants of sexual practice and belief and the cultural tools by which social actors make sense of themselves as sexual beings. I adopt the concept of cultural schemas—which the sociologist Mary Blair-Loy, following William Sewell, defines as the virtual aspects of social structure and as "ordered, socially constructed, and taken-for-granted framework[s] for understanding and evaluating self and society, for thinking and for acting"[25]—to identify and describe what I call *sexual schemas*.[26] This term refers to the publicly available and partially internalized understandings from which individuals draw sexual meanings.[27] Also with regard to both structural determinants and cultural tools, I am influenced by theoretical approaches that build on the work of the sociologist Pierre Bourdieu to elaborate concepts such as sexual fields and erotic capital.[28] Those concepts are helpful to understand how my participants learn about, perceive, and negotiate the rules of the game in specific sexual contexts. They also extend the reach of Gagnon and Simon's concept of sexual scripts by facilitating analysis of structural inequalities in sexual contexts, including those inequalities that may shape cross-racial sexual dynamics. In addition to the above theoretical approaches, like other sociologists of sexuality I borrow from the work of Michel Foucault—and subsequent developments in queer theory—to comprehend, in the most general terms, the constitution of sexual subjectivity in the modern West and its relation to both power and knowledge.[29]

Sociologists and other scholars in the interdisciplinary domain of sexuality studies have examined a wide range of themes that influence the stories I tell in this book: the political economy of sexuality; sexual rights and sexual citizenship; the social and legal regulation of sexuality; the spatial dimensions of sexual geographies; the globalization of sexuality; sexual culture; the race and class dimensions of sexuality; and gay and queer Latina/o studies, among others.[30] Yet ironically, sex itself—or more precisely, eroticism, passion, and the bodily experiences of what I call the sexual moment—is at risk of becoming a forgotten topic in sexuality studies. In my work, and certainly in this book, I attend closely to the embodied details of sexual practices and desires, because I see these as just as thoroughly "social" as the other topics to which social scientists attend.[31]

As a general conceptual framework for the book, I draw from the growing body of scholarly work on the topics of sexual migration and queer diaspora, as well as the scholarly literature that has attended to interactions between the global North and the global South—specifically in relation to sexual globalization and the links between colonialism and sexuality. I discuss this general conceptual framework in chapter 1.

Later, in specific chapters, I bring into my analysis other literatures, including those on the topics of sexuality and gay identities in Mexico and Latin America, Mexican migration, sexuality and space, sexual citizenship, sexual passion and eroticism, sexuality and power, and sexuality and race. For now, I turn to discussing the specifics of my study, which I called the Trayectos (Spanish for "trajectories") Study. I describe how I selected my research site, as well as the methodological choices that informed the study's design.

The Research Setting

The border zone in general is an ideal place to study queer sexual migration—indeed, in a recent analysis of US census data, Amanda Baumle observes that "a greater proportion of male same-sex partners in the border areas emigrated from Mexico than did different-sex partners," suggesting the prevalence and salience of gay sexual migration in such areas.[32] Among border cities, San Diego offered a particularly appropriate setting for my present study. Sitting at the crossroads between Mexico and the United States, San Diego not only is a major American city (at the time of my study, the seventh most populous in the United States) and the most developed along the US-Mexico border; it also lies just a few suburbs north of the border with Tijuana, the sixth-largest city in Mexico. And both San Diego and Tijuana have well-developed gay cultures. San Diego constitutes an important point of entry and place of settlement for Mexican immigrants, and is the location of the busiest border-crossing point in the world.[33] It has a visible and well-organized gay community that provides entry into US gay life for newly arrived gay immigrants. It is also a city where the presence of Mexican and Latino men is sizable, leading to much sexual and romantic intermingling between Latino gay immigrants and American men. And finally, the San Diego metropolitan area is politically diverse: the central city and the predominantly Latino southern suburb of Chula Vista vote Democratic, while the rest of the suburbs in the county are known for their conservatism.[34]

The Methods and Data

Máximo's story, like the many others appearing in the pages of this book, is part of the data collected in the Trayectos Study, a large ethnographic research project that used qualitative methods to analyze the sexual migration experiences of self-identified gay and bisexual Mexican male immigrants in San Diego, California. I directed the Trayectos Study, but it was conducted by a team that included three ethnographic interviewers besides myself (Jorge Fontdevila, Victoria González Rivera, and Jaweer Brown), a coinvestigator, support staff, academic consultants, and others who assisted with tasks such as recruiting participants and coding interview transcripts. Trayectos was funded by the National Institutes of Health and included a particular interest in the social and sexual contexts of HIV risk among the immigrant men.[35]

The most significant form of data in the Trayectos Study came from in-depth, semi-structured interviews with 150 men, the majority of whom returned for a follow-up interview a year after their initial interview (for a total of 265 interviews). The other main source of data was the participant observation that my research team and I conducted in venues where Mexican gay immigrant men socialize. These data collection activities took place between 2003 and 2005. Altogether, they yielded a database of more than twelve thousand pages of text that I have analyzed in order to write this book.

It is important to note that by emphasizing interviews, I placed the focus of my work on the analysis of narratives that individuals were led to provide about themselves—accounts produced out of intense, and sometimes quite emotional, intersubjective encounters between participants and interviewers. The fact that participants' memories of their upbringing and sexual socialization in Mexico generally lined up with the findings of the extant scholarship on Mexican sexualities gave us confidence that these retrospective accounts could be trusted; the fact that participants spoke to us in quite detailed and often graphic terms about sexual matters belied the claim made in some quarters that sexuality is an especially difficult topic to study by means of interviews; and the fact that participants were willing to divulge material that sometimes cast them in a bad light reassured us that they were not simply telling us what they thought we hoped to hear. However, interview data—like all forms of data that researchers produce or compile—have both strengths and limitations. I endorse Michèle Lamont and Ann Swidler's advocacy of "a pluralistic and pragmatic position, which reaffirms that the selection of methodological approaches should depend on the questions being pursued, to be assessed on a case by case basis."[36] As these qualitative researchers note, interviewing as a method poses distinct advantages, including the possibility of systematic "comparison across contexts, situations, and kinds of people" (something I performed with my three groups of interview participants, described below), as well as the ability to unearth "emotional dimensions of social experience that are not often evident in behavior."[37] Yet precisely because no method of social investigation is perfect, I also "triangulated" my findings from interviews with those from participant observation, the other research method that I and my team employed.

The Interview Participants

We recruited our interviewees in a wide variety of gay and non-gay venues throughout the San Diego metropolitan area, both in person by bilingual recruiters trained for this purpose and through the use of take-away cards, posters, newspaper advertisements, Internet postings, and "snowball" recruitment by those already contacted for the study. To determine their eligibility, we screened potential participants on-site or when they called a toll-free number that appeared in our promotional materials. Altogether, we screened 332 men in order to reach our goal of 150 participants.

These 150 men were divided into three distinct groups. First and most important, we sought out eighty self-identified gay and bisexual Mexican men who were migrants to the United States.[38] For Mexican men to qualify, they had to be eighteen years of age or older; have been born or raised in Mexico;[39] have migrated to the United States within the previous ten years; self-identify as gay, homosexual, bisexual, queer, or other labels denoting a non-heterosexual identity; and have had sex with men in the previous six months. Most of the men in this sample ($N = 77$) self-identified as gay or homosexual as adults (these two labels of identity are often used interchangeably in Mexico), and the remaining three thought of themselves as bisexual. Three described themselves sometimes as gay or homosexual and other times as bisexual, and another three simultaneously self-identified as gay and transgender. The study did not recruit heterosexually identified men who have sex with men, whose identities and lived experiences are considerably different from those of the self-identified gay and bisexual men in this sample.[40] However, our participants often referred to sexual encounters involving those men.

The result of our recruitment effort is perhaps the largest and most diverse ethnographic sample of Mexican gay and bisexual men to be studied to date in any context, in terms of both their geographic origin within Mexico and their social class positions. They came from fifteen of the thirty-one Mexican states plus the Federal District (Mexico City);[41] some grew up in large urban areas, others in medium-size cities, and still others in small towns or rural areas (*rancherías*); and they vary in terms of their social class position, education, and skin tone and ethnic features. Although the majority of these men were in their twenties ($N = 33$) and thirties ($N = 34$) at the time of their interviews, their ages ranged between twenty and fifty-seven years, meaning that they came of age in quite different moments within Mexico's rapidly shifting sexual cultures of the past few decades. Moreover, their exposure to different varieties of expression of same-sex desires in Mexico was furthered, in many cases, by travel or internal migration within that country. Indeed, before moving to the San Diego-Tijuana border region, about one-quarter of the eighty Mexican participants had moved from small towns or small cities to larger cities within Mexico, several for reasons directly related to their sexuality. The life circumstances of a few others took them from larger to smaller places and then back to larger ones, at each step encountering different ways in which same-sex desires were incorporated into local social life.

In addition to the eighty Mexican participants, my research team and I recruited a second group, consisting of thirty-six US-born gay and bisexual Latinos. To qualify, these men had to be eighteen years of age or older and currently residing in either San Diego County or the Tijuana area, and they had to have had sex with a man in the previous six months. As I noted earlier, the inclusion of this second group gave me the ability to determine how the experiences and perceptions of Mexican gay immigrants differ from those of US gay Latinos whose formative socialization was into ethnic communities in the United States. Also, given that some of our immigrant participants had sexual and romantic relationships with US-born Latinos, interviewing members of the latter group gave us the opportunity to explore perceptions of such relationships from the perspective of the "other side," as it were.

Finally, we recruited a third group: thirty-four gay and bisexual non-Latinos (men of any other ethnicity) living in the San Diego area who were born or raised in the United States and who had been involved in recent sexual or romantic relations with Mexican or Latino men. Interviews with these men gave us an important vantage point on cross-ethnic and cross-cultural relationships that we could juxtapose to the stories the immigrants told about their sexual and romantic experiences with men of other ethnicities.

I and the three other ethnographers (all of whom are fluent in both Spanish and English) conducted the interviews. Our interviews lasted two and a half hours on average and were conducted in the participant's preferred language. Each one consisted of an in-depth exploration of the participant's family background, sexual history, migration history, incorporation into San Diego's gay life, preferred sexual practices and types of partners, history of HIV testing and current HIV status, perceptions of HIV risk, current life and social networks, and current and past sexual or romantic relationships, among other topics. At the end of the interview, participants completed a short exit survey that we used to collect basic demographic and behavioral information.

We employed a number of methods to stay in touch with each interviewee over the subsequent year, resulting in great success in bringing back our participants for follow-up interviews after one year had passed. Overall, 115 of the original 150 participants returned to complete a follow-up interview. This second wave of interviews fulfilled several functions. In part, it allowed us to assess changes in the immigrants' lives over the course of an additional year spent living in the United States, though in practice we found fewer changes of significance than we had anticipated. But in addition, the follow-up interviews provided a rare opportunity to address inconsistencies noted in the original interviews and to raise new questions that analysis of the first wave of interviews had sparked in our minds.

Interview Data Analysis

After the digital audiotapes of the interviews were transcribed verbatim and the transcripts were spot-checked for accuracy, we summarized each interview to record its most salient points. Then a group of coders trained for this task systematically assigned a series of relevant codes to each interview using QSR N6.0, a qualitative software package.[42]

Once all interviews had been coded, we were able to use the qualitative software package to analyze the entire sample—for example, by searching for all instances of specific individual codes, or by searching for concatenations of more than one code. After identifying patterns within the coded text, we selected passages to illustrate the most relevant themes (as well as to represent variations in lived experience according to the various themes detected). However, in order to avoid a simplistic analysis of decontextualized quotes from our interviews, we then took many of the most illustrative passages and recontextualized them within the broader details of the individual cases from which the passages were drawn. In other words, we constantly moved back and forth between "narrow and deep" analyses of individual lives and "broad and shallow" analyses of patterns cutting across individuals. In addition to the coded transcripts, we created analytical summaries of each individual interview that helped us to identify the most relevant themes.

Participant Observation

I and the other three ethnographers (in various combinations) conducted more than three hundred hours of participant observation over the course of fifty-four distinct sessions at twenty-six different locations in San Diego County. Generally speaking, these locations, selected after an exhaustive mapping of venues in the area, fell into three categories: gay bars and clubs, gay-identified public events and meetings, and events held at religious or social service agencies. In our visits, we paid attention to our first impressions of the venues and clientele, key events or incidents that occurred, and anything that the patrons we spoke with perceived as significant. In our field notes, we recorded information about the setting, the people present, our specific interactions with attendees, and our interpretations and evaluations in relation to study themes. These ethnographic experiences generally corroborated the accounts of our interviewees while giving us firsthand knowledge of the places and contexts to which they referred.

Ethical Concerns

Careful consideration of research ethics was essential in a study of this kind. In the process of obtaining informed consent from our interview participants, we presented a detailed explanation of our commitment to confidentiality and the specific measures we were taking to ensure it. (These included asking participants to avoid mentioning information during the interviews that could identify them; maintaining all interview materials in locked file cabinets; obtaining signed confidentiality agreements from study personnel; obtaining a Certificate of Confidentiality from the US National Institutes of Health, which guarantees that our research records cannot be subpoenaed by a court; and erasing all identifying information from our records once the interviews had been completed.) I believe that these trust-building measures contributed to the remarkable candor that characterized our participants, who spoke freely not only about sexual matters but also about legal matters such as their immigration status.

The Plan of the Book

The organizing logic of this book is to trace what I call pathways of desire, beginning with close attention to points of origin of the migration experience and then examining the whole arc of that experience. Before delving into my empirical material, chapter 1 discusses how sexual migration has been conceptualized, as well as the theoretical gaps that the literature has left to be filled. The same chapter also explicitly links sexual migration to the topics of sexual globalization and sexual colonialism, drawing connections that I develop further over the course of my analysis and that help me formulate my conclusions.

In chapter 2, I begin my exploration of the arc of sexual migration by considering my Mexican participants' points of origin in Mexico. Drawing on their narratives about their lives there, and the recent academic literature on male-male sexualities in that country, this chapter examines the many different worlds of Mexican male same-sex desires and the different sexual schemas by which Mexican men orient themselves. My participants' experiences in Mexico not only shaped their erotic lives and social identities but also generated the pressures and aspirations that inspired them to migrate. I also review the extent of social change in Mexico in recent decades with regard to sexual matters in general and gay issues in particular, and I consider the implications for both gay lives and sexual migration. Then, in chapter 3, I scrutinize sexual migrants' particular imaginaries of gay lives elsewhere. I analyze the wide range of factors that propel some Mexican gay men to migrate to the United States while also revealing the complexities that lie beneath the stated appeal of sexual freedom and the depiction of contrasts between the United States and Mexico.

Chapters 4 and 5 track my participants' journeys to San Diego. First, in chapter 4, I consider the forms of assistance that permitted gay migrants to leave their homes in Mexico and travel to the United States. Building on the migration studies literature and the concept it calls a "culture of migration," I describe a "gay culture of migration"—the lesbian, gay, bisexual, and transgender (LGBT) social networks and social capital facilitating the cross-national movement of many of my participants. The story continues in chapter 5, which examines how my participants managed to get into the United States—the political economy of crossing. I describe three different patterns: one principally involving middle- and upper-class immigrants, one involving those lacking economic and cultural capital, and a third involving border residents.

In chapters 6 and 7, I analyze how Mexican gay migrants found their way to gay San Diego, and how—and to what extent—they acquired "sexual citizenship" within it. Chapter 6 describes the considerable variability in how my participants made their way to Hillcrest, San Diego's primary gay neighborhood, or to other places in the city and county where gay life could be found. Here the differences in sexual socialization in

Mexico, as well as differences in geography and social class background, proved highly salient: while some of my participants arrived already well informed about the nature of gay life in American cities, others found the whole idea of a gay neighborhood to be a foreign concept. Chapter 7, coauthored with Steven Epstein, further considers what it means to become a citizen of a new gay social world, especially if one is not a legal citizen of that country. We consider how immigrant gay men construct new forms of belonging in Hillcrest, and how their process of "learning the ropes" of social and sexual interaction (often with the help of those we call "cultural ambassadors") goes hand in hand with a process of learning their rights. But we also analyze the practical constraints that hem in gay migrants and keep them from a full sense of belonging.

Chapters 8, 9, and 10 all deal with the complexities of my participants' lives in San Diego, particularly their sexual and romantic lives, with attention to both the structural forces that impinge on them and the cultural patterns and schemas they adopt. These chapters emphasize the changes these men experience in new social and sexual contexts, as well as the implications of the racial dynamics they confront and the various vulnerabilities they experience. Chapter 8 begins by analyzing specific patterns of change in the sexualities of my participants—a discussion that links back directly to my description in chapter 2 of their diverse origin points within Mexican society in general and within its distinctive cultures of same-sex desires in particular.[43] I then analyze the discourses of attraction among my participants, examining the patterns that emerged with regard to the races and ethnicities of men that gay Mexican migrants found desirable and sought out. This theme continues in chapter 9 with analysis of what I call the discourse of Latino sexual passion. I investigate the prevailing idea among all three groups of my interviewees that Mexicans and Latinos are more passionate than Whites, and I consider this discourse as both a collective sexual reputation and a sexual racial stereotype.

Then, in chapter 10, I explore the dimensions of power that structure cross-racial sexual and romantic relationships. I consider how the vulnerabilities associated with power imbalances can be further heightened when immigrants find themselves in unfamiliar sexual contexts whose rules they have not fully grasped. I round out this discussion by returning to the trope of Latino sexual passion and considering its functions as a response to such vulnerability. I show how gay Mexican immigrants, in the absence of power to fully shape the contours of their lives in the United States, invoke the notion of sexual passion as a badge of honor and as a discursive tool to launch a broader critique of mainstream American society.

Finally, in the conclusion, I return to the larger themes of the book. I recap how a careful analysis of the entire arc of "pathways of desire" sheds new light on the phenomenon of sexual migration in a way that contributes both to the broader literature on migration and to that on the globalization of sexuality. I close by considering the practical implications of my analysis in an important domain: sexual health, HIV risk, and HIV prevention.

ONE

Conceptualizing Sexual Migration

Around the time that I was beginning to conceive of the present study, I came across a newspaper article in the *SF Weekly*, a free newspaper in San Francisco.[1] In the article, "You Can't Be Gay—You're Latino: A Gay Latino Identity Struggles to Emerge, Somewhere between the Macho Mission and Caucasian Castro," reporter Joel P. Engardio sought to highlight what he saw as an inherent incompatibility between gay and Latino identities even in sexually liberal American cities such as San Francisco. Engardio interviewed Mexican and other Latin American gay and lesbian immigrants who had moved to San Francisco—immigrants who, he argued, had migrated to the United States because it was impossible for them to adopt gay identities in their home countries. Upon their arrival, they soon realized that even in San Francisco, their Latina/o and gay identities were somewhat incompatible.

Engardio's account of a young man called Miguel caught my attention. Miguel told the reporter that he had migrated to San Francisco from Guadalajara, Mexico's second-largest city, because "in Mexico, gay doesn't exist." More specifically, he maintained that being a man with same-sex desires in Mexico implied behaving "in a way that seems stereotypically gay. In that case, he says, you may exist, but 'you're not considered a person.'" Miguel imagined that the only options available in Mexico for a gay man were to become overtly effeminate and endure discrimination, or else hide and live a double life under constant fear of being discovered. Engardio argued that Mexico's staunch conservatism explained why Miguel and others like him were unable to adopt gay identities in their home country: "In his conservative Mexican hometown, the Catholic Church has such a strong hold on the common culture it is difficult to find a drugstore that sells condoms. Homosexuality is not even open for discussion." As a result, "when Miguel became convinced he could never be happy in Mexico, he emigrated to San Francisco. It was the gay mecca, he was told, the place where he would be accepted, as is."

The finality of this straightforward explanation for Miguel's transnational relocation surprised me, especially because it so easily accepted the notion that it would be impossible for anyone to be openly gay in Mexico. Given this presumption, it would be logical for a man such as Miguel—as for any other gay Mexican man, for that matter—to leave. But absent in this simple explanation for Miguel's sexual migration was any recognition of the profound sociocultural transformations I had witnessed and analyzed as part of the research on sexuality that I had conducted in Guadalajara—Miguel's hometown—around the time that Miguel was coming of age. Ironically, at the time this article appeared, I was in the middle of writing my book *The Night Is Young*, where I discuss just how much things were changing in Guadalajara in relation to sexuality. For one thing, gay and lesbian sexualities and lives had grown increasingly visible, to the point where Guadalajara was sometimes referred to as the San Francisco of Mexico.

To be sure, that city was known for being conservative and intensely Catholic—along the lines described by Engardio—as well as the cradle of many quintessential and heteronormative Mexican traditions. So Guadalajara, as I describe in my book, was a complicated and contradictory place. But gay and lesbian people—particularly gay men—had become ubiquitously visible there and were crafting lives that resembled gay culture in many world cities, even if local expressions of that culture were not completely identical. One simple illustration of the growing visibility of gay culture in Guadalajara at the time was the inclusion of gay bars and dance clubs, along with HIV/AIDS community–based groups, in the weekly entertainment supplement of a prominent mainstream local newspaper. As I wrote in my book, "By 1995, anyone could easily access information about the location and characteristics of the gay clubs in the section called 'De ambiente' [a label that referred to the gay milieu in slightly veiled, coded fashion]," and by 1999 the gay bars and clubs "appeared under the rubric 'Fuera del closet' (Out of the closet)."[2] Had Miguel consulted this supplement—which in Guadalajara was equivalent to the "Time Out" entertainment guides in other world cities—he could have learned about his hometown's many options to explore a gay identity. And he would have been able to see the many ways in which gay men expressed themselves—he did not have to behave in any particular prescribed ways in order to be gay.

However, unlike the thousands of gay men and lesbians who regularly attended gay venues in Guadalajara, Miguel did not find his way to the city's gay culture and community. Instead, he concluded that it was impossible to be gay there (or, for that matter, anywhere in Mexico). Why had he been unable to adopt a gay identity in his hometown? Why had he felt that he needed to leave Mexico altogether, and become a sexual migrant in the process, in order to be gay?

If we go back to Máximo's story from the introduction, it contains some clues that may provide some initial answers to these questions. Máximo had a gay life and a circle of gay friends who gathered regularly in his house in Hermosillo, but he was incapable of confronting the pressures emanating from his immediate heteronormative social and familial circles. His anxiety seemed partly connected to his fear that his relatives and coworkers might learn of his homosexuality. Thus, Máximo not only felt impelled to pretend that he was straight within his everyday work and family life but also had to carefully manage and control who knew his sexual orientation—he had to make sure that this information stayed within his gay circles. He was burdened by both the vulnerabilities of leading a double life and the enormous amounts of energy required to sustain it. And the pressure had become so great that he thought the only way to alleviate it was to leave Hermosillo and start anew somewhere else, away from his relatives and other people who had long known him as a straight man.

Note that Máximo, unlike Miguel, did not blame his city or his country for his own inability to be openly gay there. But like Miguel, he credited his new life in the United States with giving him the possibility of finally achieving an integrated and fully open gay life and identity. And, as we will see, many other Mexican participants in the present study did believe that by migrating to the United States they had achieved a kind of sexual freedom they felt would have been hard for them to acquire in their home country, especially while living near their families and longtime friends and acquaintances, who knew them as "regular," straight men.

For instance, Raimundo (born 1967), who like Máximo grew up in Hermosillo, said that he migrated to San Diego "for personal reasons; wanting my life as a gay man to be more open and more relaxed." Similarly, Melchor (born 1972), who originally had been from the northern state of Chihuahua but grew up in the border city of Tijuana, said that he "wanted a change" because in Tijuana he felt "very stereotyped" within his immediate straight social circles. He "felt tired and lonely (although I had my friends)," and most important, he had been aware since early on about his "sexual tendencies," leading him to realize he would never fully fit in the straight life he was leading. As he put it:

I felt I would find more respect here [in San Diego], because in Tijuana I had to hide my sexual preference for years, in school, with my friends. . . . When my friends saw a homosexual, they would say, "Let's beat him up." And I thought, "If they just knew that they have one standing here right next to them!"

Finally, Crispín (born 1980), who had grown up in Mexico City, mentioned that he stayed in the United States in part because his family in Mexico "did not really accept me as I am." However, he had never actually told them that he was gay.

Notably, these men emphasized their personal situations within their immediate social circles as the circumstances they felt most immediately would prevent them from achieving sexual freedom. And their assessments of their personal situations told them they would be better off leaving for a new location where no one knew them and starting a new gay life. Máximo had considered going to Mexico City or other Mexican cities, but the first option that the other men thought of was moving to the United States. Closely analyzing why many of these men could not imagine crafting an openly gay life for themselves within Mexico—especially given that other gays and lesbians did just that, as the social conditions surrounding homosexuality were rapidly shifting in their home country—and why they assessed that sexual freedom would be readily available to them only in the United States, is a central goal of this book.

Transnational Migration and Sexuality

Beginning around the mid-1990s, a number of scholars became interested in the connections between transnational migration and sexuality (particularly gay or queer sexualities).[3] As Benigno Sánchez-Eppler and Cindy Patton note in the introduction to their edited collection *Queer Diasporas*, "Translocation itself, movement itself, now enter the picture as theoretically significant factors in the discussion of sexuality." The term *translocation* in this statement refers to the back-and-forth relationship between the local and the global in sexual identity work, as well as the actual transportation of those identities across geographic space. Implied in this dual definition of translocation—in terms of both embodied identities and geography—is the notion that "when a practitioner of 'homosexual acts,' or a body that carries any of many queering marks moves between officially designated spaces—nation, region, metropole, neighborhood, or even culture, gender, religion, disease—intricate realignments of identity, politics, and desire take place."[4]

Queering Migration Studies

These kinds of concerns emerged in the work of scholars in the social sciences and humanities who had become interested in the transnational sexual migration of gay men and lesbians as part of a series of studies that were brought under the rubrics of queer migration and queer diaspora.[5] As scholars began to raise important questions about both the place of sexuality in migration studies and the place of migration in sexuality studies, the effect was to link two bodies of work that had previously remained separate. For instance, in the introduction to an edited collection published in 2005, Eithne Luibhéid notes that "despite rich scholarship about the causes and consequences of international migration, there has been little consideration of how sexual arrangements, ideologies, and modes of regulation shape migration to and incorporation into the United States."[6] The articles in this collection seek to address how sexuality shapes migration processes; how "concerns about sexuality shape US immigration control strategies and constructions of citizenship"; how migration transforms "U.S. queer communities, cultures, and politics"; and how sexuality can be "a source of conflict within migrant communities, and between migrant and U.S. communities."[7] As these interrelated foci suggest, researchers studying the United States were examining the links between sexuality and transnational migration at the level of state policy and institutional formation—for instance, in terms of immigration policies that excluded homosexuals, or domestic policies that turned American gay and lesbian citizens into second-class citizens by denying them the right to sponsor their partners for US residency or naturalization. And they were also conducting on-the-ground analyses of the lives of gay and lesbian immigrants that examined the processes of these migrants' incorporation into host societies.

This literature painted a picture of immigration as one of the policy arenas deeply shaped by state concerns about homosexuality, and it further suggested that absent consideration of those concerns, it is impossible to understand how the contemporary state in countries such as the United States came to take its current shape. This idea of a mutually constitutive relationship between homosexuality and state formation has been perhaps most compellingly argued by the historian Margot Canaday in her book *The Straight State*, which treats the domain of immigration control in the twentieth century as one of several important sites where the policing of sexuality has been linked to the expansion of state capacities.[8] Other scholars have also considered specific immigration policies that regulated homosexual inclusion and mobility, including attempts to establish boundaries between "good" and "bad" sexual citizens,[9] as well as the shifts in asylum policy generated by the emergence of the legal field of LGBT asylum beginning in the 1990s.[10] Moreover, through attention to individual queer immigrants, the literature has generated helpful understandings of their motivations and processes of incorporation into their host societies (including into gay communities in countries such as the United States and Canada). It also has shown the importance of treating those immigrants "not simply as sexual subjects, but also as racialized, classed, gendered subjects of particular regions and nations that exist in various historic relationships to US hegemony."[11]

Indeed, Lionel Cantú's study with Mexican gay immigrants—which is the most direct precursor of the present study—began to examine how those men's migration to Los Angeles is "influenced by sexuality," and in turn how "sociostructural and migratory factors" shape their sexualities after migration.[12] Cantú simultaneously aimed to account for the processes through which "Mexican gay immigrants adapt to, negotiate, and resist the constraints of their marginalization (in terms of their sexual orientation, gender, race/ethnicity, class, and legal status)" in the United States.[13] And he challenged "the presumption that Latin American society and culture are more oppressive and therefore create greater stress for queer individuals."[14] In *Pathways of Desire*, I have adopted but also expanded this framework, particularly with a goal toward further developing and theorizing the concept of sexual migration.

Gaps That Remain

Overall, this significant body of scholarly work has paved the way for the analysis in the present book. However, the literature has also left some significant gaps in our understanding of sexual migration (and more specifically queer migration or queer diaspora)—gaps that my research seeks to address.

One such gap concerns the need to examine the wide range of lives and experiences both before and after migration, and to attend to the complete trajectory of migration. The pioneering empirical studies that examined the lives of queer immigrants have produced nuanced descriptions of their post-migration incorporation into gay communities,[15] but those studies typically were not designed to systematically analyze immigrants' lives pre-migration, the diversity of their lived experiences, or the social, political, and cultural sexuality-related changes taking place in their home countries.[16] For instance, in *Global Divas*, Martin Manalansan provides background information about the cultural schemas of sexuality and gender to which his participants were previously exposed in the Philippines—including an indigenous schema based on *bakla* identities (a local Tagalog term that, according to Manalansan, signals "effeminate mannerism, feminine physical characteristics . . . and cross-dressing" among men), which contrasted with the global gay identities his participants encountered while in the Philippines or later in their diasporic setting in New York.[17] He notes that some of his participants favored strategies of sexual silence that are consistent with the *bakla* identity, while others incorporated the strategy of coming out that is seen as prerequisite for being openly gay. Yet because of Manalansan's primary focus on the immigrants' lives in New York, his work does not systematically examine how the specific pre-migration lived experiences of his participants influenced their subsequent processes of incorporation into New York's gay life.

A similar example is provided by Lionel Cantú's study. As I mentioned above, Cantú was critical of a dominant cultural framework in the United States that would suggest that Mexican gay men migrate there simply to escape a backward sexual culture in Mexico (as is implied by the article that opened this chapter). His desire to learn about gay issues in Mexico prompted him to take a two-week research trip to that country to do fieldwork and conduct some interviews with Mexican gay men who were not immigrants.[18] During his short stay in Mexico—and similarly to what I myself found in my own research in Guadalajara in the 1990s—Cantú became convinced that Mexican male homosexualities were more diverse than many Americans assumed, and this information gave him a backdrop against which he analyzed his immigrant participants' efforts to find "their way home," as he put it, in the United States.[19] However, like Manalansan's study, Cantú's was not designed to explore the diversity of his immigrant participants' pre-migration experiences, nor was he able to systematically link those experiences to their equally diverse post-migration sexual lives. He therefore did not analyze with sufficient detail how they had changed sexually after relocating.

Cantú's and Manalansan's studies lead me to note a second gap in the literature, which concerns how best to account for cultural differences, both between home and destination countries and among sexual immigrants themselves. Such differences make themselves manifest in a number of ways that are important for the study of sexual migration. First, imaginaries of the contrasting sexual cultures of destination countries may prompt sexual migration in the first place. Second, cultural differences among immigrants may create distinct patterns in how sexual immigrants become incorporated into their receiving communities. And third, the varying degrees of sexual change experienced by sexual immigrants may depend in part on how similar or different their new cultural contexts are from those they experienced in their places of origin. By giving greater consideration to cultural diversity among the immigrants, we can challenge the pervasive assumption that gay or queer immigrants from the global South leave places where local attitudes toward male homosexuality are necessarily more "traditional" and possibly "pre-gay," as well as a sense that they become exposed to modern, globally distributed ideas about gayness only once they have arrived in a country such as the United States.

It was in reaction to such assumptions that Cantú voiced suspicion of reified accounts of Latino sexual culture (a point with which I agree).[20] He opposed "the manner in which 'culture' as a focal argument not only obscures other structural dimensions that shape Latino men's lives but also pathologizes our 'culture.'"[21] Cantú worried that stereotypical understandings of Mexican sexualities had the effect of "othering" Mexican and Latino gay men.[22] For those reasons, he initially downplayed the notion of sexual culture in favor of a political economic framework that he called a "queer materialist paradigm"—a framework he thought would facilitate accounting for power dimensions imbricated in the mutually constitutive relationship between sexuality and migration.[23] But after going to Mexico, Cantú realized that culture can indeed play "an important role in the lives and identities of gay Latino men."[24] Yet despite this realization, he did not find a way to reconcile the two approaches, in part because his materialist approach seemed to depend to some degree on the dismissal of cultural understandings.

This last issue points out yet another gap in the literature, the absence of a balanced framework that can help us link cultural and structural explanations for sexual migration—for simultaneously analyzing the roles played by structural and cultural factors at all stages of the migration process. Such a framework enables us to get past the idea that sexual immigrants come from locations whose sexual culture is "backward," and helps us see how immigrants' own cultural understandings may become assets for them in their new locations. An example of this latter possibility is provided by Martin Manalansan's account of Filipino gay immigrants' transposition of Filipino cultural expressions to New York, where they used them as tools to launch a critique of the discrimination and stereotyping they encountered in the local mainstream gay community, and therefore also as tools of empowerment.[25]

A final, related, gap in the empirical literature concerns an insufficient understanding of the racial dynamics of the sexual and romantic interactions in which gay immigrant men engage post migration. Previous studies have alluded indirectly to those dynamics, as well as to effects of the racialization of gay immigrant men in the United States and its consequences for their sexual lives. But they did not examine in any significant way the patterns of cross-racial attraction or the effects of power inequalities that emerge in cross-racial relationships.[26] These all are among the conceptual and theoretical gaps that *Pathways of Desire* is meant to address.

Sexual Migration and North-South Interactions

Beyond its specific focus on sexual migration, a study such as my own also has implications for a broader understanding of North-South interactions in relation to sexuality. It invites discussion of additional literatures that have addressed those interactions, namely the literatures on the globalization of sexuality (developed by scholars such as the political scientist Dennis Altman and the geographer Jon Binnie) and on colonialism, sexuality, and queerness (developed by humanities scholars such as Anne McClintock, Robert Young, John Hawley, and Ann Stoller, as well as sociologists such as Joane Nagel).[27] These bodies of scholarly work have operated with very different emphases that have yet to be reconciled.

The scholarly work on sexual globalization has focused primarily on forms of global exchange, while the work on colonialism and sexuality has emphasized the historical use of sexuality as a tool of colonial power that helped to justify, in the eyes of the colonizers, the domination of the colonies. These two emphases can be brought into closer conversation, and a nuanced focus on sexual migration can help clarify how.

Local and Global Sexualities

In the 1990s, coinciding with a time when "globalization became a key buzzword,"[28] sexualities scholars such as Dennis Altman began to note "the emergence of 'the global gay,' the apparent internationalization of a certain form of social and cultural identity based upon homosexuality."[29]Altman had in mind gay men and lesbians in locations around the world who were "young, upwardly mobile, sexually adventurous, with an in-your-face attitude toward traditional restrictions and an interest in both activism and fashion."[30] He more graphically described them in these terms:

Images of young men in baseball caps and Reeboks on the streets of Budapest or Sao Paulo, of "lipstick lesbians" flirting on portable telephones in Bangkok or demonstrating in the streets of Tokyo—none of which are fictitious—are part of the construction of a new category, or more accurately the expansion of an existing Western category, that is part of the rapid globalization of lifestyle and identity politics, the simultaneous disappearance of old concepts and invention of new ones.[31]

Central to this view is the notion of increasingly global commercialization and commodification of sexuality, as well as their strong links to global capitalism. Also central is the idea of an "expansion of an existing Western category," which implies the exportation of sexual schemas associated with the "global gay" that are produced in countries such as the United States and disseminated to the rest of the world.[32] This expansion is facilitated by the acceleration of mechanisms of exchange that include communication technologies that instantaneously transmit ideas about sexuality; the increasing circulation of global capital and "the vast apparatus of consumerism" that expand the reach of global sexual schemas; and, important for my present study, the growing numbers of people who cross transnational borders.[33] Transnational movement—including through migration and "the large-scale movement of people from the 'third world'"—is therefore considered to be one of the ways in which more and more people become exposed to the sexual ways of the global North.[34]

An irony, of course, is that as the global exchange of capital and culture has expanded, national borders have become increasingly entrenched, and border controls increasingly are meant to limit the free circulation of people who are deemed illegitimate border crossers (not the expatriates, tourists, and others who have ready access to the visas and other documentation that legitimizes their transnational movement, but the less fortunate migrants and refugees who often lack proper documentation). As Eithne Luibhéid and others have argued, state control of its borders "significantly regulates sexuality and reproduces oppressive sexual norms that are gendered, racialized, and classed."[35]

Such limitations on cross-border movement notwithstanding, when defined in terms of global exchange and transnational movement, the notion of sexual globalization raises some important questions to consider as we delve into the material in subsequent chapters of *Pathways of Desire*. First, to what degree is the notion of "the global gay"—and the constructions associated with this cultural schema—responsible for triggering the imagination of Mexican gay immigrants-to-be? Can we safely assume that, as the newspaper article at the beginning of this chapter suggested, imaginaries about the existence of the global gay that originate elsewhere are powerful enough to trigger an exodus from places where people perceived it as not being present? Somewhat paradoxically, these questions contradict another central concept in the literature on sexual globalization, which has to do with the notion that the so-called global gay is emerging everywhere, including in unlikely places. If that is the case, why, then, would sexual migrants feel a need to leave their home countries? In the case of Mexico, for instance, why would gay men want to leave when they might find locally emerging forms of the global gay within their home country, at least in large cities such as Mexico City, Guadalajara, and Monterrey?

To be sure, one of the concerns emerging in relation to the notion of sexual globalization involves the question of whether it will eventually erase the local specificity of sexual cultures.[36] Research conducted in a number of locations suggests that is not the case. For instance, recognizing the local specificities of gay cultures in China, the anthropologist Lisa Rofel has explicitly sought to implement "an effort to forestall the rush toward a discourse of homogenous global identities."[37] But she notes that despite the diverse ways in which same-sex desires are embodied and performed in China, "still the temptation to conclude that a singular 'global gay identity' has come into existence and that China offers one more instantiation of it appears virtually irresistible."[38] On the other hand, proponents of the notion of sexual globalization have expressed sensitivity toward the specificities of local sexualities, and have acknowledged that the changes produced by sexual globalization are "simultaneously leading to greater homogeneity and greater inequality."[39] This statement contains some clues that may be helpful in explaining diversity among sexual migrants, as my own case will show.

Over time, a consensus seemed to emerge about the need to account for both the "local" and the "global" in analyses of sexual globalization—to consider the full complexity of how contemporary sexualities are shaped, in both the global North and the global South. Consensus has implied that sexualities in many locations have become simultaneously local and global, or "glocal."[40] In this sense, "the global gay" is itself constantly reinterpreted and adapted at the local level; consequently, viewing "gay" as simultaneously global and local need not be a contradictory proposition.[41]

Defined in this way, the notion of "global gay" has provided a general scaffolding flexible enough to be adapted locally. Scholarly work along these lines has generated fruitful conceptual developments for my analysis in subsequent chapters of *Pathways of Desire*. For instance, in my earlier work in Guadalajara, I expressed the overlaps between, and coexistence of, local and global sexualities by describing the development of Mexican "sexual hybridity," a concept I adapted from Néstor García Canclini's theorization of cultural hybridity.[42] Similarly, Tom Boellstorff proposed the notion of "dubbing culture" to describe local interpretations of gayness in Indonesia that are at once aligned with global sexualities and culturally specific to that country.[43] Also, working in Thailand, Peter Jackson noted that the emergence of "commercial spaces in major cities commonly called 'gay scenes'" are "just as intimately related with each other as an interlocking global set of spaces as they are with the national cultures within which they are located."[44] Jackson further observed that "if one focuses on the indigenous discourses within each of these widely separated spaces, then instead of global homogeneity, one is impressed by local specificity and difference."[45] Finally, also linked to this way of thinking about sexual globalization is the perception that its processes "operate unevenly," an idea that links back to the notion that sexual globalization "does not lead to homogenization."[46]

The Directionality of Sexual Globalization

Note that the various analyses to which I referred earlier focus on cultural processes triggered by the arrival of a global gay schema from countries in the North—particularly the United States—to countries in the global South. Such a focus leaves open a question about the cultural processes that may unfold in reverse, when gay sexual migrants from the global South relocate to sites in the global North, carrying with them their own versions of glocalized sexualities and gayness. Such cultural processes have not been thoroughly explored.[47]

Sexual migration from the global South raises questions about the directionality of sexual globalization. It challenges to some degree a widespread understanding of sexual globalization as involving a unidirectional transfer of sexual schemas from the global North to the rest of the world—a prevalent view even when scholars have expressly sought to avoid comparisons between countries that are based on a strict, and implicitly hierarchical, "modern"/"traditional" binary.[48] The temptation to rely on a modern/traditional dichotomy indeed remains high, especially when depictions of some countries' sexual cultures as "traditional" are meant to characterize them as static, homogeneous, and premodern (as in the depiction of Mexico in the newspaper article I discussed above).

But if we consider the evidence that "glocalized" forms of "sexual modernity" have emerged in many countries of the global South, should we not also contemplate the possibility that those same countries may be putting into play their own forms of glocalized sexual modernity[49] within a global context? Specifically in the case that concerns me, might not gay Mexicans' contributions to sexual globalization become evident when they travel or relocate to the United States and interact sexually and romantically with "the locals"? The possibility thus exists that sexual migrants from the global South are not merely passive recipients of the sexual schemas they encounter in the global North. The question, then, is also whether there are any lessons that those immigrants can offer to their interlocutors in the global North. These are all issues that *Pathways of Desire* takes up by considering the incorporation processes of Mexican immigrants into gay San Diego, as well as the day-to-day interactions they have with others there, particularly American gay men.

Colonialism, Race, and Sexuality

Once we have begun to consider interactions between immigrants and the locals, we are forced to examine the dynamics of interpersonal and sexual relations taking place between citizens from countries having quite unequal power. This is a theme that the literature on colonialism and sexuality brings to the fore, although usually by focusing historically on the interactions that took place within the colonies, or, in more contemporary terms, between a "new class of expatriates"[50] from the former colonial powers and the citizens of the now independent former colonies. As Dennis Altman has noted, these are the expatriates that replaced "the colonial class who ran the European empires from their redoubts in Delhi and Algiers."[51]

We know less about the reverse situation—about the interpersonal and sexual interactions that take place between immigrants (that is, citizens of the former colonies) and "the locals" (citizens of the former colonial powers) in the global North. How does unequal power play out in those interactions? How does the often disadvantaged social position of immigrants—particularly those who are vulnerable because of their race or ethnicity, or their undocumented status—influence their sexual and romantic relations after migration? And how do disparities of power at the interpersonal level affect what the immigrants expected to achieve by migrating transnationally?

These questions require a focus on power and power disparities—a focus that can be facilitated by the tools developed by the literature on sexuality, colonialism, and postcolonialism. However, as Anne McClintock has noted, the degree to which the notion of postcolonialism is relevant in thinking about countries such as Mexico that stopped being European colonies long ago is somewhat unclear. In those countries, as McClintock also noted, a more pressing concern may be the cultural imperialism exercised by economic and cultural powers such as the United States, a notion indirectly related to the effects of globalization (and sexual globalization).[52] Invoking a colonial/postcolonial framework is nonetheless helpful for my purposes because of its emphasis on examining transnational "imbalances of power" that have been sustained by long histories of unequal exchange. As Robert Young has proposed, such power imbalances

are consistently articulated through points of tension and forms of difference that are then superimposed upon each other: class, gender and race are circulated promiscuously and crossed with each other, transformed into mutually defining metaphors that mutate within intricate webs of surreptitious cultural values that are then internalized by those whom they define.[53]

This is part of what Young has labeled "colonial desire,"[54] which, he argues, appears in its modern form as "cultural interchange and diversity."[55]

In other words, the awareness of power brought about by a colonial framework facilitates an analysis of the unequal relationship between the United States and Mexico, and by extension between Americans and Mexicans. It proves helpful for highlighting dynamics of "power and resistance"—indeed of simultaneous admiration and resentment.[56]

However useful this perspective may be, it is important to remain aware that all too often, analyses based on a colonial/postcolonial framework seem to have overemphasized one aspect of the connections between colonial powers and the former colonies, namely how the colonies were and continue to be oppressed (materially and culturally) by unequal relations of power. The same overemphasis might apply to settings characterized more by forms of cultural imperialism. This may come at the expense of considering forms of agency that respond to Gayatri Spivak's provocative and oft-cited question about whether "the subaltern can speak"—and, in the case that concerns me, more specifically whether the "*gay* subaltern" can speak, to follow John Hawley's own provocation.[57] The question that remains is whether it is possible to examine what the (ideally no longer just) "subalterns" have to say about the sexualities and sexual cultures they encounter in the "metropolis" (to use language that is common in colonial studies). And, as Homi Bhabha has observed, can this speaking back be recognized in the forms of hybridity that emerge at the "the moment in which the discourse of colonial authority loses its univocal grip on meaning and finds itself open to the trace of the language of the other"?[58] Can the voices of the so-called gay subalterns therefore be captured by analyzing their interactions as they become part of urban gay communities in a place such as the United States? As they interact with the sexual cultures that prevail there? (Of course, in doing so we must be mindful that the notion of "sexual culture" itself can be problematic insofar as it has been burdened by a history of colonial racism, exoticism, and the construction of "the Other.") As Ann Laura Stoller has suggested, this analysis requires focusing not solely on the colonized but also on how the sexual cultures prevalent in the North are seen through the eyes of the peoples from the South—that is, a view from the South.[59] That is a view I have striven to capture in *Pathways of Desire*, particularly as my analysis brings attention to processes of cultural exchange, as well as to the racial dynamics and disparities of power that emerge in the context of sexual and romantic relations, just as the literature on colonialism and sexuality has highlighted.[60]

Two other implications of this approach are worth drawing out. First, in analyzing cross-racial interactions, it seems crucially important to take into account dynamics occurring at the macro or structural levels, in terms of interaction between countries, states, and societies, and also at the micro (and more intimate) level of cross-racial and cross-cultural sexual and romantic interactions. Joane Nagel has provided an excellent example in her conceptualization of "ethnosexual frontiers," which she describes as "the borderlands on either side of ethnic divides; they skirt the edges of ethnic communities; they constitute symbolic and physical sensual spaces where sexual imaginings and sexual contact occur between members of different racial, ethnic, and national groups."[61] Second, like

Tom Boellstorff and in contrast to scholars such as Jon Binnie, I therefore do not perceive an intrinsic incompatibility between a sexual globalization framework and a queer postcolonial framework—especially if, in the process of putting the two into dialogue, we are mindful of the various caveats and conceptual reformulations I have discussed throughout this section.[62]

Toward Further Conceptualization of Sexual Migration

This chapter shows that the phenomenon that I and others have called sexual migration is not as simple as it might appear at first sight. Contrary to the argument made by the newspaper article I discussed at the beginning of the chapter, understanding why gay Mexican men move to the United States requires more than assuming that they leave their home country merely because they cannot be gay there.

Conceptually speaking, the goal of *Pathways of Desire* is to address the gaps in the literature I have discussed, and produce a deeper and more nuanced understanding of sexual migration. To do so, I make use of the tools provided by the literatures on sexual globalization and colonialism and sexuality. By placing a study of sexual migration explicitly in dialogue with those literatures, my goal is to contribute to our understanding of the broader cultural and political phenomena in which sexual migration is embedded. I now move into analyzing empirically the sexual migration of Mexican gay and bisexual men to the United States, and this discussion begins with an examination of their sexual lives in Mexico.

TWO

The Many Mexican Worlds of Male Same-Sex Desires

As a teenager living in Mexico City, Marcelo (born 1970) first encountered the world of sex between men at the age of fifteen while riding the extensive public transportation system in Mexico's vast, chaotic, and populous capital. His sexual awakening took place in the back of a crowded city bus, where a man began rubbing Marcelo's leg, which Marcelo found deeply arousing. Soon afterward, he discovered that such forms of contact were common among gay working-class men, especially in the subway system:

To get to my high school . . . I had to take . . . the Metro, the subway, and that's where I really began to meet other men. Because you should know that the Metro gets very crowded downtown. People are packed in very close to each other. . . . And at some point I detected which were the key points for cruising. . . . You notice where [sexual touching] happens [to you] the first time and you keep going there, and you realize in what train car things happen.[1]

These events put Marcelo on a path to find and become immersed in Mexico City's extensive gay culture. By the late 1980s, when he had openly adopted a gay identity, the city's gays and lesbians had come to think of their identities, their cultures, and their institutions as standing in a relatioship with a global gay and lesbian movement that had become visible during the previous two decades.[2]

Growing up far from the metropolis, Eliseo (born 1962) first encountered a local world of sex between men in an altogether different manner. In his small coastal town of three thousand people in the Mexican state of Nayarit, teenagers commonly engaged in sexual games as they socialized with one another. Eliseo's first sexual contact took place at approximately fourteen years old, with a male cousin. Later, he also had sex with some of his town friends. He recalled that a group of his friends would gather to watch television, and one inevitably would remain after the others had left and suggest *echar un palo* (a colloquial phrase for "sexual intercourse"). Eliseo also described a broader small-town male culture that seamlessly and informally incorporated same-sex sexual encounters as part of homosocial relations.[3] Moreover, he talked about the visible presence of a group of gay men (identified by their effeminacy) who gathered in the town's plaza:

The same *chavos* [guys] that gathered in the plaza invited others. We would organize parties. We would go to the fields for a *lunada* [a nighttime gathering under the moonlight], to drink and to play guitar. It was something really beautiful. And *las copas* [the drinks] would lead to sex on the beach, the fields, or by the river. It was really nice.

After *secundaria* (junior high school), Eliseo left his small town and migrated to Tepic, the state capital. There he established a sexual connection with a man whom he kept casually encountering around the city, and who eventually talked to him and invited him to his house, where Eliseo penetrated him. During his time in Tepic, he learned about Mexico City's gay life, but he never was curious enough to travel there to see it. Later, he moved to other locations within Mexico, and along the way he learned about urban gay life in larger cities there, including Tijuana. But he never sought to see those places with his own eyes. Eliseo first came in contact with any sort of urban gay life when he finally migrated to San Diego.

However, other Mexican men first encountered institutionalized gay life right in the midsized cities where they grew up. In the late 1990s, Venustiano (born 1975) found it in Irapuato, his hometown and a city of 340,000 people in the conservative central Mexican state of Guanajuato. As he recalled:

I got to the bar and I thought, "How could I possibly go in?" . . . But I worked up the courage and I went in. . . . As I entered they asked me: "Where are you going? Upstairs is *de ambiente*[4] and downstairs is normal." So I went upstairs to hook up [*ligar*]. Even when I am this ugly, [men] bought me drinks; they asked me to dance. Three men asked me, but I didn't like them. As one of the security guards went by I asked her: "Is it really OK for men to dance with each other here?" She says: "Yes, that's right." I responded, "What a strange place!"

What were the various pathways that led Mexican men such as Marcelo, Eliseo, and Venustiano to acquire gay and bisexual identities? What brought them to find gay groups, cultures, and communities within Mexico before migrating? The answers to these questions are centrally important to the story I tell in this book. First, immigrant participants' lived experiences in Mexico dispel a commonplace view that Mexican gay men's sexual migration to the United States can be explained simply as the consequence of a lack of options to be gay in Mexico, as suggested in the newspaper article I discussed in chapter 1. Second, Mexican men's diverse experiences in Mexico show the importance of considering immigrants' lives in their home countries in order to fully understand the diversity of their lived experiences in the United States after migration. Third, and related to the previous two points, gay Mexicans' diversity confirms the inadequacy of a widespread view that the sexual cultures in sending countries such as Mexico are universally "traditional," conservative, and static. Finally, my participants' cases highlight the importance of considering differences among them, especially in terms of their social class position and geographic (urban/rural) origin. Such differences help explain the range of sexual lives and cultures that Mexican gay immigrants encountered in their home country before migrating,[5] and in turn they will be helpful in understanding the diversity of their post-migration experiences. They thus create a launching pad for subsequent analysis of the sexual migration of Mexican gay men to the United States and their incorporation into gay San Diego.

Mexican Male Homosexualities

In the United States, both academic and popular understandings of Mexican male homosexuality have been heavily influenced by the important early works of the American anthropologists Joseph Carrier and Clark Taylor.[6] Carrier's account of the heavily gendered interpretations of male homosexuality he observed in Guadalajara in the late 1960s and early 1970s led him to formulate the *pasivo/activo* model, which Taylor later also confirmed in Mexico City in the late 1970s. This sexual schema[7] has influenced both US scholars' and popular discourse about Latino male homosexualities for almost four decades, especially after the publication of Tomás Almaguer's oft-cited article "Chicano Men: A Cartography of Homosexual Identity and Behavior" in 1991.[8]

According to the interpretive logic of this schema, Mexican men who have sex with men can be divided into two groups: *pasivos*, the effeminized, socially stigmatized, receptive partners during anal intercourse, and *activos*, who are thought of as the *pasivos'* masculine and non-stigmatized sex partners. The *activos* are assumed to take the "male" role as inserters during anal intercourse while retaining a status as "normal," "regular," or "straight" men (*derechos* or *bugas* in Mexican gay lingo).[9] And beyond these gendered sexual roles, the *pasivo/activo* model encapsulates a more general sexual schema that is regarded as preceding the "identitarian transit," the "major transformation in the trajectories of subjectivity and collectivity" we typically associate with a modern gay historical moment—which, in reference to Mexico, Rodrigo Parrini and Ana Amuchástegui relate to a transition from *puto* (fag) to *gay*.[10]

The problem is that when used alone for describing all Mexican male homosexualities, the *pasivo/activo* model reifies Mexican understandings and practices of male homosexuality (and Mexican sexual culture more generally) and depicts them as necessarily "premodern."[11] Hence, it also curtails the possibility of considering a wider range of Mexican homoerotic subjectivities, including those centrally based on the adoption of gay identities. Indeed, gay identities are often represented by an alternative form of sexual categorization that is primarily defined in terms of attraction (or "object choice," in a borrowing from psychoanalytic theory).[12] In other words, the sole use of the *activo/pasivo* model hampers our ability to examine the incorporation of a global gay sexual schema into the Mexican world of homoerotic desires, and it keeps us from giving due consideration to the variety of gay subjectivities, identities, venues, enclaves, groups, and communities that are recognizable throughout Mexico, which the recent literature on Mexican sexualities has extensively described and analyzed.[13] This literature has generated nuanced accounts of Mexican gay subjectivities that are not constrained by the assumptions of a "premodern," "pre-gay," and heavily gendered *pasivo/activo* model—accounts that instead have incorporated heavily gendered Mexican male homosexualities within a broader universe of Mexican male same-sex desires and gay subjectivities.

My research in Guadalajara in the 1990s—also the main site of Carrier's original research two decades earlier—showed that such incorporation led to the emergence of hybrid interpretations of sexuality that combine criteria and understandings from both a gendered classificatory system and one based on object choice.[14] My findings in Guadalajara led me to formulate the notion of "sexual hybridity" as a way to capture the often seamless mixing of so-called traditional and so-called modern interpretations of sexuality, as well as Mexicans' adeptness at adapting "global" discourses of sexuality to their local contexts.[15] This notion relates to what

Richard Parker, working in Brazil, earlier referred to in terms of coexisting sexual cultures,[16] and Tom Boellstorff, working in Indonesia, later called "dubbing culture."[17] It also suggests that the diversity of sexual subjectivities in Mexico can be seen as simultaneously global and local, as representing a range of sexualities that have become "glocalized."[18]

Similarly to other countries, including the United States, the origins of a contemporary sense of local "gay modernity" in Mexico can be traced back to the early decades of the twentieth century. In 1901, the Mexico City police raided a homosexual ball that is commonly referred to today as the famous "Dance of the 41"[19]—an event that, according to the renowned Mexican intellectual Carlos Monsiváis, marked a symbolic first outing of the urban homosexual world in Mexico and the full emergence of awareness about male same-sex desires in Mexican culture and society.[20] Furthermore, as described in a memoir by the well-known Mexican poet and essayist Salvador Novo, by the 1920s a relatively well-developed homosexual subculture already existed in the city.[21] And some evidence suggests that by the late 1950s and early 1960s, the incipient signs of what became a "gay community" in the 1970s were already present.[22] Unfortunately, this history has not yet been fully recorded as far as I know, at least not in the same way as in the historical projects conducted in other cities such as New York, San Francisco, London, Berlin, and Philadelphia.[23] Of course, Mexico City does not represent all Mexico, but as my participants' narratives will show, what happens there is often emulated in other parts of the country.

In the remainder of this chapter, I describe and analyze the varied patterns of interpretation of same-sex desires in Mexico that emerged in the narratives provided by Mexican gay immigrant men in my research. My discussion is organized around participants' geographic location, which along with their social class position proved relevant for recognizing differing understandings of same-sex desires—different sexual schemas—to which these men were exposed in their home country before migrating.[24] For the purposes of my analysis, I have grouped immigrant participants in three general categories according to whether they grew up in large cities, small to medium-size cities, or small towns and rural areas. The locations (fig. 1) where they were raised and became sexually socialized include the country's three largest metropolises, Mexico City, Guadalajara, and Monterrey; other large cities such as Tijuana, León, Ciudad Juárez, Torreón/Gómez Palacio, and Toluca; medium-size and small cities such as Cuernavaca, Ensenada, Culiacán, Mexicali, Cancún, Hermosillo, Tepic, La Paz, Uruapan, Durango, Mazatlán, Minatitlán, Puerto Vallarta,

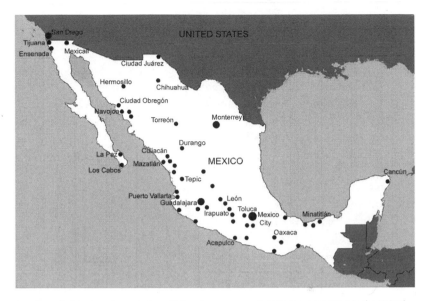

1   Places in Mexico where study participants grew up or lived before migrating to the United States.

Navojoa, Ciudad Obregón, and Los Cabos; and small towns and rural areas in Mexican states as diverse as Oaxaca, Michoacán, Veracruz, Sinaloa, Guerrero, Baja California, Nayarit, Sonora, Morelos, Tabasco, and Jalisco. As this list attests, immigrant participants came from a wide range of locations. Moreover, they were diverse in terms of their class position, which influenced not only their socioeconomic status but also their social and cultural capital in regard to homosexuality and gayness, and in turn the pathways they had followed as they explored their same-sex desires and acquired gay or bisexual identities before they migrated to the United States.[25]

Gay Life in the Big City

In large Mexican cities, the pathways toward acquiring gay identities and coming into contact with gay cultures are multiple and readily available. Upon realizing their sexual interest in men, participants who had grown up in large Mexican cities were often able to find others who, like them, were constructing gay lives that were primarily or fully defined around their same-sex desires. I now return to Marcelo's story.

Marcelo: From Underground Gay Venues to Institutional Gay Life

Marcelo grew up in a working-class family in an area of Mexico City he described as one of the "barrios bravos" (tough neighborhoods) in the city's center. He provided further details about his sexual awakening in the back of a crowded bus. On that occasion, a man, who Marcelo estimated was around thirty years old, had rubbed Marcelo's leg with his hand.[26] "He electrified me, he made me very nervous," Marcelo remarked.

Of course I didn't move . . . but I was sweating. . . . I was practically terrified, but at the same time I consented. . . . I remember that I had to get off at my stop to go home, and instead I stayed in the bus. I couldn't even get up. . . . [Eventually] I thought, "I can't do this anymore, I have to get off." By then I was all wet and aroused. Nothing else happened, in spite of how much the man smiled at me. . . . Perhaps he also realized that I was terrified, and he didn't dare do anything else.

Soon after this incident, Marcelo discovered that sexual touching of this kind also happened in the jam-packed cars of the Metro. Now he was attuned to his own homoerotic desires, and he started making direct eye contact with men who he hoped would touch him. Eventually, someone he met on the Metro invited him to a public steam bath where sex between men was known to happen.[27] Subsequently, Marcelo gained access to a range of locations that were part of an assortment of underground yet institutionalized public sex venues where men sought sex with each other in the city. In addition to buses, the Metro, and steam baths, these included certain movie theaters (often ones showing porn films for straight audiences), streets or plazas, cruisy bathrooms in shopping malls, and parks. In them, Marcelo met a mix of gay-identified and non-gay-identified men.

As Marcelo came of age, he became involved in leftist political organizing. Through this work, he met gay activists, one of whom invited him to join Cálamo, a local gay and HIV/AIDS group, and to attend the 1988 Mexico City Pride March.[28] The march had originated a decade earlier as a result of the early Mexican gay activists' participation in broader leftist political marches and causes. Juan Jacobo Hernández, a longtime activist and one of the founders of the movement, noted on his Facebook page in 2013 that that year marked the thirty-fifth anniversary of the first political march in which openly gay male activists participated. He wrote:

On this date, July 26, 35 years ago [in 1978] the *homosexuales* of the "Frente Homosexual de Acción Revolucionaria" [FHAR—Homosexual Front of Revolutionary Action] went out on the streets. We demonstrated publicly for the first time as part of the march that commemorated the anniversary of the Cuban revolution and the 10-year anniversary of the 1968 [student] movement in Mexico.[29]

As Hernández noted, these early gay and lesbian demonstrations in Mexico City were initially tied to broader leftist politics, but they soon became independent and symbolically linked to the Stonewall uprising in New York, the International Gay Pride Day, and a political period that emphasized gay liberation.[30] Reflecting this significant shift, in 1980 the Mexico City Pride March was moved to Saturday, June 28, so that it would coincide with the global commemorations of Stonewall.[31] Today, the march is one of the largest public events in Mexico City, and attracts hundreds of thousands of participants.

Back in 1988, when Marcelo first attended the march, displaying one's homosexuality publicly was regarded as exceedingly risky socially,[32] so for him this was a crucially defining time:

I was avid to know the gay social core. . . . I started participating in a gay social life, from inside the ghetto, very involved in the bars and discos, but also with [gay] friends in other types of places, in other activities. . . . That was the beginning of my gay social life, and the beginning of my farewell from a straight social life, because in the nineties my life centered completely on gay society. . . . Even my jobs in the nineties were more with people in the gay ghetto. . . . The last one was in an art gallery owned by a gay friend of mine. Everyone who went there was gay.

Marcelo's participation in leftist political organizing led him into the city's more institutional gay spaces—to the gay political groups, the Pride March, the gay clubs and bars, and even to businesses that specifically catered to gay people—and gave him access to exclusively gay social circles. His narrative suggests that these developments also put him in closer contact with middle-class gay circles within the country's capital.

Before the Internet, this pathway toward an urban gay identity, as expressed by the Mexican men in my research, sometimes began with a same-sex sexual initiation during childhood or adolescence (involving sexual encounters with neighborhood or school friends, or with older men, including relatives), followed by a subsequent, sometimes unexpected discovery of underground urban gay sexual spaces, which in turn led to making gay friends, entering institutional gay spaces, and joining gay social networks.[33] In some cases, however, the order in which these events occurred was reversed, depending on when any given boy or man happened to meet others who were already attuned to the local gay culture. Marcelo's case thus nicely demonstrates that by the 1980s, many men in large cities in Mexico were becoming openly or semi-openly gay and participated in increasingly visible urban gay communities. Nonetheless, Marcelo later decided to migrate to San Diego for sexual reasons.

Crecencio: The Working-Class Suburbs

Crecencio (born 1962) grew up outside Mexico City in Ciudad Nezahualcóyotl (popularly referred to as "Neza"), a massive, working-class suburb of more than one million inhabitants that originally developed through irregular settlements.[34] Similarly to Marcelo, he discovered gay cruising on the Metro, where at the age of nineteen he met a gay man who also lived in Neza. Soon afterward, he met a man on a bus in Neza, and they became boyfriends. In this relationship, Crecencio initially penetrated his partner, but later the two started switching roles. This was a significant development, given that these men were immersed in a working-class urban sexual culture that was often assumed to lack the sexual role versatility regarded as a marker of more egalitarian, middle-class gay relationships, which Susan Kippax and Gary Smith characterize as "sexual democratic."[35] Eleven years into the relationship, Crecencio became curious about attending a gay disco, which he acted on when a gay cousin invited the couple to Spartacus, a gay club in Neza.[36] Later, he visited another club in downtown Mexico City, El 14, which had a reputation for being frequented by soldiers. Crecencio said of these clubs:

These were my favorite places, because there are others . . . that are more for people with an attitude, who just go to show off their bodies and . . . to make fun of others [estar perreando a los demás].[37] I never liked that. El 14 was a more homogeneous environment. More hombres [real men][38] went there, more mujeres [women]. . . . I think it was 70 percent homosexual and the rest [men] who say they're not [homosexual]. I identified more with this place, as well as with Spartacus, where everyone does whatever they want. There are no limitations.

As suggested by this comment, Crecencio had become critical of middle-class gay discos, where he felt he did not fit in (he mentioned such venues as Butterfly, Anyway, El Antro, and El Taller, all of which were active when he lived in Mexico City). These were the venues that he thought of as populated by "people with an attitude." His critique highlights the fact that, although urban gay bars and culture may have a democratizing effect (which is how Marcelo experienced them), they also reproduce social class stratification, which is manifested in terms of taste, types of clientele, and class-based attitudes. Of course, such precise stratification is possible only in places with a wide range of options.

Edwin: A Middle-Class Experience

In contrast to Marcelo and Crecencio, Edwin (born 1974) grew up in a middle-class Mexico City family. He first gained entry to the city's gay culture (*"el ambiente gay,"* as he called it, or "the gay milieu") at the age of fourteen, and experienced sex only after meeting his first boyfriend a few years later.

As a child, Edwin had enjoyed the physical sensations he felt when wrestling with a boy his age during childhood games, and he also became slightly infatuated with this friend. He recalled that when he was fourteen, he was returning by bus from vacationing with his sister at the Pacific Coast resort of Acapulco. He began talking with a fellow passenger, a gay man in his late twenties. Upon their arrival Mexico City, this man offered to introduce him to his gay and lesbian friends. Edwin cheerfully recalled this as his first contact with gay people:

When we returned to Mexico City [the man from the bus] introduced me to this young [lesbian] woman, who said, "If you want to come by, we're here every weekend." I liked their circle, so it didn't take me long [to return]. I came back the following week, and . . . those youths started taking me to parties, to bars, those types of things.

Edwin decided to come out of the closet (*"salir del closet,"* in his own words). He first disclosed having same-sex desires to his mother, whom he described as a very strong woman:

I told her, "You know what? I want to talk with you, because I feel a little bit like I am lying to you." . . . She and I had very open communication. . . . For that reason I told her *que era homosexual* [that I was gay], and that I am attracted to my own sex. . . . She simply said, "That's something I can't change. I only ask you to respect my house; this is your house, and as long as you are a righteous person, you will never have problems here." I told my dad, too, who somehow also accepted me. And they told my siblings. All that really helped me; it helped me see life differently. I was always very aware, very centered in terms of what I wanted.

Edwin had waited to have sex until he had his first boyfriend at age nineteen, in part because his lesbian friend had always protected him: "She would say, 'You are too young. If someone approaches you, and you want to do something with him, do it. But if you don't, tell me and I will set things straight.' So I felt protected." In discussing his first relationship, Edwin remarked:

It was very cool [*muy padre*] . . . because I really loved this person. We met on the street in Mexico City on my way home from school. I met him and we started dating. Obviously, by that point I already knew what a [gay] relationship entailed.

In his twenties, however, Edwin's explorations of his professional interests and same-sex desires put him on a pathway that had been unimaginable to him earlier, and which brought him first to Cancún, then to Spain and Germany before he eventually moved to San Diego for sexual reasons.

Norberto: Finding Gay Culture in Mexico's Gayest City

Norberto (born 1982) acquired a gay identity in Guadalajara, Mexico's second-largest city, and widely regarded as the gayest in Mexico.[39] He had not yet come into contact with Guadalajara's extensive gay culture when he left at the age of fourteen to join his mother in San Diego. Before he left, however, two of his uncles had separately targeted him for sex.[40] With one, he said, he enjoyed the interaction (although he found it confusing). Sex with the other had been forced, and had made him bleed during penetration. Norberto said he left those experiences behind when he moved to San Diego. Yet contrary to what might be expected, his first contact with gay culture happened not in San Diego but in Guadalajara, when Norberto returned for a visit at the age of eighteen:

I called a phone number [I got from a flyer] and asked where I could make gay friends. I remember the flyer was for a march. It said: "Join the march and come to fight for our rights." So I called, and I told them I wanted to meet people and make friends. They invited me to an office. "Come here, you can meet people and talk with them." But I never found them. What did I do? I went downtown and went to . . . a small plaza where I saw a person. . . . A transsexual.

This may have been the same downtown plaza in Guadalajara that I discuss in my book *The Night Is Young*, which constituted a daily gathering spot for working-class gays and lesbians.[41] The person Norberto met there introduced him to gay men who came to the plaza, and they took him to several of Guadalajara's gay bars. Norberto was surprised about how open gay men were in his hometown, something he never had imagined. Paradoxically, recalling that homosexuality was not openly discussed in his family when he was growing up, Norberto also said that "in Mexico we're very close-minded."

Fidel and Rogelio: Gay Lives in the Mexican Borderlands

Fidel and Rogelio grew up in Tijuana, a city of 1.7 million that is the largest Mexican city along the US-Mexico border. Fidel (born 1971) left his family home as a teenager and became independent. He discovered gay sex before learning of a large gay culture in his own city. When Fidel was seventeen, a friend of his brother's who was visiting asked if he could stay over. Fidel had two beds in his bedroom, so they each took one. However, in the middle of the night, this young man proposed that they sleep together to keep each other warm. This gave them the occasion to touch each other and have sex, which in turn led them to establish a one-year relationship that ended when Fidel's boyfriend decided to migrate to Canada. Fidel went back to being single. He had no knowledge about how to make contact with other men like him, but soon afterward he stumbled upon a cruisy park near his home:

One day I was there smoking. I saw . . . many men who were walking around, but I didn't pay attention to them until one approached me and started talking to me, and then asked me if I wanted to have sex with him. I didn't agree to do it, but then I began paying attention and realized that the men there were usually gay men. . . . I never did anything in the park, because it was kind of new to me and I was scared.

Fidel became alert to the comings and goings of men in this space. Around the same time, one of his cousins issued an unexpected invitation:

One day he asked me, "Do you want to go to a discotheque? But it's a little different." I said, "OK, let's go." I had never been to one. When we entered, I saw many men kissing, embracing. I felt somewhat uncomfortable, but he [the cousin] told me, "Relax, it's normal."

These events marked Fidel's official entry into Tijuana's gay world. Eventually, he realized that an even larger gay enclave existed in San Diego, right on the other side of the border. Indeed, for participants who lived at the border, San Diego was often more of a magnet than the more distant gay worlds of Mexico City or Guadalajara.

Also in Tijuana, Rogelio (born ca. 1967) ran away from his family home when he was twelve. He explained, "I simply wanted to have my own money, my freedom—to do whatever I wanted." Three young gay men welcomed him into their household. He shared a bed with one of them, an eighteen-year-old, and he ended up having sex with him. Rogelio's roommates introduced him to Tijuana's gay life. But when he turned eighteen, he decided to move out of that household and go live with a straight friend. Soon afterward, he developed a sexual attraction to straight men: "I started playing soccer. I started hanging out . . . doing things that *straights* [*said in English*] do. . . . I began leaning toward straights, toward people who were *hombres* [real men]." Rogelio then started having sex with some of his straight friends.[42]

He eventually shifted back to having sex with gay men in San Diego. However, he also decided to maintain a sex life involving straight-identified partners in Mexico. As he put it, "[I have] my straight friends in Tijuana and my gay friends in San Diego. . . . I have no problems. Each in their place. Each in their world." For Rogelio, his participation in these two distinct worlds of same-sex desires, and the way he used the US-Mexico border to separate his gay life in San Diego from his sex life involving straight men in Tijuana, were merely some of the various possibilities offered to him as part of his binational, urban gay life.

Budding Gay Life in Midsized Cities

Venustiano: Entering the Gay World in Conservative Irapuato

Like their urban counterparts, participants who came of age in midsized cities in Mexico accessed well-established gay venues in their locations, so they did not have to travel to larger cities to experience institutionalized gay life. One interesting example is provided by Venustiano, whose case I introduced briefly at the beginning of the chapter. Venustiano grew up in the outskirts of Irapuato. After years of feeling internally conflicted about his same-sex desires, he learned about a local gay bar, and it provided him an entry into the local gay culture. But he did not check out the bar immediately; it took him a while to finally make the decision to go there. One night, when he was "burning inside" with desire, Venustiano secretly left his family home, flagged a taxi, and asked the driver to drop him off within walking distance of the bar. As he approached his destination, he was extremely nervous, and he hesitated. But he was also simultaneously full of anticipation, and began debating with himself whether to enter the bar or leave. Thankfully, a young man he knew happened to walk by just then. The man greeted him by simply saying, "See you inside," which Venustiano took as a fateful sign that he should finally cross this threshold and discover a world he yearned to know.

The pathway that brought him to this moment had begun some weeks earlier, when he spotted a magazine with an attractive man on the cover at a newsstand in the center of town, "A [Mexican] gay magazine, that is," Venustiano explained. "I was working up the courage to buy it. I was trying to buy it quickly and disappear, so that the merchant wouldn't see my face. I bought it and read it." That such a magazine was openly sold at that newsstand was itself an indicator that Mexican urban gay culture had already arrived in his hometown. The magazine gave Venustiano a glimpse of Mexican gay life, but not the specifics of where to find it in Irapuato. However, it unexpectedly made it possible for him to get the information he wanted later on:

Another day, when I was there again, I saw an older man [*un señor*] who bought [the same magazine]. I thought, "Wow! That's the first step." The second [step] was to follow him. He realized that I was following him, and he stopped in the next block. I was scared . . . but I crossed the street. He said, "What's up?" "Nothing." . . . I told him my story; he told me his. He was married and he had two kids. . . . I let him go . . . but [before he left] he told me, "You know what? There's a restroom where people go to *buscar ambiente* [seek sex with men]."

Venustiano started frequenting this restroom and having sex in hotels with men he met there. He thought of these contacts as "shameful," but also as a stage toward obtaining information about the local gay bar that he ended up attending. Soon after visiting the bar, however, Venustiano decided to migrate to the United States, which he saw as the next step in his pathway of desire. But, unlike other men in my study, when he migrated he originally had not planned on pursuing a gay life in the United States. Rather, as I will describe, in San Diego he hoped to find a woman he could marry.

Adriana: Gay and Feminine in La Paz

In La Paz, a midsized city on the coast of the Sea of Cortez (population 215,000), Adriana (born 1962) found gay culture through quite a different path. Her first sexual encounter took place when she was thirteen and involved a boy her own age who, she said, later identified as gay. At the age of fifteen, Adriana befriended two gay men who taught her how to "feminize" herself (Adriana had been dressing in male clothes and going by her original male name). They plucked her eyebrows and recommended that she start injecting female hormones. These bodily transformations put her in touch with an extremely gendered world of same-sex desires.

Adriana identified as a gay man. She clarified that her friends were "not *travestis* [but] *gais*."[43] As a child, she had been an effeminate boy who was teased by others for her demeanor, but she never wanted to become a woman; she saw her effeminacy as related to her same-sex attraction. Asked if she identified with the term *transgénero*, Adriana sharply responded, "No, I am a *homosexual*." She then added, "I'm not going to say that I'm a woman, because I'm not a woman. I know perfectly what I am." She had grown breasts but kept her penis: "Cut it off? I'm not crazy!" She negatively judged post-op trans women, and said that "there's something wrong in their head." As it turns out, she was also being practical in not having the surgery: she viewed her penis as an asset in her job as a sex worker, because straight-identified clients often asked her to penetrate them.

In addition to working as waiters, Adriana's gay friends in La Paz engaged in sex work on the side, dressed in female garb. After her own transformation, these friends suggested that she start doing sex work with them in *la zona de tolerancia*, the red-light district. There Adriana encountered a larger network of *jotas*—whom she labels using the feminine form of the derogatory term *joto* (fag), which is used throughout Mexico to refer to effeminate men—and she also began to meet masculine male clients in the street. Previously, she had helped her family financially, and she continued to do so as a sex worker. But out of respect for her mother, who was aware of the changes in her work life, Adriana refused to give money directly to her. Instead, she always asked one of her siblings to bring the money home. Her brother, ostensibly jealous of Adriana's ability to support the family, would protest: "Yes, because [she] makes a great deal of money with her ass," to which Adriana responded, "Sure, but how much does [that money] solve your problems?"

In her new social network, she also met "more polished" cross-dressing sex workers from Mexico City, and she decided to join them when the police ordered that group to "leave town." As they traveled through different places in northwestern Mexico, the group experienced considerable police harassment, was arrested multiple times, and was repeatedly asked to provide sexual services to their jailers. Eventually, Adriana returned to La Paz, at which point she decided to move to Tijuana, a city she imagined would be more tolerant of the kind of sex work she was involved in.

The Reproduction of Big-City Gay Life in Midsized Cities

Adriana's story is reminiscent of the cases discussed by Annick Prieur in her ethnographic account of young transvestite men in Ciudad Nezahualcóyotl in the outskirts of Mexico City.[44] By the time that my participants came of age in the 1980s and 1990s, many of the same forms of gay culture that existed in large Mexican cities had begun to be replicated in midsized cities such as Irapuato and La Paz. Options there may have been fewer than in the large cities, but they nonetheless facilitated a sense of local gay culture and became a focal point for tight local social networks of gay men.

For instance, Claudio (born 1977) described the two gay discos he knew in the city of Oaxaca, and indicated them as places where "everyone knows each other." Commercial establishments were emerging as a more middle-class and institutionalized complement to the informal social networks of gay men and the public gay gathering places predictably found in many small and midsized cities, including the central historic plazas in many locations. These plazas provide a central gathering spot where many local residents, particularly those who are working-class, socialized.

An illustration of the gay life in Mexican plazas was provided by Facundo (born 1967), who had grown up in Durango but moved to Tijuana at the age of sixteen. Facundo explained that he had to travel extensively in Mexico for business purposes. Whenever he went to a new city, he would try to obtain information about where to find gay people by consulting the listings in Mexican gay magazines or, in the absence of these, by looking for gay people in the city's downtown plaza:

It's very common in Mexico, that people give you information of any kind. One time I went . . . to a plaza, and I asked a gay man . . . you could tell he was gay: "You know what? Where is there a [gay] place?" And he gave me a complete tour.

In this comment, Facundo referred to a plaza in Guadalajara—possibly the same plaza where Norberto first met gay men and which I encountered in my previous work in Mexico[45]—but he also found that the strategy of looking for gay men in the central historic plazas was effective in many smaller cities and towns throughout the country.

Gay cruising of this informal, but nonetheless institutionalized, sort was also moving into commercial spaces as chain establishments opened branches in smaller cities. One interesting example involves the magazine section of Sanborns, a widely recognizable national chain of restaurants and department stores originally founded in 1903 as an American-style drugstore by a pair of American brothers in downtown Mexico City.[46] Efraín (born 1965), who lived in the northern border city of Mexicali, described how "you go to Sanborns. . . . It's famous throughout the country . . . the Sanborns cafés, as cruising places." Similarly, Bernardo (born 1967), talking about Tijuana, explained how the rituals unfolded in the magazine/bookstore section of his local Sanborns: "You pretend to be reading the magazines, you get it? But you are trying to hook up." These gay cruising strategies, originating in the Sanborns branches in Mexico City decades before, had become recognizable in newer Sanborns branches throughout Mexico.[47] Moreover, these various expressions of urban gay culture were being exported to smaller cities, towns, and even rural areas, where they acquired their own local flavor.

Town and Country: The Gay Cultures of Small Places

Small towns in Mexico are typically seen as the repositories of national traditions and old-fashioned cultural understandings, including sexual ones—not as centers of gay life. That does not mean, however, that same-sex desires are absent in these places. But they are assumed to be expressed in quintessentially old-fashioned ways, the representation of which was perhaps most dramatically achieved in the esteemed Mexican director Arturo Ripstein's 1978 film *El lugar sin límites* (*Hell without Limits*). The story in this film centers on the tormented sexual liaison between "la Manuela," an effeminized *travesti* (who might be best described in contemporary terms as a trans sex worker) who owns the town's brothel, and Pancho, a young *macho* who cannot come to grips with his emotional connection with and sexual attraction to Manuela.[48] The relationship unfolds as part of an intricate plot meant to yield an incisive critique of 1970s-style Mexican rural politics. When, in a moment of passion and drunken stupor, Pancho kisses Manuela in front of his male buddy, and his friend reacts negatively to what he is seeing, Pancho's predictable way of saving face is to pursue Manuela down the dark streets of the town and kill her. Manuela's tragic end, which can be anticipated from the beginning of the film, is presented as inevitable.

According to my participants, although such old-fashioned, highly gendered culture is still widely recognizable in small-town and rural Mexico, in recent decades small towns have experienced changes in their sexual cultures, including some related to the emergence of local forms of gay culture.[49] However, as we will see in the cases that follow, to be able to recognize those shifts we must look beyond the more stereotypical versions of Mexican highly gendered homosexuality, and take into account the degree to which those highly gendered sexualities are becoming hybridized.

Emilio and Ezequiel: Shifting Gendered Roles in Small-Town Mexico

Emilio (born 1979) and Ezequiel (born 1970) grew up in the same small coastal town in Nayarit, the Mexican state where Eliseo, quoted at the beginning of the chapter, described interacting sexually with his teenage friends. Emilio and Ezequiel's town is not far from the world-renowned tourist resort of Puerto Vallarta, considered to be the gayest resort in Latin America.

Emilio had his first sexual experience at the age of twelve with a young man from a nearby town, whom Emilio called a *mayate*.[50] Emilio described *mayates* as men who "are supposedly *straight* [*said in English*] guys . . . who like to have sex with homosexuals." These men typically "don't really like to suck [perform oral sex] . . . they only like to get sucked. And when the sucking is done, they *bend you over* [*said in English*] and they want to stick it in." Emilio recalled how he met this man:

[He came] to the town's fiestas. . . . I clearly remember. We left the party, and it was my first experience. He took me to his pickup truck and he made me suck him off. I sucked him off and the guy came, that was all. . . . [He was a] very attractive guy. He was around eighteen years old.

As my colleague Jorge Fontdevila and I have noted elsewhere, the phrase "they bend you over," which several participants used in characterizing *mayates*, summarizes the displeasure they later felt about the impersonal nature of their encounters with straight-identified men.[51] According to my participants, *mayates* guard their sense of masculinity within same-sex sexual encounters and distance themselves from homosexuality by strictly enforcing certain roles: they penetrate or receive oral sex, but do not reciprocate; they do not allow their partners to touch their genitals or buttocks, and they never touch their partner's genitals or caress their bodies; and they do not kiss or openly express any affection for their partners.[52]

This description works as an ideal type. Yet comments from several of my participants make clear that reality is often more complicated. For instance, Emilio said that his first sex partner openly told him that he was very attracted to him, and also wanted to kiss him all the time. Similarly, Ezequiel, who defined *mayates* as "men who like *jotos*," described encounters in which *mayates* would ask to give him oral sex or the *beso negro* ("the black kiss," a reference to anilingus, or "rimming," as it is commonly known), and also asked to be anally penetrated, which surprised him. Also surprising to him was discovering that he himself would become greatly aroused when these men, who thought of themselves as masculine and straight, transgressed expected sexual roles, encouraging him to take roles he felt were reserved for those partners.[53]

Ezequiel's sexual life had begun with some sexual exploration at age seven with a thirteen-year-old boy who asked him if he wanted to play "making love." However, when he was a bit older, he began to engage in sexual contact with masculine-acting boys his age that he called *mayatillos* (young *mayates*), and he embraced an effeminate style, developing a reputation as *joto*. He was one of the participants in my study who had been labeled as gender nonconforming since his childhood. Yet he challenged local gendered expectations by being interested in soccer and other so-called boys' sports. His friends, puzzled, would ask him, "How can you be *joto* and like soccer?" As Ezequiel explained, soccer not only allowed him to retain a reputation as "one of the guys" but also facilitated sex with masculine boys. He described how this happened:

My favorite thing was to go to the beach to play soccer with my friends. The last one who stayed . . . with that one [I had sex]. That was the plan that we all had. We would go to the beach. It would be around fifteen of us. We would finish the game, and everyone would say, "Let's go." And I would say, "Not me, I'll stay for a while." And I would swim along the shore, about half a kilometer, and I would come back to see who was the last one to stay. When I came back, one would still be there waiting, and with him I [had sex]. That was the business.

Ezequiel further indicated that in addition to sexual pleasure, *mayates* expected other rewards in the form of gifts or even money, an expectation confirmed by my other participants. Emilio, in describing this sexual culture, estimated that there were around 150 known *homosexuales* in his town (interestingly, in this estimate he explicitly included all the *mayates*, suggesting his own shift toward a gay schema in which *mayates* would be considered to be *homosexuales* or *bisexuales* in their own right).[54] Nonetheless, Emilio's and Ezequiel's interpretations shifted soon afterward as they began to participate in the international gay scene at the nearby resort of Puerto Vallarta.

Valentín: Gayness and Class Distinctions

Yet not all small-town sexual cultures in Mexico follow these highly gendered (albeit shifting) sexual prescriptions. For Valentín (born 1975), raised in the professional middle class of a small town in the southern state of Tabasco, sexual socialization was quite different. Valentín's sexual life had begun at age twelve when mild sexual games with a neighbor his own age led the two first to mutual masturbation, and then some years later to mutual anal penetration. Their sexual interactions happened in Valentín's home or in the fields. Valentín mentioned that his boyfriend—his *noviecito*—later became closeted and eventually married a woman whom both had known to be a lesbian.

Valentín explained that his middle-class world existed within a small Mexican town because of the presence of a state-owned company, the reason his father had brought his family to live there in the first place. Indeed, his family home was located in a neighborhood populated by professional families in which one or both parents worked for the company. According to Valentín, the presence of these middle-class families in the town had generated two contrasting, separate, and yet coexisting worlds, one rural and another that had been transplanted from urban Mexico. Sexuality in his middle-class, professional world seemed to him quite different from sexuality in the town.

Valentín recalled that when he was in *preparatoria* (high school), middle-class *homosexuales* would organize social gatherings in their family homes—gatherings at which the host's parents would be present:

We would get together in friends' homes, where parents knew that their children were *homosexuales* or *lesbianas* and allowed these parties to happen so that they could also watch over them. I am referring to [families] with an educational level that would be . . . let's say, high, for Mexico.

They would also invite straight classmates (whom Valentín called *bugas*, using the slang term for "heterosexuals" commonly used by gays and lesbians throughout Mexico) so that "no one would think anything weird about the parties." He explained that they "mixed . . . so that [people] wouldn't become suspicious. . . . We would invite friends [who were popular in school] . . . the classic school heartthrob or the sexiest girl." But parents were well aware that the core group of friends involved *homosexuales* and *lesbianas*.

Valentín thought of the parents' attitudes not as pragmatic tolerance but as full acceptance. As he explained:

The place where I lived was very small, but fortunately people moved to live there from many parts of the country. . . . So, it was a tiny town where everyone knew each other . . . [but] these were all educated people with university degrees and an open mind.

But outside the professional, middle-class section of town, the situation was different. "They only have low-end places, *cantinas*, dives, whorehouses—those are the only [local] places frequented by *homosexuales*," Valentín noted. Showing an overt disdain toward effeminate men in the poorer sections of his town, he described them as

lowly educated people, really closed-minded, the classic ugly homosexual. . . . The repressed homosexual who tries to be a woman, dressed really horribly, who also acts horribly . . . in front of anyone; [men] from an underworld, who drink or take drugs, and who dress up as women.

The tension between these two sexual worlds, divided by social class and education, is rather evident in Valentín's narrative, as is his perception that small-town culture was backward, while an imported, middle-class urban culture was forward looking.

Justo: Emerging Gay Cultures in Mexican Towns

These tensions were also patent in other cases, including that of Justo (born 1971), who was raised on a ranch near an agricultural town in the state of Jalisco. Justo's story shows, first, that a local sense of gay culture is emerging in small Mexican towns. But it also demonstrates that these towns may have not one but multiple same-sex cultures, varying by social class, and that one way in which these class-specific cultures may be shaped is through men's divergent experiences when partaking in gay life in nearby large cities. Finally, Justo's story suggests how gender-based sexualities may be changing in ways that open the door for the performance of more fluid and less predictable interpretations of sexual and gender roles.

Starting around the age of nine, Justo began participating in sexual games involving boys his own age—cousins, a neighbor, and later a friend. He first realized his interest in boys when he became infatuated with an elementary school classmate. His teacher noticed him staring at this boy—which he did constantly—and asked him to stop. Justo later understood that his interest in boys made him different from other boys. His mother would try to make him be more masculine, going so far as to tell him she thought he was a *puñal* (fag), and that she knew he did not want to tell her. Justo also learned other derogatory terms that people used to refer to people like him: *maricón* (faggot); *marica* (sissy); and *joto*, a word he associated particularly with the harsh and direct language of Mexico City.

When Justo was eighteen, he discovered that certain adult men in his town participated in a local culture where same-sex desires could be openly expressed. He first encountered this world when he needed a haircut and the local barbershop was closed. A young woman who saw him standing outside the shop offered to take him to a hairstylist she knew. Justo was surprised to find one of his male cousins there, who upon seeing him immediately asked, "What are you doing here?" As it turned out, Justo's cousin was dating the male hairstylist and immediately revealed this information to Justo, noting also that he was aware of the rumors circulating in the town about Justo himself. Playfully, the cousin told him, "*Ya somos primas*" (We are now female cousins). He then proceeded to interrogate Justo about his personal life, which initially made Justo uncomfortable. "I'm not out, as they say, out of the closet. I am still staying low, under the water," he told his cousin.

Justo soon learned that two core gay social networks existed in his town. His new gay friends from one group were the "well-known [gays] in the town," "the town's high class," and the town's "divas." These men disdainfully referred to the second group as the *eléctricas* (using the feminine of *electric*), a term reflecting their sense that these men were *corrientes* (a word that means "current," as in electrical current, but also means "ordinary" or "vulgar" when referring to people). The nickname was meant to delineate a strict class distinction.

Because Justo was regarded as more masculine than most of his gay friends in the town, people started thinking he was these men's *mayate*. These friends met socially in the town, but when they wanted to go out they typically drove fifty miles to attend the cosmopolitan gay clubs of Guadalajara. Thinking about the first time he entered a gay club in that city, Justo recalled:

I was shocked . . . [*laughs*]. I [previously] thought there were only six of us, six to ten of us in the whole world. When I saw the bunch of *jotos*, I thought I had died and gone to heaven! I said "Wow!"

In Guadalajara's gay bars, however, his group tried to maintain a sense of small-town, middle-class dignity:

We went to Guadalajara, to the best clubs, to the best bars. But five of us would go, and five would come back together. That is, we went dancing, drank, met people, but never left [the bars] with anyone else. By contrast, the guys from . . . the other group that they called the "eléctricas," you always saw them enter and leave the bar with someone different. They went in and out; sometimes three different times in one night. From that perspective, I am glad that I hung out with [my] group.

Justo later revealed—contradicting himself—that in fact he had several one-night-stands with men that he met in those gay clubs, as well as a short affair with a Guadalajaran doctor. But he also noted that in contrast to his own group, when the *eléctricas* went to Guadalajara they would choose to go to "*bares de mala muerte*" (low-end dives) and to straight bars, suggesting differences in style and taste regarding same-sex desires as well as the second group's emphasis on seeking straight men for sex.

Nonetheless, in his own town, Justo also had an affair with a man who could be seen as a *mayate*. This man owned a car repair shop, and Justo said he wanted to believe that he was a bisexual:

He was with me, but he had a girlfriend so that people wouldn't suspect him. In fact, I would drive him in his car to see his girlfriend. While he was with her, I would take his car for a ride. . . . I would [later] pick him up, we would have sex, and then he would drop me off at my house.

Justo's partner later married his girlfriend, which Justo said bothered him, but he preferred this situation over losing his boyfriend. In Justo's own mind, he was the one in charge in this relationship. "I'd thought that I was using him as a sexual object, instead of being in love with him. . . . When we broke up, we just broke up. I didn't cry. He just left." This interpretation contradicts the expectation, in a heavily gendered world, that the one in charge would be his very masculine, straight-identified boyfriend.

To be sure, that the couple did not always play by the perceived rules of a sexual world defined by sharp gendered differentiation is further exemplified by the fact that Justo's partner explicitly pursued the subversion of expected sexual roles. In addition to working in his car repair shop, this man was a *charro* (a cowboy) in the local rodeo (*charreada*). One time, while his partner showered before the show, Justo was ceremonially preparing his rodeo costume (which Justo seemed to think of as a female role). "I had his clothes ready on the bed: his shirt, his pants, [and] his underwear," he said. Justo did not anticipate what happened next:

He came into the room stark naked. I could tell something was up. So he approaches me and throws me on the bed and he starts undressing me. I said, "Hey, what's going on, we need to go." He responded, "I want something new with you." I said, "What?" And I started getting the shivers, wondering, "What is he going to do to me?" And then he sits [on my penis] and I say, "What are you doing?" He answers, "Shut up, I want to know how it feels."[55]

This was the first time Justo ever penetrated someone. His reaction was to start giggling nervously. His partner, who had never been penetrated, kept asking him to be quiet. "I wasn't enjoying it. He was. You could see it on his face." Despite the awkwardness of the moment, in the end they both were able to ejaculate, and then they left for the rodeo. Justo ended this story by noting, "At the rodeo he was hanging out with a girl . . . he bought her flowers . . . after doing that with me!"

Further evidence of shifts in the local organization of sexuality comes from Justo's description of his job as a deejay at the local disco, which was owned by one of his cousins. It was a "regular" disco (meaning that it was a straight, not a gay place). However, toward the later part of the evenings, groups of working-class gay men would often arrive to drink and dance.[56] When these men appeared, people in the disco would shout things such as *"Ya llegaron los jotos"* (The fags have arrived) or *"Ya nos metieron una putiza"* (a play on a colloquial phrase that would normally mean "being beaten up," as represented by the word *putiza*, but that in this case is a joke about having a group of *putos*, or fags, take over the place). Yet although people would make jokes about the *homosexuales*, they did not antagonize them, even when, in Justo's opinion, the gay men danced rather effeminately (*torcidos*, meaning "bent"). He added:

At the end of the night, when the disco closed, many [straight] guys would stick around and chat with [the gay men] and then would leave with them [to have sex]. So, they criticized them in front of others, but at one or two in the morning, when the venue closed, they left with them.

Justo's narrative therefore suggests that despite being ostracized, gay men in his town could express themselves publicly and were seen as part of the local social fabric. And yet, those with "more class"—as Justo put it—tended to live more discreet local gay lives, and often felt they had to travel to Guadalajara when they wanted to express themselves openly. In Justo's own case, despite the growing visibility of gay men in his town, he felt compelled to leave after an unexpected incident resulted in the forced disclosure of his sexual orientation to his father, culminating in Justo's departure to the United States.

———

The narratives told by Mexican men who grew up in small Mexican towns suggest that the sexual cultures there have more to them than what can be inferred from the stereotype of highly gendered Mexican sexualities. They relate to what Rodrigo Parrini and Ana Amuchástegui have called "the globalization of certain imaginaries that bring to the most distant places in the country a plural and diverse world, in terms of identities, sexuality, and subjectivity."[57] And, as some of these cases also indicate, Mexican small towns are not isolated from changes taking place throughout Mexico. The anthropologist Matthew Gutmann has made this point in discussing gender relations in the country's rural areas: "No longer can investigators rest content with the antiquated portraits presenting rural areas as hotbeds of little more than insular gossip, envy, and clan squabbling."[58] As my data show, this statement also applies to the sexual cultures surrounding male homosexuality.

Mexican Sexual Diversity

When the US anthropologists Joseph Carrier and Clark Taylor carried out their original research in Mexico, both recognized that a wider diversity of interpretation of same-sex desires was already present in their two sites, Guadalajara and Mexico City. But their research sought to show what was distinct anthropologically about Mexican sexual cultures, so they highlighted the heavily gendered interpretations associated with the *pasivo/activo* model.[59] It is thus not surprising that only this sexual schema made its way into the American imagination about Mexican male homosexualities, especially given that Mexican culture is often stereotypically depicted in the United States as "traditional," religious, macho, and unchanging. Over time, its use to sweepingly characterize Mexican male homosexuality has had the unfortunate effect not only of exoticizing Mexicans, but also of contributing to the perception that Mexican sexual cultures are premodern, static, and backward in comparison with the more enlightened, modern, dynamic, and global sexual cultures imagined to characterize the United States and other rich countries of the North.[60]

As I have noted, my previous ethnographic research in Guadalajara problematized the notion that Mexicans rely solely on the prescriptions of the *pasivo/activo* model in interpreting male same-sex desires.[61] Similarly, other Mexican scholars, including Guillermo Nuñez Noriega, have launched important critiques of this model (while at the same time acknowledging the significance of the research that generated it).[62] But when the Spanish-language version of Carrier's 1995 book *De los Otros* was published in 2003, he insisted that very little had changed in regard to Mexican homosexualities since he first arrived in Mexico in 1968. That is, Carrier ignored the fact that in the span of those three decades, Mexican urban gay cultures had diversified and expanded, becoming more visible and institutionalized in many locations, and the "Mexican sexual system" had become increasingly varied.[63] Indeed, by the 1990s male homosexuality had become a topic that was fairly openly discussed in Mexican society, including in the mass media, and the Mexican gay and lesbian movement, first organized in the late 1970s, was on its way to achieving major political successes that crystallized over the following decade.[64]

Moreover, as I have described, over that time span it had become clear that the *pasivo/activo* model alone did not do justice to the more expansive landscape of same-sex desires and forms of homoeroticism as painted by the Mexican immigrants' narratives in this chapter. The Mexican men in my research articulated gendered forms of male-male sexual interaction as well as localized versions of global gay culture. And, as my colleague Jorge Fontevila and I have demonstrated elsewhere,[65] they also reported forms of homosocial homoeroticism that are neither heavily gendered nor directly linked to a gay sexual schema (and are represented here particularly in participants' accounts of encounters they had engaged in with neighborhood friends during adolescence).

Some numbers help to clarify this picture. By the time that the 80 Mexican participants in my study left Mexico and/or began to participate in San Diego's gay life, 12 were engaging exclusively in highly gendered same-sex encounters that conformed to the *pasivo/activo* model; 41 were engaging in interpretations and practices consistent with contemporary views of Mexican gay identities; 2 were expressing their same-sex desires in ways consistent with the "homosocial" sexual schema; 23 fit what we called a "combined" sexual schema (which involved going back and forth between the highly gendered sexual schema and one of the other two—homosocial or object choice/gay—or among all three, according to

Pre-migration Sexualities

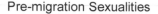

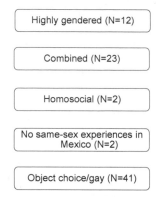

Highly gendered (N=12)

Combined (N=23)

Homosocial (N=2)

No same-sex experiences in Mexico (N=2)

Object choice/gay (N=41)

2 Mexican men's sexualities before migration (*N* = 80; this number includes three participants who lived in Mexico but regularly crossed the border into San Diego).

specific sexual contexts, situations, or sex partners); and 2 had not yet experienced sex with a man in Mexico (fig. 2).[66] As we will see in chapter 8, these data describing sexual patterns before migration are important for understanding the shifts in sexualities that Mexican immigrant men experienced once they had begun to enact their same-sex desires in San Diego.

Beyond these numbers, the narratives offered by my study participants, along with the scholarly literature, lend credence to the commonsensical perception that those who live in Mexican urban areas may have greater exposure to so-called global understandings of sexuality than those who live in small towns or rural areas. The same could be said of Mexicans who are more socially and economically privileged when compared with those having fewer resources in each location. However, as some of the cases reported here suggest, various other sociocultural issues also contribute to participants' exposure to different forms of sexual practice. Included in this list are the social processes facilitated by the contact between Mexicans and foreign gay tourists, especially at the internationally oriented resorts of Puerto Vallarta or Cancún.[67] Another example involves the presence in rural areas of urban middle-class professionals who work for large Mexican companies, as exemplified by Valentín's case. A third concerns the contact between Guadalajara's gay men and men from surrounding rural areas in Jalisco, as described by Justo. A fourth involves the interclass exchanges and forms of gay solidarity facilitated by sexual interaction at urban underground gay venues in many locations, as exemplified by Marcelo's case. And finally, we must also consider the effects of the proximity to the US-Mexico border for those living in northern Mexico, as in the cases of Fidel and Rogelio. Beyond the examples covered in this chapter, other instances of interesting forms of urban/rural and inter-class contact and exchange relate to the widespread presence and mobility of Mexican military and naval personnel, and the upward mobility of individuals who transitioned from rural agricultural economies to the service industries in regional development centers or state capitals.

Taken together, the variety of contextual and situational as well as so-cially and culturally infused interpretations reported here makes it hard to speak of Mexican male homosexualities in the singular. And, as later chapters will show, understanding this diversity is crucial for explaining different Mexican men's sexual motivations for migrating, as well as the variety of experiences these sexual migrants have after arriving in the United States.

Change and the Resistance to Change

In closing, I want to highlight two additional issues relevant to my discus-sion. The first has to do with the progressive changes surrounding homo-sexuality that had already been under way when many of the Mexican immigrant participants were leaving Mexico, and which have acceler-ated and become further institutionalized since then. The second issue is opposite the first: the persistence of homophobia in Mexico, and its possible exacerbation as the country began to enter a period of increased violence, crime, and impunity.[68]

In terms of progressive change, most of the immigrant men in my study relocated at the time the topic of male homosexuality was being brought squarely into the open in Mexican society as a result of an emerg-ing AIDS epidemic in Mexico that initially affected gay men primarily.[69] This unfortunate development had the effect of producing competing, often loud, discourses surrounding AIDS and homosexuality—discourses reflecting the voices of both progressive and conservative social actors.[70] By the early 1990s, both AIDS and homosexuality had often been dis-cussed on television and radio talk shows and national newscasts. Gay male characters had become visible on Mexican *telenovelas* (soap operas) and other television shows, sometimes in a manner that sought to pro-duce a change in attitudes from the audience.[71]

By the early 2000s, the mainstream television networks had mostly adopted the view that promoting gay rights is a signifier of cultural prog-ress. In 2004, when an international organization created the International

Day against Homophobia, it was thus not hard for the mainstream Mexican media to jump on the bandwagon and respond to a call to commemorate it.[72] Moreover, locally produced representations of gay modernity in the media were inspired and often complemented by those appearing on foreign television shows and movies that made their way into Mexico, and the influence and availability of global gay representations further expanded as access to the Internet and social media increased.[73]

With regard to politics, Pride Marches have grown in size while spreading throughout the country.[74] A small number of openly gay and lesbian politicians have managed to serve in political offices.[75] And the federal government has increasingly supported policies and created programs to reduce discrimination directed at LGBT people.[76] Finally, the country has seen steady progress toward the approval of same-sex marriage, which is now legal in Mexico City and several Mexican states. This development has taken place in part because of several rulings by the Mexican Supreme Court, which not only declared that same-sex marriage is constitutional and issued case-by-case injunctions allowing individual same-sex couples to marry in several states, but also recently ruled that state laws defining marriage as between a man and a woman are unconstitutional.[77]

At the same time, as in many other countries, the pervasive effects of homophobia have persisted, as evidenced by the stream of reported cases of antigay violence and even murder, particularly of men perceived as feminine and of trans-identified individuals.[78] Homophobia was certainly a theme that emerges in some of the Mexican immigrants' narratives for the present study. Their reports of homophobic incidents include cases of abuse by local authorities, including one narrated by Aurelio (born 1977), who described the harassment he suffered at the hands of the Tijuana police (which several study participants described as particularly repressive and corrupt).

Aurelio said that two policemen stopped him and his boyfriend as they strolled in a park, and asked them to show identification. Aurelio was not carrying his ID card, and this became an excuse for the policemen to force the couple into their patrol car and drive them around for three hours while making fun of them, beating them up, and even stripping them naked at one point. "You feel powerless and very scared," Aurelio noted. In relation to this experience, he argued that it was hard to be gay in Mexico—a difficulty he associated with Mexican machismo—unless you were rich (imagining that wealthy Mexicans would be more accepting of homosexuality or have more power to avoid homophobia). Other participants who were detained by the police reported that they had to perform oral sex on them before the officers let them go.

Edwin, too, blamed machismo for Mexicans' homophobia, but singled out Mexico City as a more cosmopolitan place regarding gay issues. Yet despite his middle-class status, he himself was attacked while walking with friends in Mexico City's Zona Rosa (the Pink Zone), a commercial neighborhood where gay men have been openly present for several decades (and where Amberes Street, with its large concentration of gay bars, discos, restaurants, and other businesses, is now regarded as the core of Mexico City's visible gay community).[79] Edwin painfully recalled:

Suddenly, a car full of guys stopped. They got out, carrying guns, and they started insulting us. [They said,] "You're *jotos*, right? *¡Pinches jotos maricones!* [Fucking faggots!]" And they brutally started beating us up as if we had done something to them or attacked them. But our only crime was being there.

Although cases such as this often remain unsolved—to a certain extent because of what Mexican gay activists note as a bias among criminal investigators, who have tended to dismiss antigay crime in Mexico, and the murders of gay men in particular, as "crimes of passion"—some evidence indicates that the local discourse may be shifting as notions of *crímenes de odio* (hate crimes) and *crímenes por homofobia* are beginning to filter into Mexican public policy debates.[80]

Of course, homophobia and antigay hate crimes occur in many countries. Yet, in thinking about countries such as the United States, we seem prepared to accept that despite the inequality that gay people still suffer, the path toward greater equality is inevitable and a matter of time and generational change. Why, then, is it often hard for many people to imagine the same trajectory in countries such as Mexico? Furthermore, if progressive change surrounding homosexuality is indeed taking place in Mexico, why would individuals such as the immigrants who participated in my study decide to leave because of their sexuality? What, then, shapes the phenomenon of *sexual migration*? And how do shifting cultures and structural conditions figure in its production? These are all questions I take up in the chapters that follow.

THREE

The Contours of Sexual Migration

Octavio (born 1977) was raised in a small town in the southern Mexican state of Guerrero after his immediate family had relocated there from Mexico City when he was seven. Octavio realized early in his life that he was physically attracted to boys. Around the age of nine, he became sexually and romantically involved with an older male teenager, a handsome *campesino* who worked in the fields with Octavio's father. Because Octavio was perceived as normatively masculine, for a long time no one suspected that he was sexually different from other boys. But his same-sex relationship, which lasted approximately eight years, eventually came to the attention of some of the adults in his family, and it greatly upset them. One of Octavio's brothers became particularly angry, saying that he could not believe "that one of his brothers . . . had turned out to be a homosexual." This brother physically attacked Octavio for that reason, but Octavio fought back.

The relationship ended when his partner, by then in his twenties, decided to migrate to the United States. In Octavio's town, young men were expected to make the journey north at some point in their lives, as part of what sociologists have called a "culture of Mexican migration."[1] Octavio stayed, but his curiosity about emigrating was later sparked by returning gay migrants who depicted the United States as more sexually liberal than Mexico:

I heard them talking, saying that in this country *homosexuales* are not discriminated against—not like in our town. In Mexico, there are many places where people discriminate. . . . They treat them badly; they beat them up, just for being *homosexuales*. And [these migrants] said that that doesn't happen [here]; that here one can dress as a woman or walk down the street as what one is, gay, and no one says anything. And then [there's] also the economic aspect: that here with the little work that you do you can make it. . . . That if you work one week you have enough to get along . . . even when you may be overwhelmed by the rent. With the work that you have, you can get along and dress as you like, and be freer, let's say, *como homosexual* [as a gay man]. All that started getting into my head.

Ideas about American sexual liberalism and the sexual freedom presumed to reign in the United States, combined with the economic promises of migration, became ingrained in Octavio's mind.[2]

Octavio had become concerned that in his hometown he would never be able to be himself. He worried because "as one gets older, if you don't have a girlfriend, if you don't marry . . . people start harassing you." He already had experienced some discrimination. "People shouted insults at me in the street," he said. They had called him *hijo de la verga* (son of a cock), or threatened him by shouting things such as *"¡Joto, muérete!"* (Die, fag!) as he passed by. "One time they even tried to beat me up," Octavio recalled. "Thank god two other people happened to walk by, and they defended me. . . . They were going to beat me up for being homosexual." He therefore began to think seriously about leaving his town and relocating to the United States. Soon afterward, the circumstances aligned themselves perfectly for him to do so.

Central to Octavio's and other Mexican gay men's narratives about their reasons for migrating are their desire and search for sexual freedom, which they described in terms of the full realization of an openly gay identity, and which they imagined they could attain by moving to the United States. In my study, all 77 of the Mexican participants who lived in the United States were asked during their interviews to explain why they migrated, and they provided a number of different reasons (often more than one in each case).[3] Fifty-nine said that they migrated transnationally for sexuality-related reasons. In that group, 44 listed exclusively sexuality-related reasons (12 also had economic motivations, and 3 also had family-related motivations). Moreover, among the 44 who listed exclusively sexuality-related reasons, 36 talked explicitly about their desire for sexual freedom (fig. 3). As Rodolfo (born 1972) put it simply, "I came to live what I am . . . I came to do what I couldn't do in Mexico: be myself."[4]

Thus, the notion of sexual freedom centrally informs the phenomenon that I and others have called "sexual migration." This concept underscores

Motivations for Migration

Sexual motivations (N=44)*

Economic motivations (N=5)

Family motivations (N=7)

Sexual and economic motivations (N=12)

Sexual and family motivations (N=3)

Sexual, economic and family motivations (N=4)

Unknown or unclear (N=2)

* Includes 36 who talked about sexual freedom

3 Mexican gay immigrants' motivations for migration (*N* = 77).

the crucial role that sexuality can play as a motivator for transnational relocation—a point that has been increasingly noted in sexuality studies but continues to be missed by many immigration scholars.[5] Moreover, in the case that concerns me, often attached to the notion of sexual freedom is an assumption that many people, in both Mexico and the United States, believe to be true. The assumption is that LGBT people can live their sexualities more freely and openly in the United States than in Mexico because, when compared with Mexico, the United States is a more sexually liberal and enlightened country—a view suggested in the newspaper article I described in chapter 1.

This chapter focuses on Mexican gay men's narratives of sexual migration and their conceptions of sexual freedom. I describe a wide range of factors, including family and work life, romantic desires and relationships, and sexual health concerns, that structure these narratives and prompt these men to uproot themselves and begin new lives in the United States. Along the way, I problematize the overarching comparison between Mexico and the United States that these narratives so often invoke. Beneath the surface of gay immigrants' simple imaginaries of American sexual liberalism lies a more complicated story involving a constellation of circumstances that these men encounter within their immediate families and social circles. These circumstances prompt them not only to leave their places of origin but also to conclude, in many cases, that the sexual freedom they crave is not to be found at all in their home country. At the same time, for these men—and for their supporters in the United States—depicting the United States as sexually liberal and enlightened, and Mexico by contrast as sexually backward and oppressive, is an attractive proposition. It provides them a simple explanation that others may accept at face value and see as logical given circulating stereotypes about the two countries. Then there is no need to explain and confront the more complicated, and often painful, specific circumstances that make these men leave their homeland.

Mexican Gay Men's Imaginaries of American Sexual Freedom

The comments by gay returnees that Octavio overheard seemed fueled by a national stereotype that paints the United States as a country where individualism reigns and, sexually speaking, anything goes. In a sense, this image is the modern, sexualized version of the early twentieth-century "standard immigration mythology," which included the fantasy that the streets of American cities were paved with gold.[6] How gay immigrants described what they saw in the United States contrasted sharply with what Octavio was experiencing in his hometown. It confirmed for him that if he stayed, he might never find sexual freedom in the same way that he imagined it might exist in the United States. Furthermore, those comments likely concretized for him images that reinforce the sexually liberal reputation of the United States and circulate widely in Mexico—images that, as I have shown in my previous work, are transmitted, among other sources, by American movies and television shows available to many Mexicans.[7]

Similarly to Octavio, other Mexican gay men had received blanket messages about American sexual liberalism, including Gonzalo (born 1958), who first learned about San Diego's gay life from acquaintances. They told him:

Go there. There are many gays there. You can be freer, you can work wherever you want, no one calls you *joto*,[8] and no one makes fun of you. No one robs you. If someone insults you for being gay, you call the police and the police will defend you.

Here we see also an emphasis—arguably a rather idealized one—on institutionalized state protections for same-sex sexuality.

It is noteworthy that, having grown up in Tijuana, just south of San Diego and directly across the US-Mexico border, Gonzalo had previously encountered a well-developed gay life in his own city. He had also experienced the extensive gay life and cultures of Mexico City, where he moved at the age of twenty-three to get away from a man in Tijuana who had rejected him. While in Mexico City, Gonzalo had become openly gay. Unfortunately, he also was diagnosed as having AIDS, which prompted him to return to his hometown, assuming that he would soon die. Back in Tijuana, where his family still lived, he missed the independence he had achieved in Mexico City, and he also missed its extensive gay life. By deciding to cross the border and move to San Diego, Gonzalo sought to recover his sexual independence in a city with a well-developed gay culture, and at the same time he hoped to find access to HIV treatments that he feared might not be obtainable in Mexico City or Tijuana. Interestingly, although Gonzalo had experienced gay life in one of the world's largest metropolises and had achieved sexual independence and self-determination there, his decision to cross the border into San Diego was still fueled in part by the imaginary of the gay panacea in the United States that his acquaintances had painted for him.

Others were exposed to less overblown perceptions of the sexual liberalism of the United States, and yet they, too, had assessed that it offered greater sexual freedom than could be experienced anywhere in Mexico. As Joaquín (born 1981) put it, "I fled Mexico in some way to come here to express my sexuality. I knew [gay] expression and all that was freer in the United States." Born in California to Mexican immigrant parents but raised in a small city in the Mexican state of Michoacán, Joaquín had never considered returning to the United States until he became aware of his sexual attraction to other men.

Finally, some Mexican men had experienced urban American gay life firsthand before they decided to migrate, and they had been impressed by it. Reinaldo (born 1963), who grew up in Tijuana, began attending gay bars in San Diego around the age of thirty. "I liked what I saw," he said. "Many people having fun freely, and many handsome men." Prado (born 1972), who was from Sonora and lived in Tijuana, attended his first San Diego Pride Parade when he was twenty-five. "I was encouraged when I saw the parade with so many floats, and so many people watching it," he said. "I thought Tijuana was very gay, but here there were so many more gays." As these comments suggest, for these men the greater range of possibilities for being gay that they perceived was available in an American city such as San Diego was based not on an imaginary but on their own experiences as foreign tourists. But interestingly, while they understood that an openly gay life existed and was possible in Mexico, and while they also recognized that American gay freedom in its most visible forms was enacted mainly in certain zones of certain cities, such complications to the narrative did not prompt them to engage in more fine-grained comparisons of the United States with Mexico.

Venustiano: An Altogether Different Imaginary of American Sexual Liberalism

The previous section shows that when Mexican gay men talk about American sexual liberalism, they refer most frequently to the possibilities of an openly gay life and the many options to be gay they imagine exist in the United States. However, an altogether different imaginary of American sexual freedom was articulated by Venustiano (born 1975), the man from Irapuato whose case I discussed in chapter 2.

Like others, Venustiano had heard that Americans were very sexually liberal in comparison with Mexicans. But when he began to consider the possibility of migrating, he did not imagine that he would move to the United States to adopt a fully open gay identity. Instead, he entertained the idea of meeting a sexually liberal American woman who would accept him as a gay man and marry him. Indeed, Venustiano decided to migrate at a time when he had become concerned that his family might find out that he was gay. He feared that as he aged, it would become harder for him to explain why he had not married a woman. He was already feeling a strong pressure to marry, and he responded to this pressure by lying about having girlfriends.

One time, as Venustiano was telling one such lie to his sisters-in-law, his father interjected, saying, "in front of them, that it was about time that I got married. I felt so bad!" Venustiano thought: "What can I do? The years are piling up and all my friends are getting married, and I know I can't marry and I can't stay either." He was startled to hear his father make such a blunt statement. "In that moment, my brain turned into mush. I told him I was going to the US and that I was going out with a girl."

Venustiano thus convinced himself that he was leaving for economic reasons, just like his brother had before him: "When my brother left, I realized that he made much more money. On top of that, he could have two separate jobs." But in reality, Venustiano's sexuality and his desire to find a liberal American wife were his main motivations for leaving:

I was getting older. I was . . . almost twenty-five. My siblings were all marrying, and I was staying behind. At that time, I didn't fully understand. When one has a problem, one always looks for an exit, and my exit was to find a woman—a woman who would want me knowing that I was homosexual. I wanted the company of a woman—not just the company, but [also] to cover the sun with one finger [*taparle el ojo al macho*—that is, to engage in deception].

Venustiano saw this strategy as preferable, both morally and practically, to what he had seen other gay men do in Irapuato. They would marry an unsuspecting woman and then secretly pursue their same-sex desires on the side. He did not want to live a life of lies or affect the life of a woman who did not know about his being gay. But he was also convinced that he had to marry a woman if he wanted to remain involved in his family life, and he did not want to give up his same-sex desires. So, he had a thought: "Who would want me this way? Maybe a lesbian or a woman who is very open-minded." Where would he find this woman? More likely in the sexually liberal United States, he reasoned. But Venustiano's fantasy of marrying a woman never materialized. Once he arrived in San Diego, he encountered a different kind of pressure he had not anticipated—the pressure to conform to particular ways of being gay that did not include the idea of marrying a woman. I return to this part of Venustiano's story in chapter 7.

The Constraints Created by Family Life

Venustiano's case also points to a major force behind the sexual migration of Mexican gay men: their desire to leave familiar contexts (in both senses of the word) in order to achieve greater sexual independence. They construct what Katie Acosta, in referring to Latin American lesbian immigrants, has called "a borderland space to express their sexuality"— a place of their own separate from that of their consanguineous family lives.[9] Moreover, many imagine that with an international border separating them from their families in Mexico, they will be in a better position to manage how much their families learn about their same-sex desires and gay lifestyles. They also think that being away from their family homes will protect them from stigma, including within their families, and in turn will protect their families from stigma in their hometowns and immediate social circles.[10] As in Venustiano's case, this constraint within immigrant gay men's family lives is closely linked to heteronormative expectations, and to a desire among the immigrants themselves not to jeopardize the family harmony. This harmony, they feel, depends in part on leaving those expectations untouched. Such accord is sometimes left intact by relying on "sexual silence" and tacit tolerance as strategies for managing sexual diversity within family life, as my previous work in Guadalajara has shown.[11] That is, family members sometimes follow complicated scripts that allow them tacitly to express tolerance toward (and even acceptance of) gay and lesbian relatives while carefully ensuring that their sexual differences are never openly verbalized.[12] The use of sexual silence and tacit tolerance as management strategies, however, differs sharply from expectations of "coming out" that are central tropes in a global gay discourse.[13]

Venustiano clearly did not want his sexuality to affect his family or his family relationships, so he felt that his relatives were the greatest constraint on his being openly gay. Other Mexican participants shared these concerns. Teodoro (born 1966) said he left his hometown of Guadalajara in search of sexual freedom, but his narrative also reveals a clear concern with avoiding familial repercussions. "I didn't come due to economic need," he said. "I never had more than I needed, but I never lacked anything either. My life was good in Guadalajara." Teodoro was instead concerned about the lack of respect for gay people that he felt was pervasive in Mexico:

For example, [in San Diego] people don't mess around with you, they treat you the same whether you are homosexual or not. In Mexico . . . they don't send the police, but they make fun of you, they criticize you. They don't say it to your face, but as soon as you turn around [they mumble], "*Pinche puto!*" [damn faggot]. Or just for being homosexual they say you're a *sidoso* [a pejorative label applied to people with HIV/ AIDS, derived from the Spanish acronym for the disease, *SIDA*]. Or because you're homosexual they want to grab your behind or try to make you touch their package. Here in San Diego I learned that you can live as you want and [people] will respect you.

Like others, Teodoro did not want to risk mistreatment for being gay while he still lived with his family, so his main motivation for leaving Guadalajara and moving to California was in fact his desire to leave home. As he put it, "Coming here meant leaving my family home, [seeking] freedom." He ended up first moving to Orange County, but he soon realized that the presence of his cousins and other relatives there had not relieved him of the family pressures and scrutiny he wanted to leave behind. In Orange County he did not achieve his much-desired opportunity to start a new life under conditions involving greater anonymity, independence, and self-determination.[14] He was still under the watchful eyes of his relatives, and he feared that if they learned, or even suspected, that he was gay or was doing anything connected to gay life in California, this news would rapidly travel back to Mexico.[15] As we will see in chapter 4, Teodoro wound up finding the sexual freedom he sought not in California but in Tijuana, Mexico.

To be sure, Teodoro knew that he could have achieved the same result in large cities in his home country. "I could've also moved from my hometown, Guadalajara, to Mexico City or to Monterrey if I had had the opportunity," he explained. But my sense is that his justifying to his family his relocation within Mexico would have been harder for him, at least initially, than saying he wanted to move to California, especially since a number of his relatives had moved there before him. And his family could simply explain to others that like many other Mexicans and like other members of his family, Teodoro had left to try his luck in "El Norte." Thus, moving to the United States solved a number of Teodoro's dilemmas simultaneously.[16] In fact, we should further note that his decision to leave his family in Mexico was motivated not only by a desire to avoid social stigma should he be found out as being gay, but also to protect these relatives from the potential shame and social stigma of having a gay son and sibling.

Protecting Families and Oneself from Social Stigma

One interesting example of the use of distance to protect one's family is provided by Inti (born 1978), who grew up in Ecatepec, a working-class suburb of Mexico City. Inti moved to San Diego at the age of seventeen, aided by a cousin who gave him the money for the journey. He explained his desire to leave Mexico in these terms:

I imagined that I would have more freedom to be as I want—to express myself more, to go out and not be worried—because in Mexico everyone knew me . . . and I knew that bad people would [eventually] shout insults at me in the street. And I worried most that they would do so when I was with my parents, or that they would insult me and my mother would hear it.

Inti's utmost concern was that antigay attitudes in his neighborhood could affect not only him but also his parents. That had already happened once. In school, a boy called him a *maricón* (faggot) in front of his mother.[17] "I didn't care, but I did care that my mom was next to me," Inti said. When this happened, his mother said nothing. She simply kept on walking. Her silence is highly indicative that Inti's gender and sexual nonconformity was tacitly handled in his family.

Like other Mexican gay immigrants, Inti arrived in the United States holding a preformed perception of American sexual liberalism. Describing his interest in San Diego, he explained: "People told me that it was nice, that it had many beaches, and that people are great toward everyone [*muy buena onda*]." Inti saw several advantages to making the migration. He imagined that he would encounter greater sexual liberalism, and the possibility that he might meet US White men was especially appealing. But the key motivating factor was his wanting to enact his same-sex desires openly while protecting himself and his family from social stigma.

However, as we will see in chapter 9, we may want to qualify the notion that men like Inti migrated for the altruistic reason of protecting their families. Given their location in a society that strongly values family and collective life, it may be more accurate to say that some of these men have felt it was *their obligation* to protect their families (even when their families were often the main source of their sexual stigma). Some of the men who spoke about protecting their families possibly thought it was the right thing to say. And they may have been especially inclined to position themselves as protectors of the relatives they were, in fact, leaving if they believed that their family life was an important source of core values that continued to shape them and in which they took pride.

The Mexican Family as a Source of Antigay Stigma

Ironically, for several men the very same families they sought to protect constituted the main source of their antigay stigma.[18] Humberto (born 1975), who grew up in a small town in Guerrero, recalled that during his upbringing, his father reacted violently if he or his brothers did anything their father considered unmanly:[19]

My father would tell us that if we swept the floors, cooked, cleaned the dishes, or made the beds, if we did feminine tasks . . . that those things were for women. He would be unforgiving about seeing us do such things; he would hit us and mistreat us. On the other hand, I would see my uncles who would ask my male cousins to sweep, cook, and nothing [bad] happened, and my uncles were all men.[20]

Humberto's father also threatened his sons by telling them that he would kick out any of them if they turned out to be a *joto* (fag). For that reason alone, Humberto wanted to get away from his family and find a place where he could live his life without fearing his father, and without the overall pressure he had also begun to experience from other family members:

I wanted to leave due to my family, because they harassed me, they could see what I was doing. . . . I wanted to leave because I didn't want to continue acting [as they expected me to act]. I already knew my situation; I knew that I was gay and that I liked men.

But at the same time, Humberto felt compelled to protect his family. As he put it: "I wanted to get out of there. I wanted to be far from my family . . . to not harm them emotionally. Do you understand? That people would start talking, 'Your son is like that.'"

In this poignant case, the father's rejection of unmanliness—and, by extension, of male homosexuality—seemed rooted in a kind of old-fashioned machismo. In other cases, however, families reacted negatively to homosexuality for other reasons, including their religiosity. Hernán (born 1971) said that while living with his family,

I couldn't be gay . . . I could not come out of the closet [*salir del closet*]. I always lived a life that wasn't mine. . . . That wasn't for me. I didn't want to be living what is not really me. That's why I opted to come, because my family is Evangelist and I had to always go to church. And I felt under a lot of pressure.

Members of his church constantly tried to match Hernán up with women, and his own brother had a hard time getting used to the idea that he was gay. Hernán thus decided to leave for San Diego as a way to relieve the pressure he felt. "I want to feel the way I was born: free. I no longer want to feel oppressed. That's how I felt when I was [living] there [in my family home] . . . . Now that I came here, I feel freer," he observed. (Note that contrary to stereotypes about Mexican religiosity, Hernán did not grow up in a Catholic family, although conservative Catholic families may exert the same kind of negative pressure on their LGBT children.)

Finally, similar to what happened to Humberto, concerns about unmanliness had also influenced Hernán's situation. He had studied cosmetology in Tijuana; his father and his grandfather had tried to convince him that such a profession was not one for men, so they refused to pay for his classes. Hernán therefore took a job at the age of sixteen in order to support his education. In the end, however, after he left for San Diego, his father eventually softened, even asking one of Hernán's boyfriends to take good care of his son. Hernán assessed that after leaving Mexico, he at last had been able to maintain a good, respectful, and cordial relationship with his family.

Beating the Gay Out of You: Pressure and Violence as "Corrective" Strategies

For other gay immigrant men, family pressures had turned into actual forms of violence. Living in Tijuana, Prado was constantly harassed by his brothers, who blamed him for acting effeminate. His sisters, too, were angry with him, because boys at school teased them on account of his behavior. And his father, a construction worker, constantly insisted that he should "walk like a *machito*, and behave like a man," and forced him to do "manly" things. Moreover, Prado's classmates regularly called him names and waited for him after school to beat him up. "They thought they could beat [the gay] out of me," he said. Friends and relatives who enacted this kind of bullying saw it as corrective; they felt that it would help boys such as Prado "turn into a man," meaning also that they thought they could prevent these boys from becoming gay.

By the time that immigrant men who experienced such a regime of violence and harassment became teenagers or young adults, they not only had learned to hide their same-sex desires and sexual attractions but also had become aware that disclosing those feelings could generate new waves of violence and overt antigay stigma within their immediate social and family circles. Leaving Mexico therefore seemed a much more appealing option. As in Hernán's case, they expected that the distance created by their departure would eventually help relatives and friends come around and accept them (or at least stop harassing them). These cases could be read as confirming that Mexico is a traditional, religious, macho, and homophobic country. But two caveats are in order. First, these forms of bullying are by no means exclusive to Mexico. In the United States, for instance, such behaviors have generated widespread concerns about bullying at schools that targets boys perceived as unmanly (which may have more to do with the generalized policing of masculinity than with actual concern about a boy's sexual orientation, as the sociologist C. J. Pascoe has found).[21] Second, not all relatives of "unmanly" Mexican boys and men harass them. Some help their gay family member migrate, reacting supportively to what they perceive as the danger of violence toward him and, in the process, becoming accomplices who promote his departure from Mexico.[22]

Complicit Families: The Production of Sexual Exile

Some of the families who tacitly tolerate or openly accept their relative's gayness, but also fear that the situation may turn out badly for him if he stays, help create the conditions for their relative to go into a kind of sexual exile—or "sexile," as Manolo Guzmán more generically has described "the exile of those who have had to leave their nations of origin on account of their sexual orientation."[23] My own use of the term, however, is more specific. I think of sexual exile as involving situations in which others expressly compel their family member to leave Mexico, believing that if he leaves, they can avoid both social stigma and public disclosure of his homosexuality. They thus in effect "exile" their gay relative for the imagined benefit of all involved. Rather than promoting full local acceptance and confronting social stigma, their complicity in fostering migration demonstrates that "the closet is a collaborative effort," as Carlos Decena has noted.[24] These features of sexual exile are nicely illustrated by the following two examples.

Justo: Becoming a Sexual Exile

Justo (born 1971), whose case I discussed in chapter 2, had achieved a fairly open gay life in both his small hometown in Jalisco and the nearby city of Guadalajara. He was indeed content with his life in Mexico, but he nonetheless migrated to San Diego at the age of twenty-five. The event that triggered this decision had taken place six years earlier, when his father learned that Justo was pursuing sexual and romantic relations with men. "The first one who found out was my dad. I was nineteen. He found [a card I had written in response to] a letter from a person I was dating," Justo said. That his father had read his personal correspondence was unusual, because the family had a strict rule that everyone must respect everybody else's property and privacy. "I don't know what happened this time. I had left my bag after coming back from school. . . . He went through my notebooks, and he found the card and he read it." Justo's father broke the family rule because he felt the need to confirm his suspicion about Justo's sexual orientation. Justo continued:

I was coming back precisely from seeing my [gay] friends. He said, "I am reading this— forgive me for reading it, but at the same time it is good for me to learn this, because many people had already told me. There was gossip, but I wanted to hear it from you. I want to know what you feel. Why did you write this?"

Justo's father asked him if he wanted to talk, and also asked him how he felt. Justo responded, "What the card says, [that's what I feel]." The dialogue continued awkwardly:

Father: Have you ever been with a woman?
Justo: I don't want to be with a woman.
Father: Why not?
Justo: I am not attracted to women.
Father: I know a house where we can go and you can be with a woman [alluding to a bordello].
Justo: No, dad, I'm sorry but no. I am nineteen years old, and I know well what I want. This is what I want.

At that point, Justo's father acknowledged that he was familiar with what his son wanted. "I have a friend who is like you," he said, "and I know he's suffered a lot." Justo knew who this friend was, because the man was openly gay and because Justo's mother used to joke that he would eventually steal her husband from her. Justo's father then finished the conversation by stating:

You know how his life is. He suffers a lot. But if that's what you want, I support you. You will still be my son. But, *mijo* [a contraction of *mi hijo*, "my son," and a term of endearment], I'll ask you just one thing. If you ever plan to do something that could shame the family, don't do it here. That's the only thing that I ask of you. For me and for your grandfather, who, as you know, he is well known here.

Justo simply replied, "Yes, I understand." In telling this story, he paused at this point and then said, "In fact, that's why I came here. That's why I'm here."

Justo felt fortunate about his father's reaction, which he believed differed from that of other gay men's families. "I am grateful to God that he helped me. That is because my dad was educated and he was not a brute. . . . There are parents who beat up their gay children [when they find out] because they are so uneducated, they don't understand." He had forgiven his father for reading his private correspondence, and was ultimately glad that the incident had led to the fateful conversation that in some way initiated his journey to the United States. As Justo's father had made clear, he would support his son and accept his decision to lead a gay lifestyle as long as he pursued it outside their town. All along, Justo's father understood why his son was leaving—after all, he was the one who had planted the seed for this to happen. But he also worried that

Justo would go wild in the United States. Influenced by old-fashioned stereotypes about male homosexuality, he feared that Justo might become an overtly effeminate *maricón* there. Justo said, "He would tell me: 'You're not wearing a wig there, are you? You are not wearing makeup.' I would respond: 'No, dad, I don't do that.' 'Alright, son, that's fine. Each to his own, but I was curious.'" In the end, Justo seemed quite amused as he recalled his father's concerns about his life in San Diego.

Tadeo: Sexual Exile, Fear, and Abuse

In another interesting example, Tadeo (born 1976) also went into sexile due to his homosexuality, but under very different circumstances. He had been born in San Diego to a Mexican mother and a Spanish father, immigrants who decided to bring their family to live in Guadalajara when Tadeo was three years old. His family were Jehovah's Witnesses who were deeply involved in their socially conservative religious community in that city. Thus, strictly speaking, Tadeo was not an immigrant, but he had lived in Mexico his entire childhood and thought of himself primarily as Mexican. His exile to San Diego was precipitated by a very unfortunate event that took place in his family home when he was seventeen. Tadeo described this event in somewhat imperfect English:

One of my older brothers [age twenty] had a kind of a party at our house. I was at school that day, and when I went back home . . . he was with his friends in the house and they were drinking. My brother . . . asked me to get a drink, and I told him, "You know I never drink." He insisted, and I said, "OK, give me a beer." . . . He [had] put some kind of pills inside to make me sleep. . . . And I knew it, when I [felt] sick. I knew . . . to call the ambulance and I knew how to call the paramedics, [for them] to take me to the hospital right away. So that day I was kind of knocked [out], then I went to my room, called the emergency [phone number]. I hang up and I just fall down. I forget about everything. When I woke up it was the next day, and I was in the hospital.

Tadeo explained that when the paramedics arrived, they found the door open and walked in. "They get in the room and they find my brother and his friends in my room. I was naked and all of them were naked. In my room! Obviously, something bad was happening there." He added, "They were playing with me. They were starting [to play] with me."

After learning of the sexual abuse, and aided by the doctors and psychologists at the hospital, Tadeo decided to press charges. His brother and his friends ended up in jail. Tadeo then was harassed for having taken legal action against them, because they all were from prominent church families: "All these guys were sons of people with names in that religion, even my brothers and me, because my father was one of the elders in that place." The incident had turned into a church scandal. Soon afterward, his attackers were released from jail, "because they didn't do anything, they were just abusing of me." They claimed at that point that the whole thing had just been a joke.

Understandably, Tadeo's parents felt caught in the middle, as the incident pitted two of their sons against each other. Tadeo said, "My father at that time was . . . he didn't want to do a lot, a big scandal with my brother and his friends. He was, like, 'You are my son; he is my son. I am in the middle.'" Once the situation had settled down, Tadeo's mother became convinced that Tadeo had to leave. "[She] starts saying, 'You know what? You have to go. I don't want you to suffer here.'" Moreover, three months had elapsed since the incident, and Tadeo was in bad psychological shape. "I didn't want to see anybody, I was so depressed. I even tried to kill myself, because I . . . was so confused. I [couldn't] believe that my brother would be doing that to me, and I was angry, I was confused. I was so bad, so depressed."

Tadeo left for San Diego, where his parents had relatives and friends. He had never lived in the United States, but being a US citizen by birth, San Diego seemed like a good alternative. There, at the age of eighteen, he began to explore his same-sex desires on his own terms.

––––––

From the explicit facilitation of sexual exile to the creation of insufferable conditions that push their gay relative away, Mexican families greatly contribute to gay male immigrants' motivations for leaving their home country. These motivations often are obscured by simpler explanations that emphasize these men's expressed desire to pursue sexual freedom in a more liberal place. As I already have suggested, the problem with giving such explanations, and stating that it is not possible to be gay in Mexico, is that they seem to invite no further questions. As the sociologist Orlando Patterson has noted, the discourse of freedom works as effective cultural shorthand because its virtues are taken to be obvious: who could be against freedom?[25] Once migration has been framed as a quest for freedom, then it is easy just to assume that sexual freedom exists in the United States and is not available in Mexico. But then we miss the point that these men did in fact have options to acquire a gay identity in Mexico, but felt unable to do so within the immediate constraints of their families and social networks.

To be sure, when Mexican gay immigrants go beyond relying on the trope of sexual freedom in explaining their motivations for migration and begin to reflect more deeply on the roles that their families played in their departure, they are opening Pandora's box. They risk contesting the positive, if stereotypical, belief that Mexican family life is benevolent compared with American family life. As we will see in chapter 10, this is a belief that these men themselves tend to endorse: they are proud to come from a culture and society they view as strongly valuing a collective orientation, where family life is prominent and always treasured. So, questioning the idea of the benevolence of Mexican families touches a nerve. That they would feel the need to leave because of how their families reacted to their sexuality—or how they thought their families might react—forces Mexican gay immigrants to grapple with the contradictions of their own individual family lives. But such reckoning is unnecessary if, instead, they stick to explanations that juxtapose a sexually liberal United States to an always traditional and conservative Mexico. Then the problem is defined in terms of Mexican culture and Mexico as a whole, not the dynamics of their own immediate families, neighborhoods, and social networks.

Institutional Forms of Homophobia in the Workplace

As important as they may be to an understanding of sexual migration, homophobia and antigay attitudes within the family and immediate social environment are not the only sources of antigay discrimination that prompted Mexican gay men to leave for the United States. Some of them also experienced more institutionalized forms of antigay discrimination. I already referred to some of these forms in chapter 2, where I discussed police harassment in Tijuana. Another disturbing example of institutionalized homophobia is the prevalence of staunch heteronormative expectations in the workplace, which can pose insurmountable barriers for gay men in terms of their career development and self-fulfillment.

Santiago (born 1967) strongly suspected that his being gay cost him his job as a reporter at a newspaper in his hometown in Sonora, and this put him on a path to relocate to San Diego. "Perhaps I'm being a bit paranoid," he said, "but I think they fired me for that reason . . . for being a homosexual." Santiago was not openly gay in this job, so he could not be sure whether his sexuality played a role in his dismissal. Given how he saw other gay men generally being treated in his hometown, however, he felt his suspicions may be justified. His case exemplifies the difficulties of separating a suspicion of discrimination from actual discrimination when a person is living, and working, in an environment he perceives as hostile toward him for being gay. The situation seems clearer in the case of Leopoldo (born 1967), who described how limiting it was for him to be an unmarried man who held jobs in private companies in Mexico. "When I was laid off," he explained, "I started looking for a new job, and I had to start lying. Why? Not being married at my age, no one wanted to hire me. In Mexico, unfortunately things happen that shouldn't happen."

Leopoldo learned this lesson in a harsh way when he began interviewing for a new position. "For one job I was in the final stages [of the hiring process], and they were about to make me an offer. [Then] they asked me, 'Are you married?'" Leopoldo responded that he was single. At that point they simply told him, "Oh, OK. You know, this position is only for married people." Leopoldo interpreted this rejection as related to the assumption that unmarried people represent a risk: "They believe that if you're not married, you're unstable—that if you're single you will be out partying every night. . . . For me, that's not a good reason [not to hire you], because I know married people who are more unstable than any single person." After being denied this job, Leopoldo learned that he had to be more strategic. "In my next interview I had to start lying. When they asked me, 'Are you single or married?' I would reply, 'I don't know how to answer that. The thing is that I am engaged, and I am getting married in four months.'" The hiring person would respond with something like "Ah, you're getting married . . . congratulations!" Leopoldo would then boastfully strengthen his point by saying, "By the way, if I take this job I will need to take some time for my honeymoon." "Yes, of course, don't worry," he would hear in response. "It was a total lie," Leopoldo declared. "I thought, 'Well, if they give me the job, in two months I will tell them that I found out that my fiancée was cheating with another man and I left her.' I would make up something new."

Through these experiences, Leopoldo became fully aware that companies often assumed something was wrong with a twenty-nine-year-old man who was single and had never been married, including the likely possibility that he was gay. Therefore, he thought that this policy of suspicion toward single men was a way of weeding out gay employees. As he put it:

At my age, in Mexico people start wondering [about why you're single]. And I don't care if people learn that I'm gay, but it worries me if they don't offer me the job [for that reason]. In that case, I can't do anything, because in Mexico I couldn't even sue them.

This comment alluded to an absence of strong job-related antidiscrimination policies in Mexico—protections afforded by the City of San Diego and the State of California, though in fact the Employment Non-Discrimination Act, which would protect LGBT people against discrimination in the workplace at the federal level, has been stalled in Congress for many years (so the issue of protections against antigay discrimination in the workplace has been left for local jurisdictions to legislate). Leopoldo also realized that in his particular field in Mexico, his chances of ever being able to disclose his sexual orientation were practically nonexistent: "If you're openly gay in Mexico, there are many jobs that you would not get, they would [simply] not hire you." He felt fortunate that headhunters eventually recruited him for a job in San Diego, which brought him to the United States with a work visa. "In the United States, it doesn't matter if I am married, single, gay, or straight.[26] They can't even ask me, and they don't care. So I'm not limited by my marital status," he said. He felt more protected in San Diego, although he seemed unaware that the protections he enjoyed in California were not yet available in many US locations.

Note that Santiago and Leopoldo mentioned economic and job-related motivations for migrating to San Diego, but in both their cases their sexualities also played a major role. This combination of factors demonstrates a significant intertwining of economic and sexual motivations for migration, which characterized some of my other study participants' reasons for leaving Mexico.

Men and Romance as Catalysts of Migration

So far, I have focused on the connections between migrants' stated desire to pursue sexual freedom, the role of their families, and concerns, among both immigrants and their families, about antigay discrimination and homophobia. For some immigrant men, however, another powerful, sexuality-related motivation for migrating to the United States was their actual romantic relations with men, in Mexico and in the United States. This motivation was reported by seventeen men in my study, most of whom had adopted gay lifestyles and participated in gay communities in Mexico. This focus on same-sex romantic relations takes us beyond the more common focus on male-female relations in studies that have examined love and romance as catalysts of transnational migration.[27]

Among the Mexican immigrant men in my research, romantic relations influenced their desire to migrate in two different ways. One involves men who were sexually attracted to American men or who followed a partner to the United States. The second reflects a desire to get away from boyfriends and ex-boyfriends in Mexico, or from situations of failed love in which romantic interest was not met with reciprocation.

Relationships with American Men

When asked why he migrated to the United States, Eliseo (born 1962) simply answered, *"Los güeros,"* meaning "the blonds." By this he meant White Americans more generally, as the word *güero* is often used in Mexico to describe anyone perceived as having European features, regardless of the color of their hair.[28] "I'm very attracted to them; I practically moved here following them," he elaborated. He added that his attraction to *güeros* was complemented by the expectation of "a better lifestyle. . . . One hears that life is better here, although it has its limitations in relation to some aspects; but here we are, waiting to see what happens in the future." When Eliseo decided to migrate, he had become infatuated with a "tall, blond Mexican" that "looked like a gringo." This man had moved to Los Angeles, and Eliseo thought of looking for him there. But he ended up staying in San Diego instead, hoping that he would meet a US White partner in that city.

The dynamics of cross-racial same-sex attractions will be a focus of chapter 8. For now, I simply want to note how some Mexican immigrants' ideas about nationality, ethnicity, and physical appearance were sometimes entangled with imaginaries of gay life in the United States. Others moved to the United States motivated not by a general fantasy of the type of men they might meet there, but by their desire to accompany an actual boyfriend. Some of those boyfriends were indeed US Whites. For instance, Néstor went to live with a US White man who lived in Palm Springs. This man later developed symptoms of AIDS and told Néstor to move out and return to Mexico. Néstor recalled that his boyfriend said to him, "You go, you go, you go." He asked him why, and the boyfriend plainly stated, "I'm really sorry, but you have to go. Why? Simply because you have to go." Néstor said that he received no explanation, so he just left.

The partners of other Mexican men, however, were not White Americans. Matías (born 1975) moved from Tijuana to live with an Asian American boyfriend of Japanese and Filipino background who spoke Spanish. They had met in that city, where people called this man *el chinito*, "the little Chinese." When Matías first saw him, though, he told him, "You don't look Chinese to me." Still other immigrant men had moved to follow their Mexican American or naturalized Mexican immigrant partners. Fausto (born 1971), for instance, met a Mexican immigrant at a party in National City, a heavily Latino/Mexican suburb in the southern part of the San Diego metropolitan area, not far from the border. He later decided to migrate to San Diego, motivated by a desire to live with this partner, among other reasons. In these two cases, Matías and Fausto had lived or grown up near the US-Mexico border, so it was not hard for them to meet Americans. By contrast, Valentín (born 1975) moved to San Diego to follow an American partner whom he met in Cancún. As I described in chapter 2, Valentín was from a small town in the southern Mexican state of Tabasco, but later moved to Mexico City, where he lived an openly gay life. Then he moved to Cancún, where in a gay bar he met his boyfriend, a Mexican immigrant who had become a naturalized US citizen. "I saw him drinking with his cousin," he said, "and then I saw him at a gay disco and I approached him. We were [together] some time in Cancún to decide if we wanted to form a couple."

After three weeks together, Valentín knew that he wanted to be in a relationship with this man. He felt they were compatible in terms of their styles and their shared emphasis on good communication. But his decision to follow his boyfriend to the United States was also triggered by a desire to improve his economic and personal situation. "For me, it was a good opportunity, because [in the United States] the standard of living is higher—although many people have to scramble—and for other reasons: people here are more protected," he said. By this he meant that the United States had more antidiscrimination protections for gay men. Valentín was aware, however, that such protections often did not extend to undocumented immigrants. He noted, "Harassment, however, doesn't fully stop; I mean . . . if you are illegal they can sexually harass you in your job for being homosexual, and because you're illegal they [can] take advantage of that."

It is noteworthy that at the time of my study, the Defense of Marriage Act (DOMA) was still the law of the land, and same-sex marriage was not yet available in California. Hence, participants such as Valentín could not imagine that a stable relationship with an American man might, in itself, lead them to obtain full citizenship rights in the United States. That, of course, changed in 2013 once the US Supreme Court had thrown out the central provisions of DOMA, and the Department of Homeland Security began to grant immigrant visas to the foreign spouses of gay and lesbian Americans and US permanent residents in states that had approved same-sex marriage laws.[29] Yet because of its Proposition 8, California was not one of those states. More recently, the right of Americans in binational same-sex couples to request permanent residency status for their spouses was extended to all fifty states as a result of the 2015 US Supreme Court decision that eliminated all remaining state-level bans on same-sex marriage.[30] With regard to the right to bring a foreign partner to live in the United States, binational same-sex married couples are now finally on a par with their heterosexual counterparts.

Leaving Mexican Men Behind

Partners also figure prominently in the migration narratives of several other men in my study. But in these cases, their main motivation for leaving Mexico was a desire to get away from an ex-boyfriend, or from a man who did not love them back. One dramatic illustration is provided by Facundo (born 1967), who traveled extensively within Mexico for business purposes. He had been in a relationship with José[31] for more than seven years in his hometown of Tijuana. The couple was tacitly accepted by Facundo's family. "I slept in his house—where there was only one bed—and José came to my [family] home, and he slept with me in my bedroom. . . . For example, if I went [alone] to a family party, [everyone asked,] 'Why didn't you bring José?' Everyone associated me with him." Facundo observed that all in his family "accepted him as my friend [mi amigo]." The word friend is often used euphemistically within Mexican families to refer to a male relative's boyfriend or partner.[32]

Facundo's relationship with José ended abruptly. On one occasion, when he was leaving on a trip, he missed his flight. The next available flight did not leave for several hours, so he decided to go back to José's house and wait there. "I found him with one of my friends in bed," he said. This "was a tremendous shock. I trusted him. I felt both had deceived me." Facundo broke up with José on the spot, which was not only extraordinarily painful, but also made Facundo utterly depressed to the point of becoming suicidal. His family noticed right away that he was not well. "I was in really bad shape. My family [started asking,] 'What's wrong? What's happening? Where is José?'" When Facundo simply answered, "He's gone," his family wanted more details: "How come he's gone? Where did he go? Did you fight?" "They figured it out," Facundo said. Concerned, one of his brothers decided to break the thinly veiled silence of Facundo's sexual orientation and relationship, although he still did so indirectly and without naming what he suspected. "[He] told me, 'Let's talk openly. I know what this is. Confirm it.'" Facundo said that he responded, "I have nothing to confirm; life will be the same, but yes, I am gay." To make matters worse, José then started stalking him.

Facundo's depression and a suicide attempt landed him in the hospital. At that point in the crisis, his kinship support system kicked in, in full force. His family asked him to leave Tijuana. They told him, "You are going to San Diego, because you need to start your life over and meet new people, because this whole thing is really harming you." With Facundo's sexuality now in the open, the family made arrangements for him to move in with a cousin. "My cousin lives in San Diego," he explained, "and she told me: 'Come here. [José] lives in Tijuana. He won't come here looking for you or to harm you.'"

Facundo's case illustrates that sexual migration can be triggered by a desire to leave painful situations of failed love behind or to get way from a previous partner. His story also shows that kinship support systems may be more likely to play a role when the gay member of the family has disclosed his sexual orientation to them, and the family is tolerant, if not outright accepting, as we have seen. Not unlike Justo and Tadeo, Facundo became a sexual exile with the help of his family.

HIV Care: Migration as a Matter of Life and Death

A final sexuality-related motivation for migration involves HIV-positive gay men who left Mexico seeking medical care. This motivation fits within the broader picture of sexual migration, not only because sexual health is often a component of sexual identity but also because of the connections between HIV stigma and antigay discrimination, as the cases that follow demonstrate. Sixteen Mexican men mentioned HIV care as a reason for migrating to the United States, and among them HIV was the sole reason that five mentioned. For instance, Claudio (born 1977) lived in Oaxaca when he first tested positive for HIV. He was originally from a small coastal town and later moved to the state capital, where he became aware of his same-sex desires and began to participate in Oaxaca's gay life. He decided to test for HIV after his first boyfriend was diagnosed as having AIDS. In Oaxaca, Claudio had no access to any information about HIV/AIDS services in the United States. But neither did he seek those services locally, and he feared that if he stayed his health would simply wither away. He recalled, "I thought to myself, 'I need care, I can't remain like this. I need treatments.' I had this idea of coming here. . . . No one had told me that help was available here, but my heart said to me, 'Go, you will find help there.'" When Claudio made this decision, he had not yet experienced any symptoms associated with the disease.

In contrast to Claudio, Efraín (born 1965), who lived in Mexicali, waited a full nine years after testing positive for HIV before he took any action to pursue HIV treatments. When he finally began to develop symptoms of AIDS, which suggests that his immune system had become badly damaged, he decided to cross the border into California. Efraín explained:

I started feeling badly; I started having diarrhea and vomiting. And, as you know, services [in Mexico] for people with my condition, for persons who are positive, can't be compared [to those in the United States]. So, I sat with my parents and told them, "I either go to the US to seek treatment and prolong my life, or I sit here waiting to die." I believe that if this hadn't happened, I would not be alive in Mexico.

Why would someone like Efraín wait so long to seek treatments for his condition? The answer may lie partly in his perception that AIDS treatments were scarcely available in his city, and partly in his fear about AIDS stigma, and by extension antigay stigma, as the case of Néstor next demonstrates. Such fears link a search for HIV care to a trajectory of sexual migration.

An even more dramatic case involves Néstor (born 1961), who reached a highly advanced stage of AIDS while still living in Ensenada, a city approximately seventy miles south of the US-Mexico border. After he had first experienced symptoms that concerned him, Néstor saw a local doctor, who encouraged him to get an HIV test. The result came back positive. The doctor offered him some treatment and counseling.

Fearing rejection from his family, Néstor decided to keep his condition secret. Over the next few years, his situation worsened to the point that, after several hospitalizations, the doctors at the state hospital where he was receiving care finally gave up. According to Néstor, "A doctor was examining me. I told him, 'I still feel sick.'" The doctor responded, "We've given you everything. We can't do anything else. You must go home." The doctor then told the supervising physician that his patient did not want to go home. From her desk, Néstor recalled, the supervisor shouted, "Let his family take him home. He'll be admitted and discharged continually until one day we will not have him here ever again." Néstor felt terrible hearing this pronouncement. "She was suggesting that I was going to die—that there would be a moment when I would finally not return because I was dead. And then they could finally be rid of me."

The first doctor apologized, but he nonetheless did not admit Néstor, sending him home in an ambulance. Not knowing what Néstor's condition was, everyone at home was quietly worried. Néstor finally told a close friend that he had AIDS, and then he told his siblings. As his situation worsened, he again demanded to be admitted to the hospital, threatening to sue if they did not take him. The doctors unhappily acquiesced and placed him in an isolation unit. However, in this otherwise inhospitable hospital, Néstor found a doctor and a social worker who treated him with respect and tried to cheer him up, care which Néstor found humane. A different doctor, however, insisted that Néstor had to go home, telling one of his sisters that there was nothing else that could be done. Néstor's sister asked the doctor what the family could expect. He responded, "He's going to die. When? I don't know. He won't last long." Néstor listened to this conversation in which he was being spoken of in the third person, as if he were not in the room. As he was being discharged, this same doctor told him scornfully, "If your siblings don't want to take care of you, sue them," and then he turned away, laughing.

As they left the hospital, Néstor's sister wondered aloud whether they should try to bring him to San Diego. The doctor whom Néstor liked approached her:

I overheard you saying that it might be possible for you to bring him to San Diego. My advice is that you do, because here your brother is not going to last long. I assure you we already did everything humanly possible. I see him in very bad shape, and if he stays here he will die. Do anything that you can to bring him to the United States.

Néstor's siblings were now aware that he had AIDS, but they still lied to their mother and told her he had cancer. They wanted to help him, and decided to bring him to an AIDS hospice in Tijuana where he could at least die peacefully. But his sister was not ready to give up. As they left him in the hospice, Néstor recalled that she said something along the lines of "As long as you're alive and your heart is beating and your eyes are open, I will fight till the end. Don't give up. I haven't given up myself." One of Néstor's brothers stayed behind and, perhaps sensing that the end was near, told Néstor that he knew about his being gay, adding that he wanted him to know that he could count on his support.

In the hospice, Néstor finally lost his will to live. But then his brother and sister arrived unexpectedly, announcing that they were bringing him to San Diego, where they had managed to get an appointment at a clinic. Néstor had become incontinent by then, so his sister put a diaper on him and dressed him. He could no longer walk, so he had to be carried to the car. They headed to the border, crossed into the United States, stayed in a hotel overnight, and went to the clinic the next morning. The doctor who examined Néstor there told them, "His situation is difficult, but we don't think it's impossible. We will do everything we can for him to improve." Néstor was hospitalized for a month, and was, he felt, "*un paciente muy latoso*" (a difficult patient).[33] As the doctor predicted, however, his condition was treatable. After having been sent home to die in Mexico, Néstor survived in San Diego.

It is hard to know what would have happened to men such as Efraín and Claudio if they had stayed in Mexico, but Néstor clearly had been dying in an AIDS hospice by the time that his siblings brought him to the United States. For him, and possibly also for other HIV-positive men, migrating proved to be a matter of life and death. Their fears about their uncertain futures in Mexico were justified, particularly if we consider the disparities in HIV-related health care and treatments that existed between Mexico and the United States at the time they made their decision to leave. The situation has perhaps improved in Mexico since then; in fact, recent Mexican administrations have claimed that universal coverage for HIV treatments is now a reality throughout the country. But Mexican AIDS activists regularly contend in the media that that has not occurred. This is one situation in which, despite the limitations of the US health care system, lifesaving state-administered programs such as the one in California, established partly in response to the strong demands of AIDS activists, proved to really make a difference.[34]

It is also worth noting that not all the HIV-positive immigrants believed they had acquired HIV in Mexico. Efraín, for instance, had lived temporarily in Colorado, where he had unprotected sex with a partner and tested positive just a few months later. Similarly, Hernán (born 1971) tested positive for HIV five years after migrating from Tijuana to San Diego. Néstor was unsure of where he became infected with HIV, given that he had had unprotected sex with men in both countries. His trips across the border were mostly "to party," as he put it. This issue is important, because those who supported the immigration policy preventing HIV-positive people from entering the United States (which was lifted in 2010)[35] often argued that HIV-positive immigrants were bringing the virus with them—a claim that more progressive commentators saw as xenophobic, particularly in light of the high prevalence of HIV in the United States.

The Intertwining of Sexual, Economic, and Family-Related Migration

Although the accounts I have presented throughout this chapter highlight the connections between transnational migration and sexuality, they also indicate that sexuality-related motivations for migration are often intertwined with economic and family-related ones (fig. 3). This mix is indicative of the view that "sexuality is not an all-encompassing reality but one that intersects with and through other social, economic, and cultural practices and identities," as Martin Manalansan has noted.[36] In my study, 19 Mexican participants who cited sexuality-related reasons for migrating also discussed economic or family-related motivations (12 sexual and economic, 3 sexual and family-related, and 4 all three; see figure 3).[37] As we have seen, Valentín moved from Cancún to San Diego following a boyfriend, but also was attracted by the economic opportunities he might encounter in San Diego. Bonifacio (born ca. 1975) similarly moved from Tepic to Tijuana at the age of twenty-one at the urging of a cousin who had hired a *pollero* (smuggler) to cross the border, with the main goal of finding work. But he also stated:

Being gay . . . there's more freedom [here]. Not like in Tepic, where it's so limited. There are [gay] bars, but life is limited, there's discrimination. . . . There are movie theaters, but it's risky, to be hiding. I thought, "I like it here; here's my life."

Finally, in Aldo's case (born 1971), he relocated from Ensenada to San Diego at the age of sixteen, motivated by three intersecting reasons. First, back home in Mexico he was experiencing tremendous economic problems. Second, he was concerned that his family might find out about his homosexuality. And third, he wanted to get away from an older partner whom he had tried to blackmail, and who had threatened Aldo in return.

To be sure, a few participants moved to the United States exclusively for family-related reasons (six talked about having been brought to that country by their families before they were even aware about their sexuality), and five referred exclusively to economic reasons. But even among the men who moved for economic reasons, their same-sex sexualities played a role by convincing them to stay once they had arrived in the United States. An interesting example of this is provided by Cuauhtémoc (born 1961), who moved to San Diego after losing his job in Mexico. Cuauhtémoc was primarily motivated to make money to send to his wife and children, to cover

the needs of my family; my children were growing. One thousand pesos was not enough for school, clothing, food, and all that. It wasn't enough. So I decided to come, to migrate here to the United States.

In Mexico, however, Cuauhtémoc engaged in clandestine sex with men during business trips, usually by sitting in the back of the bus during overnight journeys and waiting for another man who wanted sex to sit next to him. In San Diego, he came into contact with the gay community, prompting him to change how he thought of himself. Gay men encouraged him to adopt a bisexual identity, which Cuauhtémoc did. He rapidly moved from being a labor migrant to becoming a sexual migrant as well, and his homoerotic explorations ended up convincing him to stay permanently in San Diego.

I now turn finally to two cases—those of Edwin and Marcelo—whose stories show an even more thorough intertwining of economic, familial, and sexual factors that prompted their migration. Their stories also nicely exemplify the blurred boundaries between being an immigrant and being an "expat," a title often denied to Mexicans living abroad, as they are typically presumed to be immigrants or migrants.[38] Edwin and Marcelo certainly could be seen as both "sexual migrants" and "global gay expats."

Edwin and Marcelo: Mexican Gay Men as Sexual Migrants and Global Gay Expats

Edwin (born 1974) had led an openly gay life in Mexico for many years, first in Mexico City and then in Cancún, where at the age of twenty-five he changed professions. He went from being a business administrator to becoming a dancer, which was his real passion. Edwin recalled that this "was a big decision, perhaps the biggest decision of my life." It led the way to a whirlwind of global experiences that brought him to several countries. Cancún, Edwin felt, had indeed opened the world for him:

I loved [Cancún]. I liked it so much that I thought, "This is me. I'm not giving this up." You meet . . . many people; you learn languages, learn about other cultures, and socialize in new social spheres. And that's exactly what I did.

But then, when his German boyfriend decided to move back to Germany, Edwin felt it was time for him to relocate to Europe as well to be closer to him, and he was able to secure a job in Spain in the same hotel chain for which he had worked in Cancún. Later, Edwin moved to Germany to be with his boyfriend. But their relationship eventually soured, and he took the time to return to Mexico on the occasion of his mother's sudden death. Sensing that he might not come back, his boy-friend threatened to travel to Mexico and make a scandal if Edwin did not return.

Back in Mexico City, Edwin realized he no longer fit in his family's life: his greatest supporter, his mother, was gone; his father was indifferent to him; he had no job or money; he had lost his sexual freedom; and the threat issued by his German boyfriend loomed on the horizon. He therefore chose to start his life afresh by following a new path. Edwin decided to go to the eastern United States, where he had friends, as a means to make enough money to eventually move back to Europe, a place he loved. But he had a brother in San Diego, and he stopped to visit him on the way to the East Coast.

In the end, Edwin never left San Diego. He found a job in a hotel, started attending a gay support group, found a new boyfriend, and, most significantly, tested positive for HIV. Realizing that his immune system had suffered considerable damage and that he could obtain HIV treatments in San Diego, Edwin decided to stay; but he was ambivalent about this decision. He felt that his life was "now tied to the United States . . . because I know that here is where I could have a longer life. In Mexico, the resources aren't there." At the same time, he deeply regretted becoming an undocumented immigrant, which betrayed his image as a middle-class Mexican. Edwin bitterly remarked:

I arrived here with my visa, and one could say that my status is regular. But I don't have a work permit. I am illegal; I'm working illegally. So I am trying to legally process a work permit. If I am going to stay in the United States, I don't want to be like any other bracero.

Edwin was judgmental of undocumented migrants, and he disliked the proximity of San Diego to Tijuana, because he felt that the *tijuanenses* who crossed the border to work in San Diego cheapened labor, making it hard to survive on an immigrant's salary. He also imagined, perhaps unrealistically, that his situation might be different if he were able to move to a different US city such as New York.

Similarly to Edwin, Marcelo had acquired a global sense of gay culture in Mexico City, as we saw in chapter 2. However, in contrast to Edwin, his start in Mexico had been quite modest. His family was originally from Michoacán, a state that, as Marcelo put it, "is 100-percent migrants"—a clear exaggeration meant to highlight his sense that many of its residents had lived at some point or another in the United States. However, his mother broke the family tradition of migrating to the United States by taking Marcelo with her to Mexico City after divorcing his father. "I am *chilango*, *chilango* at heart,"[39] he declared, and credited the city with giving him the opportunity to live an openly gay life. "My education, my upbringing, all took place there, and that's where I became open toward sexuality," he proudly asserted.

Marcelo thrived on his reputation as a rebel and a wanderer, which prompted him to travel to the United States to see it with his own eyes. Beginning in 1992, he went to California as a tourist, "always short trips, back and forth." During those visits, he befriended American gay men who kept inviting him to come back, and he also took the opportunity to attend conferences organized by LLEGÓ, the now-defunct National Latino/a Lesbian, Gay, Bisexual and Transgender Organization.[40] Marcelo also thought of himself as an innovator, and had taken it upon himself to bring American gay iconography back to Mexico City. "I was fascinated," he said.

This was the early nineties, and, for instance, the [gay] rainbow flag was not yet a fad in Mexico. No one knew it. I was one of the first gays who brought back a bunch of rainbow flags to give to my friends to bring to the marches, or who wore rainbow-colored jewelry. In fact, I love that symbol, I always did.

He also claimed that he had been the first to propose the idea of a "White Party"[41] to a Mexico City gay bar, leading the bar to organize the first global gay circuit party ever held in Mexico.

Before visiting California, Marcelo had imagined that he would encounter "a perfect world, a gay world; that pink-colored world that we all have in our heads." Though later he realized that his fantasies about an American gay utopia were blown out of proportion, he still liked very much what he saw in California. But he was not yet thinking about migrating. A few years later, however, his income dropped. He also broke up with a boyfriend and became depressed. At that point, he began to think about moving to Los Angeles or San Francisco, although he ended up in San Diego.

For both Marcelo and Edwin, migration was prompted by sexuality-related motivations that figured centrally in their desire to relocate, but were clearly intertwined with economic, family-related, and, in Edwin's case, health-related motivations. But an additional important feature of their migration narratives is that they contain both "traditional" factors assumed to motivate Mexicans to migrate, and lifestyle factors that the literature has associated more readily with "expats" from rich countries who are usually not thought of as "migrants."[42] These cases question a common stereotype about citizens from so-called developing countries who relocate transnationally. They challenge the notions that Mexicans do not move for lifestyle reasons, that they are necessarily working-class, and that therefore they are immigrants and not expats. As we have seen, their stories resemble those of other middle-class, global gay expats.

Marcelo's case is particularly interesting in this regard because, had his family stayed in its hometown in rural Michoacán, he might well have joined the flow of working-class rural Mexicans to the United States and become a "typical" Mexican migrant instead of a global gay expat. But his life in Mexico City, and in particular his gay life, changed all that.

Expanding the Notion of Sexual Migration

The cases I have discussed in this chapter show the importance of adding sexuality to the list of factors that can lead individuals to cross borders and begin new lives. Yet they also demonstrate that the simple notion of sexual freedom as a motivator for transnational sexual migration is insufficient to capture the complexity of this phenomenon. Even so, immigrants themselves rely on it very commonly in their accounts, including those in my own study, much more than their American counterparts. Indeed, among the seventy American men who also participated in my study, most of them migrants to San Diego from other parts of the United States,[43] none invoked the notion of sexual freedom. Some certainly moved for reasons related to sexual freedom—including wanting to get away from their families—but they named their motivations differently in terms of independence, self-sufficiency, and expectations that as adult men they would make a life for themselves. And some also depicted San Diego as a draw in itself, because of its gay community, its physical beauty, and its weather. But a discourse of sexual freedom is absent from their narratives.

By contrast, among Mexican gay immigrants "sexual freedom" operates as a kind of shorthand for a complicated constellation of factors connected to their lives and imaginaries before migration. As my findings indicate, this notion of sexual freedom must therefore be unpacked if we are to fully understand how transnational sexual migration is produced. First, for Mexican gay immigrant men, concerns about their families figure prominently—how their families will react to disclosure of their sexual orientation; how they themselves are to avoid stigma, discrimination, and the consequences of homophobia within the family; and how they can protect their families from social stigma. Also associated with these concerns is a preoccupation with how best to manage their same-sex desires within the immediate social networks in which they grew up. Taken together, these primary concerns often lead men to decide that it would be difficult for them to live an openly gay life in Mexico as well as achieve sexual freedom in their own hometowns.

Why, then, don't they move out of their family homes but stay in Mexico? Why not seek independence within their hometowns or by moving to other Mexican locations? Of course, many do precisely that, but the men in my study took a different path. Why does transnational migration become their preferred option to seek their sexual freedom? To answer this question, we must turn to the rest of the interrelated reasons that become embedded in these men's notions of sexual freedom. First, as we have seen, many are exposed to an imaginary about the greater sexual liberalism of the United States, which may make that destination more salient in their minds, despite the opportunities for pursuing a gay life afforded by larger Mexican cities. Second, when Mexican men migrate to the United States, people take it for granted that they do so for economic or family reasons, which makes it easy for these men to say they are migrating for the very same reasons as everybody else. In other words, their transnational migration does not invite uncomfortable questions about their lifestyles and sexualities, or about family disharmony, as might moving out of their family homes without being married or without having a good job- or education-related reason. Third, transnational migration is seen by these men as having the advantage of providing them greater distance, both physical and symbolic, from their families. This distance then combines with the presence of an international border that participants in my study often perceived as a buffer that may facilitate privacy from relatives' prying eyes and prevent gossip about them from reaching their hometowns or families in Mexico. As I will discuss later, the border sometimes also provides them with a symbolic separator of identity that allows them to live their sexualities differently in Mexico and the United States. However, as we already have seen, these imagined protections are somewhat of a fiction, particularly when these men have relatives or hometown acquaintances living in the same US locations as they.

Beyond the notion of sexual freedom, my participants' narratives also suggest the importance of carefully considering the role played by transnational aspects of love and romance; the pursuit of sexual desires; class position and the lure of travel for those with more economic and cultural capital; and even a desire to obtain HIV treatment in shaping these men's sexual migration.[44] And we must consider as well that a number of these men perceived that migrating to the United States would benefit them both sexually and economically in ways that domestic migration within Mexico might not. Such intertwining of sexual and economic factors supports the idea that sexuality-motivated migration must be understood as entangled with a broader political economy of migration, as Lionel Cantú proposed in an earlier study.[45] Yet, as demonstrated by a number of examples in this chapter, sexuality alone—and the constellation of factors encapsulated in the notion of "sexual freedom"—can be sufficient to motivate some Mexican gay men to engage in transnational sexual migration. Therefore, the place of sexuality in motivating gay immigrants' transnational relocation cannot, and should not, be minimized; and although some of these men could be regarded as labor migrants, it would be a mistake to consider them exclusively, or even primarily, as such.

Finally, a number of Mexican gay men take advantage of existing transnational family networks or link their sexual migration to processes of transnational family reunification—in other words, they use the resources provided by the Mexican culture of migration, which again signals that their sexual migration is linked to the broader political economy of Mexican migration.[46] But others rely instead on the supports provided by gay communities and transnational LGBT networks, both in Mexico and abroad, calling attention to an altogether different culture of migration. I examine these issues more fully in the following chapter.

FOUR

A Gay Culture of Migration?

After he had been thinking about migrating for some time, a concrete opportunity arose for Octavio (born 1977) to leave his hometown in Guerrero. His father, who was already living in California, sent money home to pay for two of his sons to join him. Let us recall that Octavio had overheard gay returnees exalt the sexual liberalism of the United States, and their comments triggered his imagination, making him wish he might one day experience firsthand the wonderful gay life in California that these men had described. But his father did not have Octavio in mind when he sent the money to his family. Instead, he expressly requested that Octavio's two older and heterosexual brothers be the ones to join him in San Diego. But one of the brothers refused to migrate, and Octavio immediately volunteered to take his place. Their father, unaware of the switch, was quite upset when Octavio arrived in California. "When I came, my father became very angry," Octavio recalled, "because I wasn't the one he wanted here with him. He wanted my other brother, the one who stayed behind." What upset their father the most was not that his other son did not want to migrate, but rather that Octavio had done so, especially because he was very opposed to Octavio's sexuality.

Octavio's experience with his father is reminiscent of Cymene Howe's observation that "although lesbians, gay men, and same-sex couples may have family in the United States, they may not have familial support [to migrate] because of their sexuality."[1] Howe further emphasizes that these migrants "potentially lack the kin networks, as well as the social and financial support associated with kin networks, in both their countries of origin and their countries of destination, that prove so critical to nonlesbian and nongay migrants."[2] Central to this view is a sense that, as the sociologist Douglas Massey has indicated, "kinship is the most important base of migrants' social organization and family connections provide the most secure network connections."[3] Octavio was able to use the assistance his father provided, but only because his father was not told that Octavio would be the one going to California instead of his older brother.

But Octavio's case is not altogether anomalous. Like him, other Mexican gay men indeed have benefited from the *culture of Mexican migration*, a label that refers to migration processes involving places in Mexico—primarily towns, but possibly also some urban locations—that have had large numbers of transnational emigrants.[4] In such places, proponents of this concept have noted, is a well-entrenched cultural expectation that young people—particularly young straight men, but also some women—will relocate temporarily or permanently to the United States at some point in their lives.[5] And, as suggested by Massey and his collaborators, their migration is facilitated by migrant networks, which generate forms of social capital that individuals can access in order to organize their own migration.[6] Furthermore, these migrant networks are assumed to depend not only on family kinship but more broadly on *paisanaje*, "the sharing of a community of origin," which creates a sense of bonding and obligation toward others from the same community or town.[7] Once migrant networks become established, they generate migration flows that are perpetuated across generations, resulting in a self-sustaining culture of migration. Octavio indeed grew up in a town in Guerrero that fit this description—a place where it was common for young men to emigrate, and for previous immigrants such as his father to help others migrate, particularly their own relatives and most specifically their sons.[8]

It is not altogether clear whether Octavio would have been able to migrate were it not for the money his father had sent home. By the logic of Howe's observation, he might have been forced to migrate on his own. However, as we will see in this chapter, other Mexican gay immigrants have succeeded in obtaining support from their families and migrant networks within the Mexican culture of migration. And, unlike Octavio, some of them did not have to go about it surreptitiously.

But it turns out that assistance from families and conventional migrant networks is only one part of the story. Some Mexican gay men are able to tap into other forms of aid provided by an alternative social network—one that involves LGBT people, in both Mexico and the United States. This network includes Mexican gay and lesbian immigrants who help new gay migrants relocate to the United States.

Consequently, I emphasize two patterns of support—one involving blood relatives that has been much discussed in the migration literature, and another involving LGBT people that has escaped notice by migration scholars. Interestingly, for the Mexican participants in my study, these two sources seemed equally important overall. Among the 77 Mexican men who had lived at one point or another in the United States,[9] 37 reported being helped exclusively by family members or having relocated to the United States together with their families. By contrast, 35 had received support exclusively from LGBT people, including gay and lesbian acquaintances and friends as well as boyfriends and sex partners. And one, Emilio, was aided both by blood relatives and by LGBT people, because the assistance came from a gay brother and a lesbian sister. The remaining 4 men migrated on their own without the help of any blood or LGBT kinship networks.

Drawing on these findings, I argue that to fully account for the range of support that Mexican gay immigrants receive to migrate, we must consider not only the Mexican culture of migration but also alternative networks that contribute to what could be called a "gay culture of migration." My analysis thus brings into focus the role of LGBT kinship networks, understood in terms of both gay relationships and—following the anthropologist Kath Weston—LGBT "families of choice."[10]

Gay Men and the Mexican Culture of Migration

Similarly to Octavio, a number of other Mexican gay men participating in my study who came from towns with well-established and substantial flows of emigrants accessed the very same resources available to their heterosexual counterparts. Siblings, parents, uncles, aunts, and cousins were all mentioned by immigrant men as they spoke about the people who helped them migrate.[11] Crispín (born 1980), who lived in Mexico City, began to think about migrating when a cousin who lived in his parents' hometown in Guerrero—a town that seemed to have a large number of emigrants—offered to bring him to California. This cousin painted a rosy picture about how easy it would be for the two of them to get into the United States. "He told me some beautiful fantasies, that I was going to migrate for free, and I don't know what else . . . and that he would join me," Crispín said. During a visit to Guerrero, Crispín had become so excited about this possibility that as soon as he returned to Mexico City he told his mother about his plan to go to the United States. She approved of this plan, and he swiftly returned to Guerrero to take his cousin up on his offer. His cousin, however, had just been boasting—he may have felt the need to do so given the culture of the town—and did not really intend to migrate any time soon.

Hearing Crispín express his disappointment, his mother decided to activate an altogether different part of their family kinship network. Crispín's godmother lived in a suburb of San Diego, and his mother decided to contact her. The godmother's response was straightforwardly positive. She simply said, "Yes, send him to me. . . . I'll answer for him." Similarly to Octavio, for Crispín the help to migrate arrived from someone already living in the United States—in this case someone related to him not by blood but by the social obligations of *compadrazgo*.[12]

By contrast, in other cases the family members who helped gay immigrants leave Mexico were not in the United States but in Mexico itself. That was the case for Armando (born 1981), who grew up in rural Oaxaca, where he had a troubling childhood characterized by constant sexual abuse from an early age by older boys. In order to protect his family's reputation, Armando had secretly carried the burden of his abuse for years. During that time, he had been blackmailed by other boys his own age who asked him for money in exchange for keeping quiet about his damaged sexual reputation. Armando often paid bribes to those boys, or alternatively silenced them by seducing them. By the time that he came of age, Armando had been forced by his circumstances to have sex with dozens of boys and teenagers in his town. Given this unbearable situation, he became convinced that the only way to put an end to his ordeal was for him to migrate, at which point he pleaded with his adoptive parents for help.[13] "Either you send me, or I go on my own," he told them vehemently. Noticing Armando's firm determination, his parents agreed to pay a smuggler one thousand dollars to bring their son to San Diego. They made this arrangement from Oaxaca, deep inside Mexico and several thousand miles away from the US-Mexico border, using the informal network of services related to the Mexican culture of migration.

My participants' narratives also confirm that people who live in small towns in Mexico—or whose families have connections to small towns—are not the only ones who benefit from family kinship and migrant networks. Indeed, some men who lived in large Mexican cities similarly reported being aided by relatives and others in their immediate kinship networks who had left Mexico before them. However, as Fussell and

Massey have noted, it is unclear whether the help provided by relatives in larger cities generates or reflects enough momentum for it to be considered part of the Mexican culture of migration.[14]

One example is provided by Inti (born 1978), who, as I indicated in chapter 3, migrated at age seventeen for sexual reasons, with the encouragement of a female cousin who had already moved to San Diego with her parents and siblings. The economic situation of Inti's family was reasonably good and stable, so Inti never thought about migrating for economic reasons. As he put it, "[Our situation] was OK. . . . We had enough to eat, and we always had [money] to go out or go shopping. We never had a problem with money." Inti's cousin told him that in San Diego he could move in with her family:

I thought about it for a long time. . . . My cousin wanted me to come to San Diego, because she wanted me to study here. She is someone I really got along with in Mexico. Her family moved to San Diego about fifteen years ago. And she said, "It's really pretty there. People are [nice]," all that. I got the image that San Diego was great.

When his cousin issued this invitation, Inti was already imagining that San Diego might provide him greater sexual freedom, help him reduce the potential of social stigma for himself and his family, and provide him with opportunities to meet White American gay men. But when the time came for him to announce his decision to leave, his official reason was that he wanted to be with his cousin and study in the United States. Inti spoke with his parents about his plan, and his father was initially reluctant to let him go: "He thought I would start doing drugs." But in the end, Inti prevailed. His cousin paid his ticket to Tijuana and sent someone to pick him up there. Upon his arrival, as is common among those who had been helped by relatives in the United States, Inti lived the first year with his aunt, uncle, and cousins. But then he was able to move out and find his way into San Diego's gay community.

———

As the examples in this section show, gay Mexicans do tap into the Mexican culture of migration and receive assistance in migrating from the very same family and migrant networks that help other Mexicans make the journey from Mexico to the United States. But, like Armando and Inti, they sometimes feel that to acquire these resources they must conform to heteronormative appearances and expectations. Other men were denied family support because of their non-normative sexualities. For instance, Bonifacio (born ca. 1975) believed that his half-sister, who was already a US citizen, had refused to help him migrate to the United States because she did not accept him as a gay man and did not want him to join her. But such rejection was not always the case. Both Tadeo (born 1976) and Justo (born 1971) received help from relatives who were fully aware of these men's sexual orientation. However, it is worth noting that in these cases, relatives who came to their aid were living in Mexico and hence were helping them embark on a kind of sexual exile they felt to be for the good of everyone involved. In other words, they were helping migrants not to move in with them but rather to move away from them.

Moving Once and Then Moving Once Again

When gay men rely on the Mexican culture of migration—while often pretending that they are "regular," straight men—they may face an un-welcome surprise: at the other end of their migration, they may find themselves surrounded by relatives and others from the very towns they left behind. This leaves them unable to achieve the freedom from family scrutiny and self-determination they hoped for, which complicates their goal of seeking sexual freedom. For that reason, they sometimes have to move twice.

An eloquent example is provided by Hilario (born 1965), who started his life in León, a large city in central Mexico. His father had migrated initially without documents to Watsonville, one of the largest agricultural centers in California. His mother stayed behind in Mexico with the children. When his father became a US permanent resident, he began the process of obtaining resident visas for his wife and children. His goal was to bring the whole family to Watsonville. But then the family was involved in a tragic car accident that killed both parents, coincidentally as they were all driving from León to the US embassy in Mexico City to get their papers.

After the death of his parents, Hilario, who was six years old at the time, went to live with his grandmother and other relatives in a poor neighborhood on the outskirts of León. (Hilario said that they lived in an adobe house, a building material often signifying very modest means in Mexico.) Three of his older siblings decided to fulfill their father's dream and migrated permanently to Watsonville. The younger five children, including Hilario, remained in Mexico. However, one by one they eventually moved to Watsonville, except Hilario. As he explained:

I was happy in Mexico; I liked life there, in spite of all that it lacks, its discomforts. . . . I went to university. I had my group of friends, none of whom were gay, but they were my friends. . . . I had lived all my life there; I had my customs, the friends I partied with, the language, all those things. All that motivated me to stay there.

When Hilario was still in college, he traveled to Watsonville for a sister's wedding, at which point his siblings tried to get him to stay:

They all started telling me; they tried to convince me: "Why don't you stay here already? You can go to school here." . . . And I would answer, "No, I need to finish college." They told me, "At least stay for six months, a year; you take a leave from college and then go back and finish." And that's what I did.

He returned to Mexico to finish college, but some years later took another trip to Watsonville, this time after losing his job in León. By this point he had befriended a gay man in León, but was not yet familiar with that city's gay life. But once he was in Watsonville, a much smaller city, Hilario felt greatly constrained. "I felt oppressed," he said. With his siblings and the rest of his family there, he could not get himself to explore gay life. "So I started getting very depressed. . . . I didn't know what was happening. . . . [And] so I began to go to therapy." His instinct was to contact an AIDS organization, and they referred him to a local gay therapist, who turned out to be a man of Mexican origin.

This therapist opened a new world for Hilario: first he invited him to a gay Latino support group, and then he took him to gay clubs in Monterey and Oakland. Hilario eventually had sex with a man he met in one of the clubs. Around the same time, he began to feel the need to start over so that he could fully explore this gay life to which he was finally gaining exposure. He had a friend in San Diego, and he went to visit her. Liking what he found there in terms of gay life, he came to the conclusion that moving there would finally give him the opportunity to explore his sexuality more freely and independently. Like other participants in my study, Hilario saw San Diego as a city that afforded him the space to experience gay life without worrying about what his family might think. Before leaving Watsonville, however, he was encouraged by a new therapist to disclose his sexual orientation to his siblings. Hilario managed to reveal this only to the sister whom he trusted the most.

Perhaps even more poignantly, Teodoro (born 1966)—who, as I described in chapter 3, migrated with a cousin to Orange County, California, right after finishing high school—was unable to find in his new location the sexual freedoms that he craved, and which he had imagined would be available to him in the United States. His problem was not that there was no gay life in Orange County, but that he was surrounded by cousins and other relatives who assumed him to be heterosexual, and he was incapable of telling them his true orientation.[15] His male cousins had tried to incorporate him into their lives and into their immediate Mexican immigrant community. As part of their efforts, they would constantly invite him to join them on outings to clubs featuring table dances, where Teodoro was expected to engage in the same activities in which they participated with the women who worked there. Teodoro found it enormously frustrating to have to pretend that he was enjoying himself—as his cousins assumed any straight man would—especially after having migrated precisely in search of his sexual freedom.

Luckily, he was able to take advantage of the 1996 immigration reform policy (also known as the amnesty policy), implemented soon after he had arrived in the United States, which allowed him to legalize his situation and become a permanent resident. This development also made it possible for him to travel freely back to Mexico. On a flight to Guadalajara, he overheard two gay men talking about gay Tijuana. Up to that point, Teodoro had been unaware that Tijuana was one of the cities in Mexico that had a well-developed gay culture. He decided to seek it out, stopping there on his way back from Guadalajara. This stopover also gave him an opportunity to visit his grandmother, who lived in that city. He recalled, "I got to my grandma's house, and that same evening I immediately went in search of one of the [gay] places."

Teodoro began to travel back and forth between Orange County and Tijuana: "At first I went only on weekends. I finished work and I ran to Tijuana." He justified his trips by saying he had met a woman there, and, besides, he could also say he wanted to visit his grandmother. As he got to know gay life in Tijuana, he also gained the confidence to explore gay life in San Diego. Teodoro eventually decided to relocate, this time from Orange County to Tijuana, where he finally found the sexual freedom he had long desired. Although he became familiar with San Diego's well-developed gay community, he had no particular interest in participating in it and did so only sporadically. He usually crossed the border for other purposes, including participating in my study.

Hilario's and Teodoro's cases demonstrate that the imaginaries of sexual freedom that bring Mexican gay men to the United States are not always immediately confirmed, particularly in situations in which, by relying on the Mexican culture of migration, they cross the border only to find that the same pressures they experienced in Mexico still surround them. As Carlos Decena has indicated, Latino gay immigrants have an "investment in being part of ethnoracial networks, to transit in worlds where the expansion of a person's erotic, social, cultural, and economic prospects are possible without rupturing these contested and conflicted but cherished and necessary connections."[16] Yet, as the cases I have discussed demonstrate, sometimes they come to realize that some level of rupture with their previous networks is necessary for them to live their sexualities more freely. Of course, as Teodoro's case shows, such separation can sometimes be achieved not by relocating elsewhere within the United States but by moving to a different location in Mexico. For Teodoro, Tijuana, and not San Diego or Los Angeles, ultimately gave him the space he felt he needed to adopt an openly gay identity and finally live his sexual life in the way he desired. Over time, as for many *tijuanenses*, San Diego became the place where he went to work, and was the main reason for him to cross the US-Mexico border.

A Gay Culture of Migration

In other cases, Mexican gay immigrant men participating in my study benefited from support from other LGBT Mexicans who had migrated to the United States before them, as well as from LGBT Americans who helped them move to, and get settled in, the United States. As a prerequisite for these men to obtain such assistance, they must have been previously incorporated into LGBT networks, and must also have been in contact with transnational LGBT networks or at least have known some LGBT people who lived outside Mexico.[17] In other words, they must already have possessed a particular kind of gay social capital.[18] These forms of aid remain invisible within mainstream (and largely heteronormative) studies of Mexican migration, in part because in those studies sexuality is considered, if at all, only insofar as it pertains to heterosexual marriages.[19] By examining LGBT forms of social capital and the supports for migration that they generate, my analysis thus expands the purview of Mexican migration research.[20]

The Role of Mexican Gay Friends

A number of Mexican participants received help in migrating from Mexican gay friends,[21] acquaintances, and ex-boyfriends who had previously moved to the United States and who catalyzed their relocation. Those individuals often played multiple roles in helping Mexican gay men move to California, and some in fact were the ones who first suggested to them the idea of migrating. Being sexual migrants themselves, they told my participants, and demonstrated through their own experiences, that migrating could also be a possibility for them. And then they subsequently provided the migrants-to-be with various forms of support to make this happen. To illustrate this pattern, I focus on the experiences of three participants: Braulio, Marcelo, and Justo.

Braulio (born 1977) ended up in Tijuana after leaving his hometown in Oaxaca and then moving around Mexico. When asked how he arrived in San Diego, he initially said that he did it on his own. By this he meant that he had no family who could help him. As he himself put it, "I didn't even have family. . . . I don't have relatives here." As it turns out, however, Braulio did not migrate by his own means. One of his ex-boyfriends, who lived in San Diego, played a major role in facilitating Braulio's relocation across the border. Braulio explained: "I called my friend, because he lives here in San Diego. He had been my boyfriend. . . . I met him at Extasis [a large gay dance club in Tijuana]." He described this man as a "white Mexican." When Braulio asked him for help, the man took him to meet his godmother, a nun that knew smugglers who crossed people over the border. Braulio recalled, "She said, 'OK, I will help you find someone who doesn't charge you too much.'" He spent everything he had to cross, and his friend was waiting for him right on the other side.

In contrast to Braulio, Marcelo (born 1970) received help from Mexican gay friends with whom he had no history of romantic or sexual involvement. Marcelo, whose story I described in chapters 2 and 3, first went to California as a tourist when a Mexican gay friend invited him to visit. He then made subsequent trips, staying with gay friends for a few months at a time so as to make the most of his investment given the expensive cost of travel from Mexico City. He briefly considered the possibility of migrating, although initially he fantasized that he might move to San Francisco, which he described as "a city of the [gay] community," or to West Hollywood, also a well-known gay enclave. But Marcelo had never seriously considered migrating to the United States until much later, after a painful breakup with a boyfriend and the ensuing depression, and amid concerns about his low income in Mexico:

I had [gay Mexican] friends in San Diego, and I began to contact them via the Internet. "How are you?" . . . (Typically for me, I was exploring first.) "Hey, I would like to take the step of moving there. What do you think?" "OK, perfect, go ahead, come." "What would I do there?" "Well, see, there's this and this option." I started planning [my departure].

Marcelo finally left Mexico in late 2002. One of his gay Mexican friends drove to the Tijuana airport to pick him up and bring him to San Diego (Marcelo had a passport and a US visitor visa). Once they had arrived in the city, this same friend helped him get a job in the hotel where he worked, and also told him how to buy false papers so that he could be hired. Marcelo initially lived with this friend and his boyfriend.

Finally, Justo was similarly aided by LGBT friends, specifically a binational lesbian couple he met in his hometown in Jalisco. One of the women was Mexican and had family in the town. The other was American, and the two lived together in San Diego. As their friendship with Justo developed, the couple invited him to travel with them to the Baja California resort town of San Felipe. While there, they asked him how he went about finding gay life in his hometown. Justo explained that he usually went to the state capital, Guadalajara, when he wanted to participate in that. (He did not tell them that additionally, he had a network of gay friends in his hometown, as we saw in chapter 2.) The women then asked him, "Do you want to come to the US? There [gay life] is very open; very, very open. People don't bother you; they don't mess around with you. People respect you. Because . . . they can't put you down for being gay. Think about it, it's your decision." They also encouraged him to get a visa, which Justo did right away.

The second time that they met in San Felipe, these friends invited him to continue to San Diego with them. They also told him that they wanted to make a deal with him. "What kind of deal?" he asked. The Mexican woman explained:

We are trying to have a child, and we don't want to have it with someone we don't know. We could go to a . . . sperm bank . . . and do an insemination. But we really like you . . . the *americana* really likes you. She says you're very intelligent. . . . And if you can help us, we can get you papers. We'll get you residence.

In essence they proposed that in exchange for his sperm, one of them would marry him in San Diego so that he could obtain US permanent residency.

Justo eventually accepted their offer, but once he had arrived in San Diego, things did not go well. He complained that his friends did not host him in their home, putting him up with a cousin of theirs instead. They also became incredibly controlling, and constantly tried to make him fearful of the *migra* (as people call the immigration enforcement agents). All this prompted Justo to distance himself from these women and find his own path in San Diego. But they nonetheless had played a crucial role in helping him decide to migrate.

Support Offered by Potential Boyfriends

Other gay Mexicans were beneficiaries of American gay men—mostly US Whites—in the context of budding love affairs in which one or both of the partners had become infatuated. One example is provided by Augusto (born 1972), who was helped by a White American man whom he met during a trip to San Diego. At the time, Augusto had a rocky relationship with a boyfriend in his hometown of Culiacán, Sinaloa. After a fight, he decided to take a vacation trip to San Diego, which happened to coincide with that city's LGBT Pride celebration. While there, Augusto had a short affair with the American man who later helped him move. This man was the roommate of the boyfriend of one of Augusto's gay friends from his hometown who now lived in San Diego. The two met through a somewhat intricate friendship network of American and Mexican gay men in San Diego.

Before migrating, Augusto had worked in Culiacán at the local branch of a national bank. He was so taken by his affair in San Diego that, upon returning from his vacation, he requested a transfer to a branch in Tijuana so he could continue seeing the American man. Augusto was encouraged by the fact that this man had clearly become infatuated with him, too. In fact, he had asked Augusto to stay. Augusto was pleased with this development, because he felt especially attracted to US White men, and he did not want to miss this opportunity of being in a relationship with one. Moreover, the man had continued to pursue him. "He called me every day," Augusto said. "He called the bank where I worked, he called me at home—every day."

In the end, the bank denied Augusto's request for a transfer. Undeterred by this setback, he quit his job and decided to move to the border region anyway. He sold his car and bought an airplane ticket to Tijuana, and then he asked the American man to pick him up at the airport and bring him to San Diego. His partner welcomed him into his home, which he shared with a roommate.

Unfortunately, their relationship did not prosper. Six months after his arrival, Augusto discovered his boyfriend passionately kissing their roommate. Moreover, as he had held professional jobs in Mexico, he was unhappy about being able to find work only as a busboy. So he decided to make immediate adjustments to his life situation: he ended his relationship, moved out of the household, and eventually obtained a more professional position in Tijuana. Augusto started crossing the US-Mexico border every day from San Diego to Tijuana to work, and then back to San Diego to sleep and live his gay social life. He effectively reversed the more common pattern of daily movement among Mexican border residents who live in Tijuana and informally work in San Diego, returning home to their families at the end of the workday—another example of how sexuality complicates the usual patterns of migration and cross-border experience.

Similarly, Toribio (born 1971) received help from a US White man he had first met on the beach in his hometown, the resort town of Mazatlán. He described this man as "not good looking" but with "an amazing personality." "And that really attracted me," said Toribio, who was twenty-one years old when he met this man. The two went out on a few platonic dates in Mazatlán, and Toribio started falling in love. Eventually they had sex, which Toribio described as "a very good experience" and also the first time that he was "versatile." The American man then returned to California, but the two stayed in touch. As Toribio put it, speaking in English during his interview: "So he called me and . . . he said that he needs me, that he loves me . . . that kind of love that I can't live without you." The man said to him: "I want you to come over and meet me in the United States. I live in Hollywood." This dazzled Toribio. "Hollywood. Oh my God! It was, 'Pretty woman, walking down the street,'" he sang, recalling the well-known tune and the movie of the same name. "And I remember watching the movie and saying, 'Yeah, I want to go there.'"[22]

Toribio asked his grandfather for advice about what to do, and his grandfather simply and pragmatically told him, "Well, this is probably what you're looking for."[23] Toribio therefore accepted the American man's offer, and the man sent him the bus fare to Tijuana. Once there, Toribio ran into a man he knew whose uncle was a smuggler. His American partner drove down to Tijuana to meet him, and he also got to meet the smuggler. Then he waited for Toribio on the US side of the border, and together they drove north to Los Angeles.

Unfortunately, once Toribio had arrived at the man's home in Hollywood, he realized that the story had been too good to be true: "I learned that he had another three [Mexican] guys just like me living with him." Toribio went on: "He had told them all the same story, and now they were illegally in the United States and living with him and serving him, the *señor de la casa* [the man of the house]." Noticing Toribio's obvious disappointment, the American man said, "But you're the one I love." This did not convince Toribio, who rapidly decided that he needed to flee this situation. Before he left Mazatlán, a friend who lived in San Diego had given him his gay brother's phone number in Los Angeles in case he needed anything. Toribio decided to use this lifeline. Crying on the phone, he asked the Mexican man for help. The man's response was unequivocal. He said, "Don't worry, I will come and get you." And he did.

––––––

The cases I have presented in this section demonstrate that Mexican gay men's sexual migration is often bolstered by a transnational gay network that can play a central role in prompting them to imagine gay futures elsewhere and then convert that goal to reality.[24] Significantly, these support networks involve not only American gay citizens (or citizens from countries other than Mexico) but also Mexican gay immigrant men who help their gay acquaintances and friends relocate. To be sure, sometimes LGBT supporters have their own agendas and cannot be counted on, leaving migrants feeling exploited, disappointed, and disillusioned. But in other cases, those who come to the aid of Mexican immigrant men help them purely for altruistic reasons.

Emilio's Gay Family Network

One final interesting case is provided by Emilio, who, as I indicated in chapter 2, grew up in a small coastal town north of the international (and very gay) tourist resort of Puerto Vallarta. After experiencing the gay culture of Puerto Vallarta, Emilio returned to live in his hometown. Eventually, however, he decided to leave Mexico, a decision largely prompted by the aid he received from a gay brother and a lesbian sister, one at each end of his migration path and both eager to help him. Although this case is unique, it points to potential overlaps between migration based on blood kinship and migrant networks, on the one hand, and LGBT-supported migration, on the other. The case therefore suggests that the two patterns need not be seen as mutually exclusive.

Emilio's gay brother had migrated to San Diego earlier, and lived there with his American boyfriend. Their lesbian sister, who remained in their Mexican hometown, had become increasingly concerned about how their father treated Emilio. Consequently, she pleaded with their gay brother in San Diego, and convinced him that the best thing for Emilio would be to leave their hometown and move to the United States. Emilio recalled that his sister told their brother something along these lines: "Bring him over and help him. The way Dad treats him here will never change." After she had taken the initiative to make this request, Emilio became excited about the possibility of moving to San Diego. "I wanted to be here, I wanted to learn English. So it was constantly in my mind. I said to myself, 'I will succeed [at leaving],' and I did."

Emilio was fortunate to have a gay and lesbian support network within his own immediate family that paved the way for him to become a sexual migrant. I find it interesting that, unlike the two gay boys in the family, Emilio's sister did not migrate. Instead, she avoided stigma by living a heteronormative life (she was married to a man and had two children with him), but she had disclosed her sexual orientation to her two gay brothers and went to gay bars when she was with them. Their father, therefore, did not mistreat her as he did Emilio and their gay brother. This avoidance of stigma may also be related to lesbians' greater social invisibility in Mexico, which ironically may sometimes protect them from the kind of family-based violence and harassment that Emilio and other gay men in my study experienced.[25]

Emilio's case raises the question of whether his siblings would have helped him in the same way had they not been gay or lesbian themselves. That is, would he have received the same open, kinship-based aid from straight relatives as part of the Mexican culture of migration? It is difficult to know the answer, but a prerequisite for that to happen, as we have seen in other cases, would have been for Emilio to either "pass" as heterosexual or have straight relatives who accepted him as a gay man. His case also indicates how little we know about such overlaps between blood-kinship-based migratory assistance and LGBT-supported migration. Of course, the main reason for that lack of knowledge is that most studies of Mexican migration never think of asking about sexuality-related factors and motivations.

The Combined Role of Migrant and LGBT Networks

My findings reveal that in addition to a generic (and largely heteronormative) Mexican culture of migration, a separate "gay culture of migration" has been put in place by gay immigrant men and their LGBT supporters—supporters who are located both in Mexico and in the United States. Earlier studies of Mexican gay migrants hinted at the existence of such a culture. For instance, Lionel Cantú noted that approximately half the twenty Mexican gay immigrant men whom he interviewed used "preexisting gay networks" to migrate.[26] Similarly, in a study of twenty-four such men in Los Angeles, James Thing found that "most of the men who identified as gay prior to migration and who had access to gay transnational networks did engage those connections for migration."[27] He also concluded that "of the men who did not identify as gay prior to migration, none employed transnational gay social networks for migration."[28] These scholars, however, did not develop this theme further.

My findings are generally consistent with Thing's, but they also differ in a significant way. Although the Mexican participants in my study who were attuned to Mexican gay culture were indeed better situated to draw on LGBT networks, some of them still depended primarily on non-gay immigrant networks, in part because those networks were already in place and were easier to rely on. But, as we have seen, to obtain the assistance provided by non-gay networks they usually had to minimize the role of their sexuality and sexual orientation and pretend to be just like other immigrants from their towns who were seeking to move north. And then they engaged in largely heteronormative pathways of migration. This will become clearer in the next chapter, where I discuss the means by which Mexican immigrant gay men entered the United States.

The present research further establishes that the LGBT individuals who help Mexican gay men migrate to the United States are quite varied. They include immigrants' gay and lesbian relatives; gay Mexican migrants who later helped others like themselves to migrate; acquaintances made during vacation trips to the United States or when those individuals vacationed in Mexico; boyfriends and former boyfriends; and casual sex partners. These social actors seem generally motivated to help gay immigrant men for altruistic reasons, but some of them also have their own interests and personal agendas—agendas ranging from infatuation and romance to situations that involve exploitation.

Finally, although my immigrant participants who relied on LGBT networks often came from urban centers or tourist resorts in Mexico where they had come into contact with well-developed gay cultures, not all had. Some immigrants from other geographic backgrounds were nonetheless able to tap into resources provided by LGBT networks. Meanwhile, the fact that the immigrants from urban areas typically did not migrate without assistance calls into question Fussell and Massey's assumption that immigrants from Mexican cities are not in a position to benefit from dense network ties.[29] In this case, the ties may simply be of a different sort, which indicates the importance of attending to kinds of networks beyond the traditional ones studied in immigration research. Indeed, very few of the Mexican men in my study, including men from urban areas, migrated without help. This point also suggests that expanding how we think about migrant networks—including attention to LGBT networks and forms of LGBT kinship and solidarity in the case of gay immigrants—may lead us to qualify Howe's point quoted earlier about the lack of kinship-based supports for LGBT immigrants.

Having considered both the motivation to migrate and the networks that buoy this decision, I now turn to describing and analyzing the actual pathways that Mexican gay men follow to get to the United States. As we will see, their trajectories of relocation are just as varied as their social positions within Mexico—in terms of location, education, class, and even looks.

FIVE

Departures and Crossings

In their book *Immigrant America*, the sociologists Alejandro Portes and Rubén G. Rumbaut note that "moving abroad is not easy, even under the most propitious circumstances. It requires making elaborate preparations, enduring much expense, giving up personal relations at home, and often learning a new language and culture."[1] Add to that list the mix of emotions and uncertainties that gay sexual migrants may experience as they move abroad with a yearning for sexual freedom—with the hope that they may find sexual autonomy and self-determination, and also protect themselves and their loved ones from shame, humiliation, and the threat of violence—and we can begin to better understand how momentous it may be for them to uproot themselves from their home country and community and move to the United States.

As can be surmised from stories I included in preceding chapters, Mexican gay men's paths of relocation to the United States are diverse, in terms of both the means by which they entered the country and the degree to which their paths were planned. A number of the men in my study had been looking for some time for a way to leave their family homes and start a new life elsewhere. They put plans in motion when they thought the conditions were propitious to do so. Others, by contrast, did not have a concrete plan for departing—they only had a fantasy of possibly doing so—and sometimes they left Mexico abruptly when the conditions for relocating presented themselves unexpectedly. And for still others, moving transnationally had been the last step of a long journey that brought them first to various locations throughout Mexico, until they reached a point at which they decided it was time for them to try their luck in the United States.

While some of the men in my study could be seen, at least partially, as labor migrants, others might be more accurately described as lifestyle migrants.[2] And some qualify for both designations. Taken together, Mexican gay immigrants' accounts of their departures from Mexico tell a story about both the politics of sexuality and what Lionel Cantú called "a queer political economy of migration."[3] They highlight the many social inequalities associated with both transnational migration and sexuality, especially given that the actual means by which these immigrants left Mexico and entered the United States reflect their specific social situations in their home country before they embarked on their transnational journeys.

Three distinct patterns of experience emerged in my study, and the chapter is organized around those patterns. One involves men who had a middle-class or higher social class position in Mexico, as well as high levels of social and cultural capital. These men were typically successful at obtaining Mexican passports and US visitor visas, which reflects their privileged social status, their higher levels of education, and their ability to negotiate institutional bureaucratic systems. A few were even able to acquire work visas or student visas, which fully legitimated them for extended stays in the United States. Moreover, participants with passports and visas could enter the United States formally at official border-crossing points or by flying directly into any of the international airports in US cities.

By contrast, men who did not have the same level of economic resources or cultural capital often experienced their entry into the United States very differently. They typically made their way to the border, hired smugglers (known as *coyotes* or *polleros*), and crossed into the United States informally without any documents, sometimes enduring very difficult situations along the way. And yet, some men in this group had the "right" looks and words to present themselves convincingly as US citizens or permanent residents to border agents at formal border-crossing points, and were thus formally ushered into the United States without having documents to prove their status.

Finally, a third group is composed of Mexicans who lived or had lived just south of the border. Those Mexican border residents who qualify have access to special border-crossing cards that allow them to visit San Diego temporarily to go shopping, visit friends and relatives, go to restaurants and movie theaters, and attend cultural events, among other social activities.[4] LGBT *tijuanenses* who have these permits can also regularly attend

San Diego's gay clubs, visit gay friends, meet sex partners, and spend time with boyfriends on the US side.

The presence of these Mexican border residents, including their LGBT counterparts, is generally welcome in San Diego, in part because it is seen as good for the local economy. Indeed, Mexicans spend large amounts of money in that city's shopping malls, restaurants, bars, and dance clubs, among many other locations.[5] But the border permits have some conditions. One is that Mexicans who use them are required to remain in the "border zone" and not travel beyond a certain distance from the border—a distance that varies by state, but that in California is twenty-five miles.[6] Not all border residents abide by this rule, however. The other is that Mexicans who hold border-crossing permits are not supposed to work while in San Diego. Yet many do.[7] Together, the Mexican immigrants who live permanently in San Diego and the *tijuanenses* who cross daily provide a large source of cheap labor on the US side. In other words, as Richard Kiy has noted, by spending money and working in San Diego, "the Mexican immigrant community is making enormous contributions to the San Diego regional economy."[8] This view can be extended to include the positive economic impact of *tijuanenses* who cross the border regularly to spend money and work. For all those reasons, even local San Diego residents who strongly oppose the Mexicans' presence in that city strongly benefit from such presence. Mexicans help keep down the cost of many local services that would otherwise be much more expensive. For considerably low wages, they cook the food that many local Americans consume in restaurants; build their homes, offices, and businesses; tend their gardens; and clean their homes, among many other activities.[9]

In this chapter, we see once again how attending to the phenomenon of sexual migration has the effect of *queering* migration studies by highlighting less explored aspects of the migration experience. Scholars have emphasized the crossings that fit in my second category of that experience and, to some extent, my third, and these are the sorts of migration stories that inform popular stereotypes as well. And it makes sense that Mexican migrants motivated primarily by the desire for economic betterment would be disproportionately (but not necessarily) working-class. The fact that my participants included such a high proportion of middle-class men tells us something about the aspiration for sexual freedom—that it cuts across class divides in countries of origin, even as it manifests itself differently according to social class.

The sections that follow detail the three patterns of Mexican gay men's relocation to San Diego I outlined above.

Formal Arrivals at US Entry Points

Among my participants, the group who crossed the US-Mexico border formally comprises 43 men. Among them, 35 arrived at entry points with a Mexican passport and a US visa, 3 had become US residents through their family ties before entering the United States on their own, and 5 had been born in the United States and brought to Mexico as young children, where they were raised as Mexicans (these 5 men had a birthright to US citizenship). In this section, I focus on the formal border crossings of the 35 Mexican-born participants who entered the United States with passports and visas.

These men could arrive by airplane and be admitted into the country at a major international US airport—an option not available to their undocumented counterparts. Some, however, still chose to travel first by air or land to Tijuana and then cross by land at a border-crossing point. The majority held visitor visas allowing them to engage in business (B-1 visa), tourism (B-2), or both (B-1/B-2).[10] These visas also made them eligible to stay in the United States for a maximum of six months, but they could be readmitted into the country multiple times: they could spend extended periods in the United States as long as they left before the six-month limit and then came back, and did not work while in the country. In effect, some of them had become quasi-formal US "permanent tourists."

Many among them indeed ended up overstaying their visas or accepting jobs while in the United States, which in essence turned them into undocumented immigrants. For all practical purposes, they had become no different from those who had first entered without documents, and they were likewise subject to the risk of deportation. But the fact that they held passports and visas, and also had formally been admitted into the country, made an enormous symbolic difference to them, and allowed them to distance themselves from those Mexicans who entered the United States without documents.

Some of these men also took explicit steps to protect their image as tourists. For instance, Roy (born 1969), who lived with an American boyfriend in San Diego, had avoided doing any paid work while in the United States. In addition to protecting his visitor status, he viewed this measure as necessary for him to be able to pursue asylum based on his HIV status, which he hoped might allow him to become a permanent resident.

Roy supported himself informally by bringing in Mexican products to sell in San Diego and then bringing back American products to sell in

Mexico. His back-and-forth travel also helped him avoid overextending his visitor visa. But in effect, his permanent place of residence was San Diego. In addition to the money he made from selling products, Roy received assistance from his American boyfriend, who provided him with housing and some additional financial support. In order to remain an active community member in San Diego, Roy volunteered at nonprofit organizations and took some classes at a local community college, all of which he felt were within the rules of his visitor visa (although technically, a student visa should have been a prerequisite for him to enroll in any classes).

Roy's explicit avoidance of paid work also served another function: it seemed to reflect his sense of himself as an upper-middle-class Mexican (and a member of a *familia bien*, a well-to-do family). Maintaining this social status seemed crucial for him to avoid being seen as a stereotypical undocumented Mexican immigrant or perceived as having moved to the United States for economic reasons. Moreover, he emphasized that he did not get along with the "majority of Mexicans who live here," whom he described as *mojados* ("wetbacks"). He told himself: "That's not what I am." And in some ways, his assessment was right. Despite Roy's spending most of his time in the United States, officially he was not breaking any rules, and he had never had any difficulties being readmitted into the country, because he had the right documents. Furthermore, he had been able to obtain these documents in the first place because of his social class position, his cultural capital, his level of education, and his looks. As he put it:

What happens is that, as a tourist, I have a good record. And my family in Mexico is upper-middle-class—as they would say here. We traveled to Disneyland as tourists ever since I was a kid; I have studied in Europe and Canada. That is, I am one of the few Mexicans here, I believe, with the [right level] of education. Thank God I am lucky that way.

He added that because of his fair skin and other physical features, people in the United States always thought that he was from Spain and not from Mexico. In the end, however, Roy could not fully maintain his sense of distance from other Mexican immigrants. Aware that in reality he was bending the rules somewhat, he concluded, "I am part legal and part illegal."

In another example, Toribio (born 1971) crossed the border without documents the first time he entered the United States. Later, however, he succeeded in obtaining a passport and visa. By then he had been aware that he needed to take steps to maintain his new immigration status. He decided to live in San Diego with his boyfriend, but also to cross the border into Mexico each day during the workweek to his middle-class job in a Tijuana hotel. Hence, he left the United States regularly and was readmitted at the end of each workday, and he had a regular income while also avoiding working in the United States.

Toribio reported that a majority of the officers at the border-crossing point already knew him and were aware that he crossed the border daily. He explained, speaking in imperfect English:

Those guys would look at me with my [hotel employee] name tag on the border. . . . They would see me every day crossing the border with my passport in my hand. And they'd say, "Oh, how was the hotel today?" "Oh, very good. How you doing, guys?" And I would know them by name, because they were there all the time. . . . I was never asked "Where are you going?" because I would probably say, "Oh, [I'm going to] my boyfriend's house." I never had anybody be mean to me . . . it was obvious to them that I had my name tag, and you can see the hotel standing from here that I worked right there. They really didn't care where I was going, because I had my passport and I was legally crossing, and they'd see me every day, it was obvious.

One time, when Toribio returned after a vacation trip abroad, the border agents told him that they had missed him and had been wondering where he was.

Toribio eventually became tired of commuting across the border, which had become very taxing and was affecting his relationship, so he took a job in San Diego. This effectively turned him into an undocumented immigrant, but that is not how he saw himself. He said, instead, that he was "sort of legal," especially because he was still free to cross the border back and forth with his Mexican passport and visa. Like Roy, as a middle-class Mexican Toribio felt that his being grouped with undocumented Mexicans would be not only potentially stigmatizing but also inconsistent with his true identity.

Both Roy and Toribio were involved in long-term relationships with American men. The irony is that had they been in relationships with American women at the time, they could have married their US partners and obtained US permanent residency. But, as I indicated in chapter 3, this right had not been granted to binational same-sex couples until 2013 in states that had approved same-sex marriage, and in 2015 in all fifty states.[11]

Finally, other Mexicans were able to secure visas that allowed them to work (H-1) or study (F-1 or J-1) in the United States, and they could remain legally in the country for as long as their visas were valid. One example is provided by Leopoldo (born 1967), who entered the United States with a work permit he obtained through his job with an American headhunter firm. When he had lost a job in Tijuana, this company helped him find a new job there. Seven months later, one of its recruiters reached out to him, indicating that the firm had liked his style during his interview and was offering him the chance to work for it. The company also offered to pay for the costs of processing his work visa. Leopoldo seized the opportunity, telling himself, "OK, I am going to San Diego, because there I can build a future." He speculated that there he might encounter less discrimination against unmarried men than in the firms for which he had worked in Tijuana. (I described Leopoldo's experiences with those Mexican companies in chapter 3.)

As suggested by the various examples included in this section, Mexicans who enter the United States with US visas tend to be better educated and more middle-class, and come more frequently from Mexican urban centers, when compared with their undocumented counterparts. They possess the cultural and social capital to adopt identities as global tourists, foreign workers, or international students, and thus they can avoid being seen as stereotypical Mexican migrants. Their passports and visas become available to them because of the legitimacy that their social class position, education, or looks afford them, particularly in the eyes of US consular officers who make decisions about visas. Ironically, the cost of obtaining those documents, while not trivial, is typically lower than the amounts that their undocumented counterparts have to pay smugglers to get into the United States.

Undocumented Crossings

The Hills of San Diego

Many of the men who came from Mexican towns having a strong culture of migration[12] assumed that their only option to enter the United States was to do so informally, without any official documentation. Of the 80 Mexican gay men in my study, 23 described first heading to a location along the US-Mexico border and, once there, developing a strategy to cross into the United States without documents, often guided by smugglers who charged them hefty amounts of money for helping them cross.

One dramatic example is provided by Octavio (born 1977), who described his trip from Guerrero to California as a "beautiful journey." He and his older brother traveled by bus for three full days to Tijuana. Every new place that the bus went through amazed him. "It was a very beautiful experience," Octavio reminisced with pleasure. When they finally arrived in Tijuana after traveling two thousand miles, Octavio was shocked by that city's level of activity, and he particularly marveled at the presence of female and transgender sex workers openly looking for clients in broad daylight in the red-light district.

Octavio's father had hired a *coyote* to bring his two sons over the border. The crossing was difficult. It involved four days of walking with a group of men over hills and down deep canyons, suffering from incredible cold and very little food or water, while being chased by and having to outsmart the border patrol.[13] They finally arrived at a predetermined spot on the US side where several cars were waiting, and Octavio was piled into a car's trunk with three other migrants. The smugglers dropped them off in a northern suburb of San Diego—a location that seemed to Octavio like a completely different world, despite its being a mere sixty miles north of Tijuana. Once there, he and his brother were delivered to their father, who became very angry upon seeing Octavio emerge from the car. As I discussed in chapter 4, in the father's eyes, the Mexican culture of migration that brought young men from Mexican towns to the United States was not supposed to include the gay ones.

Like Octavio, Toribio described a difficult crossing into the United States the first time he came at the age of twenty-one. (As we saw in the previous section, later in his life he managed to get a passport and a visa, which allowed him to cross the border freely and regularly.) After he crossed the border, a man instructed him and others to get in a van, "men lying down underneath, and women on top." The man wanted a lady traveling with a boy to "sit in the front so that they see a woman with a child in a car, no problem." Toribio recalled then feeling a deep sense of regret:

So they put us all on top of each other and the car drove [away], and my heart was pounding. . . . I felt so stupid, because I kept thinking to myself, "Why are you doing this? You have a perfectly good life; this is not something that you need to be doing."

Octavio and Toribio both succeeded in crossing on their first attempt. Others, however, were caught and deported multiple times.[14] But they persisted, and they eventually succeeded. Claudio (born 1977), for instance, attempted to cross over the hills four times, and each time he was caught and deported. It was not until his fifth try that he could make it to a preset meeting point, where smugglers brought him to Los Angeles.

From there, he returned to a northern suburb of San Diego, where one of his siblings lived. Similarly, Narciso (born 1983) was also caught and deported several times, and during one of those crossings managed to make it safely to a van that was waiting for him, but then some ranchers fired multiple shots at the vehicle. (Narciso did not know who these men were, but at the time the controversial vigilante groups that eventually became the Minuteman Project were beginning to form; border vigilantes promoted the idea that US civilians should take border control into their own hands.[15]) Thankfully, no one inside the van was hurt.

But not all the stories of crossing the border over the hills are as dramatic. Inti (born 1978) had been completely unaware of what to expect when he made arrangements to cross. He was simply told to wait in the dark and then walk under the border fence. A car awaited him on the other side. Inti saw this experience as quite normal: "I didn't have a single document. I didn't have a passport, or anything. Just like all other people, I think." Moreover, some of those who were caught and deported reported that sometimes the border patrol officers were friendly and pragmatic. When Venustiano (born 1975) was caught, the officers simply told him, "Better luck next time." But for many, crossing in this manner was quite humiliating. As Humberto (born 1975) put it, "It was such a horrible experience, crossing through the hills. You feel pursued; you feel as if you stole something or killed someone."

Informal Crossings at the Formal Border-Crossing Points

Although the images of Mexican immigrants walking over the hills or traversing the desert are quintessential in representing their migration to the United States, undocumented gay immigrants sometimes use other methods, including some they enact right at the heavily guarded formal crossing points. The specific strategies they thought would work for them individually signal important differences among immigrant men in terms of their social class, physical appearance, and cultural capital. Some participants in my study felt that because of their looks, they could possibly get away with pretending to be American citizens or US permanent residents, while others assessed that their looking stereotypically Mexican and working-class made them immediately suspect—that if they tried to pass as legitimate border crossers they would likely be questioned, caught, and rejected as inadmissible.

This latter group included Adriana (born 1962), whose story of feminization and acquiring a gay identity in La Paz I recounted in chapter 2. In order to get to San Diego, she had to resort to hiding in the trunk of a car. "I got a pill to calm down. I took it, and I was very relaxed," she said. When Adriana climbed into the car's trunk, she realized that a young woman had already gotten inside. Then the car left for the border. Adriana described the events that followed:

Through the vents I could see the lights at the crossing point. The driver turned up the volume of his radio, and I fell asleep due to the pill. I was snoring, and the other girl was covering my mouth. How embarrassing! When I woke up, I was in Chula Vista [on the US side]. They woke me up with a nice cup of coffee and breakfast. "Get up, we're here," they said.

The smuggler charged Adriana $1,700 for this crossing.

In another similar case, Rodolfo's (born 1972) smuggler put him inside the trunk of his car with two other people and waited for a tip from someone positioned at the checkpoint; that person's role was to tell the smuggler which lane to take based on his knowledge of, and instinct about, the individual border agents. In this case, success depended on the credibility of the person driving the car—whether she or he seemed trustworthy to the agent, or raised any suspicion. The role of the immigrants was to remain quiet and do nothing that could attract attention to the car's trunk.

Other participants, however, dared to take the high risks involved in jumping the border at the crossing point. As Teodoro (born 1966) put it, he "crashed" the border by jumping a wire fence at the border-crossing point and then dashing across the eight lanes of traffic of Interstate Highway 5, in plain view of the border crossing. His aim was to reach the trolley station and board a train to San Diego, which he managed to do. Similarly, Braulio (born 1977) was instructed by a *coyote* to cross the border and run with him against traffic on the outbound side of the freeway. They jumped the freeway divider and ran across the remaining freeway lanes, aiming to reach a fast-food restaurant where Braulio's American boyfriend was waiting to pick him up.[16] Braulio said that the border agents saw them doing this, but by the time they called someone to pursue them, the smuggler and Braulio had already changed shirts and disappeared into the crowd.

These border-crossing methods were all incredibly risky, and they led to experiences that contrast greatly with those of undocumented participants who entered the United States by passing as US citizens or permanent residents. Such men were aided by either their looks, which were less stereotypically Mexican working-class, or their ability to modify their appearance so that they "looked" legitimately American, middle-class, or both, at least to the border agents. Emilio (born 1979), for example, had a gay brother living in San Diego who encouraged him to head to the border-crossing point and pretend to be a US citizen. To ensure Emilio's success, his brother brought him nice clothes meant to give him a middle-class, professional look. He also told him to get near a group of Americans returning to the United States on foot. His specific instructions: "When you see a group of Americans, you get [mixed in] among them, and when you get to the checkpoint, you say *US citizen*." Emilio chose to cross at two in the morning, when many young Americans return to San Diego after partying in Tijuana. In Emilio's own words:

So I learned that word, *US citizen*, and I crossed among a group of Americans. . . . The agent saw me and didn't say anything. I said, "*US citizen*," and he responded, "OK." He opened the door for me, and I didn't have to pay anything—I didn't have to pay a *coyote* or anything. You know, it was luck; but maybe immigration wasn't as alert then as they are now due to 9/11.

Crossing had been so easy that Emilio later felt comfortable going back to Mexico on a vacation trip to Puerto Vallarta, knowing he would return to San Diego afterward. Upon returning to the border, he tried to use the same method that had worked so well for him before. This time, however, he dyed his hair blond, wore blue-tinted contact lenses, and headed to the border checkpoint. These strategies demonstrate that Emilio associated a middle-class Mexican or American status with whiteness. However, the border agent was not convinced that he was a US citizen and started asking him questions. Emilio described the event, mixing Spanish with imperfect English (the words he said in English appear in italics):

The American started asking me, "*Where are you going*?" I said, "I'm going to San Diego." "*Where are you come from*?" I said, "From dancing, from the club." And he asked me, "*Where were you born*?" I said, "In San Diego." "*How it is called, the hospital where you were born*?" I didn't know what to say. He got me, and I became nervous and started stuttering. He said, "*Come with me*." So I went to the office, and they checked everything. I didn't give my real name, I gave a false name, but they checked my ID, my fingerprints, and they locked me away.

Emilio was deported, but he did not give up. Soon afterward, his brother borrowed someone's permanent residence card and brought it to him. He dyed Emilio's hair black to match the ID owner's, and he gave him a cell phone. He advised Emilio to use the phone as he approached the checkpoint so that he would look more relaxed and legitimate. Emilio selected a line where the agent seemed to be asking no questions, showed the permanent residence card while pretending to be talking on the phone, and walked back one more time into the United States.

In these crossings, which involved interactions between Mexican gay men and border agents, Emilio and others who pursued similar strategies were concerned about looking respectable and middle-class so that they would be seen by the border agents as having a legitimate immigration status to enter the United States. But interestingly, they were not concerned about passing as heterosexual. This may be related to the fact that these men first crossed the border in the late 1990s; the policy that excluded homosexuals from entering the United States had been lifted in 1990.[17] This makes their experience of crossing different from that of people like Sara Harb Quiroz, a lesbian and US permanent resident who was stopped at the border in 1960 for "looking like a lesbian," as reported by Eithne Luibhéid.[18]

Finally, Eliseo (born 1962) relied on his looks to accomplish a leisurely crossing along the beach at the westernmost end of the border fence, where it reaches the Pacific Ocean. As he walked across, he was never stopped by the border patrol:

I had the idea of walking along the beach. I was wearing shorts and had a shaven head, and I could pass as White because I looked blond. . . . I walked on the beach and I crossed and I came here, and I am here ever since then.

As these accounts show, the strategies used by the Mexican gay immigrants in my study who lacked the required documentation to formally enter the United States are not dissimilar from those used by other Mexicans, and are also varied. Moreover, they are often quite risky. And notably, as these men enacted such strategies—particularly in border crossings involving smugglers—they usually did so alongside "regular" straight Mexicans on their way to try their luck in the United States, and so they simply did not advertise their homosexuality. In other words, they crossed the border by blending in with the larger body of Mexican undocumented immigrants—a migration process that is largely heteronormative—and keeping quiet about their sexuality and motivations to move to the United States.

Many of these undocumented Mexican gay men never considered the possibility of entering the United States formally as temporary visitors by obtaining a Mexican passport and a US visa. They may have assumed that their applications would not be approved—indeed, for some this had been their prior experience. Or they may simply have been influenced by the fact that most Mexican immigrants they knew personally had crossed without documents.

Their stories also suggest that looks, social class, and cultural capital mattered in terms of how these immigrants crossed the US-Mexico border. Those who could fashion themselves as "Americans" or middle-class Mexicans could pretend to be US citizens or US permanent residents, and sometimes successfully crossed without being suspected. For this latter group, the cost of crossing was much lower, at least compared with the hefty amounts that other immigrants had to pay to their *coyotes*, not to mention the hardships and risks associated with such methods.

Border Lives

The third pattern of Mexican gay men's relocation to San Diego involves men who obtained the privilege of crossing the border based on their status as longtime border region residents. Fourteen Mexican participants in my study are included in this group. Most of them eventually decided to stay permanently on the US side. For instance, Fermín (born 1977), who had attended school in San Diego while living in Tijuana, had grown tired of the long time it took to cross the border every morning.[19] When he lost his border-crossing card, he decided it was time for him to stay in San Diego. He welcomed being in one place, but he mourned having to give up his work as freelance writer for a Tijuana newspaper, which he saw as contributing to that city's culture and arts. In San Diego, the only job that he could find was as a helper in a supermarket.

Participants who were border residents but continued to live in Mexico were convinced that whatever San Diego could offer them was insufficient for them to relocate. Their cases are a reminder that most Mexican gay men, including many who live in border cities, are content to remain in their home country, pursuing gay identities and enacting their same-sex sexualities there. Those in my study who chose to live on the Mexican side of the border viewed San Diego's gay life as a complement to the gay lives they were enacting in nearby Mexican cities such as Tijuana, Ensenada, or Mexicali. Oscar (born 1976) had lived in Tijuana for thirteen years when, at the age of twenty-one, he began to cross the border. He noted that it was common among Tijuana college students to supplement their income by informally working weekend mornings at San Diego's swap meet. After work, he would remain in San Diego and go to a cruisy adult bookstore he discovered. There he could engage in casual sex, after which he would return to Tijuana to continue his life in that city. Oscar did not want to move to San Diego permanently because, as a high-skilled worker, he wanted to work in his area of training, and he thought that such a position would be hard to find in San Diego without having a proper work permit. He feared that in San Diego he would have access only to the kinds of low-paying jobs that many *tijuanenses* perform on the US side of the border.

Similarly, Sabino (born 1967) had a boyfriend and a good job in a bank in Tijuana. But he was motivated to visit San Diego regularly because he was especially attracted to White Americans. As he put it, "I'm intrigued about meeting a gringo, an American young guy." He and his boyfriend had an open relationship, but Sabino did not seek sex in San Diego, in part because he was concerned about language barriers, and in part because he did not know the rules of street cruising and feared getting in trouble with the police. When he went to San Diego to be interviewed for my study, he joked that his boyfriend would surely ask him, "How many *güeritos* [blondies] did you see today?" "As if I could count them!" Sabino remarked, laughing.

Finally, Teodoro's story challenges the idea that sexual migration at the US-Mexico border always involves relocating from Mexico to the United States. As I described in chapters 3 and 4, he initially moved from Guadalajara to Orange County with a cousin, only to find that he could not freely enact a gay identity while being surrounded by family there. So he moved to Tijuana after learning of its well-developed gay culture. By making Tijuana his new home, Teodoro became a border resident who was fairly openly gay on the Mexican side. Having become a US permanent resident after his initial undocumented crossing into California, he now also formally crossed into San Diego regularly for work and other activities, including sporadic participation in that city's gay life.

The Political Economy of Crossing

The moment of entering the United States functions symbolically as a time when differences among gay Mexicans—their varying social class positions, urban or rural origins, levels of education and cultural capital, and racial features and looks—become most starkly evident. This view of the border emphasizes its role as a clear point of demarcation between the United States and Mexico that keeps people from these countries separate through complex processes of filtering. This view is different from, although not altogether incompatible with, a more romanticized conception of the US-Mexico borderland region as a privileged space where hybridity and cultural contact among dissimilar peoples create unique forms of welcome liminality.[20] In my participants' narratives, the emphasis is instead on the idea of the border as an intense point of scrutiny where agents of the state are charged with deciding who belongs and who is deemed inadmissible, who is allowed in and who is excluded.[21] In this view, the border emerges as a site where designated social actors—border agents, customs officers, and the border patrol—not only have considerable discretionary power, but often make subjective decisions and assess a person's trustworthiness based on criteria that may rest on strong racial and class-based stereotypes.[22]

Such subjectivity also applies to decisions made in consular offices that foreign individuals visit to request visas to enter the United States.[23] Indeed, being granted a visa is considered a privilege reserved for those foreigners—Mexicans included—who convincingly present themselves to US consular officers as possessing the means and having the right reasons to travel to the United States, as well as the demonstrated intention to return to their home countries after temporary visits. Although there is nothing wrong with such requirements, consular decisions are not necessarily objective. Evidence suggests they are often largely subjective and left to the discretion of individual officers. In addition, such decisions cannot usually be reviewed or appealed, which opens the door for the enactment and perpetuation of biases that can go unchecked.[24] Like decisions about admissibility that are made at the border at the moment of crossing, decisions about who receives a visa often seem to be influenced by assessments of race, national origin, social class, and even an officer's sense of affinity with individual applicants or subjective judgments of their likeability.

For those reasons, some Mexican men in my study felt that even a middle-class status offered them no guarantee that they would be granted a visa. Justo (born 1971) had heard horror stories about the kinds of documentation applicants had to show to persuade American consuls to approve their visa applications, and commented that several of his friends as well as his own brother had been denied visas. When he himself went to apply for one, he made sure to be well prepared with any documents he thought he might be asked to provide. The consul, however, did not ask him to show anything. "The consul liked me," Justo said. "She asked me, 'How are you, cutie?'" After the consul learned that Justo worked for a bank, she told him to return the next day to pick up his passport. Not knowing whether this meant that the consul was approving his application or rejecting it, Justo offered to show her any documents she might need to see, but the consul responded that that was not necessary. When he returned, his visa was approved and ready.

Justo perceived that the outcomes for specific applicants at the American consulate are fairly arbitrary. But he also felt that looks do matter, and that that is one way in which being a gay man was possibly an advantage—which in his mind meant, somewhat stereotypically, that gay men pay more attention to their grooming and their self-presentation. In the end, despite his fears, his experience seemed to confirm to him that his middle-class status and education level had helped him obtain his visa.

With his passport and visa in hand, Justo found that crossing the US border into California was simple, and so he traveled back and forth repeatedly even after he had moved to San Diego permanently. And yet, later and unexpectedly, he also experienced the arbitrariness of the US admissions system. One time, when returning to San Diego from Tijuana, Justo had an altercation with a border agent who instantly and permanently altered his immigration status. Justo had felt unhappy about how the agent was treating him and, according to him, made the mistake of raising his voice. The agent responded by crossing out the visa on his passport and telling him, "No more San Diego for you." She then called a supervisor, who took Justo away and told him, "Please excuse her; she's having a bad day." But Justo's visa had been officially revoked on the spot at that border agent's discretion, and his status instantly shifted from "Mexican tourist with an approved visa" to "inadmissible alien." All that the supervisor at the border could do was encourage him to go back to an American consulate, explain what had happened, and ask it to renew his visa.

Justo went straight to the airport and took a flight to Guadalajara. Unfortunately, renewing his visa proved difficult this time around. The consul who interviewed him was less receptive and rejected his application, simply telling him to try again a year later. Feeling that he was being denied the life he had constructed for himself in San Diego, Justo traveled back to Tijuana, paid $1,500 to a smuggler, and crossed back over the hills into the United States. He faced the enormous cost disparity between formal and informal border crossings to which I referred earlier: as an undocumented Mexican, he had to pay much more money to enter the United States than as a documented one.

If we take into account complications such as these which can arise in obtaining a visa, it should not be surprising that many Mexican gay men participating in my study never considered applying for one. Many lacked the cultural capital to even imagine obtaining a passport and visa. And if they had considered the possibility of getting these documents, they also often assumed that their dark skin and working-class or rural looks—which they thought made them look stereotypically Mexican— would render them ineligible for a visa. Without documents, they then felt forced to pursue informal ways of entering the country, often putting themselves at the mercy of smugglers and undergoing very harsh conditions. Hence, their migration experiences contrasted enormously with those participants who were able—and who typically assumed it to be their right—to obtain the proper documents to enter the country formally and officially.

It also seems clear that for many of these men, obtaining a passport and visa was not part of the script presented to them within the Mexican culture of migration. For Octavio, for instance, the idea of getting proper documents had never crossed his mind, possibly in part because the men who emigrated from his town usually just headed over to the border without any papers. He and others thus accepted that their chances of entering the United States might be better if they simply followed the same path as every other immigrant who had left their towns. Crossing the border without documents was one of the prescribed steps of their journeys north.

Other men, including Armando (born 1981), who grew up in Oaxaca, would have considered obtaining the proper documentation in Mexico. But they pessimistically, if also realistically, assumed that instead of facilitating people's transnational movement, governments were invested in curtailing it. Armando complained that entering the United States with a *coyote* "is not the best way to enter a place to progress. . . . There are other means, there are forms, but sometimes the governments don't let you access those forms, they put up very costly barriers. They prevent you from doing it."

That I have recounted such divergent narratives of crossing from Mexico to the United States reflects somewhat the dynamics of migration spurred by reasons connected to sexuality. Because the motive of sexual freedom is distributed randomly along the class hierarchy, my participants were more diverse in their class backgrounds than might typically be the case in a study of Mexican migrants. The different pathways that Mexican gay men followed to reach the United States not only mark profound dimensions of social inequality among them but also influenced their experiences upon arrival. Notably, these pathways affect Mexican gay men's ability to find and become incorporated into San Diego's LGBT community. That is the topic of the next chapter.

Finding Gay San Diego

When Narciso (born 1983) first arrived in San Diego around 2001, his half-brother found him a place to live in a collective household of young immigrant Mexican men in a central neighborhood of the city. Having no knowledge about San Diego's gay community or where to find gay men there, his sexual life was initially limited to occasional sexual interactions with two of his straight-identified roommates—interactions involving kissing and mutual oral sex while they watched porn movies together. Eventually, Narciso heard that San Diego had gay bars and dance clubs, and also learned that they were clustered in a specific part of town. He set out in search of this area, "by myself, but I never found it. I imagined a street full of men dressed as women; that's what I imagined." His only point of reference was that the gay bars were near University Avenue, which (unfortunately for him in this situation) happened to be one of the longest streets in the city.

As Narciso traversed the length of University Avenue, he hoped to spot that utopian place where he imagined all men would be walking around dressed as women. He was deeply disappointed not to find it. As he explained:

I always had a map. I had heard a lot about the famous University [Avenue]. I had a map in my hand, and I was always looking for University, and I walked all along University up to Fifth [Avenue] . . . and I never found the place.

By arriving at the corner of University and Fifth, Narciso had indeed reached the core of Hillcrest, known throughout

4 The Hillcrest sign at University and Fifth Avenues, San Diego.

San Diego as the geographic (and symbolic) center of the city's LGBT community. But he did not know the name of the neighborhood he was looking for, so the fact that Hillcrest, like a number of other San Diego neighborhoods, was marked by a gigantic sign did not help him (fig. 4). Furthermore, his preconceived idea about what San Diego's gay area might look like prevented him from realizing he had made it to his destination.

Narciso's inability to recognize San Diego's gay neighborhood, even when he was standing right in the middle of it, reflects an unrealistic imaginary about what an American urban gay area might look like, at least during the daytime. Narciso lacked the cultural capital to pick up on the more conventional markers of so-called liberated gay territories in American cities (as well as in many locations around the world). He did not recognize the ubiquitous rainbow flags taped to windows or flying outside doorways. Nor did he spot the many gay stores and businesses in the area. Finally, not having had contact with Mexican urban gay communities before his departure from Mexico, he imagined explicit gender nonconformity as the sole iconic marker of gayness in a liberated area. He therefore did not realize that many of the people walking by him in Hillcrest were likely gay or lesbian.

This chapter focuses on the varied ways in which Mexican gay immigrant men first encounter and become incorporated into LGBT communities in US cities such as San Diego. The speed at which both experiences occur depends on the imaginaries and degree of knowledge about American urban gay life they bring with them, which in turn seem related to their lives in Mexico as well as their urban/rural origin and social class position. Like Narciso, other immigrant men from my study were largely unfamiliar with the signifiers of global gay culture while they lived in Mexico, and for them the process of finding Hillcrest, and the LGBT community in San Diego, was often very drawn out. By contrast, Mexican men who had participated in institutionalized gay life in their home country or visited global gay enclaves during their travels abroad often arrived directly into Hillcrest or its adjacent areas—including North Park, which at the time of my study was becoming recognized as a more affordable gay-friendly neighborhood (and also one known for its ethnic diversity, and that was attracting more Latino and African American LGBT people). Indeed, many of the men who arrived in Hillcrest and North Park instantly began to participate in LGBT activities. Their experiences of incorporation into San Diego's LGBT community are thus not altogether different from those of American gay men, including both those who grew up in the San Diego metropolitan area and those who moved there from other parts of the United States.

My analysis of these two patterns shows that for some Mexican gay men, the mere idea of a gay neighborhood is extremely foreign. At the time of their arrival in San Diego, they had little knowledge about the social processes that permit LGBT people to stake out geographic areas in US cities, or about their creation of clear symbols of gay citizenship that LGBT people are expected to recognize. (I explore the theme of "sexual citizenship" in detail in the next chapter.) But for other Mexican gay men, the notion that places such as Hillcrest existed is common knowledge. They arrived understanding that American cities such as San Diego had well-developed gay communities, and sometimes they had the opportunity to see gay neighborhoods for themselves. And yet for a portion of even these men, some of the specific expressions of US urban gay culture they encountered in San Diego were previously unknown to them, and in some ways also unimaginable.

I must note that most of the men in my study first arrived in San Diego at a time when gay neighborhoods indisputably had considerable salience as part of American urban LGBT life. More recently, a debate has ensued about whether this is still true—that is, whether Americans have entered a "post-gay" era in which sexual identity is simply less consequential as an identity marker and in which openly gay men and lesbians carve out lives well beyond the confines of so-called gay ghettoes.[1] In a post-gay world, it is unclear whether "gayborhoods"—now sites of gentrification and the influx of young, straight families in many cities—continue to play important practical or symbolic roles as part of American gay culture. Even if the post-gay argument is overstated, it may still be the case that the functions served by gay neighborhoods have changed from earlier eras. Yet while the social and urban changes that have prompted such considerations likely had already been under way by the time my participants found Hillcrest, once they did so they mostly felt they had found the core of San Diego's LGBT community. And thus they used Hillcrest as a reference point to discuss their gay lives in the city, both to praise what they liked and to criticize what they did not about San Diego's gay life. But sometimes they also referred to other gay enclaves and expressions of gay culture within the San Diego metropolitan area that provided them with alternatives to gay life in Hillcrest.

The timing of my study is significant in another way as well. Those of my participants whose first arrival in San Diego was some time ago had encountered its gay life before the Internet was available to provide instant capacities for data retrieval. At the time of my study, some who had arrived during the Internet age, plus others who had been in San Diego for some time before that, had begun to conduct online searches and experiment with online dating and sexual hookups (although not all of them liked this method for meeting men, which some found impersonal). And still others lacked easy access to computers. Moreover, at the time of their arrival none of these men had yet experienced a world in which smartphones place enormous computing power in the hands and pockets of ordinary people as they traverse the cityscape—affording them not only instant information retrieval but also apps that use GPS to connect them easily with nearby potential gay friends and sexual and romantic partners.[2] For those reasons, my results certainly would have looked different in some important respects if I had studied people who first migrated in the mid-2010s.

In what follows, I continue my examination of the group of men who, like Narciso, had not known about the existence of gay neighborhoods such as Hillcrest before they arrived in San Diego. I then turn to the experiences of immigrant men who, by contrast, rapidly became incorporated into San Diego's LGBT community because they knew to seek it out and knew how to find it. Along the way, I analyze how Mexican participants defined the LGBT community in San Diego, and I also compare their experiences with those of their American counterparts, both Latino and non-Latino. Throughout, I argue that gay Mexican immigrants' experiences in places like Hillcrest cannot be grasped absent an understanding of the social and sexual particularities of their individual pre-migration lives in Mexico—and therefore, perspectives that homogenize Mexican immigrants or neglect their lives before migration cannot explain their range of experiences as they become incorporated into new worlds.

"Oh, Yes, It's Here": Stumbling upon Hillcrest

As I described in chapter 2, Norberto's (born 1982) first contact with gay life took place in Guadalajara at age eighteen during a visit there, after he had lived in San Diego for four years. At the time, he did not know where to find gay people in San Diego. Sometime after his trip to Guadalajara, however, he overheard a classmate describing Hillcrest in derogatory terms as a gay area:

I learned [about Hillcrest] when I was in school. I remember that I was talking to two boys, two classmates, and one said, "There are many *jotos* [fags] near where I work." And I was startled [*me quedé así*]. . . . I was wondering, because I didn't know anything. I [then] tried to participate in the conversation to find out where that place was. I asked, "And where do you work?" . . . I remember he mentioned Fourth Avenue. "Where is that?" He says, "You go down University until you reach Fourth Avenue, and you see a sign that says Hillcrest . . . many *jotos*."

Norberto immediately acted on this information. He recalled getting home, "and given that I wasn't working then, I said [to myself], 'I'll go there.' . . . So I started walking; it was a long walk." That was a long walk indeed. Norberto and his family lived near the intersection of University and Forty-Sixth Street, four miles away from his destination. When Norberto finally reached the Hillcrest sign, he was initially very disappointed. "I walked all the way there and I thought, 'I don't see anything, I don't see anything.'" But then he noticed something that told him he might be in the right place. "As I began to walk back, I saw two guys embracing and I thought, 'Oh, yes, it's here.'" Like Narciso, Norberto did not initially recognize the most visible signifiers of an American gay neighborhood—the rainbow flags, the gay businesses, and the storefronts. But he was able to confirm that his journey on foot had not been in vain when he saw two men interacting physically with each other in a way that told him they were gay.

It is noteworthy that Norberto found Hillcrest boring during the day, when the neighborhood's life appeared to him as conventional and mainstream as that of many other middle-class neighborhoods in San Diego. (That is probably one of the reasons why Narciso, quoted earlier, had not recognized the area as "gay" when he went there for the first time.)[3] Other men indeed were startled by, or marveled at, the expressions of same-sex intimacy that could take place in Hillcrest during the day. But Norberto did not see anything out of the ordinary, and therefore started going to Hillcrest at night. Then, by contrast, older men (*hombres mayores*, whom he described as being around forty-five years old) often stopped to offer him a ride as he walked through the neighborhood—an action that suggests these men were trying to pick him up for sex.

Being twenty at the time, Norberto, much like many American teenagers, acquired a fake identification card so that he would be allowed into the dance clubs.[4] He first went to gay dance clubs in Los Angeles, but after a Mexican immigrant friend he had met through a gay phone line gave him information about the San Diego scene, he began to patronize gay bars in Hillcrest also. He became especially keen to go to Latino Nights at the various clubs that hosted them weekly. "I really like it with the Latinos," Norberto said. "I don't go out to bars where, let's say, I only find *americanos*, either blond[5] or Black. I don't know why that doesn't attract me." He also liked shopping for clothes in Hillcrest—which he did together with a female friend. But over time, he became disillusioned with the neighborhood because of what he perceived as a troubling attitude among gay men. "The people who live there . . . I feel they are very arrogant," he said. "They think they're everything. I don't like them. They're smug. For a while I stopped going there for that reason." Norberto also felt that the LGBT community in San Diego was a small community where gossip reigned. "When someone has sex with someone, everybody finds out."

Norberto was not the only participant who first learned about Hillcrest through derogatory comments made by heterosexual people. Alfaro (born 1971) similarly heard about Hillcrest at age twenty-four when, driving through the neighborhood, his brother commented, "Look, I worked there, and it's only gay people." His brother also pointed out an adult bookstore and explained, " 'In that place, they'—my brother called them *jotitos*—'they look at magazines and look for big cocks [*vergotas*].' . . . And he would tell me, 'Don't ever come here, because they will corrupt you.' " This did not stop Alfaro, who eventually was brought to an adult bookstore by a Mexican male friend whom he thought was straight. But he did not venture in without considerable trepidation: "You know, the first time I entered [such a place] I was really scared."

Narciso, Norberto, and Alfaro were all secretive about their same-sex desires within their own (mostly Mexican/Latino) communities at the time they first stumbled upon Hillcrest, and so they learned about the gay neighborhood only by chance. By contrast, Inti (born 1978), who moved to San Diego on his own at the age of seventeen, was able to meet and befriend gay classmates in his high school, and these friends told him about Hillcrest. "They asked me to go out with them. They took me to Hillcrest and things like that." A gay classmate asked him to join a gay group. "He had a group in the high school that supported gay people. They organized a meeting every Thursday.[6] . . . And I said yes, and I got to know more people."

Interestingly, immigrant men who stumbled upon Hillcrest—as well as others who arrived in San Diego not knowing anything about where to find gay people in the city—often recalled their utter surprise at the realization that San Diego had not only a well-developed and well-organized gay culture but also a specific area regarded as a gay neighborhood. And some were even surprised that specific bars and dance clubs for gay people existed. Crispín (born 1980) expressed this idea in the following terms: "When I saw a gay place, I was shocked. I thought, 'How could this be?' . . . I didn't know there were [gay] bars, gay places." He was someone who had no previous contact with gay life in Mexico before migrating, despite having grown up in Mexico City (which may be explained by his having been around sixteen or seventeen years old at the time).

The Contrasting Experiences of American Gay Youths

The stories told by Mexican immigrants such as Norberto, Alfaro, and Narciso about how they first found Hillcrest share some commonalities with stories narrated by American men in my study who grew up and came of age in San Diego. However, there is a notable difference. American young men originally from San Diego, including its suburbs, had multiple opportunities to learn about Hillcrest as they grew up, and often were fully aware of the existence of urban gay neighborhoods since quite early in their adolescence. Even if they did not know anything about Hillcrest per se, they assumed that as a large American city, San Diego would have a well-developed gay culture and a gay area. For them, it was just a matter of time before they would find out where the local gay community was located, and they anticipated that would happen when they became old enough to participate.

For instance, Elio (US Latino, born 1973) began to go to Hillcrest's gay clubs and bars as soon as he reached the legal drinking age. This was a simple decision for him. "I just knew where the gay neighborhood was. . . . Just [about] everybody in San Diego knows Hillcrest is . . . gay," he said. "I went to a gay club at twenty-one because I wanted to go, I was curious. And [I] realized [right away] that the guys were really good looking . . . and they worked out a lot." On his first night out, Elio ended up at Rich's, one of the large, mainstream gay dance clubs.[7] He found it by simply "driving by. I'd see a lot of gay guys in line, and you could tell they were gay." However, he recognized that no matter how easy it had been for him to join the gay community, when he had first gone to Hillcrest he still lacked some basic knowledge about the symbols associated with the American LGBT movement. "I didn't know the colors of the flags; I didn't even know they had those symbols back then."

Similarly to Elio, Doug (White, born ca. 1980) first learned that Hillcrest was a gay neighborhood when he was ten years old:

My mom used to work up here on Fourth . . . I mean, I didn't know anything about it, but I used to go to her work sometimes, and she'd have me, like, walk down to get some bagels. And, like, she told me it's a gay neighborhood: "It's so colorful around here," and so, I kind of knew.

Keith (Mexican American, born 1969) had a similar experience. When he was a child, his grandparents took him regularly to a fast-food restaurant in Hillcrest that was located across from one of the gay clubs, the Brass Rail:

It probably wasn't until college that, you know, I would come back . . . to the neighborhood. . . . It's like a gradual progression: you don't just start swimming in this little pool and then jump straight into the ocean, sort of.

Other men had picked up on the information about Hillcrest from the local media. Adam (US Latino, born 1983) learned about Hillcrest when, as a teenager, he was watching a television show. "They were doing, like, a bio on, like, gay neighborhoods or something like that." Although watching this show in his family home in a San Diego suburb made him very nervous, he did not change the channel. "And I remember being in my room, kind of like having the TV on low volume, but I was still watching."

However, much like the Mexican immigrants whose experiences I described earlier, some American men had indeed stumbled upon Hillcrest. For example, Scott (US White/Latino, born 1973), who grew up in Calexico, on the border with the large Mexican city of Mexicali, found Hillcrest "by accident; pure accident." He explained: "I got off the wrong freeway, the wrong time, and I turned around and I . . ." But then he paused and clarified that despite his having stumbled upon Hillcrest, he already knew of its existence. " 'Cause we had heard, like, well there's a place in San Diego where there's gay people."

Although becoming an active participant in a gay neighborhood such as Hillcrest was a new experience for these American men—coincidentally, all were around the age of twenty when this happened—they already knew what to expect. They thus possessed the cultural capital that made it simple for them to find that neighborhood and begin to take part in its life. That was not the case among some of the Mexican gay immigrant participants in my study, for whom the very idea of a gay neighborhood was completely new. Indeed, some of them initially knew only the primarily Mexican/Latino sections of San Diego, and it was only later—in some cases years after arriving in the city—that they learned that it even had a gay neighborhood.

Nonstop Arrivals

The experience was very different for their counterparts who had been attuned to global LGBT culture and politics before leaving Mexico: men who knew about American urban gay neighborhoods, had already visited Hillcrest or gay areas in other American cities, or had made contact with American gay men. Those study participants became incorporated into San Diego's LGBT community and gay life much more directly and rapidly, even those from places in Mexico that had no gay enclaves of their own.

One such participant was Federico (born ca. 1969), who grew up initially in a small town outside the city of Ensenada. "I knew there was a community here," he said. "I knew how it was called, where it was located, just like I know that there are [similar communities] in San Francisco, Miami, New York, Los Angeles . . . in many places, but I hadn't been to one."

As a teenager, Federico lived briefly in Long Beach, California. Then, upon arrival in San Diego at age eighteen, he wasted no time looking for the LGBT community. He said he did so "immediately . . . that's what I

did: I became integrated into the community." He also sought out Latino gay support groups:

Without knowing anyone, without having a job or anything, I arrived at that group
and I introduced myself. And then I attended regularly. And I got a job, [and] I started
getting involved in the art and painting worlds, without ever leaving the community.

Support groups of this sort play an important role in fostering feelings
of community among Latino US and immigrant gay men in San Diego.

Heriberto (born 1973) shared Federico's sense of urgency. Before moving from Durango, he had been in touch with a friend in San Diego who
spoke highly of the city. Heriberto explained that "in relation to the *ambiente* [the gay world], he told me that there are many clubs. 'You have
to go and see,' he said. 'San Diego is very cool!'" Excited about this possibility, Heriberto began to investigate what he could expect to find in
San Diego. "I started compiling information about San Diego while I was
still [in Durango]," he said.

By the time Heriberto arrived in San Diego, he had learned about San
Diego's LGBT Pride and about the gay dance clubs, but he did not yet
know of the gay neighborhood called Hillcrest. "As soon as I arrived, my
friend . . . the person who received me, told me: 'Look, I will take you to
the gay places here. Hillcrest—that's the name—is a gay area. You can hold
hands [with a man].'" As part of this tour of gay San Diego, Heriberto's
friend took him not only to Hillcrest but also to one of the gay bathhouses
and to the Metropolitan Community Church (MCC), a nondenomina-
tional LGBT church that has congregations throughout the United States
and abroad. With this information, Heriberto had all his bases covered: he
learned where he could socialize with gay people, find sex, and explore his
spirituality, all within the contours of the local gay community.

Heriberto detected differences between gay life in San Diego and the
gay life he knew in Mexico, which he summarized by stating his sense
that American gay men were unapologetic about their freedom to express
themselves as they wish:

Here I find it to be, how should I say, more intense. . . . People express themselves more
easily here. For example, in the clubs in Mexico, in Durango specifically, you can't take
off your shirt. . . . In Durango, Guadalajara, Monterrey—all large cities—you can't take
off your shirt.

But he also noted that in Mexico, gay men had some freedoms that US
gay men did not. As an example, he mentioned that in Mexico, men could

smoke inside the clubs, while in the United States that is forbidden.[8] Like Heriberto, other Mexican participants similarly found it paradoxical that the United States had more individual freedoms at the same time that it also was more restrictive in relation to individual expressions such as making noise, smoking where you please, or having loud parties at home until late.[9] However, as a nonsmoker, Heriberto welcomed US tobacco control measures.

As a final example, when Marcelo (born 1970) moved to San Diego after having led an openly gay life in Mexico City (see my description of his story in previous chapters), he found a job in a San Diego hotel, where he met many gay people who were part of the local hotel industry. A Mexican gay man he befriended and his partner asked him to live with them. But Marcelo was unhappy to find out that this friend socialized mostly in "a straight circle" ("in Mexico, one calls it *buga*,"[10] he said). The problem was not that the friends of his friend were straight, but rather that within that straight circle his friend was not openly gay. "Everyone knows it or assumes it, but that's it, no one talks openly . . . and I don't like that," Marcelo explained. Believing strongly in the notion of coming out, he rejected the strategies of sexual silence and tacit tolerance that seemed to be operating within the group.[11]

Therefore, Marcelo decided to move into an all-gay American household composed of a White owner and three roommates, one of whom was White and two Latino. Marcelo spoke little English, and none of his roommates spoke Spanish, so he interacted minimally with them. However, by living in such a household, he felt freer to explore San Diego's gay life, which he found somewhat provincial given his previous extensive experience as an openly gay man and activist in Mexico City.

Marcelo recounted that he had no trouble finding gay venues the first night that he went out:

That [first] night I went by Brass [Rail] and it was half empty. . . . I didn't want to go in. I thought, "There's no point." I started walking on University . . . and I got to Rich's. I saw a huge line waiting to get in, and I noticed that many men were Latinos. And there was a sign that read "Club Papi."[12]

Seeing the size of the crowd, and realizing that this seemed to be a Latino event, Marcelo felt compelled "to get in line," even though he did not know exactly what he would find inside the venue:

I went in [and] paid, they gave me a CD, and I liked [the place]. I met a person that night, and I had fun[13]—we interacted with a group. . . . That was my first night [out] in San Diego, and then I didn't stop. I go to the clubs on Wednesdays, on Saturdays. I now go to the discos . . . I really like discos, I like to be part of the gay social core, I love it; it fascinates me.

Because of the cultural affinity and language, he preferred to attend the Latino Nights that took place each week in several dance clubs—including Bacchus House[14] on Wednesdays and the Brass Rail[15] on Saturdays—and he also kept an eye out for the special Club Papi parties at Rich's.

Marcelo liked some things about San Diego's gay life better than Mexico City's—including his sense that Mexico City's gay men had too much attitude—but he also perceived that in San Diego, gay men imposed some restrictions on themselves that their counterparts in Mexico City did not (his feeling about this matter is similar to Heriberto's quoted earlier). He specifically referred to feeling freer in Mexico City to bring a casual sex partner home, where his roommates generally did not care, whereas that was explicitly not allowed in his San Diego household. For him, such a household rule seemed to represent what he felt to be greater regimentation in American society.

Marcelo also visited San Diego's gay bathhouses. Yet, compared with other participants in my study, they did not dazzle him: "I got to know them, I had fun, I had a good time, but that's it. I haven't had any inclination to go back." After having been a part of the gay community in Mexico City, he seemed to think that nothing in San Diego would ever surprise him.

The ease with which Mexican immigrant men find Hillcrest and gay San Diego greatly depends on how savvy and sophisticated they had been about gay life—and about global gay culture—before migrating. Some, like Marcelo, resemble American gay men in my study who had moved to San Diego from other parts of the United States, and who assumed, or knew already, that San Diego would offer them a gay neighborhood and an institutionalized and well-organized gay culture. They know what to expect, and how to find what they seek.

But, with a few exceptions, even Mexican men who thought they knew what to expect come to realize upon arrival that being gay in Mexico and being gay in the United States can mean different things. They rapidly learn that the rules of interaction within American urban LGBT communities are not the same as in the places in Mexico that they knew. And they are often taken by surprise by some of the expressions of gay life and gay sex they encounter in San Diego. For instance, many of the participants in my study did not anticipate the existence of such venues as the gay bathhouses, the backrooms in adult bookstores, or a nude beach and its cruisy areas. As Santiago (born 1967), put it, those places were "something new for me," then added, "I swear to you that I didn't know." By contrast, the American gay men who moved to San Diego usually had participated previously in the LGBT communities of other US cities, had already visited Hillcrest, and were quite familiar with how to interact with other gay people in San Diego. Greg (White, born 1957), who was originally from Memphis, described having visited San Diego a couple of times on business trips: "I knew there was a very active gay community here, very supportive." Before moving to that city, he had lived in San Francisco, San Jose, and Reno, and was very familiar with gay life and culture in cities in California and other parts of the United States. San Diego's gay community was not essentially different from that of other American cities, men like Greg realized, except perhaps for the large presence of Mexican and Latino men. For some of them, this presence turned San Diego into an attractive destination.

Alternatives to Mainstream Gay Culture

Mainstream versus Ethnic Sexual Cultures

In many cases, people who introduce their gay Mexican immigrant friends to gay San Diego bring them to what probably seemed to them the most emblematic of that life: Hillcrest and the many institutions of the mainstream gay community. But sometimes the mainstream venues of Hillcrest are not the first gay places to which these men are led. Some are initially introduced instead to the emerging, vibrant, and distinctive Latino gay ethnic culture forming on the periphery of Hillcrest, in the less expensive neighborhood of North Park. As they gain entry to a gay ethnic enclave, they are also introduced to Latino support groups and Latino gay organizations, Latino Nights in bars and clubs in both North Park and Hillcrest, and San Diego's yearly Latin Pride event. The sections that follow describe, based on my team's fieldwork, some of the options that were available to our participants.

Latino Nights at Bacchus House, Kickers, and Brass Rail

In the mid-2000s, Bacchus House in North Park hosted its Latino Night every Wednesday. A well-known entertainer and gay activist, Franko Guillén (who used the stage name Franceska), was the regular emcee for the event. To highlight the Latino nature of the night, the bar set a table with

Mexican food. Also, in the early part of the evening, Franceska, in full drag, organized a round of bilingual Lotería, the Mexican bingo game. She asked the audience to shout "¡Jotería!" (an allusion to *jotos* [fags] and the Mexican gay world) instead of "¡Lotería!" whenever someone filled their card. She also gave a queer twist to the Mexican iconography of the game as she read out each card and added her witty commentary.[16] For instance, as Victoria González Rivera—one of the study ethnographers—noted in her field notes, when Franceska pulled out the card depicting *el catrín* (the dandy), she quipped that this character had to be gay, "because no straight man would dress that well."

Later in the evening, Franceska would emcee the weekly drag show. A variety of performers impersonated famous female singers, mostly but not exclusively Latinas. Occasionally, male performers impersonated male Latino singers, making a point of highlighting (even exaggerating) their masculinity. An additional feature of the show is worth noting: showing her activist side, Franceska often expressed political messages as she interacted with her audience, addressing, for instance, LGBT rights, the importance of voting, immigration policies, and the policies of the California government. These messages were intended to mobilize gay Latinos to act collectively on their own behalf. The drag show was followed by dancing, and the deejay played a mix of mainstream and Latino dance music.

Finally, Latino Night at Bacchus was somewhat unique in that it attracted a considerably diverse clientele in terms of gender and race. In addition to gay men, it was attended by a number of women (both transgender and cisgender), including a visible lesbian presence. And besides Latinas/os, it drew considerable numbers of Whites as well as some African Americans and Asian Americans.

Comparatively speaking, the Latino Nights at other small venues, including Hillcrest's Kickers and the Brass Rail, were more conventionally focused on socializing, drinking, and dancing. At Kickers in particular, the clientele tended to emphasize more middle-class looks and "club" attire, denoting certain class distinctions emerging within the circuit of San Diego's weekly Latino Nights in bars and clubs.

Club Papi at Rich's

Club Papi, the venue that Marcelo discovered on his first night out in Hillcrest, took place periodically at the space occupied by Rich's, the largest gay dance club in the neighborhood. This venue consisted of a front bar area where people could talk or play pool, a patio for smoking, and, as described by Jorge Fontdevila in his field notes, a "larger club space [that] was much darker than the front one, with customary disco light effects and very loud music." Jorge also noted that on the nights that Club Papi took place, the music "was a combination of trendy dance remixes of Latin rhythms and house music: Thalia's Megamix, India, Christina Aguilera, Monica Naranjo, but also Missy Eliot, 50 Cent, and B2K." Sometimes, however, the deejay switched to more Latino music, which consisted of salsa and cumbia remixed with mainstream dance beats.

Go-go boys, most of them buffed and wearing skimpy underwear, danced on elevated platforms. And on one occasion a drag queen impersonated Cher, framed by four go-go boys dancing behind her while she sang. (The presence of drag queens at Club Papi was less common, though, than at other, more working-class Latino Nights.)

A majority of those who attended Club Papi were Latino gay men, but people of other ethnic/racial backgrounds were also present. Moreover, according to our study recruiters, some attendees came down from Los Angeles, possibly following "the circuit party itinerary," as Jorge Fontdevila noted.

Club Papi was the trendiest and most mainstream of the Latino gay venues in San Diego. Yet it was also generally a friendly space, including to people who were not gay men. Victoria González-Rivera was visibly pregnant during one of our ethnographic sessions there. She described the positive reactions she received from many of the patrons. As she walked through the tightly packed crowd, gay men playfully "announced 'Pregnant lady walking through' or something like that," Victoria said. Instantly, the crowd would part around her to let her pass. Also, a security guard approached Victoria and asked "if I needed anything, maybe a glass of water or something else to drink"; he later offered to escort her to the bathroom, "since it was way in the back of the club and I had to get through the masses of people to reach it."

The Latin Pride Yearly Event

Founded in 2001 by Latino gay organizations, Latin Pride attracted much the same population of Latino US and immigrant gay men that could be found in Latino support groups and the Latino Nights in local gay bars and clubs. It was held in an enclosed area in San Diego's Balboa Park and consisted of a stage, a dance floor, food stalls, and booths and stands for various HIV and gay organizations and commercial vendors. According to the Lambda Archives website, in 2001 "the first Latin Pride Festival is held in Balboa Park. Over 2000 lesbian and gay Latinos/as attend the one-day event that is planned to be an annual celebration."[17] Two years later, in 2003, the San Diego LGBT Pride website described Latin Pride and Ebony Pride—an African American equivalent—as "splinter groups":

While San Diego Pride was making an effort to reach out and be more inclusive by changing its name to reflect the bisexual and transgender members of the community, other segments were trying to go out on their own. Ebony Pride and Latin Pride took place on August 23 and September 27 respectively.[18]

Despite its apparent discomfort with the two ethnic pride events (which did not take place on the same dates as the mainstream Pride event), the LGBT Pride organization decided to sell a pass that included admission to all three. The same website went on to say:

Although San Diego Pride was supportive of both organizations, some people wondered whether they had splintered off because they felt that they were in some way not being represented at the main Pride event. Addressing their concerns would eventually result in them coming back into the fold of the main organization.[19]

This suggests that the connections between the mainstream LGBT community and the emerging ethnic ones involved some degree of political tension.

Latin Pride was an occasion when the various community-based organizations, bars, and clubs serving LGBT Latinas/os came together in a space perceived as quintessentially Latina/o (and also one that, in contrast to the gay bars and clubs, could be attended by those younger than twenty-one). To reduce the possibility of being perceived as un-American, the organizers adopted an overtly nationalistic tone. For instance, the opening of the event in 2003 included a segment labeled "Flag Presentation." The emcee recited all the countries of Latin America, but then explicitly took pride in the event's occurrence in the United States, after which "The Star Spangled Banner" was played.

Latin Pride did not last long as a separate event, and it eventually rejoined the mainstream San Diego LGBT Pride festival. As a gesture of inclusiveness, San Diego Pride had implemented a Latin Stage and also began to print a bilingual Pride program. However, as noted in a newspaper article from 2011, an uneasy relationship between the mainstream Pride event organizers and the ethnic gay communities continued as activists launched complaints about a lack of adequate representation.[20]

Mexican Straight Bars Where Men Connect for Sex

In addition to the gay Latino venues and events, some immigrant men in my study were taken by their Mexican friends to bars where they could find the more heavily gendered forms of same-sex sexual interaction often associated with more "traditional" Mexican understandings of homosexuality (as defined by the *pasivo/activo* model I discussed in chapter 2). For instance, a friend of Prado's (born 1972) initially brought him to what he described as *"bares de mayates,* bars for Mexicans who like *jotos."* Prado described these places as follows:

There are three, four such bars nearby on University; of men who say they are *hombres,* but they like to have sex with other *hombres.* That is, they have a woman in Mexico or here, and they are really macho.

Prado noted that these bars were on University Avenue—not in Hillcrest, but not far from Hillcrest either. They were located in a primarily Mexican/Latino neighborhood and were patronized by working-class, straight Mexican men, including some who have sex with other men. In these bars, Prado learned that to be successful at meeting sex partners, he had to play by the local rules of interaction:

You sit at the bar, order a beer, a sangria, or whatever you want to drink. . . . I start doing like this [he demonstrated pulling his hair back in a feminized manner], even if I don't have long hair. You get it? How many men have you seen who would do that? None. I pull my little hair and things like that. Then, casually, when he goes to the bathroom, you put on an act and suddenly you also need to use the bathroom. So you follow him. . . . While you're washing your hands, you start with whatever: "How's your evening so far?" or "Are you drunk already?" . . . Simple things. Then they answer you or they don't.

While he enjoyed these experiences, they also gave him the impetus to seek out San Diego's more mainstream gay culture, particularly after having lived in Tijuana, where he was attuned to that city's gay life. Through a friend, Prado "found the Brass [Rail], Rich's . . . all the *chachareo* [random variety] of bars that exist [in San Diego]." He began to meet gay-identified people, and eventually found his way to the Metropolitan Community Church. The same friend showed him where to find the gay bathhouses and the adult theaters, and by the age of twenty-five, Prado had attended his first San Diego LGBT Pride parade and festival. These various activities prompted him to move to San Diego permanently.

Latino Gay Support Groups

As I mentioned earlier, Mexican immigrant men also took part in Latino gay culture by attending meetings of the Latino gay and HIV support groups organized by various community-based organizations. Soon after being taken to Hillcrest, Julián (born 1978) went to the San Diego LGBT Community Center (known as the Center), where he learned about Pacto Latino and other groups, including Bienestar and PROCABI (the Bi-National AIDS Advocacy Project). Other options included Alma Latina at the Vista Community Clinic in North County, the CASA program at the San Ysidro Health Center, and the Family Health Centers of San Diego. Some of these groups originally had formed around the specific needs of HIV-positive Latino gay men, but they welcomed everyone regardless of their HIV serostatus; other groups emerged as Latino gay support groups more generally.

Similarly to Julián, Edwin (born 1974), who was desperate to meet gay men, went out looking for a gay bar. Along the way, he was told about a Latino gay support group at Bienestar, which happened to be holding its weekly meeting that same evening. When he lived in Mexico City, gay support groups had not interested him. He found them "pathetic," because he felt they were for less sophisticated people who had not yet come out of the closet. In San Diego, however, he decided to give the group at Bienestar a try, and was pleasantly surprised to find out about the wide range of gay-related topics they discussed:

I stayed. I really liked the people [in the group]. It was a group of around ten. After the meeting, they told me they were all going out for coffee. "Do you want to join us?" So I went with them, and I came back the following week, and then returned repeatedly.

This group provided Edwin with a place for gay socialization and an entry into San Diego's gay life. Later, he met his boyfriend in the group and became a volunteer.

Two members of my ethnographic team, Jorge Fontdevila and Jaweer Brown, attended a multiple-session training program at one of the organizations—training that focused on helping participants become "agents of change." The trainees attended workshops and lectures delivered by various LGBT activists and professionals on topics such as combating homophobia, disclosure and coming out, machismo, promoting tolerance, HIV stigma, race relations, antigay defamation in the media, and LGBT and immigration activism. As Jaweer Brown noted in her field notes, the goal was to mobilize two politically disenfranchised communities, gay immigrants and US gay men of color, and teach them how they could best fight for their collective rights. Such activities were seen as an important part of gay immigrants' integration into US gay life.

A Rural Expression of Latino Immigrant Gay Culture

A final example of entry into San Diego gay life takes us some distance—geographically and sociologically—from the "gayborhood." A more rural Latino ethnic gay culture was also emerging in the heavily Latino working-class suburbs of San Diego's North County, located closer to the agricultural fields at the edge of the metropolitan area. Gay men from these suburbs sometimes traveled to central San Diego to attend gay venues, but they also organized activities nearer to home. In 2003, my research collaborator Jorge Fontdevila and I attended a fund-raiser organized by Alma Latina, which consisted of a Miss Mexico beauty contest involving men in drag who represented nine different Mexican states. The competition took place at a community recreation center in the North County suburb of Vista. Over the course of the night, the contestants competed wearing regional garb, cocktail dresses, and evening gowns. Individual performers—who appeared to be both men in drag and cisgender women—impersonated well-known Latina and Spanish female singers between each stage of the competition. At every turn, the audience members, who consisted of both LGBT people and straight families, were extremely engaged and took very seriously their role of supporting their preferred contestant with loud cheering, ovations, and applause. Along the way, the witty master of ceremonies made comments and jokes geared specifically to a Mexican immigrant audience (as when she joked that the winner would receive round-trip travel to Acapulco, *coyote* included).

The mix of LGBT people and extended Mexican/Latino families at the event was striking. Gay and lesbian couples spontaneously engaged in slow dancing and kissing on the dance floor. Around them, straight couples also danced; groups of young straight men seemed delighted when the female impersonators playfully interacted with them; young children ran all over the place despite the late hour of the show; elderly grandparents and young straight couples watched the show and simultaneously kept an eye on their children; and at least one young straight couple was openly making out in the back of the hall. Although straight people could be seen attending the gay venues of Hillcrest, at the time it would have been uncommon to see such a large presence of straight families and their children there. Here the mix was unusual, yet at the same time Latino LGBT people made it clear that this was ultimately their space, a gay Mexican/Latino event.

The existence of these LGBT Latino cultural expressions in San Diego thus challenges the stereotype that Mexican gay immigrant men necessarily must leave their families or Mexican/Latino communities permanently, and participate in mainstream gay culture, if they want to be openly gay. Although it is possible that the straight Mexican immigrant families in attendance at this LGBT event might just be part of a small, self-selected minority of straight working-class people who happen to accept gay friends and relatives, my interpretation is that what Jorge and I witnessed that night exemplified the kinds of social and attitudinal change taking place in Mexico and in Mexican communities (discussed in chapter 2).

Assuming that to be the case, this example would also challenge the perceived need among some of the Mexican study participants to move twice—first to a Mexican enclave in the United States, and then elsewhere to be openly gay. Those men assumed that the relatives, friends, and town acquaintances who surrounded them in California would reject them if they "came out." But they could not be sure about this outcome, because instead of disclosing their sexual orientation, they chose to move again to a place where they could be freer from their scrutiny. By contrast, some of the gay and lesbian Mexicans who attended this Miss Mexico beauty contest in Vista seemed to have managed to be openly gay in their own immigrant communities, at least within substantial segments of their immediate social and family circles. That was the case, indeed, for two of my participants who had been contestants. Octavio (born 1977) was openly gay in Vista, where he lived, and Armando (born 1981, who won the crown competing as "Miss Oaxaca") mentioned that he was free to be himself everywhere because his parents in Mexico knew about his being gay and were supportive.

My point is not to suggest that everyone should "come out" instead of migrate—in fact, other men probably had good reasons to believe that disclosure would have negative consequences in the immediate immigrant communities in which they lived. But it is important to keep in mind that when gay immigrants say that visible gayness would be impossible in their own communities or immediate social circles, their assessments may well be based on hypothetical fears about the bad things they assume might ensue, rather than on evidence of such negative consequences.

Networks of Incorporation: The Crucial Role of Friends and Acquaintances

Many immigrant men spoke of the crucial role that gay friends and acquaintances played in introducing them to San Diego's gay culture, to the many institutional forms that it takes, and to Hillcrest specifically. In the Latino support groups I mentioned above, they not only acquired relevant information about gay life and were "shown the ropes" of how best to participate, but also made new acquaintances and friends, including other Latino immigrants who already knew San Diego's gay scene. Gay friends also brought them to coffeehouses, the cruising areas of Balboa Park, adult bookstores throughout the city, the nudist Black's Beach, and, if they were age twenty-one or older, the various gay bars and dance clubs (especially on Latino Nights) and bathhouses. For those who were religious, their friends introduced them to religious groups that embrace LGBT people, including the Metropolitan Community Church, which had a Spanish-speaking branch, and Dignity, the Catholic gay group. Collectively, friends, groups, and organizations provided a solid platform from which Mexican immigrant men could then delve more fully into San Diego's gay life and cultures.

Making Gay Contacts

As I mentioned earlier, some immigrant men in my study already had gay connections in the city before their arrival, and so were brought directly to Hillcrest and its surrounding neighborhoods from either the San Diego International Airport or the border-crossing point. For instance, Emilio (born 1979), who had pretended to be a US citizen when he crossed the border, was picked up by his gay brother in San Ysidro and driven directly to North Park, where the brother lived. Through his brother's social network, he gained immediate access both to Hillcrest and to the Latino ethnic gay community forming in North Park around the time he arrived. Like Hillcrest, North Park was marked by a large neighborhood sign (fig. 5), and both Bacchus House and Bienestar, along with other gay clubs, were located there.

However, as we have seen, other men had not known gay men in San Diego before migrating, and arrived to live in primarily Mexican/Latino households and sections of the city. Some of these men also spoke about serendipitous contacts they made with gay men at various locations that

5   The North Park sign at University Avenue and Twenty-Ninth Street, San Diego.

are not specifically gay, including their workplaces, English as a second language (ESL) classes, and high school and college courses. Moreover, they sometimes met gay men within non-gay-specific immigrant networks and households. But because these men often felt compelled to be secretive about their sexual orientation in these "straight" spaces, their initial contacts with LGBT people in San Diego were sometimes fraught with hesitation and uncertainty. People who thought them to be gay initially had a hard time establishing an open conversation. But after they did, the floodgates opened, enabling those with knowledge about the city's gay life to introduce their new immigrant friends and acquaintances to gay San Diego.

A charming example is provided by Benito (born 1977), who described how a coworker approached him and got him to reveal that he was gay. He said that this man had circled the issue of their sexuality for a while until he mustered the courage to ask him:

[He] obviously got to the point of noticing [that I was gay]. He said, "Hey, I'd like to ask you something. . . . I don't want to disrespect you, obviously. I don't want to offend you. It's simply that, as I have got to know you, I have the suspicion . . . I feel that you are gay, right?"

Benito was shocked by his coworker's direct question and at first did not know how to respond, so he lied. "I denied it at first: 'No, how can you think that?'" Embarrassed, his coworker then told him, "Forgive me. I thought [that] you were, because I am." This made Benito reflect: "I thought, 'If he's openly accepting that he is [gay], it means he has no problem with it, that he accepts it.'" Benito also realized that if he continued to deny that he was gay, even when someone was directly asking him, he would remain isolated. So, on the spur of the moment, he opened up to this man, who ended up becoming his guide into a whole new gay world in Hillcrest.

Seeking HIV Services

Having such peer guides was particularly crucial for men who had moved to San Diego hoping they would gain access to HIV treatments. For those participants in my study, making contact with gay men in the city was an essential first step to learn about the extensive network of HIV/ AIDS services and supports that LGBT people and their allies had put in place there, which included Latino-specific and Spanish-language support groups, case management programs, HIV clinics, free HIV care, and even subsidized housing programs. Claudio (born 1977), for instance, who moved from Oaxaca imagining that he might find much-needed care for his medical condition, first made use of HIV services in the northern suburb of Oceanside. At a local HIV program, where he felt that everyone treated him very kindly, he was first retested for HIV, and then was offered medical services and referred to a local HIV support group. A woman in this group later brought him to PROCABI in San Diego, where Claudio began to meet with a case manager. In turn, this case manager gave him access to subsidized housing at a state-sponsored home for low-income people living with HIV in central San Diego. These various services provided Claudio with a "landing pad"[21] within the gay community, enabling him to become independent from his brother and his family, and also with the space to take care of himself while simultaneously regaining the freedom to be gay he had previously enjoyed in Oaxaca.

Another participant, Efraín (born 1965), had a similar experience. He first spent a brief period in San Jose but then moved to San Diego, where a friend took him to Christie's Place, an HIV/AIDS organization, where he began to attend a support group. Efraín said:

And that's where I began to network, to meet more people who had the same situation. And I found much support. The support that I did not find in San José I found it here with them. I really respect them. They helped me a lot, to get more information, to realize I was not the only one.

The HIV services that Claudio and Efraín initially found in San Diego in turn provided their gateway to the city's gay life and community. Others moved in the opposite direction. While still living in Tijuana, Julián discovered an adult bookstore on the US side of the border, and there he met a US White gay man. Julián explained that "being a closeted gay," he "didn't know where to go, didn't know there were bars." In the bookstore, he realized that it was easy to find sex there, but nothing else. He was thus surprised when this man "followed me outside and asked my name. He said he wanted to see me again, and that's how it started." The two became sexually involved, and later became best friends. This new friend showed Julián Hillcrest ("It freaked me out."). Then, upon learning that Julián was HIV positive, he also took him to the Center and put him on a path to connecting with other Latino-oriented gay and HIV/AIDS groups, including PROCABI and Bienestar.

The Role of Casual Sex Partners

It may seem unusual that a casual sex partner that Julián met at an anonymous sex venue would play such an important role in his life, but he was not the only Mexican participant in my study who reported such an experience. In Cuauhtémoc's case (born 1961), soon after he moved to San Diego he spotted through his apartment window an adult theater across the street. He saw a man come out of the theater, get in his car, and start masturbating. Having been attuned to detecting cruising places in Mexico, Cuauhtémoc imagined that same-sex encounters likely happened inside this theater, so he decided to go check it out. Inside, he met a US White gay man who gave him his phone number. They met again some weeks later and had sex. But the man also became his friend, and proved instrumental in helping Cuauhtémoc not only become part of San Diego's gay community but also obtain false papers and a job.

This man also taught Cuauhtémoc how to think about his sexual orientation. As I described in chapter 3, Cuauhtémoc had a wife and children in Mexico, where he engaged only occasionally in anonymous casual sexual encounters with men during business trips. Moreover, because of his primary attraction to women, he had refused to self-identify as homosexual. But he had never heard about bisexuality as a category or an identity. Cuauhtémoc explained:

[In Mexico,] they told me I was homosexual.[22] I would say, "No, not me. I like both women and men." So, I told . . . this [American] man. . . . I said I did not know how to define myself. . . . I told him that I liked women and that sometimes I liked to be with men, and that I didn't like it much to be penetrated, that that was not my goal, to be with a man who penetrated me. . . . And he said, "Then you're bisexual." And that's how I realized [what I am].

In the end, this connection, which started as a casual encounter in an adult theater, helped Cuauhtémoc obtain a job, gain entry to a new sexual world, and even acquire a new identity.

Immigrants' Incorporation and Their Previous Lives in Mexico

The incorporation of gay immigrants from countries such as Mexico into urban gay communities in the United States is not a simple or uniform process. How they make contact and interact with gay men and gay life in US cities such as San Diego depends substantially on the specifics of their lives in Mexico before migrating as well as their paths of relocation. Those study participants with little previous experience with and contact with gay cultures and communities had a longer path to walk before they made it to gay San Diego. By contrast, their counterparts who had been part of gay life in Mexico often went directly to Hillcrest, North Park, and other gay-friendly neighborhoods in that city upon arrival. And yet, some of these men, who often thought of themselves as savvy about the ways of global gay life, were sometimes surprised to realize that the interactions and expectations within San Diego's LGBT community differed from what they had known in Mexico. Their accounts lend credence to the notion that the global is always localized.[23]

Another important feature of the incorporation process is that specific subgroups have altogether different experiences. For HIV-positive men, their access to HIV services and to LGBT San Diego is tightly intertwined. Those who mainly stay within Mexican immigrant communities sometimes have less access to the mainstream (primarily White) gay community, and sometimes they have greater exposure to the more gendered world of same-sex desires in a few primarily Mexican and working-class venues. The existence of these venues is in itself interesting, as it shows that we need to talk about same-sex desires in San Diego—and the places, practices, and institutions they generate—in the plural. Further demonstrating this plurality is the emergence of a Mexican/Latino rural community and culture in San Diego's North County, exemplifying the possibility that gayness can be expressed even within some segments of working-class Mexican immigrant communities.

The varied patterns of arrival that my participants described suggest the complexities of the incorporation of immigrants inside gay communities in the United States. What does it mean to become a "citizen" of a new gay social world, especially if one is not a legal citizen of the country in which it is located? What rights and responsibilities are entailed in this mode of belonging, and how do newcomers learn those expectations? What specific barriers and obstacles to full inclusion do they confront along the way? These questions are the focus of the next chapter.

SEVEN

Immigrant Sexual Citizenship

WITH STEVEN EPSTEIN[1]

The previous chapter began with the story of Narciso (born 1983), who lacked the cultural knowledge to identify San Diego's gay neighborhood even when he stood at its very center. By contrast, Bernardo (born 1967) also had to wander a bit to find Hillcrest, but knew it the moment he saw it. As a *tijuanense* who was used to crossing back and forth regularly between the United States and Mexico, he was familiar with San Diego but had never been to Hillcrest until the day he took a friend's advice and crossed a border of a different kind:

> A friend of mine told me, because I didn't know very well how to get there. . . . "You take the University Avenue exit, and it will take you I don't know where"; and there I was, looking for the damn University Avenue until I finally found the exit. . . . First I went the wrong way, east instead of west, and I said, "¡Ay no! [*laughter*], this doesn't look like a gay area [*de ambiente*]." And then I said, "Okay, I'll go the other way to see if . . . ," and no sooner said than done, I started seeing the stores and everything, the flags and things like that, and I said, "Oh, yes, this is it."

Bernardo's "Oh, yes" reflects the matter-of-factness of simple recognition: the sight of rainbow flags told him immediately that he had crossed the border into the "gay nation."

This chapter expands the discussion of social incorporation launched in the preceding one to consider how immigrant gay men attempt to construct new forms of belonging within the gay urban spaces they encounter in the United States. Immigration scholars have paid scant attention to how questions of sexuality affect migrants' claims to belonging or practices of social incorporation upon arrival in their host countries.[2] Therefore, I invoke the academic literature on *sexual citizenship*, which refers to a diverse assortment of political, social, and cultural claims and struggles that link notions of sexual rights and duties to membership in nations or other political communities.[3] Scholars of citizenship often examine its working at subnational levels such as the city,[4] and accordingly, a growing number of studies have examined the dimensions of sexual citizenship in cities and towns as well as in public spaces, "sex zones," and what Nayan Shah calls the "countersites and landscapes of queer contact."[5] As Bernardo's recognition of the significance of rainbow flags begins to suggest, many of the participants in my study constructed an attachment to the United States as immigrant sexual citizens that was expressed concretely with reference to Hillcrest or other gay spaces—geographic connections to what Desforges and coauthors have called the "landscapes" of citizenship.[6] This sense of belonging mattered fiercely to them, even when they encountered racism and anti-immigrant sentiment from US White gay men within the boundaries of those spaces. In this chapter, I consider how Mexican immigrant gay men acquire sexual citizenship in places like Hillcrest—and how "learning the ropes" of social and sexual interaction in such communities can become linked to a process of learning their rights.[7] But I also consider the practical limits on full inclusion that my participants confronted, as well as some of the more coercive dimensions of citizenship that some of them had to negotiate.

Disseminating the Rules of the Game: Cultural Ambassadors of Sexual Citizenship

As we saw in chapter 6, when Mexican gay immigrant men seek contact with mainstream gay culture in San Diego, they find that having people guide them through the initial stages is extremely helpful. Indeed, some of those altruistic guides take it upon themselves to act as "cultural ambassadors" who carefully spell out for these men how things work within gay San Diego—how they can maximize the benefits of their participation and minimize the risks. Such friends "show them the ropes" of San Diego gay life, conveying local knowledge about the rights and responsibilities of community belonging. For instance, the new friend who first took Armando (born 1981) to Hillcrest was thorough in telling him what to do and what not to do. Armando recalled that this man "showed me Hillcrest, showed me all the places." But then he also explained that he wanted Armando to be careful. As Armando recalled, his friend told him:

"You know what? . . . I'm going to take you now to every place where you can go, [because] I won't always be with you. . . . Soon you'll be independent. And you will meet someone, and they will want to take you to a place, and I don't want them to take you to a place that you don't know."

When Armando turned twenty-one, his friend wanted to help him become independent from his Mexican godfather (whose family he lived with), because Armando had complained that his hosts really constrained him. "They controlled my money, they controlled my time, [and] they controlled my work . . . my free days, food, sleep, practically everything. I was a robot to them." Armando felt that his friend's help had given him the confidence to move out of his godfather's house and rent a room of his own. But his friend also wanted to make sure that Armando would explore gay life safely.

"Cultural ambassadors" also provide new immigrants with detailed advice on the rules of the game within gay venues that are unfamiliar to them,[8] and counsel them on how to maximize their erotic capital (and other forms of capital) within those venues.[9] Two interesting examples are provided by Gilberto and Troy.

Gilberto (born 1962) had lived for many years in Tijuana before moving to San Diego at the age of forty. He started crossing into San Diego when he was in his twenties, after he had obtained his first passport. Around that time, a friend who lived in Chula Vista, a substantially Mexican suburb located between San Diego proper and the border, offered to take him to the cruisy section of Balboa Park, not far from Hillcrest. In the park, his friend taught him how to find sex with men there, and explained to him the informally defined rules of the public sex venue. This friend told Gilberto:

"Look, this is Balboa [Park]. There are many guys here." . . . Then he pointed to two parts of the park. He said, "Those [men] that you see there, they have sex for free; and those here, they will charge you." And I asked, "So, if I stand there they don't pay me, and on that side they'll pay me?"[10]

Gilberto found this information helpful when he later returned to the park by himself. "One day I was around there, and I remembered that he said that there they pay, and here they don't," he recalled. Thinking about those two options, he decided there was no reason for him not to pursue sex while simultaneously making some extra money. "So I stood where they paid," he said. His success at being picked up by men in the park prompted him to pursue this activity regularly. "I started coming often—every day. And the truth is that at some point I was charging [for sex], and [men] did pay."

Troy (born ca. 1973) had heard about San Diego's gay bathhouses and wanted to find one. When he finally succeeded, he ventured in. But once inside, he realized that he had put all his effort on finding the place, and knew nothing about what actually happened there. Everything he saw was completely foreign to him. He was especially unprepared to see naked men openly cruising and having sex. Unable to cope with the newness of all that surrounded him, Troy shyly sat by himself, fully dressed, and watched the porn videos that were being projected on a screen. He recalled:

I didn't take off my clothes, but I noticed that people would show up and take off their clothes as if they were taking off a hat as they entered a home. I said, "I won't do that." My subconscious told me: "So, why did you come, then?" And I would answer myself: "No, this can't be."

Troy seemed to be conflicted and in shock, and this probably showed. A staff member, noticing that he was breaking the explicit bathhouse rules against clothing, approached him to ask him to undress. But when he realized that Troy was an immigrant who seemed completely new to the scene, the employee softened his tone:

"I can tell you're a first-timer. Come, I'll show you the whole place." He says, "We're going to become friends, so let me ask you for something." He grabbed my hand and he said, "Never, I mean never, when you come to this place, never fail to use a condom." That's what he said to me. And his words really stuck in my mind . . . I can tell you that since then, I've used condoms with everyone.

Here, as with Armando's friend, we see that local knowledge was not simply of a practical nature: those who conveyed it were committed to an ethic of protection and cooperation. Troy found the information and help he received from this staff member invaluable. It stayed with him as he continued his explorations of gay San Diego and sought to become a full member of the local LGBT community.

Alfaro (born 1971) had a similar experience in an adult bookstore. His first time there, he said, "I was surprised 100 percent. . . . I went in to see the porn films in those little rooms. I was just seeing the parade of men, all opening doors and going inside." As he was trying to figure out how the place worked, he noticed a young man who sought his attention:

He said to me, "Hello, do you want to see a film with me?" I just stared at him and said, "You know what, I'm new here. I'm a bit scared." He just laughed. He then said, "You know what, I'll explain to you how this works. Don't worry, come with me." And I left the place with him.

That men such as Troy, Gilberto, and Alfaro needed the help of the cultural ambassadors they met in various venues suggests how foreign Hillcrest and some of the expressions of San Diego's urban gay culture were to some of them.

Informal and Formal Rights

The Symbolic Significance of Seeing Men Holding Hands in Public

When my participants absorbed lessons about how to negotiate new social and sexual spaces, they appeared to progress naturally from "learning the ropes" to learning their rights. For example, when Heriberto (born 1973), who grew up in a small town, was taken by a friend to Hillcrest, shown around, and told that there he could hold another man's hand publicly (*andar de la mano*), he was simultaneously absorbing lessons about sexual rules and sexual freedom. Many participants came to see gay spaces in San Diego as protected zones within which their "citizenship" rights were respected. Even Narciso, who originally had little idea of what an American gay community even looked like, came to perceive a sense of both belonging and entitlement: "I feel very comfortable in a gay and lesbian area, like we have a right to everything." This notion of an everyday right to belong—obviously salient for immigrants, who may generally find themselves treated as lacking even the "right to have rights"[11]—seemed to resonate with my participants much more than the conceptions of rights found in more confrontational and iconic forms of US gay activism such as protests and demonstrations (about which they were more divided or ambivalent).

Indeed, among the many expressions of gay culture that Mexican immigrants first encountered in Hillcrest, it was the simple act of holding hands that stood out as most foreign to them and most surprising, yet ultimately most attractive. They were completely unprepared to see men walking down the street hand in hand in broad daylight. A striking number of my participants made reference to this practice. Compared to the rainbow flags, the displays of sexually explicit paraphernalia in neighborhood storefronts, the posters advertising gay events in clubs, the flesh bared in LGBT Pride parades, the long lines of gays and lesbians waiting to enter dance clubs, the men in drag walking around the neighborhood at night, and the gay couples that could be seen dancing inside gay clubs, for Mexican immigrant gay men the presence of male couples holding hands best symbolized a utopian world that many had previously felt they would never encounter in their lives. This practice simultaneously shocked them and, in some cases, even scared them, but also appealed to them strongly. As Sabino (born 1967) put it, when he first saw men holding hands on the street, "it freaked me out. But I also liked it."

Mexican gay immigrants seemed to perceive the image of two men holding hands as both an ideal expression of the social validation of gay intimacy and a transgression of the rules of heteronormativity (in this case the social expectation that gay men should strive to "pass" as straight in a public and heteronormative space such as a city street).[12] That no one would blink at seeing two men holding hands in Hillcrest, still less make fun of them, criticize them, harass them, attack them, or arrest them—that they could do this in the context of everyday "normal" life with no negative consequences—seemed to be the ultimate expression of sexual equality. Of course, holding hands could also be interpreted as the projection of heteronormative ideals onto gay sexualities through the construction of the "respectable same-sex couple."[13] Yet for many of these immigrant men, seeing male couples holding hands in public told them that San Diegans accepted gay people and, by extension, that the United States was a liberal country with respect to questions of sexuality. The practice also provided them with a concrete indicator for comparing Hillcrest and San Diego with the places they knew in Mexico.

When Román (born 1983) first heard that Hillcrest was known as a gay neighborhood, he immediately told a cousin. This cousin confirmed that Hillcrest was "like a gay city. I thought it was great, I don't know, like I had never been in a gay city, never, never." Among the many markers of such a sense of "a gay city," the one that Román highlighted was that gay couples could hold hands in public:

I knew [Americans] were quite open about this topic, that they had no problem being gay, that two guys could walk on the street holding hands, and no one would say anything—they wouldn't be arrested or anything—that there was more freedom. I only knew that.

Asked by the interviewer if the same could happen in Tijuana, where Román was raised, he plainly responded, "No, they arrest you. And besides, people can beat you up. I don't know . . . [they're] like ignorant animals."

Benito (born 1977) similarly recalled his reaction when he first heard about a visible gay community in San Diego. "I was . . . very surprised, because at first I thought that being gay was . . . OK, that there would be nothing for you, no stores for gays, no discotheques, nothing; being [utterly] isolated." Soon after arriving, he learned about the gay bars and stores, but most important, he remembered being told that Hillcrest was "a place where you could walk around freely holding your partner's hand—that you could express yourself just as you are. And that people would not point at you—wow! That was really shocking." When he first saw men holding hands in public, he was surprised by his own reaction at how odd the practice seemed to him:

At first, I won't deny it, I thought, "Wow, how can these people walk around holding hands and kiss each other in the street?" Obviously it was my lack of information, my immaturity probably. . . . This really made me think.

Benito's reaction, like that of many other immigrants, signals the fact that in Mexico, he never had imagined that publicly expressing same-sex intimacy might ever be possible.

Holding Hands and Ideas about US Sexual Freedom

For some participants in my research, the nonchalant way in which men held hands with each other in public signified a major difference between the United States and Mexico as a whole. On the one hand, they extrapolated what they saw in Hillcrest to the entire United States, and on the other hand they concluded that the same practice would not be possible anywhere in Mexico. Facundo (born 1967) spoke of "the freedom that exists here in relation to being gay." He then noted:

In Mexico, you can't walk around [holding hands]. . . . Here there's a street where you can hold hands, and there is no problem. In Mexico, they would stone you, you can't do that. So there's much freedom here.

Immigrant men such as Facundo acknowledged that in Mexico, gay men could be open about their sexuality in private—in gay bars and dance clubs and in the context of social networks in which it was clear that LGBT people were accepted—but not in a public place where they would have no control over who was watching them.[14] Such acts, they said, simply did not take place. And they interpreted the fact that same-sex intimacy could be expressed in public in Hillcrest as signifying that people in the United States "are more advanced than in Mexico"—as Horacio (born 1982) put it—while "in Mexico, people are more closed up."

Similarly to Facundo, Horacio assumed that if two men were to spontaneously hold hands in public in Mexico, there would be consequences. "There, if they see you doing that, people [would] say, 'Look at that *vato* [guy]. What's he doing there?'" For that reason, after he arrived in San Diego, he was pleased when he realized, "Here they treat us just like anyone else. . . . I can walk in Hillcrest with a guy and no one says anything. In Mexico, it's different . . . people are racist toward homosexuals." Note that Horacio chose to use the word *racist* and not *homophobic*. The term functioned in his statement as a generic way of describing prejudice or discrimination.

But It's Also Happening in Mexico

But not all immigrant men in my study felt it was impossible for two men to hold hands in public anywhere in Mexico, and some expressed instead a more nuanced view about their home country. They acknowledged that men could hold hands in public—and even engage in other forms of same-sex intimacy, such as embracing or kissing—in some locations. One big difference, some participants noted, was that in Hillcrest, gay couples could hold hands in daylight, not just in the late evening when no one was around—during the times when these men felt that same-sex intimacy and sexuality was tolerated. As Benjamín (born ca. 1955) put it:

In Mexico, there are still many taboos. Curiously, there are many gays in Mexico. . . . The gay discos are packed. If you go to Mexico City, there are discos everywhere. But during the day everyone is straight, and everyone is in the closet. That's the difference. Here people are gay [all day long], there are gay communities, there are gay stores, you can have your rainbow [sticker] on your car . . . , you can have the freedom of holding your partner's hand in the street. In Mexico, you can't do that. . . . You're gay only at night, when no one is watching.

This notion that one could only be gay "when no one is watching"—the sense of a separation between a world of heteronormative daytime life and a more sexually permissive time of night—resembles what many people had described to me when I conducted research in Guadalajara in the 1990s.[15] At that time, however, LGBT people in Mexican cities were already beginning to test the limits of their invisibility and increasingly seeking to be openly gay all day long, not just at night. They were challenging what seemed to be centrally at stake in this tacit separation between daytime heteronormativity and nighttime tolerance of sexual diversity: the perceived need to protect children from witnessing what was thought of as non-normative forms of intimacy and sexuality.[16]

Some immigrant men indeed recognized that same-sex intimacy was now visible during the day in some locations, including in many places throughout Mexico City. For instance, Edwin (born 1974), who had been living in Europe for a few years, returned in the early 2000s to find a considerably changed Mexico City. As I mentioned earlier, Edwin and some friends had been gay-bashed in the 1990s by a group of strangers while walking in Zona Rosa, the Pink Zone.[17] But when he returned to Mexico, he said, "I was very surprised that gay openness is now super accepted. In the same area, in the Zona Rosa, I was so surprised to see gay couples holding hands down the street." Similarly, Valentín (born 1975), reflecting on his sense that "Mexican machismo" was the main barrier preventing same-sex marriage from being approved in Mexico, noted that change concerning gay issues was nonetheless under way there:

In Mexico, it is now normal to see two guys holding hands in some parts. . . . Similarly to Hillcrest, this happens in Cancún or Puerto Vallarta. You can see that more in the tourist areas, or in the large metropolises, such as Mexico City or Monterrey, which would be equivalent to New York or San Francisco.

This greater visibility of same-sex intimacy has certainly increased in large Mexican cities. Specifically in Mexico City, in recent years I have witnessed young gay male couples embracing and kissing in many public places within the central city, including on subway platforms while waiting for the Metro to arrive, or inside the trains as they travel across the city, without anyone around them saying a word.

But other participants, including Augusto (born 1972), were reluctant to equate these changes in Mexico with what they encountered in San Diego. Singling out the tourist resort of Puerto Vallarta, Augusto explained:

Puerto Vallarta is really open. But in any case, it's not like here. Here on Halloween you can dress in drag if you want and go out in the street and have fun. . . . And I don't believe I would do that in Mexico. I wouldn't go back in the closet, but I think I would be a bit more reserved than here, because of Mexicans' mentality.

Asked what he meant by "Mexicans' mentality," Augusto simply stated, "Machista." He invoked Mexican machismo—that term so often used as shorthand for recalling the worst traits of Mexican backwardness. However, as Matthew Gutmann has shown, in contemporary Mexico "macho" is what no man wants to be called, and the word is often deployed as an insult meant to suggest that a person is old-fashioned and has lagged behind.[18]

Augusto singled out Puerto Vallarta as a place in Mexico where things were changing, although not, he felt, to a degree comparable to what he saw in San Diego. But his comments about Puerto Vallarta's increasing openness were also prescient. In 2009, just a few years after Augusto had made this comment, the owner of one of that city's gay clubs decided to organize the first Carnaval/Mardi Gras nighttime parade[19] (which, beginning in 2014, was scheduled to coincide with New Orleans' Fat Tuesday).[20] This development brought out into the streets the performance culture of Puerto Vallarta's gay bars. In its first three years, the parade, which its website described as "flashy and trashy," was "limited to the southside of Vallarta," to the "Zona Romántica," which is regarded as the center of Puerto Vallarta's gay culture.[21] But in 2012, with the "backing of the City Government," the parade was extended to the more "straight" North Side, including the city's heavily touristed Malecón (the Boardwalk).[22] In addition to floats sponsored by the gay clubs, it now included "a mariachi band, dancing horses, the *bomberos* [firefighters] and many 'straight' bars, restaurants and real estate companies that had previously refused participation."[23]

I attended the Carnaval/Mardi Gras parade in 2016, and the floats certainly included many gay men in drag (or very scantily dressed), alongside schoolchildren who also marched in the parade, and a number of floats representing the more conventional institutional and commercial groups listed above.[24] Thousands of gay and non-gay spectators viewed the parade along a route that began at one of the "straight" resorts on the North Side, passed through downtown and the Malecón (just a block from Puerto Vallarta's cathedral), and ended in the Zona Romántica. And one of the floats featured the well-known San Francisco gay stand-up comedy troupe the Kinsey Sicks, who were in the city to perform a multiple-week run of their most current show.[25]

Note that in Augusto's assessment, he also compared what people could do in San Diego (walk around in drag for Halloween) with what *he* would choose not to do if he went back to Mexico. But as this example of the Carnaval/Mardi Gras parade shows, not long after he had made those comments, many of his counterparts in Puerto Vallarta felt comfortable going out in drag or scantily dressed for this event, and not just within the "gay zone." To be sure, he clearly thought of Puerto Vallarta as one of the places in Mexico where gay culture had become ubiquitous, and recognized that there "you see [gay] couples walking holding hands. You see men kissing each other. They are on the beach holding hands." Yet in Augusto's view, what happened in that city was anomalous for Mexico and could never happen in his hometown of Culiacán—or rather, he would never feel comfortable expressing himself openly as a gay man there. He asserted:

In Culiacán, forget it. I have to be in the closet. I would never go back to live there. It's completely homophobic. They kill people often. Violence is high. . . . When I go to Culiacán, I go back to the closet, as I was before. Not with my family but with other people. . . . You never know how people will react.

Of course, it is not hard to think of places in the United States that could be described in this same way.

Clearly, there are some slippages in the comparisons that men such as Augusto made. They extrapolated what they saw in Hillcrest to the whole United States, and then concluded that the open expressions of gay intimacy they saw there could not take place in most of Mexico. They also assessed that back in Mexico, they would never engage in the forms of self-expression that *they* might be willing to enact in Hillcrest.

Hillcrest Is Not the Whole United States

Yet after traveling to other places besides Hillcrest, some gay immigrant men participating in my study developed a more nuanced view of the possibilities for gay expression in the United States. They realized that men did not actually feel comfortable holding hands on the street and displaying other forms of same-sex intimacy *everywhere*—that this happened only in particular areas. Valentín commented that he liked "Hillcrest, because it's the gay center, right?" He went on: "It's where one, incredibly, sees men holding hands, or kissing each other, like nothing. One doesn't see that in every city, but it's growing every day."

Valentín thus recognized Hillcrest as a "gayborhood"—as the kind of liberated space for which LGBT people had to fight, and which had become characteristic of American urban gay life.[26] In this perception, Hillcrest joined a list of other gay neighborhoods such as Chelsea and the West Village in New York, the Castro in San Francisco, Boystown in Chicago, West Hollywood in Los Angeles, and South Beach in Miami as the quintessentially liberated centers of this life.[27]

However, other immigrant men held unrealistic expectations about American cities such as San Francisco that had a reputation for being extremely gay friendly, and had been disappointed by them. When Hernán (born 1971) went to San Francisco with his boyfriend, he felt that people stared at them when they held hands "as if we were extraterrestrial, weirdos." This experience led him to believe that Hillcrest was more sexually liberal than San Francisco. "Here we hold hands everywhere, and I've never seen people say 'Uy!'" Hernán clarified that in San Francisco, the couple had stayed in Chinatown and never went to the Castro or any areas having a visible presence of LGBT people. He therefore made a somewhat unfair comparison between the two cities, in part because he did not seem to have a full understanding of the concept of a gay neighborhood as a distinct part of the city. Indeed, this same issue emerged in some of the comparisons immigrant men made between Hillcrest and all of Mexico, especially given that with the exception of the Zona Rosa and the Colonia Condesa in Mexico City, or the Zona Romántica in Puerto Vallarta, the notion of a "gayborhood" had not permeated the Mexican imagination.

Same-Sex Marriage and Divergent Views on the Possibilities for Social Change in Mexico

Beyond the symbolism of public but informal expressions of gayness and gay intimacy, my participants also compared Mexico and the United States with regard to the possibilities of acquiring formal, state-granted rights. Their assessments sometimes contributed to their perception that LGBT people might acquire sexual citizenship in the United States more easily than in Mexico, and arriving at this conclusion led them to think they would be better off remaining in the United States than returning to their home country.

At the time of my interviews, the topic of same-sex marriage was being hotly debated in California, and in talking about this issue 47 Mexican participants also discussed the feasibility of same-sex marriage in Mexico.[28] Among them, 26 opined that it would never be possible. They cited reasons related to culture, education, ignorance, religion, machismo, conservativeness, closed-mindedness, the Mexican mentality, and homophobia. These were men who were generally not aware, or who disregarded the pace, of sexuality-related social and political changes taking place in in their home country.[29] They responded to a question about whether same-sex marriage might be approved in Mexico with statements such as the following: "Oh, gosh! I don't think it can [happen]" (Toribio);[30] "It's hard enough here, and Mexico is a thousand steps behind" (Venustiano); or "Definitely not" (Hilario).

However, Hilario recognized that attitudes toward homosexuality in Mexico were shifting, and he cited ads that were broadcast in 2005 as part of a national anti-homophobia campaign sponsored by the Mexican federal government (the equivalent of which, incidentally, has never been implemented in the United States).[31] To be sure, other participants felt that such changes indicated that a policy such as same-sex marriage might one day be possible in Mexico. Yet this group was divided in terms of how soon such a policy might be approved and implemented. Seven felt that the foundations for same-sex marriage were already being constructed—at least in Mexico City. They referred to the freedoms LGBT people increasingly seemed to have in Mexican cities, and one, Bernardo, compared Mexico with Spain. As he put it, same-sex marriage "happened in Spain . . . [which is] as Catholic, if not more, than Mexico." Another participant, Raimundo, compared the United States unfavorably with Mexico: "I think in the current situation it would be easier [to implement same-sex marriage] in Mexico. Mexico is moving in one direction, and the US in the opposite direction." Like some others, Raimundo was responding in part to events taking place in the United States in the mid-2000s, at the height of president George W. Bush's administration, which led him to conclude that the United States was less sexually liberal than he originally thought. "Before I came, I thought the US was a very progressive country," he remarked.

The remaining fourteen estimated that it would be a very long time before same-sex marriage could become a reality in their home country. A prerequisite, as Augusto put it, is that "it would have to happen first in the United States." This view confirmed a common perception that progressive change must first be tested in the global North. And a sense of delayed implementation seemed key in other participants' assessments: "Not in the next 10 years," said Leopoldo; "Maybe in 20 years," declared Román; "Maybe in 20 or 30 years," was Efraín's estimate; and "Who knows, maybe in 30 years, 40 years, the story will be different," stated Melchor soberly.

As it turns out, the predictions of participants who thought that same-sex marriage would soon be feasible in Mexico were the most accurate.

In 2007, not long after we concluded our interviews, Mexico City and the northern Mexican state of Coahuila approved civil unions, and in 2009 the legislative assembly of Mexico City approved same-sex marriage.[32] By mid-2016 (a year after a US Supreme Court ruling extended marriage equality throughout the United States), same-sex marriage was legal in Mexico City plus nine Mexican states, which together are home to almost one-third of the national population. And in eight of those federal entities, the measure was approved not by judicial order but by the local congress—by elected officials whose continued power depends on the popular vote. Furthermore, individual same-sex couples in several other states have married through injunctions approved by the Mexican Supreme Court. These are all developments that most of my Mexican participants—and probably most Mexicans, for that matter—could not anticipate just a decade ago.

The Limits of Immigrant Sexual Citizenship

I have described how Mexican gay immigrants to Hillcrest acquire both a sense of themselves as citizens of that locale and some of the concrete freedoms that such belonging brings with it. Yet it is important not to overlook the obstacles that lie in their path.[33] In particular, my participants sometimes found themselves hemmed in by barriers that marked the tensions inherent in immigrant sexual citizenship. That is, at times their involvement in gay life jeopardized their legal status as immigrants in the United States, or else their status as immigrants limited their capacity to participate as sexual citizens of San Diego's gay community. These tensions point, in turn, to broader issues of inequality and power imbalances that I will continue to explore in later chapters.

Some participants bitterly described having discriminatory statements and behaviors directed at them by White gay men on account of their race, nationality, accent, or immigrant status in ways that clearly lessened their sense of community belonging. Several undocumented participants described problems gaining entry to gay bars because of a lack of proper identification; many others simply could not get to gay venues easily in an automobile-dependent city like San Diego, because they feared that a routine traffic stop could result in deportation if they were found to be driving without a license. (Indeed, one participant arrived late for his interview with us, visibly shaken because he had been stopped by the police on the way.)

Finally, several participants who were HIV positive noted a distinctive paradox that trapped them. On the one hand, living in the United States meant they acquired access to life-saving antiviral medication, which was provided even to those without legal status. But on the other hand, under an exclusionary policy in place at the time of our interviews and lifted only in 2010, a negative HIV test result was a prerequisite for legal residency, and therefore—barring receipt of a humanitarian waiver that was difficult to obtain[34]—it was impossible for them ever to regularize their immigration status. These HIV-positive men, several of whom had become infected while living in the United States, lived in constant fear of running afoul of the law and risking deportation that, they perceived, could mean a death sentence.

For many, the dilemmas of immigrant sexual citizenship meant living a life of trade-offs. As Crecencio (born 1962), who came from a large working-class suburb of Mexico City, expressed it:

Here I'm not as free as there . . . , because here one always has to be watching out for *la migra*. . . . In Mexico, I was very free, I could walk wherever I wanted and as I pleased. But I was free in some aspects [of my life] but a prisoner in others. And here I'm free in those other respects—that is, in my sexuality—but I'm not free in all the rest.

These poignant predicaments suggest the practical limits of social incorporation into a gay neighborhood in securing a stable sense of belonging for those living at the intersection of two stigmatized social identities.

A Normative Path for Becoming Openly Gay in San Diego

So far this chapter on Mexican immigrants' incorporation into gay San Diego and acquisition of sexual citizenship has emphasized the new expressions of gay culture and sexual freedoms that my study participants described. But Mexican immigrants also encountered specific prescriptions for how they should be openly gay—prescriptions that sometimes differed from what they desired for themselves—which greatly surprised them. Such episodes suggest the importance of understanding sexual citizenship as, to a certain degree, an outcome of projects of subject formation via the inculcation of specific norms related to sexuality.[35]

An eloquent example is provided by Venustiano (born 1975), who, as we saw in chapter 3, left Mexico in part to search for a wife who would accept him as an openly gay man. Rather than deceive a wife by having male lovers on the side, he had imagined a wife—either a lesbian or a heterosexual woman with liberal ideas—with whom he could be honest, and who would be open-minded enough to accept his sexuality.

Soon after Venustiano arrived in San Diego (where two of his siblings also lived), a television commercial advertising a heterosexual dating service caught his eye, and he called the number on the screen. "I told [the woman who answered] that I was a homosexual," he said. "'Uy!' she said. 'My advice would be for you to see a psychologist.' I said, 'I don't want to see any psychologists, what I want is to get married.'"

The person who had taken his call referred him to the San Diego LGBT Community Center in Hillcrest, which assigned him to a gay Latino psychotherapist. "He didn't understand me. To him I was nothing but a person who was quite confused," Venustiano noted. Bewildered by his client's desires, the therapist decided to pass him on to a female therapist. Venustiano liked her better. "We understood each other quite well," he said. "I felt comfortable with her. I thought, 'This is it.'" He told his therapist about his desire to meet a woman who would want to marry an openly gay man, and he then tried to persuade her to hook him up with her lesbian clients. The therapist tried to be supportive and nonjudgmental. Venustiano recalled that she told him something along these lines:

"Venustiano, I understand you perfectly. If you want to marry, that's up to you. I will counsel you and help you as much as I can. The rest depends on you. Because there are many [gay men] who are married. There are."

But she also demurred and suggested he would have to manage to find dates on his own. Then she proceeded to tell him about Hillcrest: "She started telling me that there was an area here of homosexual people and all that, and that there were bars for every kind of person." She seemed to trust that given the right incentives and counseling, Venustiano could be directed away from his fantasy of marrying a woman and would turn toward adopting a more typical path as an openly gay man.

Though Venustiano began to explore gay life in Hillcrest, for some time he remained fixed on his goal of marrying a woman. At times he participated in events organized for bisexual men and women as a strategy to keep his relationship options open. But he also became increasingly anxious about how his family members perceived him, and he suffered three months of insomnia. Finally, in desperation, he went to see his sister and confessed that he was *homosexual*. She told him that he was simply confused, and that God would help him overcome this problem. Soon afterward, Venustiano happened to see a television program about someone who "had been gay and had stopped being gay because God helped him," and he began to wonder if it would be possible for him to "change." He then passed through a difficult period in which he experienced panic attacks, made suicidal gestures, and ended up being hospitalized. Eventually, however, he resolved the crisis. He acknowledged that he was gay, abandoned his goal of getting married to a woman, and established a good relationship with his siblings:

I love my family and they love me, thank God. With a lot of effort I am coming out of the closet. But as I said to myself, "The day I come out, I'll come out through a wide-open door [*voy a salir por la puerta grande*] and with my family's support."

The ultimate resolution was a happy one for Venustiano. Still, it is worth considering how little patience the community representatives and professionals he encountered appeared to have with the particular life solution he had imagined for himself. He was taught to desire a life of authenticity and wholeness as defined by the norms of US gay liberation and the global gay sexual schema—an openly and exclusively gay life organized around the narrative of coming out of the closet.[36] His interest in a different life pattern was discounted as a psychological symptom rather than entertained as a serious possibility.

A final, small irony deserves mention in considering Venustiano's story of immigrant sexual citizenship: if he had succeeded in his original goal of finding and marrying an accepting American woman—and thus becoming incorporated into US and gay society in his own particular way—he could have become a legal permanent resident of the United States as a direct consequence, years before the US Supreme Court approved same-sex marriage nationally. Instead, as a gay man who was expected to partner only with other gay men, he remained, precariously, undocumented.

Incorporation into US gay life therefore came to Venustiano—and to other immigrant men—with a price tag. It allowed them to pursue the sexual freedom they craved, so long as they conformed to specific community expectations about what a liberated and open sexual life was supposed to be like.

The Mexico-US Border as a Separator of Identity

Venustiano's account also puts Cuauhtémoc's (born 1961) experiences in a new light. As we saw in chapter 6, Cuauhtémoc considered himself primarily attracted to women, but also had sex with men in the United States. When his American friend suggested that he should therefore call himself bisexual, the implication was that Cuauhtémoc was wrong to think of himself as a straight man, or *hombre normal*. These normative understandings of sexual identity categories influenced him, and he began to apply the term *bisexual* to himself. However, his use of the label was selective. He called himself bisexual when he participated in gay life in San Diego. But with his family, and especially when he went back to Mexico to visit his wife and children, he reverted to identifying primarily as a husband and father, and by implication also as *un hombre normal*.

Cuauhtémoc's shift in self-identification is a marker of another important feature of Mexican immigrant men's incorporation into San Diego's gay life: they sometimes do not see the gay practices, norms, and ideas they learn and adopt in that city as permanent and fully defining. Instead, some learn to navigate their two sexual worlds in Mexico and the United States according to what they understand to be the rules of the game in each location. And they are also capable of making sense of contextually based identity practices and strategies that could be seen as contradictory if we strictly assume that consistently "coming out" in all aspects of one's life is a prerequisite for calling oneself gay.[37]

These men sometimes develop the skills to use the border as a tool to enact separate lives in two separate places, trusting that with adequate management, those separate lives will never come in contact. The gay spaces into which some of them become incorporated into San Diego give them a respite from the pressures they feel in their hometowns in Mexico; but when they go back to that country, or have contact with their loved ones there, they do not necessarily take steps to alleviate those pressures. From the perspective of a normative gay schema, these men's strategies can be seen as an unwillingness on their part to leave "the closet." Yet these immigrants are deliberate and agentic in terms of the strategies they put in place to manage their sexualities in different national, ethnic, and sexual contexts. As Diana Fisher has noted, "Contrary to a popularized valorization of queer 'outness,' there is a great deal of power in the oscillation between visibility and invisibility."[38] Some, like Venustiano, end up disclosing their sexual orientation selectively to their families and friends on both sides of the border. Others, however, comfortably settle on managing, and keeping separate, their two sexual worlds. For them, the US-Mexico border becomes a convenient separator of identity.[39]

Men who rely on this strategy to manage their identities and sexualities in Mexico and the United States perceive that it helps them achieve what they wanted: the possibility of experiencing a fully open gay or bi-sexual life while simultaneously avoiding conflict with their families and protecting themselves and their families in Mexico from social stigma. These goals, as I discussed in chapter 3, are often central motivators be-hind their migration.

But it takes a lot of effort and careful management to keep their iden-tities and lifestyles separate, as these men constantly have to take steps to ensure that news about their sexual involvement with men in San Diego does not reach their hometowns and families. Furthermore, the management of these split identities seems most difficult when they have relatives or hometown acquaintances living in the same place as they in the United States. To a certain extent, this is what motivated Teo-doro (born 1966) to move from Orange County, where he had relatives, to Tijuana. And it was also an issue in Cuauhtémoc's case, because four of his siblings lived in San Diego.

Cuauhtémoc was careful not to mix his family circles with his gay ones by visiting with his siblings only in their homes and avoiding go-ing out with them as much as possible. One day, however, his two sepa-rate worlds almost collided when he was out shopping with one of his sisters and saw two transgender Latinas ("*vestidas*," in his words) whom he knew walking toward them. Normally, he would kiss these friends on the cheek, or even on the lips, as a form of greeting. This time, when he saw them approaching he cringed. "I thought to myself, 'Please don't let these two girls have the idea of stopping to kiss me!'" However, seeing that Cuauhtémoc was with a Mexican woman whom they did not know, and also understanding the tacit rules of interaction in such a situation, the Latinas passed them by without acknowledging Cuauhtémoc at all.

Achieving Sexual Citizenship: Local Possibilities and Constraints

In this chapter, we have seen how citizenship can be enacted on a local scale. Indeed, in the case of immigrant sexual citizenship, it seems plau-sible to suggest that local attachments are especially significant, inso-far as they serve as intermediate points of linkage between experiences, emotions, and encounters that are highly personal, physical, and inti-mate and abstract notions of one's relationship to a remote and often threatening nation-state. In well-bounded places like Hillcrest, immi-grant gay men can acquire a sense of their right to belong—even if in practice their enactment of this right is sometimes highly circumscribed.

At the same time, and despite most of these men's perceptions that the United States is more sexually liberal than Mexico, upon arrival they realize that the range of possibilities for expressing their sexualities and identities is constrained by normative values and expectations about what it means to be gay in contemporary American life. Hence, they also learn that if they want to participate, they have to conform to certain rules of interaction. As we will see in the next chapter, this theme also emerges when we consider how Mexican gay immigrant men's sexualities shift in San Diego, as well as when we examine how they pursue and engage in sexual and romantic interactions with casual partners and boyfriends.

EIGHT

Shifting Sexualities and the Dynamics of Cross-Racial Attraction

[San Diego] has helped me a lot, because it's helped me live my sexuality as I wanted. . . . It's changed me, because it's helped me be more open, accept my homosexuality more, and realize that I am not doing anything wrong as long as I am not harming anyone.

Like Teodoro (born 1966) in this quotation, many other Mexican participants in my study felt that moving to San Diego had significantly changed them, sexually speaking. Their assessments are consistent with a general perception in the scholarly literature that the sexualities of Latin American gay and lesbian immigrants shift after they relocate to the United States. For instance, Lionel Cantú asked his participants "if they felt that they had changed at all since migrating to the United States." As Cantú reported, "Nearly all of the men responded with a resounding yes."[1] He summarized the changes that those men experienced as related to their "racial, gender, sexual, and class identities."[2] In another study, Bianchi and coauthors succinctly noted that Latino gay immigrants "reported exposure to sexual practices that they had not encountered in their countries of origin," which "were added to the sexual repertoire of the participants."[3] They also observed that their participants' "gay lives became less compartmentalised."[4] James Thing similarly found that several of the Mexican men in his study were able to claim a gay identity only after migrating to Los Angeles, where they became exposed to an urban gay culture and community,[5] and Ernesto Vasquez del Aguila described Peruvian gay men who became more open in the United States to having a steady male lover or recognizing that they may be bisexual.[6] And, although "only a small number of men" in Carlos Decena's study of Dominican immigrant men "shared descriptions about partners and sexual histories, . . . the few who did emphasized their increased flexibility and openness with sex as linked to experiences and challenges faced after migration."[7] Decena concluded that "these men understood sexual practices to be intimately tied to the full realization of oneself through the establishment and regulation of reciprocity and versatility as kernels of a modern sexual horizon and a resignification of the models of same-sex desire they associated with Dominican identity."[8] Finally, following Gloria Anzaldúa, Katie Acosta argued that Latin American lesbian immigrants in her study recreated borderland spaces in the United States—spaces they " 'imagine' . . . to be places of fellowship and solidarity."[9]

Yet beyond this general sense that Latin American gays and lesbians change sexually and become more open about their sexualities after migrating transnationally, details about the post-migration changes they experience have remained scant. Before the present study, the specifics of what their sexual changes entail—and the question of whether and how different gay immigrants change or, alternatively, resist changing—have not been systematically investigated. Doing so presupposes close attention to the varied patterns of sexual socialization among Latin American gay and lesbian immigrants in their countries of origin, which has not been a focus of previous research, at least not with large numbers of research participants.[10] Nor has the literature provided a sense of how the changes that gay Latin Americans experience in the United States are affected by the dynamics of their cross-racial interactions—including how their attractions to specific kinds of partners shift or stay the same after migration, and what roles their sexual and romantic partners play in shaping their experiences in the United States. Those are the topics I examine in this chapter and the next.

As we will see, also important to this discussion is how the sexuality-related changes gay immigrants experience are complicated by more general shifts in their social position that result from their incorporation into US society. Latin American gay immigrants can experience upward social mobility because of greater opportunities in the United States, or alternatively "a deterioration of their class position upon arrival," as reported by most participants in Decena's study.[11] Decena further noted that "the immediacy of racial and class subordination provoke a *desencuentro*, or failed encounter, with *dominicanidad* in New York City."[12] Moreover, Latin American immigrants become racialized—even when, as Wendy Roth has noted, it has been hard to decide if Latinas/os are a separate race within the "racial schemas" of the shifting US racial classificatory system[13]—and "become 'people of color,' regardless of what their prior experiences had been," as Acosta has noted.[14] Once racialized, they often become exposed to racism and cultural stereotypes about Latinas/os in the dominant culture, and are sometimes deemed "sexual others," as Cantú indicated.[15]

In the present analysis, I consider this intertwining of sexuality-related and other kinds of changes that my participants reported, including changes they experienced as connected to racial inequality within US society. I am attentive to how Mexican gay men described changes that they perceived as beneficial at the same time that they sometimes expressed profound disappointments with their lives in the United States, the quality of their connections with American people, and their unrealized imaginaries of American equality. Indeed, the immigrant participants in my study were often ambivalent about how the benefits they felt they obtained from moving to the United States measured against the aspects of American life, and gay life, they disliked.

The Notion of Sexual Change

After migrating, practically all the Mexican participants in my study came into contact with San Diego's visible gay community (see chapters 6 and 7).[16] They felt that as part of their incorporation into that city's gay life, they became more openly gay and freer to disclose their sexual orientation, and they gained a greater sense of self-respect and self-determination. They also talked about becoming more sexually assertive, more open about being sexual, more willing to attend gay sex venues and engage in sexual experimentation, and more open to adopting various sexual practices. They reported having more sex and more sex partners, as well as being more able to find boyfriends. Some, who in Mexico had socialized mostly within straight circles, constructed new lives that involved mostly other LGBT people. And they felt more comfortable participating in gay life and going to gay bars without concern about who might see them. If they had relatives in San Diego, some also became more open to bringing gay friends home. As Benito (born 1977) put it:

I no longer have to hide . . . my siblings now know it; my immediate family, my dad and my mother, and my sisters-in-law all know it. . . . If we go together to Hillcrest and I run into someone I know, I can say hello [to him] and he can say hello [to me]. And if someone goes to [my parents] and says, "Oh, I saw your son in Hillcrest! I saw your son in the gay community!" it will no longer surprise them. Because they all know that I'm gay, you know? Now I can even bring my friends home.

Overall, Mexican participants concluded that their changes were directly linked to their relocation to the United States and, more specifically, to San Diego. They generally also connected those changes to a personal process of sexual liberation they felt was facilitated by their being in San Diego. Norberto (born 1982) indicated that "it really opens up your mind; the way you thought before is different than the way you think once you're here." In this sense, they are similar to the Mexican men interviewed by Lionel Cantú, whose participants "referred to a more liberal sexual environment as a reason for their transformations."[17] Yet given that a number of my own participants were fairly young when they migrated, it is hard to determine how much the changes they experienced are the result of their being in San Diego, and how much they reflect developmental changes.[18] Several men, including Rigoberto (born 1965), Crispín (born 1980), and Hilario (born 1965), indeed described feeling that in San Diego they had become more mature. For them, their migration may have been "one step in a series towards what might be called 'a journey to the self.'"[19] This same issue emerged in the study by Bianchi and coauthors, who noted that among their participants, "excitement about sexual opportunities and freedoms lessened over time, while their interest and investment in building a more integrated gay life grew."[20] In this journey, they argued, "it is impossible to determine from our data the extent to which this change was due to maturation, increased involvement in a gay community or acculturation into life in New York."[21] All this points to an intertwining of developmental changes and changes produced by the contextual shifts associated with migration that were often present among the Mexican gay men in the present study.

Shifts in Sexual Interpretations, Roles, and Behaviors

As my colleague Jorge Fontdevila and I have reported elsewhere, in San Diego many of the Mexican participants in my study experienced transformations in their overall sexual interpretations according to the three sexual schemas—heavily gendered, homosocial, and object choice/gay— that I introduced in chapter 2.[22] That chapter showed that Mexican par-

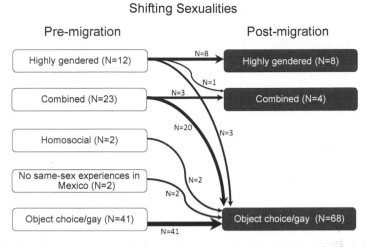

6   Shifts in Mexican men's sexualities pre- and post-migration (*N* = 80; this number includes three participants who lived in Mexico but regularly crossed the border into San Diego).

ticipants were diverse in terms of their pre-migration sexual interpretations and practices (see figure 2 in chapter 2). Post-migration, as figure 6 shows, the sexual interpretations and behaviors of a number of those men shifted. When we interviewed them in San Diego, the interpretations and practices of 68 (85%) of the 80 Mexican participants now aligned with the object choice/gay schema, only 8 (10%) exclusively retained interpretations consistent with the highly gendered schema, and 4 (5%) remained in the combined schema. No men exclusively participated any longer in sexual encounters that could be characterized as purely homosocial.

These data indicate a noticeable post-migration shift toward interpretations and practices consistent with American urban gay lifestyles. However, they simultaneously show that the post-migration changes the Mexican men in my study experienced are not uniform. Instead, after migrating, their sexual lives took a variety of different paths: some underwent profound shifts in interpretation as a result of contextual differences between the places in Mexico where they previously lived and their new location in the United States, and they moved altogether from one sexual schema to another (for example, from the highly gendered to the object choice/gay schema). Others stayed within the same schema that informed their same-sex desires in Mexico, but underwent a contextual shift in practices (for example, they remained in the object choice/gay schema but expanded their sexual repertoires post-migration). Finally, some stayed within the same sexual schema that informed their same-sex desires in Mexico and resisted the contextual pressures to re-define their interpretations or practices post-migration (for example, some kept highly gendered interpretations and practices post-migration, or gay scripts of sexual interaction they had learned in their previous locations in Mexico).

Significantly, as part of these shifts in sexual interpretation, a number of participants described altering their sexual roles, including Prado (born 1972), Aldo (born 1971), Crispín, Efraín (born 1965), and Ezequiel (born 1970). Prado, for instance, began to take the insertive role during anal intercourse in San Diego, noting that "in Mexico . . . I only allowed myself to be penetrated." He explained that in Tijuana it was hard for him to find someone to penetrate, because "*una jota no se deja penetrar por otra jota*" (a fag does not allow another fag to penetrate her[23]). His friends would tell him, "*¡Qué bárbaro!* In Tijuana, you were a *mujer* [a woman], and in San Diego you became a *chacal* [a 'jackal,' a masculine straight-identified man who has sex with men]."[24] In Prado's view, his shift in sexual roles had also made him behave in a more masculine manner. By contrast, other men, including Efraín, said that after moving to San Diego they had become more open to taking the *pasivo* role. In other words, among the men who had had well-defined sexual roles in Mexico, several converged on a definition of themselves as "versatile," which highlighted for them the role flexibilities and egalitarian relationships often idealized as part of the object choice/gay schema.

Who Changed and How Much?

The degree to which Mexican immigrant men felt that San Diego had changed them depended on their pre-migration experiences in their home country. Perhaps not surprisingly, men such as Edwin (born 1974) and Marcelo (born 1970), who had been attuned to gay communities while living in Mexico or familiar with gay communities outside Mexico, felt they did not change, or changed little, after they moved to San Diego. By contrast, men for whom being a part of a gay community was a very new experience felt that San Diego had really changed them. Their narratives suggest that in San Diego, they were like "a kid in a candy store." Norberto, for instance, indicated that everything there was new to him. "In Mexico, I didn't know anyone [who was gay]," he remarked. "I knew nothing about the topic." Yet, as we saw in chapter 2, Norberto first discovered gay life during a return trip to his hometown, Guadalajara. Nonetheless, he credited San Diego for having opened up his mind. Similarly, Tadeo (born 1976), who also grew up in Guadalajara, was completely sexually inexperienced when he left Mexico, and he learned the proper way to have sex with a man only after he migrated.

In San Diego, Norberto and Tadeo adopted the practices and interpretations they learned there. Other men, however, ended up disliking American gay practices and thus resisted changing the forms of gay interaction they previously had favored in Mexico. Instead of shifting their practices, they sought to meet men who would fit those practices, often within Latino gay venues. This group included men who, as indicated in figure 6, did not give up the highly gendered sexualities they had known in Mexico. They dismissed American gay men as effeminate and felt a strong sexual attraction toward "real men." After migrating, they sought straight-identified Mexican men in local neighborhood bars (*cantinas*) or crossed the border into Tijuana to meet such partners. They might socialize with gay men but could not imagine having sex with them, and some could not fathom how sex was possible between two gay-identified men. For instance, Humberto (born 1975) remarked:

Here in the disco . . . most are gay. They're gay because they like to be penetrated. . . . And they behave very effeminately. I don't like to have sex with these men. Sometimes I meet them, and they seem so formal [*seriecitos*, implying *masculine*], but when I try . . . oh, no! They disappoint me.

Men who resisted changing also included those who, as we will see in chapter 9, aligned with the object choice/gay schema, but wanted to preserve scripts of sexual passion they felt were very Mexican. These men perceived that many American gay men instead engaged in impersonal forms of sexual interaction they deeply disliked.

Changes in Sexual Health

The various shifts in sexuality I have discussed also had implications for Mexican participants' sexual health. Several reported that in San Diego, they learned more about protection against HIV than they had ever previously known. For instance, Heriberto (born 1973) responded to a question about whether he had changed in San Diego by saying, "Definitely; I'm much more careful in terms of using condoms. There [in Mexico] I did not have sex just with anyone, and here I do that even less so." Several HIV-positive participants also recognized that in San Diego, they had become more comfortable having sex without the fear that they would pass on the virus to someone else. For them, achieving such comfort was part of a longer process of accepting that a person can be HIV positive and still have a sexual life. Fidel (born 1971), for instance, stated, "I'm still working on that; I want to get rid of the sense of guilt. I do feel the need to have sex, but I am still fearful about possibly infecting someone, even when we're using protection."

Not All Changes Are Positive

But not all viewed the changes in sexual practices and behaviors they experienced in San Diego positively. Some men worried that San Diego had made them more prone to lose control over their sexuality, including Rigoberto, who associated having more sex there with "personal degradation" and "becoming addicted" (*enviciarse*). He felt lonely in San Diego and assessed that for him, sex filled a void left by the lack of significant connections. Gerardo (born 1971) similarly said that if he had not moved to San Diego, "perhaps I would be less *puto* [less of a slut]. That's one of the negative things." And Melchor (born 1972) and Emilio (born 1979) both were concerned about the sexual health risks they were taking. Melchor mentioned that in San Diego, he had "ended up doing what everyone else does," meaning he used less protection against HIV. And Emilio talked about having "sex without a condom, *big time; a lot of sex is easy right now, is easy around the corner, in my house, even driving* [said in English]."

Sexual Shifts and Patterns of Attraction

Some of the sexual changes that Mexican men reported seemed motivated and influenced by the men with whom they interacted in San Diego, including the new kinds of sexual and romantic partners to whom they now had access. Their choices about these partners sometimes also signaled shifts in their patterns of attraction. Some described becoming attracted to American men after moving to the United States. For instance, Fermín (born 1977) said that "perhaps the only thing that has changed for me is the type of men. Here they are Americans." Similarly, Plutarco (born 1975) said that in Mexico, he "only had sex with Mexicans," adding, "When I began to come to the US, I began to meet Americans," and this changed his attraction from Mexicans to "Whites. I'm very attracted to Americans. Tall. It's perfect for me if they have an athletic body, or if they have a large penis." However, not all Mexican men changed their preferences. Others had already been attracted to American men before migrating, particularly to US White men. Still others had always been attracted to men whose features they identified as Mexican and remained exclusively drawn to Mexicans and US Latinos after migrating.

I identified several patterns of racially based attraction. As we will see, the story is complicated, and in some cases patterns in one direction are met by counter-patterns running in the other. But examining these patterns is important for several reasons. It helps us not only grasp the sexual changes that Mexican men experienced in the United States but also understand the overall dynamics of their sexual and romantic relationships in that country. In addition, the complexity will direct us away from any oversimplified account of the functioning of racial stereotypes—an important topic I will continue to explore in the next chapter.

Moreover, as I mentioned in chapter 6, Mexican immigrants' attractions and relationships shine a light on their incorporation into US gay life. Their access to men who were different from them depended on whether they were immersed in primarily Mexican/Latino enclaves or whether they branched out from them. And their ability to participate in enclaves that were not primarily Mexican/Latino depended on whether they knew and interacted with non-Latino people, including gay men. This, I argue, is indicative of a mutually constitutive relationship between patterns of attraction, racially based forms of interaction, and gay incorporation. Finally, whether immigrant men interacted with others across lines of race and ethnicity influenced the degree to which they were exposed to new forms of sexual interaction and interpretation, but also to racism and discrimination.

In order to better understand the patterns of attraction among Mexican gay immigrant men, I juxtapose their patterns to those that emerged in interviews with American men. Gay and bisexual men in all three groups in my study—Mexican immigrants, US Latinos, and non-Latino American men who have a history of romantic and sexual involvement with Mexican immigrants—talked about being attracted to particular physical attributes they felt were more characteristic of specific racial/ethnic groups. Others, however, emphasized forms of cultural attraction that drew them to men either similar to or different from themselves. By focusing on culture, the latter group also sometimes sought to make the case that their attractions did not depend solely on racialized physical features.

As we consider these patterns, it is important to bear in mind that the participants' expressed attractions and the reality of their sexual lives are two different things; the men whom they idealized were often not the same men with whom they interacted sexually or romantically due to social barriers separating different types of men within US society. Indeed, in this chapter, and particularly in the next, the themes of social inequality and difference emerge repeatedly.

The Patterns of Attraction among Mexican Gay Immigrants

Venustiano: Latinos are drop-dead gorgeous [*guapísimos*]. What can I say?

Heriberto: I'm attracted to White people. Blue eyes. Or, as we say in Mexico, "I want a *güero* [blond] with blue eyes."

As suggested by these two quotations, Mexican gay immigrants hold contrasting opinions about the desirability of Latino/Mexican men versus *güeros*[25] or *americanos*, to use the two terms with which they commonly referred to US White men.[26] The immigrant men in my study were indeed fairly evenly divided in this regard. Among the 63 Mexican men who spoke about their attraction in racial terms, 33 expressed being attracted to White men, while 31 were attracted to Latinos/Mexicans. Also among them, a smaller proportion explicitly added that they were not attracted to men in the other group: 13 disliked Mexicans/Latinos, and 8 disliked US Whites. Only a minority ever mentioned African American men, with 13 indicating that they were attracted to them, and 12 not attracted. Even fewer mentioned Asian men (3 indicated being attracted, and 8 not attracted).

To be sure, several among the sixty-three immigrant men who discussed attraction in terms of race expressed being attracted to more than one racial or ethnic group. Fifteen also felt that race or ethnicity was not an important factor that influenced their attraction.[27] For instance, Federico (born ca. 1969) stated, "I don't have a prototype, I don't believe in prototypes," and Bernardo (born 1967) similarly stated, "The truth is, I don't have a prototype. . . . I've had opportunities to be in relationships with Americans, Latinos, and African Americans. They've all been great experiences." Finally, Leopoldo (born 1967) indicated, "I believe that all races have their appeal." But most immigrants had a clear sense of their primary attractions toward either Mexican/Latinos or US Whites.

In the remainder of this chapter, I analyze in more detail these and other patterns of same-race and cross-racial attraction, including those that emerged among American men. I pay attention along the way to the erotic capital—to use Adam Green's concept[28]—that racially based attractiveness confers on individual gay men, as well as the value that men assign to race and racialized looks as part of what Dwight McBride has called a "gay marketplace of desire."[29] I should explain that consistent with assumptions that are pervasive in Mexico, the Mexican participants tended to conceive of the United States as generically defined by its White population, thus ignoring other American racial/ethnic groups unless they wanted to refer specifically to them. They therefore used the term *americano* as a generic term to describe US Whites, and they sometimes engaged in complicated verbal gymnastics when they needed to explain that African Americans, US Latinos, and Asian Americans are Americans, too (but are not the kind of Americans to whom they referred when they used the Spanish word *americanos*).

"*I Really Like* Güeros"

Interviewer: What kind of men are you attracted to?
Isidro: ¡Ay! [*laughter*] I really like *güeros*!

Mexican men who were particularly attracted to US White men emphasized that racial difference, and a contrast in skin color between them and US Whites, influenced this attraction. As Hernán (born 1971) put it, "I really like *güeros* [*laughter*]. Look, I'm dark. I really like *güeros*." Similarly, Isidro (born 1980) said he was drawn to US White men "because [they're something] out of the ordinary, different," and emphasized that he preferred "Americans with blue eyes." This statement was repeated, almost word for word, by other immigrant men, including Emilio, who said, "I love blonds, *güeros*, with blue eyes." In these statements, "blue eyes" is a generic way of referring to light-colored eyes, and together with whiteness it connotes what these men understood as the prototype of American beauty—the "American standard of beauty," as Wilson and coauthors have noted[30]—and what attracted them most about White men. Mexican men in my study articulated their preference for these physical attributes without a hint that by emphasizing them they might be stereotyping White men. This may relate to a finding by Phua and Kaufman, who noted in a study of gay personal advertisements that compared with Blacks and Asians,

Gay White and Hispanic men are most likely to mention their skin, eye or hair color. Notably, their mentioning of these traits emphasizes their whiteness. Gay White men mostly mention their blond hair and blue eyes whereas gay Hispanic men focus on the lightness of their skin and their nonblack hair and eyes.[31]

Similarly, Wilson and coauthors have described the perception that because White men are "the norm to which racial minority MSM [men who have sex with men] compare themselves,"[32] discussion in the latter group of the physical attributes of White men involves "a lack of . . . raced-based stereotypes tied to White MSM."[33] Implicit in this observation is the idea that given the predominance of whiteness, and the power differentials between Whites and other groups, non-White men are simply not in a position to racialize White men.[34]

However, some Mexican men in my study qualified their attraction to whiteness in ways suggesting that some level of stereotyping was at play in the more generic attraction to *"güeros* with blue eyes" expressed by others. For instance, some participants clarified they were not in fact attracted to all types of White men, and explicitly rejected what they considered to be "extreme whiteness." This group of men included Efraín, who stated that he was attracted to White men but disliked those who were milky white: he was attracted only to White men who were tanned, *"apiñonados, quemaditos por el sol."*[35] This emphasis also emerged in Hernán's qualified attraction to White men who tanned when exposed to the sun, as opposed to those who turned red and looked burned (which several other Mexican gay men also said they found unattractive). Men such as Efraín and Hernán highlighted physical features that they liked and that transcended an unqualified attraction to all whiteness. By contrast, with others who simply hoped for *güeros* with blue eyes, it is hard to know whether their attraction was to a definite physical type or to stereotypical whiteness as such.

Beyond physical attributes, some immigrant men described their attraction to US White men in terms of the appeal of their culture and way of being. Isidro, who liked "Americans with blue eyes," also said that he liked "how they dress, how they are. How commanding they are. I really like how they are overall," as well as "the way they look at you or treat you." Notice the phrase "how commanding they are," which denotes a power disparity between Whites and Mexicans. Isidro then emphasized that he also liked "their language, their culture—which is not a real great culture; not really that good—but I do like them a lot." In this last comment, Isidro expressed a backhanded compliment: He liked US White culture, even when he found it to be not "that good" a culture.

. But, as we have seen, for immigrant men such as Hernán and Emilio, their attraction to White men was purely physical. And for several others, their attraction to whiteness also encompassed White Latinos and White Mexicans. As Ronaldo (born 1970) saw it, "I've always said that I like people with white skin very much. They don't precisely need to be from the United States, or Germany—I don't have anything against people of other races. It could be a white-skinned Mexican." Note how in this comment Ronaldo intertwined the concepts of race and ethnicity/ national origin. Yet despite declaring a general attraction to whiteness that transcended national/ethnic origins, he insisted he was most attracted to a stereotypical "Brad Pitt type," a man with *"ojos de color"* (colored eyes, as opposed to brown or black, which were deemed by some men ordinary and colorless). Such comments prompt a consideration of the racial stratification of Mexico and the oft-noted perceived advantages and privileges of being White (or light skinned) or primarily of European background in that country.[36] Indeed, my research team found it striking that when Mexican participants realized that Jorge Fontdevila, one the ethnographer-interviewers, was originally from Spain, they often were quick to point out that one of their own parents, grandparents, or other relatives was born in Spain, thereby highlighting the European or white side of their heritage. This may have been a way for them to establish a point of commonality with Jorge, but by contrast, no participants ever emphasized having Mexican indigenous roots. Furthermore, as Phua and Kaufman have noted, the preferential status of being White may also help explain why some gay Latino men seem inclined to emphasize the "lightness of their skin" and their "nonblack hair and eyes" in online personal ads.[37]

Sensing how his preference for Whites could be interpreted as racially charged, Ronaldo felt compelled to clarify: "That doesn't mean that I'm racist. It just turned out that way. You won't use this against me, will you? It's just a preference." Like other participants, he was wary about being perceived as racially insensitive: "I'm not racist [*laughter*]. I talk to everyone, and I treat everyone well. I don't care about race"—ending this statement by saying, "but physically I'm not attracted to Asians." His concern was not that he might be seen as stereotyping White men, but rather that his attraction to "Brad Pitt" types with light-colored eyes signaled a lack of attraction to men of color or men with darker features in terms of skin, hair, or eye color. Note also that Ronaldo emphasized that his attraction to White men was simply a personal preference.

Finally, Mexicans often felt that their attraction toward US Whites had already been in place before they migrated. Eliseo (born 1962) referred to "tourists . . . wow! I was impressed by their beauty. For me, *güeros* have always seemed beautiful." After he arrived in the United States, however, his admiration for White Americans diminished. He said, "It's no longer the same; one changes. Now they seem to me like anybody else. Some of them are good, and some are bad, contemptuous people, racist people. That's what I've sometimes felt here. In Mexico, I never felt such racism. . . . It's sad." Eliseo's fantasy had been crushed by his racialized interactions with White American gay men.

Attracted to Whites but Not to Latinos

Some Mexican immigrants who were especially drawn to US White men justified their attraction by pointing to their dislike of Latinos and/or Mexicans. For instance, Román (born 1983) described Latinos as *peleoneros* (aggressive), temperamental, and liars. He liked "a few of them. [But] many are arrogant. They think too much of themselves. They're ignorant." Raimundo (born 1967) described Latinos as "repressed," and felt that a majority of Mexican immigrants in the United States were "uneducated." "That's what I'm running away from," he explained. "I don't see the point of coming and living the same [as in Mexico]." Emilio described Latinos as "boring" and expressed a preference for dating US White men over the age of thirty:

It's not that I want them to control me, but I feel that they do have some control of the situation. I feel safer with them. They are people who know a lot, who are a bit *wiser* [*said in English*], more intelligent. They have more knowledge about things. They can hold a conversation.

Finally, Efraín explained that "Anglos" attracted him because of the way they thought:

Yes, because they have a different mentality. I don't mean to criticize my people; I love my country, as I've always said. But our mentality . . . that's why the country is in such bad shape, because of Mexicans' mentality. . . . We're always just thinking of how to screw our fellow man [*fregar al prójimo*].

He added that "above all, here in San Diego there are very handsome people," and he described White American men as "more practical" and "less complicated" than Mexicans or Latinos.

In a different but related vein, other immigrant men relied on criteria having to do with hygiene. "Look," Inti (born 1978) said. "I've had sex with Latinos, and I don't like it, because I feel that they're very dirty . . . like they don't properly wash their private parts." This difference, he concluded, stemmed from the fact that more US White men were circumcised, "which I believe explains why their private parts are cleaner." However, understanding that his comments could be viewed as racially insensitive, Inti clarified: "Of course, not all Latinos are like that. There are people who wash themselves very well and care well for themselves."

Along the same lines as Inti, Porfirio (born 1974) said that at first he was not attracted to *americanos*. "They repulsed me, because they are so pale," he remarked. "I wondered how they might smell if they don't shower. I wondered what it would like be to have sex with a *güero* given how pale they are. Better with a Mexican." Later, however, Porfirio changed his attitude: "But then I realized that Americans are cut . . . they're circumcised. And then I started liking Americans more, because they seemed cleaner." Now, he said, "I prefer *americanos*." Indeed, although some men held on to their attraction to *americanos* or to Mexicans, to whiteness or to Mexican/Latino features, after arriving in San Diego, for other men, including Porfirio, migration to San Diego altered their pattern of attraction.

Fantasy versus Reality

Several Mexican men fantasized about engaging sexually or romantically with White men, but they were disappointed that in reality they always ended up with men who did not match their attraction. Alvaro (born 1967) stated that he liked "White Latinos, and they've always turned out to be brown. I like them tall, and they always turn out short. I like blue eyes, and they always turn out to have brown eyes [*laughter*]." He felt that blued-eyed White men were beyond his reach and would never be attracted to him. When he pursued them, they usually responded by simply saying, "You're not my type." Santiago (born 1967) similarly said, "Sometimes you have a type, a stereotype—that you like someone blond with green eyes and a good body. But then you fall in love with people who are nothing like what you said you liked." Finally, Heriberto recognized that his current partner looked nothing like his idealized type of man:

I told him, "I came looking for American citizens with blue eyes, blonds, tall, blah, blah, blah." "So then why are you with me?" . . . [*laughter*]. OK, I laugh because he's sexually perfect. As I've told a friend, he's all I need, not less and not more. But I see him and he's not my type. But in terms of the sex and intimacy, he's everything.

Notice how whiteness was viewed as unreachable in these various comments, which confirm the degree to which it is idealized. No Mexican men made similar comments about having an unfulfilled desire for non-White men. Indeed, those who were attracted to men who had brown or black skin did not judge becoming sexually engaged with such men to be impossible or unrealistic.

———

Taken together, the comments in this and the preceding sections suggest that some Mexican immigrant men believe it makes no sense to travel so far from Mexico to interact sexually or romantically with the same kind of men whom they could meet in in that country. Their comments also contain class-based inflections, suggesting that middle-class immigrants feel that dating other Mexican immigrants in the United States, whom they view as working-class Mexicans, is a step down. For that reason, some middle-class immigrants seek explicitly to distance themselves from the stereotypical, racialized image of the working-class Mexican immigrant. And, as some of the quotations presented also suggest, some view their connections with US White men as possibly providing them with forms of cultural and social capital that they feel improve their chances of integrating into US society and achieving greater stability and upward mobility.[38] In the words of a Latino man quoted in a study by Horacio Roque Ramírez, such men seek to acquire "a white trophy."[39]

It is also noticeable that Mexican men generally interpret their physical attraction to White men, or their dislike of Latinos, merely as personal preferences stemming from their own desires and lived experiences. This point is reminiscent of the assessment made by participants in a study of Asian gay men in Canada, some of whom "saw their erotic desire for a white man as arising from a personal preference: there is no politics, no self-hate; it is simply an attraction."[40] Similarly, Mexican participants in my study who preferred whiteness did not link their preference to the pernicious privileging of the whiter, European side of Mexican society over the darker, indigenous one, or to the favoring of the foreign—a tendency common enough in Mexico to have acquired its own name, *malinchismo*.[41]

A few, however, did recognize that the racial attitudes to which they had been exposed in Mexico were in part responsible for their attraction to White men. Roy (born 1969), for instance, discussed the prevailing racial attitudes in his family and his region, where people constantly emphasized whiteness as a standard of beauty and a marker of higher social status:

I always had to deal with my father's family, and all had European features; my cousins and all. To me, Mexico is *malinchista*. [I was attracted to] Mexicans . . . but they had to be White or *güeros*. I appreciated dark people, as long as they were cultured and had money. But, basically, they were always Whites or *güeros*, first Mexicans, then foreigners. And this was agreeable to my friends, and also to me. [It was] a bit racist, or elitist.

Yet despite the value placed on whiteness, both in Mexico and in the United States, not all Mexican participants fantasized about it or saw it as desirable. Instead, they liked other Mexicans (and, by extension, other Latinos).

Attracted to My Own Kind

Mexican men who were physically attracted to Mexicans and Latinos often simultaneously noted that this attraction reflected a strong sense of cultural affinity that facilitated smoother interactions and relationships. This notion implied a rejection of US White culture. For instance, when asked about the kind of men he was attracted to, Máximo (born 1964) simply stated, "I love Latinos." Then he explained: "What I don't like about Americans, the American *güeros*, is that they're really cold. I am very attracted to Latino beauty." In this statement, "Latino beauty" stood for both Latino physical appearance and Latino culture, which Máximo saw as bundled together.

Implicit in Máximo's comments was a reaction against *malinchismo* and a critique of Mexicans who overly admired the foreign at the price of disdaining the local. Such a critique was also a rejection of a phrase that Mexicans and other Latin Americans often use, *mejorar la raza* (to improve the race), an allusion to the desirability of relationships with people who are whiter than oneself.[42] For example, Marcelo openly rejected the "myth that one comes here [seeking Americans]":

I would tell my friends via Internet that I had met this guy . . . and they would ask, "Where is he from? Is he American?" The first thing they think is that one comes looking for an American. I like Latinos, just like the ones I met in Mexico. Well, here they are handsomer, because they're northern Mexicans.

Marcelo's comment was meant to criticize Mexican friends who presupposed that seeking a US White man should be his priority. Yet ironically, by emphasizing that northern Mexicans were "handsomer," he also revealed that he in some ways accepted racialized standards of beauty that privileged whiteness, given that northern Mexican men had the reputation of being lighter complected and more European looking than their darker, shorter, and more indigenous-looking counterparts in central and southern Mexico. This same idea was also expressed by other men who preferred Mexicans or Latinos. For instance, Matías (born 1975) described his attraction:

White men with black hair. I also like Latinos, but not the dark ones. I like people who look more or less like me. . . . That's what I look for in a man. I might also like a blond man, but not any blond.

Like others quoted earlier, in this last statement Matías qualified his attraction to Whites, as well as an attraction to men who had light to olive skin (not pale but not too dark either), blond to brown hair (or even black hair), and light-colored eyes. These features denote a range of European origins—Caucasian, Mediterranean, and possibly even Middle Eastern—that does not include all European phenotypes. As Benito observed:

Many Anglos are *güeros*, but they are mixed with Hispanics, or with Italians, and they look Latino. Their skin is white, but their hair is black. . . . That I'm attracted to. Obviously, I have nothing against the white race, but the white race is not my favorite.

Excluded are Mexicans regarded as too dark or too indigenous looking—men who some participants referred to as *oaxaquitas*, a word that derogatorily connects Mexican indigenous looks with the southern Mexican state of Oaxaca, one of the states having the largest Mexican Indian population.

But a few Mexican participants were especially or primarily attracted to darker Mexicans, including Joaquín (born 1981), who stated he was attracted to "Mexicans, the more Indian they look—Mexican Indians, I mean, native Indians—they make me go crazy." And yet, others emphasized they were attracted to Mexicans/Latinos because they were racially positioned at a midpoint in the racial hierarchy. Venustiano (born 1975) stated that "physically, all [types of men] are handsome, but Latinos are definitely in the middle in terms of color; I prefer whatever is in the middle." Men such as Venustiano felt that they themselves were in that middle range, which led them to like men who look like them. As Octavio (born 1977) put it, "I really like Latinos, the brown skin like mine, because it's my color. I say, 'Let's eat what Mexico produces' even if we're in another country, or 'Let's eat what Mexico is exporting.'" These last few comments reveal a reaction to racialized standards of beauty that privilege whiteness and a desire to articulate a sense of racial/ethnic pride.

Such a sense of pride also extended to a pride in Mexican culture and a rejection of US White culture and styles to which I alluded earlier. Benjamín (born ca. 1955) characterized Latinos as "more complicated but very loyal," and then added, "I won't say that Anglos don't call my attention, but I prefer Latinos. Anglos are colder in their style, their culture." Immigrant men often perceived that such coldness manifested constantly in daily life, confirming that US Whites were overly practical and detached. Teodoro, for instance, said that compared with what he had known in Mexico, "relations with young *güeros* are different":

For instance, I've never liked it when I go out and I pay my part and the guy pays his part. I prefer it when I pay once and you pay the next time. I don't want them to pay for me—I want it to be even—but I also don't want it to be so cold. . . . I'm more used to sharing everything, and few *gabachos*[43] are like that.

Even more strongly, Rogelio (born ca. 1966) explained that he rejected American materialistic culture. He said, "I'm not attracted to Americans. . . . I don't like their money. I don't like them. I like Latinos." He also complained that when Americans "have a dog they say it's their child, if they have a cat they say it's their child, and they give their life to their [pet] child," suggesting with this that American people were more concerned about their pets than about other people. "And they are like lonely dogs, living alone," Rogelio remarked. "They don't love anyone; they don't love themselves. When someone doesn't love himself, he can't love someone else."

By making comments such as these, Mexican immigrants suggested that they are sexually incompatible with US White men because of cultural differences. This topic returns in chapter 9, in terms of a common perception that US White men are cold and less passionate than Latinos, a view widely shared among my participants.

The Labor Involved in Cross-Cultural Interactions

Perceptions of cultural difference between Mexicans and Americans led some Mexican immigrants to assess that bridging cultural differences involved too much work, dissuading them from pursuing relations with non-Latino men. One example of this attitude is provided by Román, who commented, "With Mexicans, I feel as if I have something in common." He elaborated, "It's not the same to have a relationship in another language, [with people of] another culture and way of thinking. And you have to adapt to all that. I say, '*Qué flojera* [I couldn't be bothered]. I'd rather stick to what I already know.'" Similarly, Joaquín explained that being "with someone that is different, [is] like learning new customs, and all that takes a lot. In terms of culture, I have enough trouble learning my own culture to try to learn another."

Moreover, the notion that it was simpler to date and have sex with Mexicans/Latinos pragmatically reflected a sense of these men's availability. Leopoldo, for instance, observed that "obviously, since my social circle is primarily Latino, I know more Latinos." Ezequiel similarly stated, "Where I go, there are only Mexicans, [and] almost no Americans." For men such as Leopoldo and Ezequiel, the possibility of meeting US White men was limited.

In addition to being surrounded by Latinos, Ezequiel appreciated Latino men's sense of masculinity, which he felt was stronger than what he saw in US White men. As he put it, "My dream has been [to be with] an *americano*. But Americans are more of a woman than us [*nosotras*].[44] . . . *¡Qué horror!* [How awful!]."

To be sure, some immigrant men in my research felt that the main obstacle preventing them from interacting sexually or romantically with US Whites and other American men was not cultural but structural, most concretely their own lack of English skills, which they saw as producing an insurmountable barrier. Norberto said, "I don't like Americans because . . . well, I imagine that being with an American, I would not have the freedom to express myself as I can with someone who speaks my language." In a similar vein, Troy (born ca. 1973) commented that he disliked that Americans "speak English and I'm not fluent. I can talk a bit, but I'm not fluent, so that's a barrier." Note that for these men, and those quoted in the previous section, it was simpler to stick to the attractions they had while living in Mexico than to explore meeting new types of men. Their attraction to their own kind signaled their resistance to shifting their patterns of attraction in the United States.

The Patterns of Attraction among US Latinos

The US Latinos who participated in my study provide a useful contrast to the Mexican immigrants. While the latter were equally divided in their attraction to US White and Mexican/Latino men, two-thirds of the thirty-six US Latinos who participated in my study expressed having an attraction to Latino or Mexican men, and only a third indicated that they were attracted to US White men. Furthermore, nine explicitly said that they were not at all attracted to White men. These men seemed more compelled to overtly state an allegiance to their own ethnic/cultural group. Roger (born 1974) thought that "there is much more of a common history . . . with someone who is Mexican." And when speaking of US White men, Scott (born 1973) said, "I can relate a lot more to the [Latino] culture than I can to the White person's culture," and then described the latter as "so different!"

I guess if maybe they're Latino, I feel more comfortable with them . . . I guess since they probably have the same upbringing . . . or whatever, we could relate better. . . . I'm probably less likely to feel I'm at risk being that we're from the same background. They wouldn't intentionally try to do me harm, being that we're both Latino . . . versus someone else from another race, or say, for instance, someone that's like white or something like that. . . . They would be like . . . more likely I would contract a disease from them, or something like that.

Here we see that Scott viewed cross-racial relations as not just uncomfortable but risky.

Like some of their Mexican counterparts, some US Latinos emphasized that beyond a sense of shared culture, they were mostly attracted to Latino physical features, which translated into being attracted to someone who looked like them. That was the case for Oton (born 1974), who stated:

I kind of like guys that kind of look like myself, so I like Latino men mostly, with a similar build, similar look; dark hair, dark eyes, you know. Some color to their skin; I guess, it's a good way to describe it.

In another example, Isaías (born 1978) first mentioned "Latinos' skin color, brown eyes, you know, I kind of like long eyelashes and dark hair. You know, Latino looking." Then he highlighted cultural affinity: "I love to hear them talk . . . I can sort of relate to them." Despite his primary attraction to Latinos, however, Isaías had a US White boyfriend, which he felt was unusual for him, because, as he put it, "I didn't think I could relate."

Some US Latinos went further and discussed very specific Latino looks and features that attracted them. Among other physical characteristics, Terry (born 1968) emphasized goatees, being uncircumcised (but with a retractable foreskin), being "dark, but not too dark," having an accent, being bilingual, and having Latino family values. "If they're family orientated, that's [the] bomb, because I like somebody who speaks to their mom or speaks to their sister, and [stays] in contact [with family], that's cool." By contrast, for him, "White men, they are a turnoff," except for military men. In his opinion, most US White men were too pale, had bad hair, and "are stuck up." Terry feared his comments might make him "sound prejudiced," which he compensated for by referring to US White men's attitudes toward Latinos: "The ones I meet, they are like, 'Oh my God, here comes a wetback, here's a Mexican guy.' They tend to look down on any people of color. And, they think they're above all, and they're not." In this case, we see a more politicized sense of racial difference that is less present in narratives about attraction offered by Mexican immigrants.

Similarly to many Mexican men, Terry added that he would approach US White men if they have "a beautiful gold-brown tan" and a nice body. In fact, he estimated that in the previous year he had had sex with more than sixty White men who had these characteristics. But even then, he did not expect that he could have a relationship with a US White man, because he felt that White men were usually not interested in relationships: "But it's like . . . tricks; *trick* means, like, hi, bye, see you later, just sex and that's it."

Some US Latinos shared with Mexicans certain class and racial biases about the kinds of Latinos to whom they were attracted, and expressed being attracted only to Latinos who were white or middle-class. For instance, Sal (born 1978) said he was attracted to Latinos only "if they look white"; Elio (born 1973) was attracted only to "Americanized," "clean-cut" Mexicans, and not to men who "look like they just crossed the border"; and Pascual (born 1966) clarified that for him, "it's tied between Whites and Latinos," but he likes only Latinos who lived on the US side of the border and who dressed better than the Mexicans who lived in Mexico. Indeed, for some US Latinos it was important to distance themselves from the stereotypical image of the working-class Mexican immigrant, which they felt cast a stigma on them as well. But a few US Latinos liked men who incarnated a Latino urban, working-class persona. Ignacio (born 1970), for example, said he felt most attracted to "the *cholo* kind . . . thuggish, you know, gangbanger kind of guys."[45] Similarly, Evan (born 1971) described Mexican men as "hot" and emphasized liking the overt masculinity and domineering attitudes of Mexican construction workers. He then clarified, "I don't like, you know, like, white-collar-type professional-job people. I like more blue-collar, construction, rough, you know, types."

Finally, the minority of US Latinos who were explicitly and primarily attracted to US White men tended to emphasize a preference for blond hair and blue eyes, and in this sense they were similar to their Mexican immigrant counterparts. But their attraction to US White men was sometimes accompanied by a strong awareness of whiteness as a standard of beauty and higher social status. Angel (born 1979) felt that his mother had taught him to be attracted to US White men. "Regrettably," he noted, "she inculcated [that] in us. . . . She would tell my sisters, 'Marry an American; you will fare better [that way].' " Still other US Latinos had developed a strong attraction to what Eugenio (born 1979) called "ethnospecific" White looks—the looks of US Italians, Greeks, and Jews—a taste that he himself acquired when he moved to New York between his first and second interviews for my study. In this regard, as we will see, Eugenio did something similar to US White men who first became attracted to Mexicans and Latinos when they arrived in San Diego.

As these various examples show, although US Latinos in my study were somewhat similar to the Mexican immigrants, more of them explicitly emphasized an attraction to their own kind (even if such an attraction sometimes did not include all types of Latino men). Having been part of an ethnic community in the United States all their lives, some of them had been exposed to more racism and were more politicized, which probably influenced their thinking that the right thing to do was to be attracted to people within your own ethnic group.

The Patterns of Attraction of Non-Latino US Men

Given that the non-Latino men who participated in my research were recruited specifically on the basis of their having recently been sexually or romantically involved with Mexican or Latino men, it is not surprising that a great majority in this group were attracted (often primarily) to Latinos, and sometimes specifically to Mexicans. In addition, a majority were White (29 of 34). For that reason, this section primarily reflects the experiences and opinions of US White men. However, I occasionally refer to comments made by the four African American men and the one Asian American man whom we interviewed.

To be sure, not all the non-Latino men in the study had a primary or exclusive attraction to Mexicans or Latinos. Some were also attracted to men of other racial/ethnic groups or said that they had no racial preference. Moreover, some plainly rejected the notion that race was a legitimate criterion for selecting sexual or romantic partners. For instance, Justin (White, born 1974) said that he did not have a "type" and instead just liked "people for people; for who they are." Another way of expressing this idea was provided by Nathan (White, born 1970), who said that he was "pretty equal opportunity, so I'm not, like, focused in on one particular kind of person or thing." Other US White men also used the phrase "equal opportunity"—presumably borrowed from the language of anti-discrimination policies—to suggest that they did not have a type. Let us recall that Mexican men expressed this same idea by indicating that they did not have "prototypes"—a somewhat less politicized metaphor. A central claim in both instances, however, is that attraction is an individualized matter, or, in Nathan's words, that "the attraction is more about the person, typically."

Yet some of the non-Latino men who emphasized being equal opportunity also recognized that they usually found themselves being attracted to Latino men. As Justin put it, "I don't necessarily gravitate toward Hispanic people; it's just how it's worked." Nathan offered a more elaborate explanation:

Moving to San Diego, I mean . . . it's [a] very Latin community here, and . . . there's a warmth I feel about . . . Latin men that can be lacking, you know, in Caucasian men or in African American men. It's sort of [a] different kind of sexuality, but I don't know. Latin men, they're just fiery.

Nathan's attraction shifted toward Latinos when he moved to San Diego. His use of the term *fiery* is also connected to the idea that Latinos are more sexually passionate than non-Latinos—the central topic of the next chapter.

Similarly to Nathan, other participants saw their attraction to Latinos as a personal preference in the context of multiple possibilities. "If I see a White guy and I see a Latin guy, my eyes are . . . I'll look at both of them, but for some reason that dark hair, dark eyes, the brown skin just . . . that's what I focus on," said Peter (US White, born 1968). And Andrew (US White, born 1972), who did not have a type, acknowledged that over time he had developed what he called "a Latin weakness." He first recognized this special attraction to Latinos when he traveled in Latin America; it was a departure from his earlier attraction to "blond-haired, blue-eyed" men. According to Andrew, exposure to Latin American men had changed him.

Other non-Latino men strongly stated that they found Latino men more attractive than any other men. As could be expected, for some of them their attraction to Latinos and Mexicans was primarily physical. But some understood this attraction in cultural terms, either because of a sense of cultural similarity or affinity, or because they appreciated interacting with someone of a culture that they perceive to be very different from their own. I discuss non-Latino men's physical and cultural attraction to Mexicans/Latinos separately in the following two sections.

"The Dark Dream That We All Have"

In justifying their attraction to Latinos, US White men participating in my study often invoked the notion that opposites attract.[46] For example, Giovanni (born 1972) explicitly said:

Just physically, I think opposites attract, or at least in my case they do. Most Latino men . . . often they have characteristics that I like, just physically—different hair, eyes, skin, . . . shape, everything. . . . Actually, an accent is also attractive to me, I think it's kind of sexy; so, all the differences. Plus they oftentimes would find me attractive as well, which is also kind of an aphrodisiac in its own way when you see somebody who is attracted to you back. That can be very intoxicating, so it was kind of mutual.

Mitchell (White, born 1964) similarly emphasized this idea. As he put it, "Well, I've always been attracted to Latin men. Maybe it's because it's the complete opposite of myself. . . . I am, like, pickled White, German or Scandinavian or whatever. I've always been . . . [attracted] to darker features."

The same notion also explained to these men why Mexican and Latino men found them attractive. For Paul (US White, born 1968), for instance, "The brown boys tend to like the blond/blue-eyed thing going on—that mutual attraction. Opposites attract." Also central to this construction was a sense that contrast was inherently attractive. US White men such as Steven (born 1974) therefore emphasized what he called "my big three . . . dark hair, dark eyes, and dark skin. That is where my eye goes first." As these various comments suggest, for both the Mexican immigrants and US White men, their desire for each other was sometimes highly racialized.

One difference between the two groups, however, is that while some Mexican participants saw the US White men they were attracted to as unavailable and unreachable, US Whites saw no problem reaching out to Mexican immigrants or US Latinos, suggesting the social disparity between the two groups. This difference also highlights what could be seen as a colonial fantasy among some US White men, which Ralph (US White, born 1940) expressed in terms of "the dark dream that we all have about this dark, handsome person." This fantasy was complemented by a sense that Latinos tended to have nice (and thus more kissable) lips as well as hairless, smooth skin, and that they were available to White men.

Moreover, several US White participants viewed dark features as correlating with social class differences that have become erotized—and which, when placed under a positive light, helped them think of themselves as the kind of person who was open to crossing the US social divide. Ray (US White, born 1971) said that the "dark-skinned guys" to whom he was attracted were also working-class and very masculine, inner-city *cholos*—whom he described as having "gelled-back" hair and goatees, and a slightly muscular build (with "just an average, normal" body).[47] However, being aware that cholos were often involved in gangs and urban crime, Ray clarified that the cholos that attracted him were not those who are "L.A. gangsters, that kind of thing, not like that." In this view, Latino cholos emerged as simultaneously alluring and possibly dangerous. This image is reminiscent of the construction of a "sexual other" that Lionel Cantú identified in the text of some gay travel books, which exploit a "colonial desire"[48] to sell to foreign gay tourists the idea that vacationing in Mexico may give them access to non-gay-identified, macho local men.[49]

Furthermore, other US White men in my study explicitly associated Latino dark features and working-class looks with the status of being an immigrant, coupled with the idea that Latinos were attractive because of their accents. Steven remarked that he liked it when Latinos "speak English with a little accent," and for Frank (US White, born 1979), a Spanish accent "just stirs something inside me; it's nice, you know, bright up from the monotony, I guess." This focus on Spanish accents symbolized a disposition toward connecting with men who had very different looks and backgrounds, but it was sometimes also motivated by fantasies related to power and domination. Finally, an immigrant status was also sometimes associated with the idea that Mexican and other Latino immigrant men were typically uncircumcised, which several US participants found appealing.[50] Edward (US White, born 1977) said that an uncut penis was "always nice," and Casey (US White, born 1974) said that he was "kind of intrigued with guys that are uncut. Not that it has to be one or the other; just curiosity, I guess." Casey connected this curiosity to a broader fascination with foreignness and difference.

———

Taken together, these various comments suggest that having dark features, being a foreigner and an immigrant, being working-class, being uncircumcised, and speaking with an accent were all characteristics contributing to the sense among US White men that Latino immigrant men—and, more specifically, Mexican immigrant men—were exotic and therefore desirable. In summarizing his attraction toward dark-skinned Latinos, Steven said:

It's . . . what's the word I'm looking for? It's foreign—that's not the word—it's very exotic. That's the word, phew! I couldn't find it! It's exotic and it's different, it goes with the body. It's a little package; not a little package, but it's a whole package, [*laughs*] not in a little package, not that, but that, too.

It is noteworthy that the word *exotic* is absent from Mexican men's descriptions of White men. And yet, some White American men who used that word saw it as a compliment toward Latino and Mexican men—as a way to summarize their appreciation for the notion that "opposites attract." They seemed unaware of the problematic legacy of the term—of the ways in which exoticization has been used historically to justify the domination of subaltern "others" in colonial settings, as has been extensively noted in the literature on sexuality and colonialism.[51]

The Magnet of Mexican and Latino Culture

In addition to being physically attracted to Latinos/Mexicans, some US White men emphasized cultural reasons for their attraction. In describing Mexicans he dated after moving to San Diego, Giovanni discussed how exciting it was for him to be exposed to a new culture that he found extremely appealing, especially given the aversion that he felt toward his own culture in his primarily White location in Oregon:

I came from such a sort of quiet, restricted background that it's nice to be exposed to a different culture. Culturally, I've been . . . I'm probably a lot more culturally aware. And culturally . . . I go back up to my family, and they could still use racial epitaphs [*sic*] about people of different racial backgrounds, including Latinos, which is something that I wouldn't even. . . . It's a shock to me if I hear it.

In another example, Andrew, who did not have a type but had developed a "Latin weakness," explained that this attraction resulted from his exposure to Latino culture. "It's more the language, too, listening to Spanish language and the music—just the culture. And also through living so close to the Mexican influence, Mexican food." In commenting on their attraction to Mexican/Latino culture, non-Latino men sought to highlight their openness and sensitivity toward a diverse United States.

Some US White participants felt that Latino culture influences Latino men's good disposition. "Am I attracted to Hispanics? No. But I admire a lot of them," said Nicholas (US White, born 1951). What struck him the most about Latino men was their personalities, which he believed became most evident when they smiled, revealing their tenderness. As he put it, "I'm very comfortable with them, I think, because, number one, I think they tend to be a little tender." Incidentally, Nicholas also felt that Asian men—whom he called "Oriental"—"tend to be that way, too."

Other participants commented that they were particularly attracted to Latinos' strong sense of connection, which they perceived as being culturally inflected. "It's just a fun community," said Peter. "They're all close knit, and I like that sense of community, the culture and stuff like that. . . . I guess it was so foreign to me and so different that I guess it appealed to me." By interacting with Latino men, some felt they had acquired a different appreciation for community and family. They referred to the pleasure involved in regularly attending Latino family gatherings, and contrasted their new experiences with those involving their own families. Indeed, several observed that they saw their own families only two or three times a year.

Nathan, who was in a relationship with a Mexican immigrant man, had become fully incorporated into his boyfriend's family. He described attending their gatherings, which consisted of "[drinking] tequila [and] making *carne asada*." He added, "When [his boyfriend is] home, he speaks Mexican or Spanish." These family gatherings also provided Nathan with a sense of the importance of family life in Mexican culture:

When I'm around his family, it's kind of different. . . . I get much more the sense of the family. That is the one thing with him, I guess . . . that I would pinpoint as being . . . more specifically Latino . . . the very strong ties with family. And it's not that I don't have those ties with my family, but to me, living a thousand miles from my dad and a thousand miles from my mom is nothing.

Nathan's boyfriend saw his family once a month, while Nathan saw his mother only "about once a year."

Mexican men perceived this cultural difference, too. Augusto (born 1972) commented that his US White boyfriend "likes how close I am with my family. He's not like that with his. He hasn't seen his mom in four to five years. And my mom came three times last year, and I also went there. I see her about four times a year." He explained that this difference did not produce "a cultural tension" for them as a couple: "He likes what he doesn't get with his family. . . . He likes everything, Mexican food, Mexican music. . . . He really likes *lo mexicano*." But other Mexican men read signs of culturally based detachment in the patterns they saw among US White men. According to Leopoldo, "You come to realize that the son sees his mom every five years, and that he has no other option but to leave the family home" (an allusion to the middle-class custom of sending children off to live on their own at the age of eighteen). For Leopoldo, all this stemmed from the fact that "Americans are more individualistic . . . less open to let you in to share something, right? It's colder."

US White men noted that they were introduced to their boyfriend's family euphemistically as his "friend." But in some cases, they acquired a somewhat more official status as uncles to the children, and sons to the parents. Ignacio (US Latino) noted that his boyfriend's Mormon family had been able to accept them as a couple, but in his own family his sexual orientation "over the years it's kind of been this hush-hush, we don't talk about it kind of thing." Ignacio decided to change this: "I told my family, 'He comes with me or I don't come at all.' And although they were a little uncomfortable at first, you know, my family has really come around by leaps and bounds." This meant that Ignacio's boyfriend was now included in family life:

My nieces and nephews call him uncle, just some of them call him aunt [Ignacio said jokingly, and then laughed]. My sister and her husband have been, for the most part, phenomenal and just treating us as equals and, you know, not any issues or anything. And even my mom now . . . calls him *mijo* [a contraction of the words *mi hijo*, "my son"], you know, and every time she talks to me she asks for him, and how's he doing. "Is he talking care of himself, is he taking care of you?" You know, so it's kind of like, okay . . . they've come to that point.

For US White men, these aspects of Latino culture were part of their attraction to Mexicans/Latinos, and complemented their physical attraction. Finally, some US White participants in my study also felt that Latino culture was responsible for producing a kind of masculinity that they found greatly appealing. Frank noted that among Latinos, "the male is more, I mean, like, uh, forceful; really, you know, just like, always the man, you know. Kinda like being dominated in a ways." He thus relied on the trope—or stereotype—of Latino machismo. Somewhat similarly, alluding to the forcefulness of Mexican immigrants in a slightly different way, Nicholas said that he admired them because they were willing to take risks:

Just because somebody is from Mexico and they're good looking, that isn't why I'm necessarily attracted to them. I'm attracted to them because they're a risk taker. It takes a lot for anybody . . . most people are afraid to quit a job, let alone pack up.

Nicholas seemed to credit Mexican masculinity with giving Mexican men the courage to uproot themselves and seek a new life in the United States. It should be emphasized that in this discussion of masculinity and initiative, the Latino and Mexican cultures were depicted in monolithic terms with little to no sense of internal variation.

Despite their generalizations, these various US White men sought to indicate that they saw more in Latino/Mexican men than just their physical attributes, and they emphasized that there was something for them to learn from interacting with Latinos and Mexicans. Notably, several of the men quoted in this section—Peter, Nicholas, Casey, and Andrew—were among the US White men who regarded themselves as "equal opportunity" and as not having a strong racial preference. They embraced their connections to Latinos and Mexicans because of a sense of cultural affinity and a shared interest in cross-cultural interaction, which sometimes meant that they rejected their own cultural upbringing as mainstream US Whites. These ideas will become even more evident in chapter 9 in my discussion of Latino sexual passion.

The Catholic Connection

For some US gay men, an additional and significant source of cultural connection to Mexicans and Latinos stemmed from being Catholic (or having been raised Catholic). Most Mexican immigrants and US Latinos in my study had a Catholic upbringing, including 58 of the 69 immigrant men[52] and 23 of the 32 US Latinos[53] who discussed their religious background. By contrast, only 12 of the 32 non-Latino men who discussed their religious upbringing were Catholic. Ten among those 12 were White (mainly of Italian, Irish, or German origin), 1 was African American, and 1 was Filipino American. Several also indicated that Catholicism made them feel a special bond with Mexicans and Latinos, especially given that they felt culturally marginalized in US society due to their religious background.

Giovanni, who grew up in a "fairly large, suburban Irish-Italian Catholic family," spoke at length about his religious cultural and spiritual connections with Mexicans and Latinos. Regarding his Mexican boyfriend, he chuckled when he observed, "I was always supposed to bring home a nice Irish Catholic girl. . . . So I got the Catholic part right, but I didn't get the Irish or the girl part right." Giovanni expressed feeling that being a White Catholic made him part of a minority. "You're really not a minority, but you are sort of still a minority . . . when it comes to being Catholic," he said, and this status generated what he saw as "a subconscious or a built-in affinity towards other people who are Catholic."

Giovanni and his boyfriend attended services at Dignity, an LGBT Catholic organization that provides gay Catholics with an alternative to the official Catholic Church.[54] His partner was "not comfortable with the priest being so openly gay," but Giovanni liked Dignity:

I always said, it's kind of funny, because it's very similar to a regular Catholic service except the priest actually acknowledges the fact that he's gay. Whereas you go to any other Catholic parish, [and] the priest is gay anyways, but he just doesn't acknowledge it.

Catholic US Whites such as Giovanni explained that their cultural affinity with Catholic Latinos depended to some degree on the shared experience of the icons, rituals, and practices of that faith, which brought them closer to Latinos than to non-Catholic Whites. Doug (US White, born ca. 1980) remarked, "I think it's pretty. I like all the rituals. . . . I like the saints and the Guadalupe, the virgin mother, or whatever, and all that." Indeed, several Mexican participants similarly expressed nostalgia for Catholic practices. Octavio (Mexican) joyfully recalled the religious images and the dances that were organized in his hometown in Mexico during the saints' feasts. Similarly, Bonifacio (Mexican, born ca. 1975) fondly remembered being a *monaguillo* (an altar boy). "That was really beautiful for me," he said, chuckling as he remembered that he and other *monaguillos* used to steal the alms when no one was watching.

Some Catholics also shared ambivalence about being Catholic in light of the church's positions on homosexuality. This sentiment is well represented in a comment by Mitchell (US White), who said that he "struggled with being gay and the church's view on it. I mean, it's okay to be gay, according to the Catholic Church, but as long as you don't act on it." Similarly, Bane (Filipino American, born 1980) stated that he went to church with his family, "just to be close," but he strongly rejected the Catholic Church's position on his sexuality: "As far as their teachings go . . . I only accept the ones I want to accept. Maybe that's a bad thing. . . . I'm not sure." The internal struggle about being Catholic and gay also contributed to the sense of cultural connection across national and racial boundaries.

Attitudes toward Blacks and Asians

Interviewer: And which is your type?

Reinaldo: Currently, tall men of the black race, with large hands and large feet; intelligent. That's what attracts me, nothing else.

African Americans and Asian Americans figure much less commonly in my participants' narratives about their sexual attraction, suggesting that most of them did not see these men as desirable partners. This finding is consistent with other studies, including one of sexual stereotyping among gay men conducted by Wilson and coauthors, who observed that "Asian and Black men were generally considered the least sexually desirable among different-race men."[55] However, some Mexican men, including Reinaldo (born 1963), developed an attraction to African Americans after arriving in the United States. He explained that he came to realize that "sex is better" with Black men, "and . . . they see you less as different; they see you almost like an equal."

Of the 63 immigrant men who discussed their attraction to men in racial terms, 13 said they were attracted to African American men, but 12 explicitly said they were not attracted to them. Some simply mentioned Black men in passing, as part of a list of racial or ethnic groups they found attractive. Oscar (born 1976) said, "I like Blacks," and then clarified that he liked men of "any race except for Chinese [*los chinos*[56]]." Lucio (born 1970) noted, "I like *morenos, negritos*," using terms commonly employed in Mexico to refer to Black men.[57] For Lucio, Black men were positioned at the top of his hierarchy of attraction, followed by Hispanics (Cubans or Puerto Ricans), US White men (*americanos, güeritos*), and Mexicans (whom he separated from Hispanics).

Some Mexicans viewed their attraction to Black men as physical and expressed such attraction in a racialized manner, often relying on common stereotypes about African American men's large penises.[58] Oscar said he liked Black men's complexions and their large penises. And Troy realized that he liked the contrast between Black men's skin color and his own. As he put it, Black men's skin "contrasts with mine divinely. They're really hot, and it's perfect." Finally, Heriberto noted that people with his same color "don't awaken anything in me. So, seeing a *negrito*, or *moreno*, as they call them here, or a White, is new. . . . So it is more interesting, more attractive."

Despite their stereotypes, Mexican men never used the word *exotic* to refer to Black men. But in contrast to comments they made about US White men, Mexican immigrants did not see dating Black men as socially advantageous. This sense emerged poignantly in comments by Justo (born 1971), who initially called his attraction to Black men "a defect." Catching himself in the interview, he added, "Well, it's not a defect, there's nothing wrong with it."

Among the American men in my study, four Whites, four Blacks, and five Latinos expressed having an attraction to Black men. In most of these cases, however, this attraction was not primary. US Latinos made comments resembling those made by Mexican immigrants and emphasizing physical attributes. Cayetano (US Latino, born 1976) said that he liked Black men's lips, and how sensual Black men were when they danced. "Generally speaking, they are also larger down there," he added. Cayetano nonetheless clarified that he preferred to date Mexican men, "in spite of the penis issue. The penis comes second." In another example, Al (US Latino, born 1959) similarly stated that Black men "got big dicks" and were "better lovers." He added, "They're more attentive, you know, they'll suck your toes and suck your ass and do all that weird, freaky shit. Just fuck you to death." In Al's case, his attraction to dark skin—"the blacker the better"—confirmed why he rejected White men. "I refuse to go with the White man," he remarked. "I just refuse to see that pink dick; it just turns me off."

Interestingly, such explicit racialization was absent in the few statements about Black men that were made by US White men. Andrew (US White) simply said he was primarily attracted to Latinos, but he would just as likely date White, African American, or Asian American men. Peter indicated in passing that he had gone out on dates with a couple of Black men. And Ted (US White, born 1949) mentioned that his attraction to darker skin color included an attraction to Black men, although he also feared them. "I've always heard so much about the Black guy that I'm scared of the Black guy," he stated. In addition to being more attracted to Latinos, these US White men may have been careful not to make statements that could be construed as racist, although, as we have seen, some did not seem so cautious about making racialized statements about Latinos or Mexicans. Because of the dominant White/Black binary within the racial system of the United States, these men may have felt that it was less acceptable to racialize African American men than Latinos.

Perhaps not surprisingly, the men who spoke most neutrally about Black men were the four African American participants.[59] (Again, these were US-born men who were recruited based on their recent history of sexual or romantic involvement with Mexican men.) Jerome (born 1969) simply called Black men "beautiful" (although he had a stronger preference for Latinos); Jaed (born 1967) grouped African Americans and Latinos together and included them under the rubric of men of color, which for him stood in contrast to White men. And Tameron (born 1962) simply stated that he had a primary attraction to Black men, including men of Afro-Caribbean origin (particularly some Puerto Ricans).

Finally, neither Mexican nor American men had much to say about Asians. Some US White men liked in them some of the same features that they liked in Latinos (and mentioned smooth, hairless skin as part of their attraction to Asians). The relative absence of comments about Asian men among the men in my study perhaps says more than their presence. Indeed, it may reflect a sense of the undesirability that, as the literature has reported, gets projected onto Asian men by non-Asian gay men—except for White men who are labeled "rice queens," whose fetishization of Asian gay men in the context of power differentials created by age and race has also been problematized.[60]

"I'm Not Racist"

Much as with comments (discussed earlier) about a lack of attraction to Latinos, some Mexican participants felt compelled to clarify that their rejection of Blacks and Asians did not make them racist. Abel (born 1979) said he was "not attracted to African Americans. I'm not racist." Similarly, Efraín stated, "I'm not racist, but I'm not attracted to Black people. I'm attracted to mulattoes, but they must have something really special. . . . But [they don't attract me] if they're Black, *morenos*."

It is also interesting that several participants insisted they did not have a racial preference, but then proceeded to state that they were not attracted to African American and Asian American men. Mauro (born 1972) remarked, "I don't have a preference. I may like brown or white men." He added, "I don't like Blacks much. But I might even like one of them. I don't have a preference." Matías similarly said that "nationality" (as a euphemism for race and ethnicity) did not matter, as long as there's chemistry. He then stated that he was not attracted to Asians. "I don't have anything against them, but they're not my type."

Some Mexican immigrant men also mentioned features of Black and Asian men that they disliked. Referring to Black men, Porfirio mentioned that "they have a strange attitude. They try to make you their way. They can do what they want, but you can't. They're jealous. . . . I do feel attracted to Blacks, but I don't like their attitude." Facundo (born 1967) said that he disliked how Blacks smell, and he saw this as "a barrier." Finally,

Isidro, who did not like "Filipinos, or *morenos*," commented that "the last time that I kissed a Filipino his breath stank of garlic." Rather than seeing this as an individual attribute, Isidro extended it to all Asians.

The fear of being seen as racist for not being attracted to African American or Asian men was shared by American participants in my study. Casey (US White, born 1974) talked about being usually attracted to "Latin guys, no blonds, no redheads, no Asians or Blacks," and added, "Not racist, just not a personal preference."[61] Ted was drawn to "good-looking Black guys," but could not get himself to have sex with one. "No matter how nice they are, and I'm not prejudiced, it's just that . . . oh, maybe I am [prejudiced], because I won't do an Oriental guy at all, period, nope! I won't even look at him. But Blacks kind of scare me." Germán (US Latino, born ca. 1953) was wary about African Americans' attitude: "I don't normally go with Black guys unless they . . . show me that . . . they don't have an attitude like most Black people have." And in Saul's case (US Latino, born 1975), he expressed a lack of familiarity with African Americans: "I wasn't raised around African-Americans, 'cause I see them on TV but never was raised around them." Asked if he could imagine overcoming this lack of familiarity, he succinctly responded, "No, no, no, no. Not at all. No. I think . . . I couldn't do it."

Contextualized Sexualities

According to social constructionist sociological approaches to sexuality, including Simon and Gagnon's well-known sexual script theory, sexuality must always be understood as contextualized, and sexual interpretations and practices as emerging from the complex dynamics of interpersonal and cultural interaction.[62] From that perspective, it should not come as a surprise that immigrants such as those in my study changed, or feel that they changed, after experiencing often dramatic shifts in the social and cultural contexts in which they are embedded. As shown by the many topics I have addressed in this chapter, these men view such changes as related to their participation in new social situations that many of them had imagined as being more sexually liberal—and, for that reason, as potentially providing them with the space and autonomy to explore their same-sex desires and sexualities more freely. Those shifts have to do with what Sánchez-Eppler and Patton have referred to as making "sense of the always poignant and sometimes hilarious labors of reinvention and renegotiation in new places, or in reimagined old ones."[63]

At the same time, these immigrant men come to realize that not everything they encounter in the United States is new or intrinsically better for them: the social conditions surrounding them in their new location are at once enabling and limiting, and as soon as they arrive in the United States they are often instantly classified as racial and sexual others, and also as alien. Moreover, that realization becomes most patent in their interactions—including their sexual and romantic interactions—with American gay men. And, as the data I have presented also show, the possibility, created by their migration, of engaging in cross-cultural and cross-racial interactions brings to the fore their questions about their own sense of attraction, and about who is attracted to them and for what reasons.

As we have seen, the topic of attraction provides us with an opportunity to observe what changes or does not change for these men, and the degree to which they either maintain forms of desire that they brought with them from Mexico or acquire new ones. Some of the immigrants in fact become more like the US Latinos: sensitive to their own racialization, and therefore wary of interactions with White gay men. Others, however, find in their migration experience the opportunity to fulfill desires that were kindled at least in part by entrenched Mexican ideas about the preferability of lighter skin. And still others discover attractions they had not previously considered, including to African American men.

An important point to consider is that in the interactions that Mexican gay immigrants participating in my study established with Americans, it was not just the former who changed. As in Nathan's case, several other US-born participants commented that their moving to San Diego changed *them*, particularly as a result of their discovery of an attraction to Mexicans/Latinos and their interactions with them. For several, a previous physical or cultural attraction to American men of southern European or Mediterranean origins shifted to an attraction to Mexicans/Latinos. These experiences point to the effects of Mexican gay immigrants on mainstream gay cultures of the United States (and, by extension, their contributions to what many people tend to see as global gay culture).

In addition, how both Mexican and American men in my study discussed who was desirable and who was not, and who was erotically attainable or not across racial/ethnic lines anticipates considerations of social inequality I examine in the next chapter. As we will see, beyond the different dimensions of attraction I discussed in the current chapter, the Mexican gay men in my study reported various forms of social inequality that they felt negatively affected them within their sexual and romantic relations with US White men. Such perceptions suggest that they were participating in stratified sexual worlds whose structures were, as Adam Green has suggested, "constituted by eroticized schemas related to race, class, gender, age, and nationality, among others."[64] Put differently, in San Diego these Mexican gay men found themselves operating in "sexual fields," or "socially stratified, institutionalized [matrices] of relations," that were not level playing fields.[65] Consequently, they experienced various forms of vulnerability within cross-racial sexual and romantic relations that stemmed from their often marginalized situation in US society, defined by racialization, economic disparities, and in many cases the precariousness of being undocumented. Finally, they often discovered that in situations of vulnerability, they may be readily sexually stereotyped. But, my data will show, they also learned how to turn around what at first glance could be seen as deep-seated cultural and sexual stereotypes—specifically those related to the trope of Latino sexual passion—and use them as a tools for their own empowerment.

NINE

The Discourse of Sexual Passion

The previous chapter suggested just how complex a matter sexual attraction can be, when it is structured and mediated by race, ethnicity, and nationality. I now take my analysis of cross-racial and cross-cultural relationships one step further by examining how racialized perceptions of difference and attraction play out within the sexual and romantic interactions that participants in my research described—that is, within "micro-level interactions organized around systematic power differentials," as Adam Green has characterized them.[1] In other words, my emphasis shifts from men's stated physical and cultural attractions to the details of their erotic encounters and practices.

The organizing principle for this analysis will be how my participants relied on the notion of Latino sexual passion to explain what makes Mexicans/Latinos sexually different from men of other racial/ethnic groups. When men such as Justin (US White, born 1974) described Mexicans and Latinos as "fiery"—as we saw in chapter 8—they were alluding to a widespread perception that those men were more sexually passionate than non-Latino men. On the one hand, in the context of describing cross-racial sexual and romantic relations, Mexican and Latino men invoked the notion of passion to identify sexual characteristics of Latinos that they felt proud of and that they thought made them more appealing to sex partners—or, following Green, that conferred on them erotic capital in the sexual markets in which they participated.[2] On the other hand, non-

Latino participants likewise referred to Latino passion in listing the characteristics that drew them to Mexican and Latino men. For instance, Steven (US White, born 1974) who described dark-skinned Latinos as "very exotic," also said the following:

Well, immediately I am drawn to that old . . . I'm drawn to them physically, because I like the darker skin and dark hair and eyes, the brown eyes . . . I like that part. So, automatically, I'm attracted to that, and if they have an accent it's always fun . . . and then they are [also] *passionate*.

In what follows, I examine how Mexican gay men defined sexual passion; the comparisons my participants drew between Mexican/Latino and US White gay men with regard to passion; and the lesser patterns that destabilize somewhat the dominant discourse. I consider the characterization of Latino sexual passion as both a positive group quality and an oppressive sexual stereotype, and I also summarize my participants' views on the sexual passion of African Americans and Asian Americans. The various ways in which my participants talked about Latino sexual passion suggest the importance of scrutinizing this construction through multiple analytical lenses, including perspectives on sexual stereotyping, collective sexual reputations, sexual tropes and discourses, and sexual scripting.[3]

By considering simultaneously the perspectives of both Mexican/Latino men and non-Latino men, this analysis seeks to bring greater nuance to prevailing views about cross-racial sexual dynamics involving White men and men of color. The literature on this topic has typically sought to highlight the conditions of racial inequality and the disadvantaged position of gay men of color in Western societies. My analysis does something similar, but also considers how Mexicans and Latinos themselves participate in the racialization of other groups, including Whites. I therefore problematize a common assumption that, while White men's attraction to men of color should be seen as consistently exoticizing, fetishizing, and sexually objectifying, the ways in which men of color express a predilection for White men merely reflect a personal preference or, alternatively, forms of internalized racism and oppression.[4] Implied in this assumption is the idea that, because of their unequal position, men of color cannot sexually stereotype White men. And yet, a potentially controversial response to the apparent disparities of interpretation regarding men of color and White men—at least within the charged racial politics of gay male communities—is that when White men are referred to with labels such as *rice queen* or *bean queen*, they are indeed being sexually stereotyped[5] (albeit often from a position of less power). In my own analysis, I simultaneously attend to the vulnerabilities created by unequal social positions within sexual and romantic relations, the various forms of agency of both White and non-White partners, and the way in which tropes such as that of Latino sexual passion can be deployed concurrently as sexual stereotypes and as tools of empowerment and cultural affirmation.

The Trope of Mexican/Latino Sexual Passion

As suggested by several of the quotations I included in chapter 8, my study participants often believed that Mexicans and Latinos were more sexually passionate than US White men.[6] As part of this view, Mexican men defined sexual passion in terms that connected this notion to particular sexual dispositions they saw as influencing how individuals expressed themselves and used their bodies over the course of a sexual encounter. Leopoldo (born 1967), for instance, defined sexual passion as follows:

Passion is when you are with someone and you feel that internal connection . . . you feel something inside you that moves you; and it moves you to be with that person. . . . [Figuratively,] you want to eat him . . . that everything that you do is not enough. You want to do more. You embrace him and you want to embrace him tighter . . . or you are penetrating him or he is penetrating you and you want it to last longer. It's like you are really connected, because sometimes you can have sex, and, OK, you undress, you lie down, whatever, and you finish, and, whatever . . . you didn't connect. . . . [Passion] didn't exist; it was simply sex for the sake of sex. So, to me, when I say "passion," it is that that moves you, that helps you connect, that makes you vibrate in the moment and makes you feel full of energy. To me, that is passion.

Like Leopoldo, many other men referred to sexual passion as a disposition toward constructing an intense and embodied sense of connection. And they felt that Latinos, Mexicans in particular, were especially adept at pursuing sexually passionate encounters. In Donato's opinion (US Latino, born 1976), passion required the "total surrender of all senses, of all control . . . it's just about the lovemaking. So you don't realize that you're touching, you just realize that it's like you have melted into their bodies." Enacting sexual passion in this way meant that lovers ought to abandon themselves to its forces, and that such abandonment in turn created the conditions to achieve full fusion, which Donato poetically described as "these red waves kind of melting behind . . . or heating into these orange clouds up into the . . . crimson sky." With such images, he associated sexual passion with warm colors, which represented a vigorous landscape of emotional expression that he felt could be achieved only through intensely passionate sex. In this view, the passionate fusion of bodies was thought to emerge spontaneously when partners allowed themselves to get close to each other. As Bernardo (Mexican, born 1967) asserted, in a·passionate moment "you feel the warmth of the person's body, maybe [also] his breathing, which makes me think, wow, you couldn't be any closer to someone."[7]

Achieving such passionate fusion of bodies, many of these men said, required what Mexicans call *entrega*—Spanish for "delivery," "devotion," and "surrender." Armando (Mexican, born 1981) defined *entrega* as "allowing the person to be a part of you in the moment, and you a part of him . . . and it has a moment in which the two get to be one." Surrender, then, was seen as volitional and unidirectional, yet simultaneously mutual and enacted with the purpose of achieving a sense of intense connection. Many of the Mexican or US Latino participants in my study assumed that sexual passion could build over the course of a sexual encounter up to the point when it reached its ultimate height, which often, but not necessarily, took the form of orgasm (ideally, mutual orgasm). This is precisely the moment of jointly produced sexual ecstasy that Donato's poetic images of "red waves," "orange clouds," and "crimson sky" were meant to evoke. Moreover, for a sexual encounter to be called passionate, men said, it required a gentle (and never abrupt) return to the space of everyday life, which participants thought could be accomplished by prolonged postcoital embracing, kissing, and cuddling, accompanied by caring conversation during which sex partners could learn more about each other and extend their intimate connection once the sexual encounter is over. Taken together, all these steps suggest a carefully crafted, agreed-upon sexual script that many of my Mexican and US Latino participants seemed to understand and to have assimilated—and one that is very similar to the ways in which Mexicans (women and men, both straight and gay) interviewed for my previous study in Guadalajara spoke about sexual passion and how they valued it.[8]

Such a carefully produced sense of intimacy, men also said, was particularly crucial for a casual, one-time sexual encounter to be called passionate—especially given that, barring some unexpected turn of events, the sex partners were aware that they may never again interact in this same manner, or perhaps may never even see each other again. According to the logic of this sexual script, if deemed passionate and thus not impersonal, the sexual encounter could then enter a person's memory as an ephemeral yet meaningful experience of intense connection. It could become a case of what, based on my participants' descriptions, I have labeled "instant intimacy." The point here is that instant intimacy is not a contradiction in terms: it can indeed be fostered and produced, meaning that sexual passion and casual sex need not be seen as incompatible. Furthermore, although in my research in Mexico both straight and gay people strongly valued sexual relations that can be described as passionate, the possibilities of instant intimacy were expressed more directly by Mexican gay men—perhaps because members of this group were also more open to incorporating casual sex as part of their sexual repertoire— and the notion emerged again among the Mexican and Latino gay men in the present study.

In other words, within a sexual script informed by the idea and discourse of Latino sexual passion, which many of my participants felt Mexicans and Latinos favor, sexual passion is not seen as possible only in the context of romantic relations and love. Casual sexual encounters can be highly passionate, romantic, and emotional—the argument goes—and need not just be fleeting moments of instrumental, bodily, and sexual pleasure.

Hot Mexicans and Cold *Americanos*

Latino Cachondez

My participants' discussion of Latino sexual passion was directly connected to comparisons between Mexicans/Latinos and men of other racial, ethnic, and national groups. Indeed, among the 122 men who discussed the topic of sexual passion, 78 described Mexicans and US Latinos as more sexually passionate than US Whites. These 78 men comprise 43 of the 60 Mexican immigrants who discussed that topic, 13 of 31 US Latinos, and 22 of 31 non-Latinos. By contrast, only 4 Mexican men believed that US Whites were more passionate than Mexicans or Latinos (although, as we will see later, some others did think that US White men could be passionate in their own way). Among the remaining 40 men who discussed sexual passion, 9 made comments that included no racial references, and 31 argued that sexual passion was a purely individual characteristic, not one of any given racial or ethnic group. (Some members of this last group were inclined to believe that the notion of Latino sexual passion was merely a cultural and racial stereotype; however, some men recognized that "stereotypes exist for a reason," as Steven [US White, born 1974] put it.)

Those who saw Mexicans/Latinos as more sexually passionate described Mexicans and Latinos using terms such as *calientes* (hot), *fogosos* (fiery), and *candentes* (ardent). Armando said that "we Latino people have that warmth . . . that ability to turn others on with almost nothing. Mexicans are—vulgarly speaking—hot." Ezequiel (Mexican, born 1970) similarly stated, "We are more *fogosos*, we have more fire than them." Notably, all but one of the nineteen participants who referred to Mexican/Latino "hotness" were Mexican themselves, suggesting the degree to which this notion circulated among gay Mexican men.[9] Implicit in this view was also a shared understanding of *cachondez*, a Spanish term that denotes the ability to use caresses, kisses, and full-body exploration as tools for building sexual passion. Describing a man as *cachondo* implies that he is skillful in his sexual pursuits. As Humberto (Mexican, born 1975) put it, "I think they [Mexicans] have more *mañas* [skills, tricks, knacks] in making love to you, in having sex with you." Horacio (Mexican, born 1982) likewise related sexual passion to how Mexicans used their bodies during sex: "Our body is very different, like . . . it arouses us; we are very hot in doing it." *Cachondez* was expected to be enacted at all stages of a sexual encounter—before, during, and after sex—for it to generate and sustain a sense that the encounter was passionate. In the opinion of Facundo (Mexican, born 1967):

As we say in Mexico, Mexicans or Latinos are more *cachondos* than Americans, a bit hotter, a bit more expressive. What do I know? For example, in the sex that I had with an American, we would have the [sexual] relation and finish, and then [he] to one side and I to the other side of the bed. With a Mexican, you finish and you embrace and it's different, it's different.

In this quotation, as in other comments made by Mexican men, "Americans" stands for US Whites.

These various assessments by my participants confirm that they regarded the construction of sexual passion as involving scripted behaviors they recognized as having the power to ignite and sustain a sense of deep intimacy; paradoxically, however, they also expected intimacy to be spontaneous and unscripted. Nonetheless, as part of the script, men outlined a sequence of actions that included passionate kissing (being "more intense with kissing," as Máximo [Mexican, born 1964] put it), whole-body interaction (as opposed to a sole focus on the genitals or on specific practices such as oral or anal intercourse), and a series of unexpected romantic gestures that must be enacted over the course of a sexual interaction and beyond.

Indeed, participants often referred to Mexicans/Latinos as *detallistas*, a word that signals their ability to implement simple romantic actions meant to suggest thoughtfulness, attentiveness, and affection, and regarded as unexpected and spontaneous. Those include lighting candles, engaging in romantic caresses, and sensually touching the other man's body in ways he might not anticipate. Men such as Ronaldo (Mexican, born 1970) talked about having "a flower or a card, a little present" to offer someone (which he also appreciated receiving), and Doug (US White, born ca. 1980) said that Mexicans spontaneously "whisper things in your ear. They'll whisper things in Spanish, 'cause they think it'll get you going. They say '*ay amor*' and stuff [like that] in your ear."

In addition, men interpreted these various actions and gestures as evidence that, compared with US Whites, Mexicans/Latinos were "more interested in what the person is experiencing," which also indicates that they were more personal, giving, and "not real self-centered," as Jesse (US White, born 1966) explained. Mexicans/Latinos were also deemed in touch with their and the other's feelings, which Toribio (Mexican, born 1971), speaking in English, described as emotionally and not just physically intimate expressions:

The spiciness? [*laughter*] I think in the intimate moment . . . it becomes more intimate than just the act. It's not just the penetration, it's [looking] them in the eye . . . feeling what you're doing, when you're touched in the right moment. "Kiss me, when you're feeling. Make me feel more." I have that in my blood. I'm going to jump in my skin. I'm not afraid of telling you what to do. It's just that part of it that I believe [is] more Latin . . . like that I have less reserve of, "Oh, don't touch that; don't touch me there; oh, that's too much kissing there." We give ourselves more. We open up. We're . . . not afraid of showing you the real me, the real who I am. "This is me."

This sentiment was echoed by Bane (Filipino American, born 1980), who said of Latinos:

There's intimacy feel to it, the way they touch you, the way they hold you. It feels really good. And you feel like he's really taking care, taking his time and taking care of . . . how you feel.

Men saw the ability to pay attention to what the other is feeling, and take care of the other, as related to Latinos' emphasis on giving themselves fully during sexual encounters. This perception circles back to the kind of surrender (*entrega*) that participants considered to be a basic building block of sexual passion. A similar sense also surfaced in comments about the importance of extended foreplay along with the ability to extend a sexual encounter beyond orgasm, which men saw as the opposite of the "the climb on, get off" pattern—to use Nicholas's words (US White, born 1951)—they felt that most US-White men were more likely to enact.

Icy US Whites

By contrast, twenty-nine men, most of them Mexicans, viewed US White men as cold, or *fríos*. But this figure is much smaller than the seventy-eight men who believed Mexicans/Latinos to be hotter than US Whites, suggesting that many participants emphasized Latino passion as a positive cultural trait among Mexicans/Latinos without necessarily observing the opposite among US Whites or devaluing them as a consequence.

A number of Mexicans expressed being surprised when US White men abruptly asked them to leave right after having sex, sometimes citing practical reasons (having an early start the next day or wanting to sleep alone) or simply indicating that sex was over and consequently their connection was over, too. As Leopoldo (Mexican) noted, they say, "We're done. It was a pleasure. See you later. Get dressed and leave, I'm done." Similarly, Hilario (Mexican, born 1965) said that "Americans are a little bit colder. They are not into caressing. And then you finish sex, and it's, like, each one to their side." And Román (Mexican, born 1983) commented that "[US Whites] come for what they want [*a lo que van*], and then they leave. They're not afraid to tell you what they want. They're very direct." This sense that US White men tended to end an interaction as soon as orgasm was reached (as one participant puts it, "You finish, and bye, bye") was seen by Mexicans as betraying an important requirement of sexual passion, and as signaling the value that US White men placed on practicality as the exact opposite of sexual passion. By this reading, these men violated the principles of instant intimacy by treating casual sex dispassionately.

Similar views were expressed by some non-Latinos as they explained why they themselves were attracted to Mexicans and Latinos and not to US Whites. Peter (US White, born 1968) indicated that "the sex with White guys that I've had, it just seems to be more like sex, and that's it, over and done with," and Tameron (African American, born 1962) believed that "for Caucasians, I think it's just the act."

Perhaps most graphically, several participants used expressions such as "wham bam," "*pum, pum*," "*bum, bum, taz*," and "*zas, zas*" to represent the expedient nature and rapid pace of this kind of sexual interaction, which they did not favor. Linked to these ideas about US White practicality and expediency was the notion that US White men tended to implement instrumental sexual sequences meant to produce self-satisfaction through stimulation of particular body parts, rather than seeking to generate whole-body involvement and a strong sense of connection and intimacy with sex partners.[10] Participants therefore suggested that US White men separated intimacy from sex, and they saw evidence of that in these men's refusal to kiss during casual sexual encounters. Saul (US Latino, born 1975) said that "White guys don't really get into the passionate kissing," and Hugo (Mexican, born 1974) indicated that "they don't know how to kiss, at least not as I like; they don't kiss you all over the whole body." In Ray's (US White, born 1971) opinion:

[US White men] don't know how to kiss. . . . They just want to get it, have sex, and that's it, finish. . . . It's not fun. It's more like a job with White guys, you know? With Latinos it's more fun, it's more adventurous, it's more . . . trying different things. But with White guys it's just the same thing, get down and dirty and then that's it.

These perceptions led some Mexican participants to describe US White men as bad lovers. Máximo remarked, "I'm not attracted to *güeros* [blonds, meaning "whites"]. I find them very dumb in terms of kissing and all that." Similarly, Hugo said he found US Whites physically attractive, but "the thing is that . . . the more attractive they are . . . the more stupid they are having sex [*laughter*]." And some blamed circumcision for White men's lack of passion. "I feel they have less sensitivity," said Joaquín (Mexican, born 1981). "I think someone with a foreskin is more sensitive toward me."

Furthermore, accompanying the overall perception that US White men were "straight to the point"—as Scott (US Latino, born 1973) put it—was a commonly expressed sense that they were not spontaneous. Participants voiced this idea by saying that they were "mechanical" (Oscar, Mexican, born 1976; Lance, US Latino, born 1967; Jesse, US White), "excessively technical" (Heriberto, Mexican, born 1973), "like a machine" (Oton, US Latino, born 1974), "calculating" (Bernardo, Mexican), and "plastic" (Roy, Mexican, born 1969). Roy went so far as to suggest that having sex with a US White man was like "being with a plastic doll." Finally, US White men were also described as uninterested in their sex partners— "they keep that self-centeredness . . . like, 'I'm here to satisfy myself,'" said Bernardo—and callous, as Melchor (Mexican, born 1972) concluded when he stated, "I've never experienced tender sex with Americans."

The perceived outcome of these cultural traits was the enactment of sexual encounters that a number of Mexican participants in my study thought of as not passionate, and that to them resembled the scripted sequences of US gay pornography. In Roy's opinion, "It's like in a porn film. ¡*Orale!* [Come on!]. . . . Doing all that ritual; it's so monotonous and flavorless." Similarly, Melchor described such a sequence in these terms: "When I've been with Anglos . . . penetrating and that's it; maybe oral sex. It's like a porn film. They start kissing. They start undressing. And they start fucking."

Challenges to the Discourse of Latino Sexual Passion

Nonetheless, these two images of the hot, passionate Mexican or Latino and the cold, dispassionate US White man were destabilized by two other, lesser patterns of interpretation that emerged in my study. A minority of participants believed that US White gay men could be sexually passionate in their own way. A few others also noted that not all Mexican or Latino men were sexually passionate.

In speaking of the idea that US White gay men could be passionate in their own way, some men emphasized that compared with Mexicans, American gay men were more sexually liberal. Although these comments referred to US gay men in general, they conveyed the sense that mainstream urban gay cultures were primarily White. By sexually liberal, participants meant that compared with Mexicans, US White gay men had adopted a wider range of partnering possibilities (including threesomes, open relations, group sex, orgies, and sex parties as legitimate possibilities); were more direct about expressing their sexual desires, and had created sex venues explicitly designed for that purpose, including gay bathhouses and sex clubs; were not shy about using sexual devices and other methods for enhancing sexual pleasure (from sex toys to recreational drugs); and sometimes were more open to enacting nonconventional sexual practices, including those associated with kink and BDSM.[11] In these assessments, men viewed the sexual liberalism of mainstream US gay culture as connected to a different way of being sexually passionate. In this view, sexual passion was perceived as related to an ability to challenge and surpass the erotic limits imposed by heteronormative sexual conventionality.

Perhaps not surprisingly, men in my study who thought of US White gay men as passionate in their own way were usually the Mexican and Latino participants who felt that their own sexual cultures were overly sexually conservative, craved participating in American gay cultures they perceived as mainstream, or were primarily attracted to US White men. Aldo (Mexican, born 1971) thought of Mexicans as sexually inhibited, and indicated that "there are Americans who are very passionate. . . . I really admire Americans. They are very liberal in bed." And Fermín (Mexican, born 1977), who reported being primarily attracted to Whites, said that "Americans are, I believe, better trained in bed." However, he followed this statement with a backhanded compliment:

They're more experimental. . . . Sex for them is more like a sport. It doesn't mean that it is more fun, but yes, more like a sport. Here they use lots of devices, such as toys. They are fanatical about that. They're more intense. . . . They do it more theatrically. . . . *And I am not saying it is not spontaneous* [*said in English*]. . . . At first I would feel inhibited, because I would say, "What's all that screaming, what's all that posturing?" Because it is like being onstage. . . . But for them, it's natural. And that's the culture of sex here. . . . It's the culture of porn films. When having sex, people want to do it like in the films. That's what I think.

This list of behaviors provided by Fermín is precisely what other participants read as a sign of US Whites' impersonal way of having sex. Indeed, other participants contrasted the romantic ways in which Mexicans liked to have sex with practices such as "hanging off the ceiling" (Octavio, Mexican, born 1977), "playing with toys . . . the dildos" (Alvaro, Mexican, born 1967), and being "dirtier" in sex (Pascual, US Latino, born 1966), all of which they saw as indicative of impersonal and instrumental sex. Along these lines, Domingo (born in the US in 1976, but raised in Mexico), talked about a partner who

started bringing up the idea of a whip, of having me tie up his wrists, things that I didn't find [attractive] . . . one surrenders more to caresses, to a more normal relation, right? With kisses, and embraces, and *apapachos* [pampering], and *agasajo* [pleasurable body contact]. And they [US Whites] go more for erotic games.

Domingo further complained that this partner wanted them to participate in orgies and sex parties, "which didn't go with me."

These comments also relate to a perception that to US White gay men, intensity and passion meant roughness, not connection. As Evan (US Latino, born 1971) said:

A White guy can only be passionate or he can be rough, but he can't be both at the same time. I don't know how to explain that. . . . It's like . . . if they want to get rough, they always confuse it with S&M, they always want to slap you or have you call them sir or some stupid crap like that. . . . A Mexican will be very dominant with you, but he doesn't want you to call him sir and all this paddle and whip crap. I don't know. It's more of a machismo, and not [an] S&M thing. I hate that stuff.

For other men, however, being macho was precisely how Mexicans/Latinos were not sexually passionate. Men who made this argument noted that in heavily gendered encounters, the *mayates*—masculine, non-gay-identified men who have sex with gay men just to get their own pleasure—showed no regard toward the male sex partners they were penetrating. In Alfaro's experience (Mexican, born 1971),

They just get there, they bend you over, they stick it inside, they clean themselves, and they leave. And they leave you there as their *pendejo* [idiot]. And you ask yourself, 'What about me? How will I finish? I also want to feel pleasure. *I want some of that* [*said in English*]. . . . But they only get their own pleasure.

For those same reasons, *mayates* often did not kiss, embrace, or even sexually touch their male partners. Bernardo (Mexican) similarly said, "I would not expect passion [with them]. . . . Obviously, the person has to be aroused to be able to cum, but there isn't anything in the way of caresses . . . [or suggesting] that they are attracted to you." He further described sex with *mayates* as impersonal: "Perhaps we are in the same room, but it is as if we were miles apart." And Inti (Mexican, born 1978) opined that "they just want to ejaculate, and they don't care if you already ejaculated, or if you are enjoying or not," and, in relationships, "they only want you to serve them . . . they just want you to . . . 'bring me this, bring me that.' . . . And I dislike that . . . it's not mutual."

Interestingly, these various perceptions about *mayates* would suggest that they would be compatible with US White men who liked rougher, more instrumental, and more impersonal sex. This idea was suggested by Robin (US White, born 1962), who indicated that some American men may "want the Latin stud, matador-type guy, which I think is pretty hot, too." The limitation, however, would be the absence of reciprocation. "If they don't reciprocate, it's really boring," Robin said pointedly, articulating what he saw as an American gay expectation of sexual role versatility that Mexican *mayates* were not assumed to accept.

But some American men did mention that they thought of Mexicans as generally more sexually aggressive than Americans. But the meaning of *aggressiveness* varied widely. Participants sometimes referred to Mexicans' aggressiveness as "roughness," which would be consistent with the image of the dominant *mayate*. Gary (US White, born 1977) said he liked to have sex with Latinos who were rough and who engaged in what he called "wrestle sex," which he found "ravishing." By contrast, others thought of Mexican aggressiveness in terms of their initiative and willingness to engage in full-body exploration during sex. As Steven (US White) put it, he liked that "Mexican natives" could be aggressive, but by this he meant that "they're more willing to explore, they're great kissers. . . . They're more open to experience." And some considered a mix of these two definitions of aggressiveness. Saul (US Latino) suggested that Mexicans could be "real strong and rough in the edges," and "aggressive to get the person to bed . . . and they confuse that with passion." But he added that "when you're behind closed doors or under the sheets, it's just this human being that wants to be loved and touched, just like everybody else."

Finally, perhaps not surprisingly, Mexican participants who had primarily interacted sexually with *mayates* in Mexico were precisely the ones who found US White gay men more caring, romantic, and passionate. "Americans are much more attentive," Inti remarked. "That's happened to me, that they are much more caring, and they ask me if I am enjoying what they are doing, and Latinos don't." And Venustiano (Mexican, born 1975) felt that *güeros* were affectionate, honest, and always "thinking about satisfying the other. . . . Maybe they are more satisfied by giving, by making the other person feel good."[12] As part of this view, US White men were generally seen as being less jealous than Mexicans, as well as, in Inti's words, "tenderer, more patient, [and] more affectionate with you. . . . If you go to a movie, they tell you, 'Do you need this?' or 'Do you want me to bring you a soda?' and you feel real good." In this interpretation, they emerge as "more *detallistas*," more caring, as Eliseo (Mexican, born 1962) put it, a view contradicting what others said about Mexicans and Latinos, which I noted earlier.

Indeed, this contradiction points to a somewhat dualistic view of Mexican/Latino men that some participants held, and which I believe is connected to the competing tropes of the macho, uncaring, non-gay-identified Mexican *mayate* and the passionate, caring, sweet Mexican/Latino gay man, each of whom was sometimes depicted as intense, possessive, and obsessive in his own way. Mitchell (US White, born 1964) described Mexicans and Latinos as "very extreme, there's no middle ground," and then went on to say:

Either they can be extremely loyal and then extremely possessive of you, or they can be the complete opposite, so they don't have a lot of middle ground. . . . I've met Latin men that are so intense that . . . all of a sudden they want to be [your] boyfriend after the first date.

This comment also suggests a perceived "darker side" to Latino passion that some participants viewed as a risk worth taking and a better alternative to a lack of sexual passion. As a participant in my earlier research in Mexico put it, "Passion is a fire that burns you, but you don't want to move away from it."[13]

Latino Sexual Passion as an Oppressive Cultural Stereotype

At first glance, the view that Mexicans/Latinos are hot and Whites are cold can be easily construed as merely reflecting cultural stereotypes. Indeed, the perception of Latino passion as a sexual stereotype seems to be linked to the image of the "Latin lover" that had permeated popular culture in the United States and beyond many decades ago, perhaps since before that fateful moment in 1921 when the Italian actor Rudolph Valentino stepped onto the silver screen dressed as an Argentine gaucho in the *Four Horsemen of the Apocalypse*.[14] The image of the dark and dangerously alluring, exotic and powerfully romantic Latin man has been in the minds of every generation, both in the United States and abroad. After Valentino's sudden death in 1926, the Latin lover reputation was picked up by others who turned it into successful careers in movies, television, and music, from the Mexican silent movie star Ramón Novarro, to the actor Ricardo Montalbán, to contemporary heartthrobs such as Antonio Banderas and Ricky Martin. This representation of the Latin lover has been faulted for contributing to enduring cultural stereotypes about the populations of southern European countries such as Italy, Spain, and Portugal, and of the Spanish- and Portuguese-speaking nations of Latin America.[15]

In my study, sensitivity to, and concern about, stereotypes could be found among all three groups of men. These participants recognized that not all men within any given cultural group were sexually passionate, and they viewed sexual passion as a purely individual characteristic. Such men indicated that "there's just different types of guys in all races" (Kevin, US White, born 1964), "everyone is different in their lovemaking" (Shawn, African American, born 1976), and "you can't generalize something like that" (Harris, US Latino, born 1963).

Some went even further. They argued that the notion of Latino sexual passion was just "a myth" (Edwin, Mexican, born 1974) and a cultural imposition that was demeaning to Mexican/Latino men. As Eugenio (US Latino, born 1979) put it, "I think that's just like exoticizing and fetishizing Latino men, 'cause . . . it is the Latino lover phenomenon. And I think [if] you buy into it enough, you're going to start believing in it." Eugenio went on to state that Latino sexual passion "is just a way to . . . hypersexualize Latinos and discredit them in . . . dominant society . . . the way to oppress them." Similarly, Ignacio (US Latino, born 1970) called Latino sexual passion a "crock of shit," but then turned this around by adding, "I think Latinos should use it to their advantage whenever they can." It is noteworthy that all but one of the fourteen participants who explicitly described Latino sexual passion as a stereotype were US born, which suggests that racial/cultural stereotyping may be a more sensitive social issue in the United States than in Mexico. In Eugenio's case, after hearing himself talk about exoticization, fetishization, and hypersexualization, he added, with a laugh and a hint of irony, "and that's my [liberal university] background coming out right there."

Comments about Other American Men

The various comparisons I have discussed in this chapter mainly involved Mexicans/Latinos and US White men (represented by Mexicans' use of the word *americanos*). However, a few men in my study talked specifically about Blacks and Asians, and although the patterns are somewhat less clear, they are nonetheless interesting. Seventeen men mentioned African American gay men. Some saw them as equally passionate to, or more passionate than, Mexicans/Latinos, while others placed them in an intermediate category between US Whites and Mexicans/Latinos. And still others spoke of African American men as not at all passionate, and viewed them as similar to US Whites. Asian Americans were mentioned only occasionally, and they were usually paired with Whites in terms of sexual passion, or seen as even less sexually passionate than Whites.

Finally, a few men differentiated between US Latinos and Mexicans by placing the former in a middle category between Whites and Mexicans, suggesting that US Latinos have become "Americanized" but still retain some characteristics that make them sexually similar to Mexicans. But Mexican men occasionally reported experiencing with US Latinos the very same cultural differences they experienced with US Whites. Tadeo (born in the US in 1976, but raised in Mexico) described in somewhat imperfect English a casual sexual interaction with a Mexican American partner. This man after penetrating him "wasn't even worried about me, how I feel, what I think about." Tadeo went on:

He just stand up and walk to the bathroom and came out of the bathroom and told me, "Are you going or what?" I told him, "Yeah, I'm going." He's like, "OK, I am sleepy, and if you're gonna leave, you better do it now." I feel so bad, because . . . that was humiliating for me.

He bitterly remarked that he did not like to be treated that way. "I'm not a hooker; he's not paying me." And he also felt used. As he put it, "I feel like somebody is using you like a rag to clean his dick." During the encounter, the man used a lot of dirty words, which he said in English. This contributed to Tadeo's sense that the sexual encounter had been rather harsh. "English is a hard language," he stated. "The words have to be aggressive to make it sound the way it is. When you are having sex, the words sound so mean. It's so hard." And he then contrasted English spoken during sex with Spanish spoken during sex: "Spanish is a soft language, it's romantic." By alluding to language differences, Tadeo suggested that Spanish speakers (Mexicans) were passionate and romantic in part because of their language (and thus because of their culture), while English made Americans (including Latinos sometimes) express themselves sexually in aggressive and impersonal ways.

Stereotypes, Cultural Distinctiveness, and Erotic Capital

Overall, the discourse of Latino passion is deemed to confer erotic capital on Mexican gay and bisexual immigrants in US settings, and yet this erotic capital is not necessarily perceived as giving them a position of greater power in their relationships with Americans, particularly US White gay men. This view is consistent with Adam Green's analysis of the relative position of "black gay men in a white-dominated, middle-class sexual field"—men who become "cognizant of their racialized erotic capital" but simultaneously "resent fetishization."[16] As Green has also suggested, men of color learn to play with the social and erotic stratification of White-dominated sexual fields, and align themselves "with a specific racialized currency of erotic capital in order to attract white partners and gain field advantage" (in other words, exercise whatever erotic capital a stratified and racialized sexual field grants them).[17]

That the trope of Mexican/Latino sexual passion might constitute a source of erotic capital for Mexicans and Latinos within a racialized sexual field points to the importance of examining my participants' narratives for the tension between passion as a sexual stereotype (with all the negative connotations conveyed by the word *stereotype*) and passion as a "true" characteristic and a cultural trait of Mexicans and Latinos (which allows passion to be viewed as a collective cultural or sexual reputation). This distinction is important to make because, while stereotypes can only be disavowed (suggesting the sense that stereotypes are by definition disempowering), collective reputations can be reconstructed and turned around.[18]

But as these men work to maintain a strong sense of cultural distinctiveness as signaled by the notion of Latino sexual passion, they are not oblivious to the actual consequences of power differentials in the relationships they establish. A common concern among immigrant men is that US White partners sometimes use their more privileged social position to the detriment of their Mexican partners—in both sexual and nonsexual contexts.

TEN

Power, Vulnerability, and Passion

One of my friends is very hairy. I mean, he's natural; I mean, he's Mexican, he has a lot of hair. And his [White] boyfriend says. . . . "I don't like touching you, so I want you to go and get . . . your body waxed." And I was, like, "Did the motherfucker tell you [*laughs*] to get waxed?" That was just shocking to me—that, I mean, he would go and get waxed. "Oh, no, I wanted to, too." I said, "Before or after he asked you to?" So, I mean, it's . . . I don't know, that's probably the reason why I'm single [*laughs*]. . . . I think things like that . . . really angered me because, to me, [it's] definitely devaluing someone when you say, "There's something about you I don't like that I want you to go and change."

Jaed (African American, born 1967) narrated this anecdote as he spoke critically about Mexican friends who were attracted to US White men and who, in his opinion, were willing to put up with White partners' arbitrary use of their more privileged and powerful position in US society—partners who felt entitled to make unreasonable requests of partners of color. Further dramatizing his point, Jaed said, "To me, it would [be] almost like cutting off my arm because that person didn't like my arm. I mean, not to that extreme, but . . ." He described this particular Mexican friend as someone who held "an ideal that if he dates somebody who's Caucasian, it brings him certain status. And I think he thinks that if I date somebody White, it's going to bring me certain status, too." For that reason, he said, he and this friend "argue about race all the time."

By his comments, Jaed seemed to imply that this friend lacked the racial awareness to accurately interpret the racial

233

power dynamics at play when this partner asked him to "get waxed." He joked that such an awareness prompted him to remain single. Then, more seriously, he related his own preference for dating only other men of color—namely Black men and Latinos, and explained why:

Being Black and gay in this community, or Latino and gay, or Mexican and gay . . . you have a totally different experience from someone who's White. And I don't . . . think we can relate. . . . And I don't want to be in a relationship where I'm constantly trying to prove my point of view, or when I come home from dealing with the stuff you have to deal with . . . you know what I mean?

Jaed recognized that "[it's] not that the person of color is automatically going to understand, but I think it's, it's better than trying to explain it to someone who . . . always had privilege and never had to deal with walking into a store and having people follow you around, after you've worked all day." He soberly concluded, "That's the last fucking thing you want [*laughs*]. . . . Coming home, and then you see the face of the oppressor that you saw in the store. . . . I just don't think, in my psyche . . . no, it's not going to work."

As Jaed's poignant comments suggest, his own experience as an African American told him that White privilege in the United States inevitably flavored cross-racial relations between White men and men of color. He saw little hope that such relations could ever be egalitarian, and so he avoided them. Moreover, he perceived that Mexican gay immigrants such as his friend often lacked the savviness to recognize racism in the same way as someone like him, who grew up being Black in the United States. Yet, as we will see, Mexican gay men sometimes sought an alternative way of responding to the inequalities and vulnerabilities they perceived.

————

In this final empirical chapter, I continue my discussion of the dynamics of cross-racial sexual and romantic relationships by focusing on the dimensions of power they can contain. This analysis highlights that gay men who participate in cross-racial relations often become adept at understanding their dynamics in both cultural and structural terms, in ways that focus our attention on both "marked" racial categories like Latino and "unmarked" ones like White. This issue relates to what Ruth Frankenberg called the "linked dimensions" of race, which she described in calling attention to the characteristics of whiteness as a distinct social construction. "First, whiteness is a location of structural advantage, of race privilege," she observed. "Second, it is a 'standpoint,' a place from which white people look at ourselves, at others, and at society. Third, 'whiteness' refers to a set of cultural practices that are usually unmarked and unnamed."[1] Moreover, whiteness is emerging as a distinct cultural and political identity, as recent political developments have placed it at the center of national debates in the United States.

Like Jaed, other participants in my study realized that the relative social standing of their sexual and romantic partners could generate power differentials between them. In addition, Mexican gay men's participation in sexual contexts that were brand-new to them—contexts where they often engaged in cross-cultural and cross-racial encounters, and where they were forced to interpret their partners' actions at the same time that they are learning the rules of the game—might heighten those vulnerabilities. Furthermore, beyond the structural inequalities and vulnerabilities produced by racial difference, participants also assigned a role to culture as a marker of difference. They thereby recognized that highlighting perceived cultural differences across racial/ethnic groups could help them conduct boundary work and articulate a sense of symbolic boundaries between racial/ethnic groups.[2] As we will see, insofar as this boundary work was carried out by Mexican men and US Latinos, their efforts constitute a reversal of what Wendy Roth has called the "boundary maintenance" by an American White mainstream that prevents Latinas/os, even those who have a "European appearance," from ever being "considered White by American standards."[3] By engaging in their own version of a kind of cultural boundary work motivated by the trope of Latino sexual passion, Mexican men developed a strong sense of cultural pride—and perhaps even of moral advantage over US White men. I therefore argue that they saw this strategy as a cultural response to their racialization within US society,[4] and as a way to "speak back to whiteness."[5] Consequently, they developed a sense that their having been socialized within Mexican/Latino culture may be culturally beneficial.

As part of my discussion, I also examine American men's (mainly US Whites') perspectives on the cross-cultural dynamics of their relationships with Mexicans. On the one hand, by highlighting Mexicans' sexual passion, and through their awareness, at times, of the structural inequalities that affect Mexican immigrants, these men sometimes explicitly sought to cast a positive light on their partners' lives and cultures. This should already be evident from my discussion in chapter 8 of the appreciation for Mexican/Latino culture expressed by some US White men in describing their attraction to Mexicans and Latinos. On the other hand, some Mexican participants reported that US White partners assumed they were superior, and took advantage of the vulnerabilities affecting immigrant partners (especially those who were undocumented).

Power Differentials and Vulnerability

Study participants understood that power differentials become manifest in many possible ways over the course of romantic and sexual relations. They realized that these differences in relationships can generate vulnerabilities for the sex partners who find themselves in a more disadvantaged position. And they recognized that power differentials are linked to various forms of inequality, including racial and economic disparities, and that those inequalities are sometimes brought into the dynamics of sexual encounters. This section examines power differentials and vulnerabilities that my participants brought up over the course of their interviews. As may be expected, these men often referred to the more disadvantaged position of Mexican immigrants (and Latinos more generally) in the United States.

My analysis speaks to the importance of attending to "the ways in which [erotic] desires simultaneously map onto and reconfigure power relations that originate in other fields," as Adam Green has proposed, as well as to "histories of subjectification and inequality" that emerge in the context of "collective erotic life."[6] These goals relate to Green's efforts to better incorporate dimensions of power into analyses of the enactment of sexual scripts.[7] As suggested by my discussion of sexual passion, the sexual interactions between American men and Mexican immigrant men that I analyzed are particularly helpful for us to observe the dynamics of interactions in which each partner is operating with a different sexual script. They are also helpful to understand how sex partners seek to make sense of each other's actions based on the logics of the cultural scenarios—to use Simon and Gagnon's terminology—to which they were exposed in their separate contexts. I therefore focus on dimensions of power that affect those interactions, first by discussing the perceived effects of financial disparities and the vulnerabilities created by some of my Mexican participants' undocumented status. Then the chapter examines two ways in which dimensions of power emerge in the context of sex itself: in the use of racialized language during sexual encounters, and in Mexican gay men's experimentation with shifting their sexual roles (particularly from being receptive to insertive during anal intercourse), which some of them see as empowering.

The Effects of Financial Disparities

Hernán (Mexican, born 1971) indicated that he was physically attracted to US White men, "but once I start interacting with them, they disappoint me." He was unhappy that, in his view, US White men used their privileged social status to dominate Latino partners. He felt that some White men thought, "I am the one with power. You have nothing. I govern you," which to him "makes no sense." Hernán described a relationship that he had with a White man from Nebraska:

We always had problems, because of differences between us. I made less money, and he looked down on me. He would order me, "We will go to this place," [or] "We're now going to speak in English," because he felt we spoke too much Spanish. I told him, "You know what, I'm not pointing a gun at you and forcing you to speak to me in my own language; I don't know why you always talk to me in Spanish."

To this, his partner would respond that he spoke to him in Spanish "because I say things to you, and you don't understand." Hernán recalled that his answer to this was, "OK, yes, but you can repeat [the same things in English] so that I can learn, otherwise I'll never learn." He did not mention, however, how or why this partner spoke Spanish, or what that said about him compared with other men who would not be interested in speaking anything other than English.

This partner had proposed to Hernán that if he moved in with him, he would support him. He wanted Hernán not to work, offering him instead the opportunity to focus on learning English and finishing school. Hernán, however, was wary about accepting his partner's offer, because he felt that it came with "an imposition of certain rules." He was thinking of a previous time when they had lived together. The partner paid the rent, which provided Hernán basic support. However, Hernán said, "I paid for groceries, I cooked, I cleaned the apartment, I washed his clothes . . . I paid my part when we ate out. I paid half of the phone and gas. All that he paid was the rent. And on top of everything, I also took care of his dog." Hernán had insisted on paying his share at restaurants despite having very little money to spare. Otherwise, he said, "when we fought . . . he would say hurtful things like, 'I'm tired of paying for you and seeing you just make an innocent face, like a boy who is waiting for me to pay.' "

Referring to another partner, Hernán again brought up the issue of financial disparities. He disliked the fact that this second partner would invite him to go out and then ask him to split the bill. For him, a more logical arrangement would be for the person who issued the invitation to pay, which he seemed to imply was customary in Mexico.[8] Hernán also recalled that this man would simply command him to go out and would not give him the choice of eating at home, which Hernán saw as an alternative to spending money he did not have. The interviewer asked Hernán whether he ever invited this partner to go out, and if so whether *he* paid the bill. Hernán responded that he had never issued such an invitation, because he did not have money to pay for both of them. Instead, he said, he would cook at home—which he could afford—and invite his partner to eat with him at his place. But even then, his partner sometimes insisted that they go out instead.

Hernán felt that these dynamics were caused by strong disparities in his relationships with US White partners, and that those disparities seemed to be exacerbated by what he saw as cultural differences concerning the etiquette of inviting and paying. He had developed a strong sense that US White men presented themselves as generous, but in reality used their privilege and power to control their less-privileged partners.

Although Hernán complained about the effects of economic disparities on relationships, other Mexican men occasionally were lured by the economic position of US White men, along with the social mobility they felt those men might provide them. Reinaldo (Mexican, born 1963) commented:

In terms of the rent, I've never seen any bills. I've always lived with my partners, and they take care of it. That's why I've chosen Americans, because they provide me a better economic position than a Mexican guy who is my same situation. That is the reason I've chosen them; and also because I like them.

Another interesting example is provided by Teodoro (Mexican, born 1966). After he ended a very unequal seven-year relationship with a man in Mexico—he had become "tired of being the provider"—Teodoro considered looking for a man who could support him:

I thought, "perhaps I can find someone who says, 'Come along, *mijo* [a contraction of *mi hijo*, "my son," and a term of endearment], I'll support you.' " The truth is that I thought that, and I also thought, "Where am I going to find him? On the other side [of the border], not here in Mexico."

This, he said, "was just a fleeting thought" that he never pursued, especially since he had an "aversion to *gente gabacha*" (a reference to US Whites).

Joaquín (Mexican, born 1981) was similarly wary of relationships with men who had more money than he. He felt that having a higher economic position encouraged older men to pursue him who otherwise would not have felt entitled. He was resentful that, as he put it, "the ones that approach me are sugar daddies." However, Plutarco (Mexican, born 1975) described a relationship with a White man that seemed based on that premise. At the time, he was twenty-nine and his partner forty-seven. Before relocating to San Diego, where his partner lived, Plutarco was living in Ensenada and traveling to San Diego to spend time with him. When visiting, his partner paid "all the expenses: going out dancing, and to dinner. I'm going to the gym here, and he pays my fees. And if I am short on money, he also pays my way to get here." Plutarco had no conflict about this, because his partner "had to understand that I'm younger; what he makes in an hour I can't make in a whole day." However, earlier in his interview, he indicated that the couple often had conflicts, because his partner "is older and always wants to be in control of things."

The Threat of Deportation

Beyond the economic disparities that made some Mexican immigrants feel vulnerable in their relationships with American men, those who were undocumented felt that their vulnerability was exacerbated by the possibility that a disgruntled partner would report them to the immigration authorities. Justo (Mexican, born 1971), for instance, said that if partners "become angry, they can just pick up the phone and get you in trouble." He claimed he had seen this happen to two separate friends, and they were deported. And whether this had actually happened or not, Justo's comment denotes a sense of vulnerability among undocumented Mexican men that is independent of whether American men would actually take action against them. Despite this sense of risk, Justo had chosen not to lie or keep his immigration status secret, and he freely told friends and partners that he was undocumented. "I know I'm playing with fire," he said.

Things happen, but at the same time, I can't live with such fear. It's enough to live with everyday fears. To be [constantly] thinking that you'll be caught and they will throw you out: Why add one more fear?

Julián (Mexican, born 1978), however, had actually experienced the threat of deportation firsthand. This happened to him after he had participated in a threesome involving a US White man and his Mexican boyfriend. During that encounter, Julián asked the US White man to stop penetrating him because he was feeling pain. The man refused to stop. After the incident, Julián felt that this man had been abusive. When he told the story to others, they encouraged him to make a police report, which Julián did. But the case went nowhere because of lack of evidence. Sometime later, he ran into this man. "He threatened me," Julián said. "He said if I went back to the police . . . if I said anything else against him, his lawyers could grab me and deport me."

Finally, Fidel (Mexican, born 1971) discussed having received approval for legal status in the United States, and said he was awaiting his documents. But he still felt that in the absence of these papers, his partner continued to treat him unequally based on the thought that "you're still not fully legal here, so I can do with you as I want." Fidel perceived that his partner's view was that Fidel "would never be an American. You may have your papers, but you will never be truly American."

To be sure, rather than using their Mexican partners' immigration status against them, several US White participants in my study were expressly concerned about the possibility that their undocumented boyfriends could be caught and deported. Peter (US White, born 1968) said he worried "to death" that his Mexican boyfriend might be caught. "And he [worries,] too," he added. "You know, he doesn't want to go back, he said it's always been his lifelong dream to live here. And, I respect that, you know." When they first met, Peter asked his partner "if he was legal or illegal. It didn't really matter, but it was good to know. And he told me that he was legal." As it turned out, however, the boyfriend was not telling him the truth. "Then, about three months into the relationship, he confessed that he had lied and he was afraid that I was going to turn him in. [That's] his reason why he told me that he was legal." When Peter posed the question initially, when his partner did not yet know whether he could trust him, his partner might have felt too vulnerable to disclose his undocumented status to him.

It is noteworthy that these events took place before the US federal government began providing visas to the foreign partners of US gays and lesbians. For that reason, at the time Peter had no way of helping his boyfriend regularize his immigration status so that they could stay together. And this is a reminder of the American partners' own inequalities (and second-class sexual citizenship) within US society.

Like Peter, other US White men who interacted with Mexican men had similarly become sensitized to the vulnerabilities undocumented immigrants faced on a day-to-day basis. Ryan (US White, born 1955) talked about a sex partner who had become very fearful because "one of his exes said they were going to call the border patrol and say he is at such-and-such house." Previously, Ryan had held strong anti-immigrant sentiments and thought that undocumented immigrants should not be allowed to remain in the country and obtain legal status. But his interactions with this Mexican man, who was now a close friend, made him alter his position.

————

These examples should illustrate the structural inequalities and vulnerabilities that stem from the marginalized social location of many Mexican immigrants in US society—a position that also has a concrete negative impact on the quality of the interactions some Mexican gay men establish with American gay men. The difficulties involved in addressing, at the individual level, the inequalities they experience in the US context may help us understand how and why the trope of Mexican/Latino sexual passion provides these men with a tool of empowerment—one that lets them acquire and maintain a sense of cultural pride. But first, I discuss how power differentials emerge in relation to the dynamics of specific sexual encounters.

Power Differences during Sex: The Perils of Mixing Power Play and Racialization

As we saw in chapter 9, some Mexican immigrant men who felt that US White men could sometimes be sexually passionate had also concluded that these men were more caring and egalitarian than the dominant *mayates* with whom they had previously interacted sexually in Mexico, whom they considered uncaring, arbitrary, and anything but egalitarian.[9] However, as Susan Kippax and Gary Smith have noted, sexual egalitarianism is not incompatible with the idea of chosen gender roles.[10] And indeed, participants in my study often viewed gendered sexual roles—which were sometimes established by unspoken assessments of who was more masculine, and thus perceived as more dominant[11]—as an issue only when they were involuntary and imposed (as in the sexual encounters involving dominant *mayates*). That is to say that my participants, both Mexican and American, often viewed sexual relations involving power differences and the roles that partners played during sex—whether they were more dominant or submissive, whether they were "tops" or "bottoms"—as consistent with sexual egalitarianism insofar as they perceived those differences as voluntary and mutually negotiated (even if that negotiation was not necessarily explicitly verbal).

A helpful illustration of these various points is provided by Ignacio, a US Latino (born 1970) familiar with both the heavily gendered sex that many *mayates* favored and the accepted rules of the American gay leather subculture (and, by extension, American BDSM [bondage, dominance, and sadomasochism]). Ignacio juxtaposed those two different styles of sexual interaction:

There may be some similarities as far as the . . . power dynamics that are involved in those sexual relationships; probably a lot of similarities, actually, now that I think about it. . . . Who's in charge, you know. . . . Who's releasing full control to the other person, kind of thing.

And yet, Ignacio also felt that the manner in which power played out in these two types of sexual scenarios was different in a fundamental way:

When you're looking at leather . . . the person who's being submissive is there because they want to be there. And when you're looking at, like, Latino, just *joto*, *puto* [a reference to the less masculine partner in heavily gendered relations], that kind of stuff, the person doesn't necessarily want to be there, you know; they're forced there. You know, they're put there by "this is the culture, this is the society" . . . attitudes of other folks; whereas in leather you're there because you want to be there.

Hence, Ignacio argued that men who participated in American gay leather and BDSM had the volition to relinquish power and control to a sex partner, while the more feminine and less powerful men in more heavily gendered sexual encounters involving *mayates* were forced to do so. This distinction resembles that described by Kippax and Smith between domination, defined as "a relation in which a person (or group) is not recognized as an agent and is unable to resist actions directed towards him or her," and "power dynamics," which involve "liberty between people" and voluntary "strategic games."[12] According to Kippax and Smith, when domination is negotiated, it can be seen as a form of power dynamics, such as in the context of leather and BDSM.[13]

In his comments, Ignacio also referred to other forms of social difference men sometimes invoke as part of the negotiated contract of consensual power play—as they construct sexual scenes of submission and domination that are meant to be pleasurable for all sex partners involved.[14] However, a difficulty is that power play and fantasy can be heavily intertwined with actual power differentials, making it hard for participants in any given sexual encounter to discern whether they have entered a safe sexual situation or one that may make them physically or emotionally vulnerable. This tension seems most evident in sexual situations in which power play is built around a sense of racial difference. Justo (Mexican) recounted his relationship with a US White partner who spontaneously engaged in racially based power play during a sexual encounter without ever asking Justo if he enjoyed that kind of interaction. Justo described how the two were mutually masturbating when his partner "became very freaky":

He started saying really creepy things . . . like, "You're my slut, you're my slave, and I'm going to hit you." When we finished I told him, "Never, ever say that again to me." He responded, "It's just that I used to have [another] Mexican partner, and he liked that."

At that point, Justo recalled simply telling him, "Well, not me."

At the time of his interview, Justo was considering leaving his partner, because he did not like the direction their relationship was taking. He described this partner as older (possibly around forty-eight years old; Justo was thirty-two) and as someone who had a really good job. The two had connected via a hookup website. Because of their financial disparities and age difference, his partner constantly asked Justo why he was going out with him, "since I'm older and you're so handsome." His partner would then express concern that Justo wanted him just for his money. "Sometimes I fear that they're looking for a sugar daddy," the man would tell him. It is unclear whether the "they" in this statement referred to young men, Latinos, or both. To assuage his partner's concern, Justo would reply, "If a sugar daddy is what I wanted, I would've said so in my online profile."

Coming back to Ignacio, a similar issue emerged for him in his own sexual interactions. (Although Ignacio was not an immigrant, those experiences are relevant here because, as we will see in the quotation that follows, White men sometimes racialized Mexican and US Latino gay men in similar ways, and thought of them as belonging in the same social category.) He observed, "It's really interesting, because in [the] leather community, people don't like playing the whole race-play kind of thing." He explained:

If you're in a scene with somebody and you cross that line about, you know, "I'm going to put you in [your] place, you Mexican, or something." . . . It's like, whooo! Sparks start to fly [laughs]. Some people like that, some people don't. So it's really interesting. It's a very controversial topic, actually. It's like people are very uneasy about that. Some people get off on it, though, you know, some people don't.

Note Ignacio's indication that in this fantasy, a US Latino man such as himself would not necessarily be seen as an American, and would be called "you Mexican."

Justo and Ignacio referred to the difficulty of separating sexual fantasy from the realities of racism. A similar difficulty was noted by participants in the study by Niels Teunis, who quoted African American interviewees who were baffled when White sex partners playing a dominant role spontaneously resorted to the use of derogatory racial epithets during sexual play.[15] For men such as Justo and Ignacio, the question seemed to arise concerning whether a dominant, White sex partner actually believed that Mexicans must be "put in their place" or were their "slaves." Those possibilities seemed to bother them and remind them of their unequal position as Mexicans or US Latinos. The uneasiness to which they referred suggests that racialized power play can be fraught with the realities of racial inequality, especially in the absence of any previous discussion between sex partners about whether a non-White partner might or might not enjoy being addressed with racial slurs. These examples also bring to the fore a sense that racial inequalities may generate specific vulnerabilities for Mexicans and Latinos in the context of cross-racial relations, particularly those involving US White partners, because of entrenched racial attitudes those partners may unreflexively deploy.

Shifts in Sexual Roles and Power

As I noted in chapter 8, a number of Mexican participants in my study experimented with changing their sexual roles once they began to engage in relations with men in San Diego. This group included some men who previously had been exclusively receptive and who began performing as insertive partners after migrating. Those men often had come to understand that self-identifying as gay did not automatically make them less of a man, any more than it necessarily positioned them as the receptive partners during sexual encounters involving anal intercourse. This role reversal was dramatic in that it not only introduced them to a new form of pleasure, but also was empowering and gave them a different perspective on the power dynamics of their sexual relationships with men. Indeed, they sometimes also realized that being the insertive partner granted them more power even within relationships defined in egalitarian terms.[16] Toribio (Mexican, born 1971) expressed this idea:

The power [that results from] hearing him moan, and knowing that for him I was the one controlling the situation. It was the power that in that moment I was the bigger one, the more powerful, and the other person was being submissive.

This sense that being the insertive partner provided a form of power—and by extension that being the receptive partner carried with it the possibility of losing power during sex—was shared by some of the American participants who grew up with the assumptions of the sexual egalitarianism of the American gay schema. For instance, Darin (US Latino, born 1980) talked about being a top as "a power thing, a control thing." He explained that because he never wanted to be in a vulnerable position, he never accepted being the receptive partner with partners he did not fully trust. "I didn't want anyone to be able to have that on me," he said. "To say that they were able to control me that way . . . and having me . . . [at] their mercy." He went on:

Like being somebody's bitch, which is usually what they try to do, [they] try to treat me like I'm their bitch. I'm not going to go there, not with my acquaintances. With people I care about, I'll do that. But that's been a very long time since I did that.

These perceptions connect back to Ignacio's observation that giving up power could be problematic when it was not part of a chosen and negotiated role—when it was a role imposed by the culture in which one was embedded. They also relate to the notion that power dynamics—which Kippax and Smith distinguish from domination—were based on negotiation, and reflected an intrinsic value placed on versatility, mutuality, and reciprocity—which, as those authors remind us, should not exclusively "depend upon reciprocated penetration."[17]

Thus, in the context of sexual encounters, my study participants were alert to how their own actions and those of their sex partners signified relative power within the relationship (regardless of whether they were referring to a one-time hookup or a longer-term relationship). As we have seen, the use of racialized language by White partners in the context of relationships that were meant to be egalitarian—where power play was negotiated, but where the question of whether racial slurs were welcome or admissible had not been part of the negotiation—generated discomfort and made Mexican/Latino partners wonder whether the sexual interaction was indeed an interaction of equals. Participants also often concluded that sexually dominating positions, regardless of whether they were negotiated or not, inevitably granted more power to the more dominant partner. And yet, some had also come to realize that as they themselves changed in the US context, they could adopt more dominating and

powerful sexual stances than before their relocation. But not all participants were capable of turning around situations of vulnerability, especially
when they were unsure about how to negotiate the dynamics of sexual
contexts that were new to them.

Vulnerability and the Newness of Sexual Contexts and Relationships

The material I presented in previous chapters revealed the details of how
newly arrived Mexican gay immigrants come into contact with new kinds
of people and settings. As they enact their sexual lives in their changed
location, they gain access to sexual contexts that are often quite different
from everything they had known, encounter novel forms of sexual interaction, and experience unanticipated forms of sexual pleasure. But as they
do those things, they also face the challenges involved in learning the
rules of the game that ensure successful participation in their new sexual
contexts, and grasping the cultural logics that inform sexual interaction
in those same contexts. Juggling all that is far from simple, especially
since there is not always a welcome wagon awaiting them at the other
end of their trajectories, and they discover instead that they have become
instantly racialized by the people around them. (This is partly why the
altruistic "cultural ambassadors," whose efforts I described in chapter 7,
become especially significant.) In other words, upon arrival, Mexican gay
men sometimes discover that the sexual freedom they imagined would
become available to them in the United States does not guarantee they
will be welcomed as equals by their American gay counterparts. Indeed,
the newness of sexual contexts and cross-cultural relations generates considerable challenges for some Mexican gay immigrants as they seek to become incorporated into San Diego's gay community. These challenges are
most pronounced among men who arrive in that city with little knowledge of American and global urban gay communities.

The Challenges of Cross-Cultural Relationships in a New Social Context

Troy (Mexican, born ca. 1973) was one of the men who stumbled upon
the gay neighborhood of Hillcrest (and also someone who, as I indicated
in chapter 7, had been aided by a staff person the first time that he went
to a gay bathhouse). When he began to explore San Diego on his own, he
arrived in Hillcrest "by mistake," meaning he had not planned on going

there or sought it out. After having a quick bite at a fast-food restaurant, he looked for a bus stop so he could go back home. However, as he was waiting for the bus he noticed a White man in "a very pretty car" who was waiting for the light to change, and also realized that the man was staring at him. At first, Troy did not know how to interpret the man's stare—he did not know if he was being hostile or friendly, and that made him uncomfortable. But then the man pulled over and asked him where he was going. This led to a short conversation between the two.

Catching on about where this interaction might be heading, Troy realized that he indeed found the man attractive ("*Me nació el gusto,*" he said in Spanish, an expression suggesting that he had developed a taste for this man). When the man suggestively stretched in his seat, Troy asked him if he was tired, and offered to give him a massage. The man simply said yes. Troy was thinking of their interaction as a hookup between equals. The man, however, seemed to have a different idea as he pulled out his wallet and threw a hundred-dollar bill on the passenger seat. Troy, shocked, thought to himself, "This man wants to buy me." For a moment he dismissed the man's action, set the money aside, and got into the car. In his mind, he was still treating the interaction as a hookup between equals. They headed to the man's house, gave each other massages, and had sex. During the encounter, the man penetrated Troy. Afterward, he offered to drive Troy home. He also told Troy that he had had a good time with him, and would like to get to know him better.

As Troy was about to get out of the car, the man asked him, "Aren't you forgetting something?" Troy thought he was asking him for a kiss, but the man pointed to the hundred-dollar bill, still on the passenger seat along with a piece of paper on which the man had written his phone number. Troy explained that he had not had sex for the money, but the man insisted that he take the bill. "Buy something with it that you like," he said. Troy then accepted the money, but told the man he would save it to pay for something the next time they saw each other. The man said that sounded perfect, and told him to meet him a few days later at a restaurant. Yet, not knowing if he would ever see this man again, Troy spent the money a couple of days later.

As he spoke about this event, Troy clarified: "I was not prostituting myself, I never asked for money." And he tried to make that clear to the man. But he was not sure if the message had come through, especially given the man's insistence that Troy keep the money. It is unclear whether the man assumed that Troy was a sex worker and was just pretending not to be one, or assumed that Troy was a working-class immigrant whom he was simply trying to help.

After debating internally whether to meet the man again or not, Troy decided to go to the restaurant on the day and time that the man had indicated. The man was there waiting. These initial interactions led to a yearlong relationship that ended when Troy's partner decided to move to the East Coast. The pair got along well over the course of their relationship, but Troy felt that the disparities between them were a real problem. Because his partner had money, was older, and had more experience, he was also the one who always dictated what they did or did not do, as well as where they went and even what they ate. He also told Troy that rather than letting groceries run out, he should feel free to grab money from the house—as there was always money lying around—and use it to replenish food and drinks. But this idea made Troy uncomfortable. He was not sure whether his partner simply trusted him or saw it as Troy's responsibility to take care of the house while the partner was at work. In addition, Troy refused to keep a copy of his partner's house keys or move in with him, in part because of his discomfort with the dynamics of their relationship, and in part because he was not used to staying in someone else's house. Indeed, for this latter reason, Troy never stayed overnight.

In the end, Troy seemed uneasy about how to interpret his partner's motives, and was constantly unsure about whether his partner was just being pragmatic about their economic differences or was using them to control him. We must consider that this was a very new situation for Troy. He had never before been in Hillcrest.[18] He had never before been in a relationship with a man. And neither had he interacted previously with White, older, or gay men. Being an immigrant with little money, Troy was constantly reminded of his vulnerable position within this relationship.

These kinds of disparities between immigrants and their US partners were not exclusive to sexual and romantic relations involving US White men. For instance, I discussed earlier the experience that Tadeo (born in the US in 1976, but raised in Mexico) had with a US Latino partner who, right after they had sex and with no preamble, simply asked Tadeo to leave. This man had not left any room for Tadeo to express what he himself wanted to do, and had not even felt it important to engage in any pleasantries or polite conversation after the two had shared a physically intimate moment. Tadeo seemed so baffled by this man's sudden request that he had simply complied. Of course, this man may have asked each of his sex partners to leave—and thus he may not have singled out Tadeo as a Mexican partner—and so his actions could have merely signaled a cultural difference between the two of them (a contrast between different sexual scripts). To be sure, Tadeo may have been operating with the expectations of sexual passion and instant intimacy that I described, and his partner may simply have made a practical decision (as in "We're done, it's time for you to go home"). However, in a context in which Mexican men perceive that they are dealing with both cultural differences and power disparities, it is hard for them to disentangle the two. Furthermore, the fact that Tadeo felt incapable of even expressing his desire to stay suggests he may have perceived his position as Mexican[19] as generating an insurmountable barrier to asserting his own preference, especially since he was in this man's own space. This relates to what Adam Green referred to as the reduced power of men of color to influence how sex unfolds (and, in the case of practicing safe sex, the "reduced power to set sexual limits on the exchange").[20]

A different example involves Cuauhtémoc (Mexican, born 1961), who, as I indicated in chapter 3, is a bisexually identified Mexican who was married to a woman in Mexico. Cuauhtémoc thought of himself as extremely masculine, and reported that because of his masculinity most people usually assumed he was straight. His immigration lawyer had assumed the same, and had told Cuauhtémoc that his masculinity would make it very hard to convince an immigration judge that he deserved to be granted asylum on the basis of his sexual orientation.[21] Cuauhtémoc also said that because of his masculinity, he was always quite dominant during sex.

In San Diego, Cuauhtémoc realized that he was very attracted to Black men, and he became curious about having sex with an African American man. However, when he finally had an opportunity to fulfill his fantasy, something happened that took him by surprise. Cuauhtémoc became uncharacteristically submissive, in part because he felt he was in a completely new situation, and in part because he perceived his partner to be very masculine, perhaps more so than he. Implicit in these assessments is the notion identified by Carballo-Diéguez and coauthors that men tend to assume that darker partners penetrate,[22] combined with the specific sexual stereotype that Black men are dominant tops.[23]

As a dominant, masculine, bisexually identified man, Cuauhtémoc was used to being the one who penetrated male partners, which he always did in casual encounters, and he always used condoms. In this encounter, however, not only did he allow the man to penetrate him—a completely new experience for him—but when the man could not find a condom, he agreed to have intercourse without one. "I said, 'ni modo' [whatever]," Cuauhtémoc remembered. "I was very aroused with him. . . . Then I regretted it." He then recalled other sexual encounters, all involving masculine Black men, during which he was receptive and unable to insist that his partner put on a condom. During his interview, Cuauhtémoc was both puzzled and disturbed by his inability to ask for a condom in his sexual encounters with these men. It seems plausible that his being in a new kind of situation, with a new type of partner with whom he felt less in control because of his perception of that man's masculinity, all factored into Cuauhtémoc's inability to use protection against HIV as he typically did.

Participating in New Sex Venues

A similar difficulty was reported by other Mexican gay immigrant men. Some participated only in the gay social contexts and venues that approximated those they had known in Mexico. Other immigrant men, however, had ventured into new sex venues about which they knew very little. Remember Troy's first experience in a gay bathhouse, which I described in chapter 7. He mustered the courage to go by himself to a gay bathhouse in San Diego, but once inside he realized he had no idea about what actually happened there or how the place worked. Along with adult bookstores, gay bathhouses figure frequently in immigrant men's narratives about their experiences in sex venues that were very new to them. Another frequent topic in these narratives: public cruising areas, including a section of San Diego's Balboa Park—known as the Fruit Loop—and the gay section of Black's Beach, the city's well-known nude beach.

In contrast to Troy, Hernán had quite a different experience when he started visiting gay bathhouses in San Diego. He had moved to the city five years earlier, and soon afterward tested positive for HIV, at which point he began seeing a doctor regularly. Hernán said that as part of his health strategy, he had become quite proficient at using condoms regularly. But when he went to the bathhouse, he found himself unable to implement the protective measures he now consistently emphasized. As he walked around the place, he noticed an attractive White man who was masturbating in his room with the door open—a sign Hernán knew to interpret as an invitation for potential sex partners. Hernán took a chance, entered the room, and closed the door. The man did not signal for him to leave, so Hernán proceeded to give him oral sex. The man then moved to penetrate Hernán, and Hernán allowed it. But with the door closed, the room was almost completely dark, and Hernán could not see if the man had put on a condom. His narrative suggests that the pair had not said a word to each other—they seemed to be enacting a script that was completely unfamiliar to him, and so Hernán could not figure out how to ask this attractive White man whether he had a condom on. Afterward, however, he realized that the man had not used one.

Hernán regretted this encounter, particularly because he believed that he had become infected with syphilis by his encounter with this man. He blamed his inability to ask for protection on his being "careless." It seems clear, however, that the breakdown of his intention to protect himself and others from sexually transmitted diseases was related to several contextual issues that were happening all at once. First, he was interacting with a man whom he felt was very handsome (Hernán, who described himself as "dark," was particularly attracted to *güeros*). Second, he could not visually check if his partner had a condom on because the room was so dark (Hernán said that when he first entered the room he had fiddled with the light switch, but the dark-blue light would not get any brighter). And third, he did not fully know the etiquette and scripts of interaction for the venue, so he was unsure about whether the man would be offended if he asked whether he had a condom. Unlike Troy, Hernán had not encountered anyone who explained acceptable and unacceptable behaviors as he navigated a sex venue that was new to him.

Of course, these kinds of situations could also happen to American men who are new to the gay scene, and some of the American participants in my study indeed discussed situations in which they felt at a loss about how to negotiate unfamiliar sex venues. But the issue seems particularly salient for many immigrant men, for a variety of interlinked reasons: the lack of cultural capital among some of them for negotiating American urban gay life; the expectations they brought with them from the places they had lived in Mexico (including those concerning sexual passion, sexual repertoires, and styles of sexual interaction); the limits placed on their acquisition of sexual citizenship as members of a gay community; the kinds of power differentials that sometimes emerged in the context of cross-cultural and cross-racial relations; and other structural barriers related to language and communication. In the final sections of the chapter, I describe particular cultural interpretations of my Mexican participants that can be viewed as a form of resistance to these various challenges: I return to the topic of Latino passion and examine Mexican immigrants' use of it as a tool of empowerment.

Latino Passion as Cultural Pride

As Mexican men sought to make sense of the sexual differences they perceived between them and their American sex partners, they often resorted to cultural explanations. They argued that their passion became instilled in the context of the Mexican family culture, and thus credited their families, and Mexican family-oriented life more generally, for helping them become sexually passionate. As Felix (Mexican, born 1982) put it, "I think it [Mexican passion] has to do a lot with the culture, you know, because there's always so much attention to the family." Raimundo (Mexican, born 1967) similarly explained his own sense of the origins of Mexican passion by remarking that "we come from very close-knit and united families."

The understanding of Latino passion as a cultural product deriving from family life reflects a series of tightly interwoven beliefs—what I will call the Mexican collectivity schema.[24] First, my immigrant participants perceived that Mexicans—even those who were gay—preserved more of their cultural traditions than did US Whites. Specifically, the logic here is that Mexican traditions of family and collectivity helped Mexicans maintain a more benevolent culture, which stood in opposition to the harsher, highly materialistic, and individualistic mainstream US-White culture, where traditional family values were perceived as having deeply eroded. Second, they felt that maintaining a strong sense of Mexican culture required strong disciplinary practices lacking in mainstream Americans. Along these lines, Mexican participants referred to how their families raised them to be "more respectful toward the elders, towards your family," as Felix opined. Such an emphasis, they felt, was often weaker or absent in mainstream US White culture. Third, Mexican participants associated the respect that families instilled in them with the survival of their more collective orientation—the fact that Mexicans learned that family and group needs came before individual interests—which in turn they saw as explaining why Mexicans valued deeper interpersonal relations. And finally, the cultivation of these strong interpersonal relationships within the family was precisely what Mexicans believed had fostered their disposition toward sexual passion—that is, a capacity for passionate expression was nurtured at an early age.

These various aspects of the Mexican collectivity schema repeatedly emerge in Mexican men's narratives about why Mexicans and Latinos were more sexually passionate than US Whites. As Ronaldo (Mexican, born 1970) put it, "[Sexual passion] is something learned, I believe from the roots that we learn from our mothers. . . . Gay Latinos are very attached to . . . learning from our mothers." Similarly, according to Benjamín (Mexican, born ca. 1955), family life plays a central role in fostering passion among Mexicans:

Family is more united. . . . If you're 18, 19, 20, 25 years old and you're gay, they just ask, "Why haven't you married?" But no one pushes you to become independent, to make your own life as a person, because in Mexico there is a saying that the united family lives better, because everyone contributes to be better.

Such comments reveal a noteworthy paradox. When Mexican men voiced them, they seemed to overlook that, as we saw in chapter 3, many among them had left their family homes precisely because they saw their families as an obstacle to achieving the sexual freedom they craved. They seemed to address this paradox by emphasizing that they had left thinking not only about themselves and their rights but also about protecting their families from stigma or social shame.[25] Their altruistic motivation for leaving further underscored their belief that, in the end, collective needs trumped individual ones within the benevolent, family-oriented Mexican culture.

Many of the Mexican participants regarded US White families, by contrast, as excelling at fostering a sense of individuality—something they believed these families could afford to promote, because they had more social and economic privilege—but with sharp detachment and shallow interpersonal relations as the result. In Gerardo's opinion (Mexican, born 1971), this played out as follows:

They [US Whites] grow up very independently, far away from the warmth of family. Mexican families are more united, not all, but they are more united. They try to stay together, struggle together. And for White people, the world presents itself as easy, and it doesn't bring them together in those difficult moments. . . . At thirteen they no longer want to live in their home.

Other Mexican participants were equally struck by what they regarded as an American cultural expectation that children would leave the family home at the tender age of eighteen, which in their view ran counter to any notion of a strong, united family. Valentín (Mexican, born 1975) succinctly noted, "In American culture, from the time they are very young, kids are with the babysitter, or in the kindergarten, and when they turn eighteen, *bye, bye.*"

Hence, Mexican immigrant men blamed US White individualism for promoting planned and calculated interpersonal relations in which individuals were perceived as using others for their own purposes, all counter to the workings and expectations of sexual passion. As Oscar (Mexican, born 1976) observed, US Whites' lack of sexual passion "has to do with the culture, because here everything is very measured, very premeditated." This impression added to a sense that, during sexual encounters,

US White gay men were more preoccupied with such matters as having to get up early the next day for work than with developing a strong sense of connection with their sex partners and fully enjoying each other in the moment.[26]

Culture, Race, and Sexual Empowerment

The uses of the trope of Latino sexual passion reveal an interesting perception among a number of my study participants: that there is a constitutive relationship between culture and sex. As their narratives suggest, many of these men believed that traditions and practices of familial life exposed Mexicans/Latinos over the course of their upbringing to culturally inflected scripts of affection and interaction that predisposed them to become sexually passionate as adults. As part of this logic, expectations of passion and affection in turn reinforced and promoted a collective orientation and a benevolent Mexican culture and family life. US White men, by contrast, were assumed to be exposed to an individualistic and overly practical culture, one that helped them become self-sufficient and sexually assertive, but that predisposed them to be overly impersonal and dispassionate in their ways of enacting sex—in terms of the sexual scripts they favored.

However, as we have seen, this a topic that invites considerable differences of opinion, at least among the men who participated in my study. Some believed that differences in sexual passion adequately described cultural differences between Mexicans/Latinos and US Whites, and the Mexicans among them often perceived that Mexican sexual passion gave them a cultural advantage as a group and something about which they could be proud. As such, the discourse of sexual passion seems empowering, acting as a kind of antidote to their racialization and the structural sexual vulnerabilities that affected them in the United States. Other participants, however, thought that the trope of Latino sexual passion is oppressive and disempowering, because it works as a problematic cultural stereotype. For this latter group, this trope is yet another way in which Mexicans/Latinos were exoticized within mainstream American society.

Following Audre Lorde, the view of Mexican immigrant men who see sexual passion as empowering seems to connect to a conception of "the erotic as power."[27] For these men, sexual passion can be regarded as providing them with a way of acknowledging "the erotic as a source of power and information," where the erotic stands for "not a question of what we do" but a "question of how acutely and fully we can feel in the doing."[28]

In Lorde's view, the erotic emerges also as "the sensual—those physical, emotional, and psychic expressions of what is deepest and strongest and richest within each of us."[29] From this perspective, whether Mexican gay men are indeed more sexually passionate than their US White counterparts seems less important a question than the fact that they believe they are—that they trust their ability to implement the scripts of sexual passion and instant intimacy that they learned while growing up (including as part of their gay socialization) in Mexico. Therefore, sexual passion can be seen as providing them with the tools to actively pursue a sense of deep connection, even within one-time casual sexual encounters. This understanding of what sexual passion can accomplish for them goes well beyond the idea, discussed in chapter 9, that the discourse of sexual passion provides Latino gay immigrants with erotic capital they can "spend" within a competitive field of sexual encounters.

As a response to the sexual scripts these men think of as characterizing American mainstream gay culture, the directness with which closeness and intimacy are expressed within the sexual scripts of passion that Mexicans learned relates as well to José Esteban Muñoz's general characterization of affect as "descriptive of the receptors we use to hear each other and the frequencies on which certain subalterns speak and are heard or, more importantly, felt."[30] Consistent with this view, the discourse of sexual passion could be seen as constituting a form of "racial performativity" that "is intended to get at an aspect of race that is 'a doing,'"[31] and consequently a form of sexual agency that emerges in the context of racialized and often unequal relationships. Sexual passion becomes, then, a way of "responding to whiteness" or, as Jafari Allen has suggested, a way in which people of color who are viewed "constantly as archaic holdouts to progressive 'sexual blindness' within emerging neoliberal multiculturalism" can "strategically or tactically use their putative deviance . . . as resistance."[32] But if this is the case, a question remains about whether the emotions inherent in the notion of sexual passion and the forms of intimacy that my participants described can be mobilized beyond individual self-awareness and empowerment and transformed into a source of collective action.[33]

By contrast, when perceived as a sexual stereotype, sexual passion emerges as a source of the disempowering effects of stereotyping that affect Mexicans and Latinos—and, more specifically, Mexican/Latino gay men—a point that some of my participants made and that also appears in the academic literature. For instance, Wilson and coauthors have defined sexual stereotyping as the "processes in which sexual stereotypes are used to ascribe sexually based attributes to a person based on their race,"[34] and also described race-based sexual stereotypes as "inferred beliefs and expectations about the attributes a sexual experience will take on based on the race of the partner involved in the experience."[35] Based on these notions, these authors concluded that when some of their participants talked about Latino gay men as more sexually passionate, they were merely stereotyping them. The same literature noted that sexual stereotypes—including the notion of Latino sexual passion—generally "persisted despite evidence that may have proven them invalid."[36] My own case suggests, instead, that it is important for us to hold on to two ideas simultaneously about the discourse of Latino sexual passion: it can be a sexual stereotype, but it can also function as a form of resistance and cultural pride.

Moreover, as I discussed briefly in chapter 9, my study raises questions about whether only those who are in a disadvantaged social position can be sexually stereotyped. Or, alternatively, do opinions about White men expressed by Latinos and men of color constitute sexual stereotypes? Wilson and his coauthors have indicated that "one of the most notable findings was the lack of within-group and between-group race-based sexual stereotypes" about White men.[37] They concluded that Latinos and other men of color are sexually objectified "and made to feel less like individuals," and sometimes also exploited, but White men are not.[38] However, given what non-White participants in my study had to say about US White gay men's coldness and culture, we need to consider more deeply whether those views constitute sexual stereotypes about White men or, alternatively, whether they merely reflect their partners' personal preferences and their attempts to resist oppression or counter the negative effects of the kinds of power differentials that I discussed. And it is possible that all the above are simultaneously active. Indeed, there is no reason why the various ways of thinking about cross-racial and cross-cultural dynamics that I have examined may not all be part of the broader dynamics of racial relations and disparities of power in US society.

Conclusion

The Arc of Sexual Migration

Pathways of Desire has shown that the full range of factors encapsulated in the notion of sexual freedom becomes visible only if we pay close attention to the full arc of sexual migration, from beginning to end—if we consider the pre-migration experiences of sexual immigrants, their motivations for migrating, the pathways that bring them to their transnational destinations, their "landing pads" upon arrival,[1] and the processes through which they become incorporated into communities in their new locations. In other words, attention paid solely to the motive of sexual freedom is not sufficient to fully understand the phenomenon of sexual migration.

As a shorthand designation, sexual freedom can end up hiding more than it reveals. This is especially true if notions of sexual freedom are relied on to make sweeping characterizations of the sexual oppressiveness of the countries that sexual immigrants left behind. That term—*sexual oppressiveness*—might accurately describe societies where the institutions of the state and organized religion, having the power to create social policy and strongly influence public opinion, have made it their business to severely curtail the freedom of sexual minorities; where homosexuality and other forms of sexual dissent are openly persecuted and declared to be antinational. But it less aptly describes many countries of the global South, including Mexico, that have instead experienced considerable sexuality-related change in recent decades, and where conservative voices are no longer in an unchallenged position to impede progressive developments.[2]

As we have seen throughout this book, the narratives offered by Mexican gay immigrants who moved to the United States force us to examine what they mean when they cite sexual freedom as their main motivation for migrating. Moreover, their diversity forces us to pay close attention to a variety of social forces—both structural and cultural—that influence their sexual migration and their post-migration incorporation into a new society.

Sexual Diversity in the Home Country

My findings demonstrate that cultural understandings of male same-sex desires in Mexico cannot be reduced to a single traditional sexual model or sexual schema. Indeed, an object choice/gay schema—which is connected to the notion of the global gay—has been taking shape in Mexico for at least the past five decades (and may have its roots in an earlier historical period). The sexualities of some of my study participants while living in Mexico were certainly informed by a highly gendered sexual schema that aligns with the *pasivo/activo* model. Indeed, most of my Mexican participants were able to recognize that schema and noted its presence in some parts of Mexico, particularly in less populous places and among the urban working class. But by the time that they left their home country, the sexualities of a majority—including those who were working-class or who grew up in small towns—had been informed by an object choice/gay schema that is often thought of as "more egalitarian."[3] Moreover, several had experienced same-sex sexual initiations consistent with a third sexual schema—a homosocial schema—that involved sex with male friends or relatives in the absence of either heavily gendered roles/behaviors or an explicit gay consciousness.[4]

Just as I found in my earlier research in Guadalajara,[5] in my Mexican participants' narratives both the heavily gendered schema of same-sex desires and the gay schema sometimes coexist in hybridized form, further confirming the manner in which a global gay schema has become glocalized and therefore adapted to reflect the social and cultural conditions of Mexico. Indeed, before participating in gay San Diego, the sexualities of almost a third of the Mexican men had been characterized by back-and-forth movement between an object choice/gay schema and one of the other two (homosocial or highly gendered)—fluidity that indicated their ability to adapt and enact sexual encounters according to specific sexual situations or contexts and their connections to specific sex partners. In other words, these men were not sexually uniform, nor were their sexualities necessarily fixed in place.

Finally, it is important to keep in mind that not all Mexican men in my study belonged to the same generation. The oldest was born in 1948 and the youngest in 1983, which means that they came of age between the mid-1970s and the early 2000s. Their stories therefore reflect diverse experiences of sexuality and migration over a period spanning almost three decades.

The Contours of Sexual Migration

Although Mexican gay men were often quick to talk straightforwardly about their motivations for migrating by expressing their desires for sexual freedom, this notion encapsulates a range of circumstances that are directly linked to individual immigrants' social and family lives in Mexico. My Mexican participants often perceived insurmountable barriers that prevented them from openly enacting same-sex desires and expressing gay identities—barriers often related to the fact that they were surrounded by relatives and friends who had known them as "straight" their whole life. Given the still-prevailing expectations of family life in Mexico, they also often felt that leaving their family homes to become independent in their hometowns was impossible, because it would invite unbearable gossip and possibly generate a great deal of stigma. By contrast, moving to the United States was easy to justify, since so many Mexicans have migrated to try their luck there. An additional advantage, some of these men perceived, would be to have the US-Mexico border serve as a protective barrier that would further allow them to pursue an openly gay life and start anew in the United States. (However, as we have seen, this expectation of sufficient geographic distance from the scrutiny of relatives and acquaintances was not always realized in practice.) Beyond these advantages, moving to the United States raised the prospect of an improvement in their economic status, and put them in a more powerful position vis-à-vis their families (particularly if they sent remittances back to their loved ones). All this suggests a constellation of issues that are encapsulated under the rubric of sexual freedom.

The contours of sexual migration ought to be approached broadly enough to account for the variety of sexuality-related issues that my participants reported. This presumes examining the intertwining of sexual motivations with economic and family-related ones, among other possible motivations for migration. Such intertwining suggests, more broadly, the importance of attending to the material and structural aspects of sexuality and migration (along the lines that Lionel Cantú proposed),[6] but without ignoring the many cultural and social issues that my analysis revealed as playing a role in the production of sexual migration.

Crucially, the situations of individual immigrants must also be contextualized within the broader historical processes of change, and resistance to change, surrounding homosexuality and LGBT rights in countries such as Mexico. But it is equally important to consider the positions that individuals occupy within the social stratification of their home countries. My data show that the social position of individual gay immigrants had a profound effect on their experiences of migration to the United States. Social differences in the home country determined whether specific individuals had access to official travel documents such as passports and visas, or whether they felt compelled to seek out informal travel methods without official documents. Many of my study participants perceived that their social class, education, and even looks influenced how they were treated at US consulates and at the border, and those issues also seemed to determine the degree to which they could either "pass" or be rejected by border agents based on those agents' own racial biases about Mexicans.

Furthermore, the particular locations and contexts in which immigrants had lived in Mexico determined the resources they could access to embark on the migration process. As my data show, those who came from towns having a long tradition of migration to the United States often relied on the very same mechanisms of support that sociologists have identified as part of a culture of Mexican migration.[7] But to draw on those resources, they typically had to pretend that they were straight. And sometimes after arrival in the United States, they discovered that the Mexican culture of migration squarely placed them in transplanted Mexican immigrant communities where they could not achieve the independence and anonymity they sought. Therefore, they had to move again.

By contrast, Mexican men who were attuned to urban gay cultures in Mexico and had gay friends or relatives in the United States were able to tap into an alternative network of support that I call a "gay culture of migration." But in mainstream studies of Mexican migration that do not recognize such a network, these men would appear to have migrated based on their own resources. This issue in itself makes clear why sexuality ought to be routinely considered in mainstream migration studies. Especially as recognition of the lifestyle factors within Mexican migration grows, more attention to sexuality would only enrich those studies.

Landing Pads and Gay Immigrant Incorporation

The same social differences that influenced Mexican participants' pathways of relocation to the United States also influenced their experiences of incorporation into US life, including their participation in San Diego's LGBT community. My findings demonstrate that the amount of gay cultural capital that individual immigrants possess upon arrival in San Diego influences how they find the local gay world, as well as how long it takes them to do so. It also influences their ability to negotiate specific gay social and sexual spaces. Generally speaking, participants who were attuned to global gay cultures, knew gay Americans, had previously visited gay areas in American cities, and made use of gay resources to relocate found their way into San Diego's LGBT community more easily. By contrast, those who initially landed in that city's Mexican communities and expected to find gay life there but did not know how to go about it or did not know any gay people in San Diego generally took longer to access local gay life.

However, being well attuned to gay life in one's home country does not guarantee an automatic grasp of the rules of the game in the gay world of a new location. Even Mexican participants who were clued in to Mexican urban gay life often discovered that contrary to what they had imagined or expected, *gay* does not always mean the same thing in Mexico and the United States. For instance, many had no inkling that whole neighborhoods in American cities have been designated as "gayborhoods."[8] And sometimes they stumbled upon Hillcrest and its LGBT community only when they happened to drive through it and friends commented that they were in a gay area, or when acquaintances made derogatory comments about Hillcrest and then they set out on their own to find it. Not knowing what to expect, some arrived at their destination and did not immediately recognize it as gay. Others recalled the awe they felt when they first saw gay couples there holding hands in public in broad daylight—an activity that acquired considerable symbolic meaning for many of them and often led them, in their narratives, to compare the possibilities for gay openness in the United States versus Mexico. Still others were struck by well-organized and institutionalized sexual spaces such as the gay bathhouses, or spoke of discovering more informal ones, such the gay section of the clothing-optional Black's Beach.

As these men began to participate in San Diego's LGBT community, they sometimes realized that in Hillcrest, as elsewhere in San Diego, they were classified as racial others. However, as members of an ethnic minority they also found opportunities to join networks of support that had formed around Latino LGBT identities. They benefited from a well-developed network of community-based programs tailored to gay Latinos, and they were able to use services provided in Spanish. For those who were HIV positive, or who became HIV positive in the United States, this same network provided them with vital services and treatments. By becoming part of San Diego Latino gay life, they also acquired new friends and became part of friendship circles that often extended beyond their ethnic community.

Finally, as my discussion showed, many of the Mexican participants also received support from members of San Diego's mainstream LGBT community, including non-Latino friends, boyfriends, and sex partners. They were sometimes helped by altruistic "cultural ambassadors," some of whom even offered them lessons in how to self-identify, as in the case of Cuauhtémoc, who learned that his desires qualified him to be called bisexual. But, as we saw in the case of Venustiano, who arrived with the idea of marrying a tolerant woman, their participation in gay San Diego also taught them the normative limits of *gay*, which at times curtailed possible alternative ways in which gay identities could be lived and organized.

Overall, Mexican participants' incorporation into San Diego's LGBT communities and gay life shaped them as "sexual citizens" by providing them with a sense of their rights and duties to themselves and their community, even when, ironically, many of them enjoyed few of the legal rights claimed by their American counterparts. At times, their immigrant status and ethnic identities positioned them as less than full members in gay community life.

These various findings suggest the importance of closely examining what is familiar and what is foreign for different gay immigrants in their new locations. On the one hand, this means not assuming that everything is new to all of them after their relocation. As my data show, making assumptions about cultural and experiential pre-migration homogeneity among sexual immigrants is problematic. But on the other hand, it also means not assuming that gay immigrants who arrive having considerable gay cultural capital already know how everything works in the gay world of their new location, or that their ways of being gay before migration are fully consistent with those they encounter after relocating.

Sexual Change

Upon their arrival in San Diego, Mexican gay immigrants, including those who had participated in gay life and communities in Mexico, reorganized their sexualities, sometimes in profound ways. The overall trends reported in *Pathways of Desire* suggest that their contact with San Diego's gay life further pushed some of them to interpret their sexualities and sexual orientation through the lens of a global object choice/gay schema. They sometimes encountered more opportunities to engage in the kind of sexual role versatility that is an alternative to being exclusively "top" or "bottom" within a gay schema; some scholars have connected such versatility to the idea of gay egalitarianism.[9] This means that some participants who previously had always been the insertive partner in anal intercourse learned the bodily pleasures of being penetrated. And others who had always been the receptive partners learned that they could take on the insertive role, and when they did so they discovered not only new forms of pleasure but also new forms of power.[10] Yet comparatively, the sexualities of other Mexican participants who had experienced sexual role versatility in Mexico as an option changed less in San Diego. They spoke instead of adaptations that had more to do with the process of learning particular sexual contexts in their new location.

Significantly, not all my Mexican participants welcomed the changes available to them in San Diego; in fact, some resisted them. For instance, a few who preferred heavily gendered forms of sexual interaction sought out venues where they could meet straight-identified Mexican sex partners. Others struggled against adopting what they viewed as highly impersonal and instrumental forms of sexual interaction that, in their perception, many US White gay men favored. All this post-migration diversity with regard to sexuality indicates that there is no single prescribed sexual pathway that is produced by sexual migration, and that it makes no sense to imagine a singular route from "traditional" to "modern" forms of homosexuality.[11]

Furthermore, my participants' narratives also reveal that they were capable of crafting new lives for themselves while simultaneously maintaining what they liked about the lives that they had lived in Mexico, which remained a part of their current experiences. These men became adept at moving back and forth between different sociocultural settings in Mexico and the United States and adapting their sexualities to both locations. And they did not always prioritize the sexual lives they had achieved in the United States. For instance, when I asked Cuauhtémoc to compare his sex life as a bisexual man participating in San Diego's gay community with his life as a straight-identified husband and father in Mexico, he unequivocally answered, "For me, [my life] there is more important, because all that I have is there. My gay life, bisexual, uhm, I could control it. As I said, I could go back in the closet, I would do it for my wife and children."

Cuauhtémoc's strategy of being bisexual in San Diego and a hetero-sexual family man in Mexico is not what would be dictated by the nor-mative expectations about "coming out" in a global gay schema. But it is the one that Cuauhtémoc envisioned as working best for him, because it allowed him to traverse the two transnational sexual worlds he inhab-ited. If pressed to give up one or the other, Cuauhtémoc claimed he would give up his life in San Diego, yet in reality he was invested in maintain-ing both identities and participating in both sexual worlds. And notably, his choice to "stay in the closet" in Mexico should not be seen as signify-ing that Mexico is sexually backward—that gay and bisexual men such as Cuauhtémoc cannot "come out" there. Indeed, his strategy is no different from that of US White, straight-identified married men who participated in interviews for a recent study of mine. They rejected the label *bisexual*, because they felt it did not accurately describe the most important parts of their lives.[12]

The Dynamics of Cross-Racial Relations

As part of their sexual explorations in San Diego, many immigrant par-ticipants (though not all) engaged in cross-racial or cross-cultural sexual encounters and relationships. While some maintained attractions they had developed in Mexico—which sometimes included fantasies about types of men with whom they had never previously interacted sexually—others developed new attractions in the United States. As suggested by my findings, the topic of cross-racial attraction, or lack of thereof, pro-vides a helpful starting point for analyzing the prevailing racial politics and inequalities in both the immigrants' home countries and the coun-tries to which they migrate. For instance, compared with their US Latino counterparts, a larger proportion of Mexican participants stated an attrac-tion to White men, while more US Latinos expressed having a primary attraction to Latino men. This difference may reflect that US Latino par-ticipants had spent their entire lives within the particular racialized dy-namics and politics of race of the United States. It may also reflect the kinds of race- and class-based privileging of whiteness that are common in Mexico.

Beyond these assessments of physical cross-racial attraction, this topic also allows examination of the role played by perceptions of cultural dif-ference and affinity. My findings show the centrality of cultural issues—including attitudes about individuality, collective and family life, sexual passion, romantic gestures, intimacy, and sexual scripts—to my partici-pants' stated cross-racial attraction and preferences. They also reveal that

Latino gay men—and Mexican gay immigrant men more specifically— have something to offer to global gay culture by introducing forms of interaction that impacted, most immediately, the non-Latino gay men with whom they came into contact, but also influenced more broadly the gay cultures of San Diego. Such an influence is most evident in the Latino Nights in San Diego dance clubs where considerable numbers of non-Latino LGBT people are exposed to a strong sense of Mexican/Latino gay culture.[13] It also surfaces in comments made by non-Latino men about the degree to which San Diego changed them culturally, primarily due to the (sometimes unexpected) degree to which they got to interact there with Mexican and Latino gay men, as well as how those interactions forced them to confront their own stereotypes about Latinos/Mexicans. As Peter put it, "I had no idea. I mean, I knew of Hispanic people, and stuff like that, but I never knew, I knew what tacos were, basically that's as far as I knew about Hispanic culture."

Nonetheless, it is important to keep in mind the tension between the perception (and celebration) of cultural differences and the pervasiveness of cultural stereotypes. Moreover, power disparities influenced by race and ethnicity are a reality in US society, and inequalities can taint the interactions between immigrant and local men. But it is equally important to consider how immigrants may turn perceptions of cultural difference into methods of individual and group empowerment—into assets and forms of erotic and personal capital as they participate in sexual fields in which they are otherwise sometimes disadvantaged.[14]

Sexual Migrants as Social Actors: Assimilation, Globalization, and Colonialism

Pathways of Desire also calls attention to the active character of immigrants' participation in US society, thereby pointing to the limitations of prevailing models of immigrant assimilation and acculturation. Such models have tended to assume that immigrants passively adopt the ways of an imagined American mainstream, and generally treat immigrant populations as homogeneous because they focus exclusively on immigrants' post-migration experiences.[15] Instead, as the sociologists Richard Alba and Victor Nee have proposed, we are in need of a reformulation of the concept of assimilation that does not view it as requiring "the disappearance of ethnicity"—that instead allows "for the possibility that the nature of the mainstream into which minority individuals and groups are assimilating is changed in the process."[16] Theirs is a standpoint that emphasizes the "plasticity of the mainstream"—meaning also that new groups of immigrants can leave their own imprint—at the same time that it recognizes that not all groups have equal opportunity to do so, "because life chances are still strongly differentiated by social class and other non-ethnic factors."[17] If we extend this view to encompass the processes of sexual migration that I analyzed, a picture begins to emerge of Mexican gay men's contributions to gay culture in San Diego, but also of the limitations on equal participation they face due to their disadvantaged position.

Mexican Gay Immigrants and Global Sexualities

In the process of articulating a "view from the South," Mexican gay immigrant men demonstrate their agency in promoting forms of innovation that may alter what we think of as "the global gay." Some questions remain about the extent to which what they promote is actually changing views about how to be gay in the United States, but the various examples I discussed in this book suggest the possibility of a more bidirectional exchange between that country and Mexico. They also challenge the assumption that sexual innovation always originates in the global North. Moreover, these ideas relate to what Martin Manalansan has called "to play with the world"—a way of referring, in his case, to Filipino gay immigrants' use of cultural understandings they brought from the Philippines to articulate a critique of the mainstream US White gay culture in New York.[18] Similarly, as *Pathways of Desire* has shown, there are many indicators that Mexican gay immigrants do not merely adopt the sexual ways of the North as they become incorporated into gay life in cities such as San Diego.

But to be able to consider the contributions that Mexicans and other citizens from the global South make to the sexualities of the North, we first need to be open to considering the degree to which their former countries are changing. Otherwise, absent that information, when countries of the global South implement sweeping sexuality-related social changes that sometimes surpass those believed to be possible in countries such as the United States, those changes are deemed hard to comprehend, anomalous, or paradoxical. One example is provided by the introduction of same-sex marriage policies at the national level in Argentina and South Africa, and at the local level in metropolises such as Mexico City, which had taken place years before similar developments were regarded as feasible in many locations in the United States.[19] Rather than seeing such developments as anomalous or paradoxical, an alternative would be to take very seriously the question raised by Aihwa Ong—Where are the centres and the margins in contemporary global society?[20]—and examine what "forms of innovation the sexual modernities of the global South may offer to the global North. Doing so will also put us in a better position to account for the contributions to cultural (and sexual) globalization of the sexual migrants from the global South.

Certainly, in the case of Mexico, its citizens have been articulating their own versions of "sexual modernity" in global settings in other ways as well. One eloquent example is the production of telenovelas—the well-known melodramas that center on ideas about Mexican family life, romantic relations, and sexuality—that Mexican television networks export to more than one hundred countries. In addition to reaching very large television audiences throughout the Spanish-speaking world (including in the United States), telenovelas are watched in translation in countries as diverse as Israel, Russia, China, South Korea, Hungary, the Philippines, and Egypt.[21] The global circulation of these cultural products has a potentially significant impact, one that may go beyond what Iain Chambers called "the return of the repressed, the subordinate and the forgotten in 'Third World' musics, literatures, poverties and populations as they come to occupy the economies, cities, institutions, media and leisure time of the First World."[22]

Arguably, what Mexican gay men bring with them to the United States has a similar effect, albeit perhaps on a smaller scale. Nonetheless, their contributions destabilize assumptions about the directionality of sexual globalization, and they do so in a fashion similar to other interactions between LGBT people from the global North and the global South. In addition to the Filipino gay immigrants in Martin Manalansan's research, other examples are provided by Richard Parker's discussion of the impact that Brazilian *travestis* (transvestite sex workers) and *michês* (male hustlers) have had on the worlds of sex work in European capitals and other locations,[23] and Mark Padilla's analysis of the profound personal transformations that result from the interactions and relationships between Dominican non-gay-identified male sex workers (*tigueres*) and foreign gay tourists visiting the island.[24] In all those encounters, like in those of my Mexican participants in San Diego, both locals and foreigners changed.

Mexican Gay Migrants and the Structural Inequalities between Mexico and the United States

The unequal power between countries such as the United States and Mexico is important to any discussion of sexual globalization. The literature on sexuality and colonialism helps bring this theme to the fore, as it provides a helpful link between the racialized sexual dynamics that characterized the relationship between colonizers and colonized and the racialized sexual attitudes that prevail in the former colonial powers. It also helps explain the tensions that emerged in my study between a straightforward sense that cross-racial attraction simply reflects the fact that "opposites attract," and an awareness of the stark disparities of power that sometimes occur within those relationships and may result in stereotypes of "the other." My findings suggest that stereotyping is not something done only by those who belong to the groups with more power and a higher social standing. However, the negative effects of sexual and racial stereotypes inevitably seem more pronounced when exercised on those who have less power in sexual and romantic relations (and who may also be sexually exoticized). It is precisely in those moments—when stereotypes are deployed as justifications for power differentials—that the dynamics emphasized by the literature on sexuality and colonialism become most evident.

However, in adopting this literature, I have realized that it is imperative to question the temporal linearity sometimes implied in the perceived transition from a colonial to a postcolonial period, as well as the notion that such a transition is relevant in the same way, at the same time, to all countries that were former colonies. Such assumptions risk lessening the potential to analyze dynamic processes of social and cultural change occurring in postcolonial societies—the very same processes that may help us alter circulating assumptions about the directionality of sexual globalization.

My study of cross-racial sexual relationships benefited methodologically from interviewing not only Mexican gay immigrants but also American gay men with whom such immigrants interact sexually and romantically. The analysis that this approach facilitated should serve to illustrate the value of examining cross-racial dynamics and dimensions of power from the perspectives of all involved. The result, as we have seen, is a more nuanced simultaneous account of the racial inequalities and forms of cultural affinity (and of cultural exchange) present in cross-cultural relations. It enables analysis of how perceptions of cultural difference among racial/ ethnic groups are critically deployed in both negative and positive ways, with results that are both constraining and empowering.

Finally, such an analysis contributes to the simultaneous consideration of both cultural and political-economic frameworks in studies of sexual migration and has helped me highlight the complex intertwining of cultural and structural issues that emerged in my participants' narratives. I believe this study makes the case that the conceptual integration of structural and cultural dimensions can be quite productive in the field of sexuality studies more generally. Indeed, several recent sociological studies of sexuality that have been conducted with an explicitly political-economic framework—including, for instance, the work by Lionel Cantú that I have cited repeatedly, Elizabeth Bernstein's excellent study of sex work and "bounded authenticity" in the United States, and Kimberly Hoang's wonderful study of global sex work and global capitalism in Vietnam—all have touched on issues that connect directly to shifting sexual cultures in global and local settings. All those cases invite more overtly cultural analyses that could be woven together with the political-economic analyses that these sociologists pursued.[25]

Implications for Sexual Health and HIV Prevention

Before closing, I want to emphasize that the focus on the arc of sexual migration is not only important for theoretical concerns and questions of methodology. It also has significant practical implications for activists, educators, practitioners, and policy makers whose work is directed at immigrants and who are charged with ensuring the well-being of the immigrant and refugee populations in their host societies. This certainly was an important emphasis of the Trayectos Study upon which this book is based, and as such it deserves its own section. In the pages that follow, my goal is to spell out how and why attending to the various conceptual issues I have addressed in *Pathways of Desire* should be not only of academic interest but also highly relevant to applied work with transnational immigrant populations.

When I first conceived of the Trayectos Study, one of my primary goals was to learn about how the often dramatic shifts in social context that result from transnational migration affect sexual health and risk for HIV among sexual immigrants. At the time I was designing my study, Latino men who have sex with men (MSM) had the second-highest rates of HIV transmission in the United States (after African American MSM).[26] In California, a large majority of HIV infections among Latinos, as well as among Mexican-born immigrants, involved male-to-male sexual contact (with figures estimated at around 70 percent in each case).[27] And even more recently, in 2014, most cases of HIV transmission among Latino men involved male-to-male sex (more than 70 percent of reported cases), as did cases among Mexican immigrant men (more than 85 percent of reported cases).[28]

The topic of HIV prevention has explicitly emerged only sporadically in my discussion in *Pathways of Desire*. However, I want to suggest that every topic I have addressed in these pages is directly or indirectly linked to the topics of sexual health and HIV prevention. Before elaborating, let me first briefly take stock of where we now stand in terms of the efforts to stop the spread of HIV/AIDS.

HIV Prevention Practice Then and Now

Since the mid-2000s, when my team and I were conducting interviews for the present study, HIV prevention measures gradually have moved away from the emphasis on changing sexual behavior—the emphasis on safe sex and condom promotion—that was most common then. Over the past decade, biomedical and pharmaceutical advances have generated a new wave of HIV prevention strategies that have been seen as augmenting what HIV/AIDS researchers call "the HIV-prevention arsenal."[29] These strategies centrally include the use of antiviral drugs, both to reduce the viral load in the bodies of HIV-positive people and to prevent new infections among HIV-negative individuals (through what has been labeled pre-exposure prophylaxis, or PrEP).[30]

These new strategies are seen by some as a corrective to the failure of safe sex and condom use alone to curb the global pandemic.[31] Yet it is worth noting that at the time that safe sex was invented by gay men,[32] it was deemed revolutionary because it constituted an alternative to more conventional public health measures that proposed, among other things, the closure of the gay baths in cities such as San Francisco and the more general idea that in light of the emerging epidemic, gay men should stop having sex.[33] Over time, however, many gay men began to view safe sex and condom use as unsustainable strategies in the long run, in part because condoms came to be seen by many as a barrier to sensitivity and bodily connection. Today, although the promotion of safe sex and condoms has not disappeared, HIV prevention educators now increasingly speak of PrEP for HIV-negative people and viral suppression for HIV positives.[34] Although technically PrEP is meant to be accompanied by condom use rather than to replace it, much of the interest in PrEP lies precisely in the possibility it raises of being able to dispense with condoms and engage in unprotected sex (though at the risk of contracting other infections besides HIV).[35]

In thinking back about the history of the behavioral approaches that preceded the new biomedical ones, it is important to recall an earlier wave of critique of HIV prevention efforts. Long before the current strategies made their appearance, sociologists and anthropologists working on HIV/AIDS had noted that the psychologically and individually oriented behavioral interventions that dominated the field of HIV prevention often seemed insufficient to ensure that people would practice safe sex consistently.[36] Those behavioral interventions typically focused on helping individuals gain awareness that AIDS was a relevant issue for them (that is, the interventions were meant to change their attitudes about HIV and prevention). And they also focused on providing people at risk with information about how to prevent HIV/AIDS transmission, and teaching them sexual negotiation skills. These were the components of interventions meant to focus on knowledge, attitudes, and behavior (KAB, in the field's lingo).

Sociologists and anthropologists argued that individually based interventions did not adequately recognize that sex is essentially a form of social interaction, and that as such it is affected by the same social and cultural issues and forms of social difference that influence many other social behaviors.[37] They noted that forms of social difference along the axes of race, social class, gender, and sexual orientation impact how sexual encounters are enacted, especially by generating power disparities between sex partners.[38] These scholars brought attention to the fact that the possession of awareness, information, and skills was no guarantee of the ability to practice safe sex due to the limiting and oppressive effects of broader social issues such as homophobia, poverty, sexism, and discrimination. And they advocated for an expansion of HIV prevention efforts in order to consider these overarching structural issues associated with inequality. They felt that HIV prevention must be contextualized in the full range of people's lives. In practice, however, most HIV prevention programs, even those that sought to incorporate these issues explicitly, often remained focused on more traditional, individually based behavioral strategies.

In the case of Latino gay immigrants, the call for greater contextualization led to programs such as Hermanos de Luna y Sol at the Mission Health Neighborhood Center in San Francisco, a program intended to produce self and group empowerment through extensive group discussion about the realities of being a gay Latin American immigrant in the United States.[39] Based on the pioneering research by one of my mentors, the psychologist Rafael Díaz, Hermanos sought to generate group processes that, among other positive effects, would increase the opportunities for Latino gay immigrant men to avoid HIV transmission.[40]

The Challenges Ahead: HIV Prevention for Mexican
Gay Immigrant Men

From a practical perspective, *Pathways of Desire* has sought to produce an understanding of the challenges and opportunities that Mexican gay immigrant men encounter as they traverse international borders and become incorporated into US gay life. I highlight here some of the lessons that we learned, which I believe remain quite relevant in today's public health and HIV prevention work.[41] After all, the medical strategies now being promoted are still behavioral strategies—they require that all people, both HIV negative and HIV positive, continue to emphasize prevention and regularly take their medications. Moreover, they are "not a substitute to the removal of the vulnerabilities that place people at risk of infection in the first place (which incidentally, overlap with vulnerabilities preventing access to treatment)," as Vinh-Kim Nguyen and co-authors have noted.[42] These scholars have also pointed out that

in the rush to paradigm shift, game-change, rollout and scale-up yet a new set of acronyms and standardized interventions, local epidemiological, political, and socio-historical context is once again being ignored, surely only to resurface later as "culture" once much-heralded interventions fail to deliver.[43]

In other words, the new biomedical strategies are still affected by larger structural and cultural issues that may limit or enhance immigrants' sexual health.[44]

The lessons for HIV prevention offered by this book can be considered at three levels: individual, interpersonal, and structural. First, at the level of individuals, it is notable how Mexican immigrant men in my study, including those who considered themselves savvy about gay life in Mexico, often encountered sexual contexts in San Diego that were quite different from everything they had known before. They therefore had to learn how best to negotiate those contexts at the same time that they had to make sure they took measures to avoid the transmission of HIV. The availability of community-based programs that were tailored to their needs, were conducted in their language, and provided them with various forms of support was essential to these participants. (Sadly, since the time of my study, one of the most popular programs, the San Diego branch of Bienestar, closed in 2011 due to lack of funding.[45]) Also crucial to some of my Mexican immigrant participants were the altruistic efforts of people whom they met and who took it upon themselves to · help them navigate new social and sexual contexts. Think of Troy, who was informed by a staff member about the do's and don'ts in a gay bathhouse the first time he attended one—guidance that also explicitly attended to how he could avoid acquiring sexually transmitted infection, information Troy felt "had always stuck in my mind." Think of how different this experience was from Hernán's, who did not have this kind of support and incurred sexual risk at his first time at a gay bathhouse—risk he believes resulted in his becoming infected with syphilis—as he was trying to learn on his own how to navigate the same kind of space.

Second, at the level of interpersonal relations, my discussion of the relationships that Mexican gay men have in San Diego strongly indicates the need in public health and HIV prevention work to pay close attention to the power dynamics that can emerge in the context of relationships. Linked to those dynamics are the complexities of negotiating sexual meanings in the course of sexual interactions.[46] In the words of Ken Plummer, sexual encounters can be seen as "stumbling, fragile and ambiguous situations in which participants gropingly attempt (through such processes as role taking, role making, altercasting and self-presentation) to make 'sexual sense' of selves, situations and others."[47] For instance, think of Cuauhtémoc's experience when he had sex for the first time with an African American man, which led him to say "*ni modo*" (whatever) when this man proceeded to penetrate him without a condom. Cuauhtémoc, who always used condoms with casual sex partners, puzzled about why he had been unable to insist on a condom this time around. It seems clear that this situation was different for him because of the novelty of being with someone whom Cuauhtémoc perceived as possibly more dominant or masculine than he, the novelty of having sex for the first time with an African American (which fulfilled a long-time fantasy), and the novelty of being in a sexual situation in which he and not his sex partner was about to be penetrated. This issue of course combines with my earlier point about the difficulties participants encountered when negotiating safe sex at the same time that they were trying to make sense of the rules of the game in sexual contexts that were new to them. Furthermore, if we add to this equation the kinds of vulnerabilities that emerged from power differentials—including those caused by racialization and racial difference—we can clearly see how fragile the intention to have sex in any preconceived (and safe) manner may be.

Also linked to the issue of interpersonal communication are the different attitudes that partners may hold about the severity of diseases such as HIV, or about whether sex partners are expected to look out for each other or just for themselves when it comes to sexual safety. Because of disparities between the United States and Mexico in terms of the availability of treatments for HIV at the time of my study, Mexican participants generally considered HIV disease deadly, while some of their American counterparts were beginning to see it as a chronic disease that one can live with. As Keith (US Latino) put it, "I know it's a manageable disease. It's no longer a terminal disease, it's not a death sentence." However, this meant that in sexual encounters between Mexican and American men, the potential existed for the risk of HIV infection to mean something completely different to each partner. The resulting discrepancies between them in terms of how they felt about the possibility of acquiring or transmitting HIV could put those determined to avoid transmission in a vulnerable position.

Similarly, Mexican participants often had been exposed in their home country to strong messages about collective responsibility, which seemed to lead participants such as Justo (Mexican), who was HIV positive, to make statements such as the following:

It scares me to infect someone else, because I know how it feels and I wish someone had told me everything. I feel like I would be taking advantage of the person. . . . I could change his life due to a careless moment, and I don't know if I could live having done that.

This contrasted with some statements made by American men who had adopted a more individualistic stance on sexual responsibility. For instance, Evan (US Latino), who was also HIV positive, said:

If they ask, then I'll disclose. But if they don't ask, then I assume that they know what they are getting into. Because they're over eighteen, they know what they're doing, they're throwing their butt up in the air. You know, people should know how to protect themselves; people aren't stupid. I think people have the right to know if they ask, but if they don't ask it's not my obligation to disclose my medical history with somebody.[48]

I do not mean to suggest that it is solely the responsibility of HIV-positive participants to take care of their sex partners.[49] But these examples further demonstrate that widely diverging meanings and interpretations can emerge in the context of sexual encounters, and those different meanings can be consequential—for example, if one partner imagines "we are taking care of each other," while the other instead assumes that "each human being has a responsibility to . . . make those decisions, and . . . take care of themselves," as Nathan (US White) put it. In such a scenario, the failure of each partner to grasp the other's presuppositions could easily create the conditions for HIV transmission.

Finally, at the level of the broader cultural and structural issues that can affect health behaviors, my findings indicate the importance of two separate issues. One relates to my argument about the need to consider the whole arc of sexual migration, which in relation to the sexual health of Mexican gay immigrants suggests helping them reflect on their sexual lives in both Mexico and the United States. An important way of triggering such reflections (which has been employed in programs such as Hermanos de Luna y Sol) involves asking immigrants questions about what has changed for them and what has stayed the same (a strategy not so different, in fact, from the one that informed our own interviews). Part of this work involves discussion with immigrants about their cultural assets—as well as about how they can turn aspects of their lives and cultures into tools that promote their individual and collective agency, and that can help them participate in redefining or transforming the sexual contexts in which they participate.

The second issue concerns the many vulnerabilities that can emerge from being in a disadvantaged social position in the United States. At a structural level, the often disadvantaged status of Mexican immigrant populations indeed calls attention to the efforts of many activists, service providers, and policy makers to ensure that while in the United States, all people, including immigrants, are treated with dignity and are given access to the resources that ensure their well-being. Of course, one domain where this concern applies is that of the pharmaceutical strategies that have recently become incorporated into HIV prevention programs, which require for their success that all people in the United States, regardless of their citizenship status, have access to adequate health care.

While I have not gone into detail here, I have indicated how every topic I have discussed in *Pathways of Desire* has implications for the sexual health and well-being of Mexican gay immigrants. My hope is that those who are interested in sexual health and HIV prevention can take up different aspects of my analysis over the course of the book and trace the implications in ways that link public health work firmly to the study of sexuality, globalization, and migration.

In a speech delivered before the 2016 Democratic National Convention, in a fleeting phrase, president Barack Obama made an indirect reference to the topic of sexual migration. Discussing Hillary Clinton's views on immigration, he described the "striving students and their toiling parents as loving families, not criminals or rapists; families that came here for the same reason our forebears came—to work and to study, and to make a better life, in a place where we can talk and worship and love as we please."[50] In recent years, variations of the phrase "to love as we please" have become a euphemism for sexual diversity in contemporary liberal American politics. "To love as we please": not to have sex as we please, not to enjoy sexual freedom as we like, but to love as we please, and to do so as part of a loving family.

I do not mean to be dismissive of this signal of inclusiveness toward LGBT people, which since the height of debates about same-sex marriage has become standard in progressive political discourse in the United States, even if to be included LGBT people have to be dressed in the largely heteronormative robes of socially acceptable loving families, married life, and assumed commitment and monogamy so that they become more palatable to a mainstream American audience. My point in bringing up President Obama's speech is to note that as part of these recent developments, the idea that people may uproot themselves and travel long distances—across oceans and difficult-to-cross borders—precisely in order to love as they please seems finally to have entered mainstream political imaginaries of the United States as a place of freedom.

Indeed, many of my Mexican immigrant participants felt that their lives had improved in numerous ways since they arrived in the United States, and that they had achieved, to varying degrees, the sexual freedom they craved, which had prompted many of them to move in the first place. But they also came to realize that life in the United States is not entirely free from care, and the racialization and social marginalization that many of them experienced, even within the gay communities where they sought to enact their sexual freedom, often surprised and sometimes also deeply disappointed them. Think for instance of Toribio, who left for Los Angeles with the promise of a life with his US White boyfriend, filled with fantasies about living in Hollywood—"pretty woman, walking down the street," he sang in his head—only to find out that he was just one of four young Mexican men with whom his boyfriend planned to live. Those are moments in which the fantasy of gay life in the United States suddenly ruptures. And yet, like many other immigrants who preceded them, these immigrants' narratives show that they are resilient. They are adept at overcoming difficulties and crafting new lives for themselves, and in the process, they are also willing to contribute what they can to those with whom they interact in their adopted country. It is my hope that this study stimulates further discussion of the complexities of sexual migration—especially as the country enters a completely different and much less hopeful political era—and that it helps us see this phenomenon, and other aspects of the global movement of people, practices, and ideas, in a new light.

Acknowledgments

First and most important, I would like to thank the gay and bisexual men who participated in the Trayectos Study, upon which this book is based. They include the 150 men who took part in formal interviews plus many others with whom my research team and I interacted informally over the course of our fieldwork. I am grateful for their frankness and willingness to talk about their sexual and migration histories, lives, and experiences. My thanks go also to the staff and volunteers of community-based organizations and other local businesses and institutions in San Diego; they made it possible for my team to conduct participant observation and recruitment at their events, and include Alma Latina, Bacchus House, Bienestar, the Bi-National AIDS Advocacy Project, Bourbon Street, the Brass Rail, the Caliph, the CASA Program at the San Ysidro Health Center, Clair de Lune, Club Caliente, Club Montage, Club Papi, the Flame, Flicks, Kickers, Latin Pride, the Loft, the Metropolitan Community Church, Numbers, the San Diego LGBT Community Center (and its Latin@ Services program), and the Top of the Park.

A project of this size could not have been carried out without the diligent efforts of my research team. I have very fond memories of our daily interactions in our small suite of offices in the Hillcrest neighborhood of San Diego, and I am deeply grateful for their commitment to the study and all their hard work. I miss our team meetings, our lively planning and analytical discussions, and our consistently collegial environment. The core team included three ethnographers—Jaweer Brown, Jorge Fontdevila, and Victoria

González-Rivera. Along with me, they conducted interviews, participant observation, and data analysis. Stephen Scott, our indefatigable, always cheery, and extremely well-organized project director, oversaw all the administrative and logistical aspects of the study. And two program assistants, Carlos Hermosillo and Vicente Mendívil, were instrumental in implementing the project's day-to-day administrative activities and providing logistical assistance to our participants at all steps of their involvement in the study.

The research project benefited from the helpful insight of the project's coinvestigator, Steven Epstein, and two academic consultants, Rafael Díaz and Gloria González-López. We also received valuable suggestions from our community advisory board, whose members were René Arias, Norma Benavides, Loc Dinh, Sergio Dorantes, Lauren Farber, Tom Gray, Antonio Muñoz, Delcy Olachea, Juan Olmeda, Teresa Oyos, Carlos L. Pargue, Víctor Pereda, Mauricio Pérez, Deborah Roseman, and Ramón Sandoval. A dedicated cadre of energetic recruiters scouted out a wide variety of locations in San Diego and helped us achieve the sampling diversity that we desired. For their efforts I thank Joshua Anguiano, Paula González, Elijah Griffin, María Rosario Mancillas, Matthew O'Flaherty, Arturo Ramos, David Ribes, Ernesto Rodríguez, and Genoveva Sánchez. Another dedicated team, mostly of graduate students from the University of California, San Diego, helped us code our transcripts: Shari Budihardjo Weignant, Paula González, Lyn Headley, Stephanie Lombard, Rigoberto Márquez, Devon Smith, Lyz Stevenson, and Tom Waidzunas. Finally, Jeff Henne and his team helped us transcribe our interviews. As evidenced by these lists, our ethnographic teamwork involved many pairs of hands.

This research could not have been possible without adequate funding, which was provided by a grant from the National Institute of Child and Human Development of the National Institutes of Health (award number R01HD042919). I thank Susan Newcomer for her encouragement, as well as my program officer, Rebecca Clark, and the anonymous scholars who reviewed and approved my grant proposal. The content of this book is solely my responsibility and does not represent the official views of the National Institutes of Health.

At the inevitable risk of unintentionally omitting some names, I also want to thank many individuals who encouraged me over the years at my academic homes, first at the Center for AIDS Prevention Studies (CAPS) at the University of California, San Francisco (UCSF); later at San Francisco State University (SFSU); and most recently at Northwestern University. I am especially grateful to my core mentors, Rafael Díaz and Barbara

VanOss Marín, who believed in my ability to follow in their footsteps. Their willingness to share their wisdom and expertise was essential for my own success at pursuing this research. Other CAPS and UCSF faculty provided me with critically important feedback, including Judith Barker, Diane Binson (1943–2015), Tom Coates, Margaret Dolcini, Susan Folkman, Cynthia Gómez, Olga Grinstead, Susan Kegeles, Steve Morin, Dennis Osmond, Tor Neilands, Nicholas Sheon, Ron Stall, Jean Tschann, and Bill Woods. I am equally grateful to my fellow participants in the Visiting Professors program at CAPS, especially Lisa Bowleg and Hirokazu Yoshikawa.

At SFSU, I benefited from my involvement in the Center for Research on Gender and Sexuality. I thank my colleagues Gil Herdt, Colleen Hoff, and Deborah Tolman; administrative staff members Tobie Kaye and Ruslan Valeev; and my research assistants Michael Díaz, Anthony Freeman, Walter Gómez, and Julia Sinclair-Palm. I also appreciated many helpful conversations with other SFSU colleagues, including Jessica Fields, Allen LeBlanc, Rita Meléndez, and Niels Teunis.

At Northwestern, I have been blessed with excellent colleagues and students, many of whom have provided me with helpful comments along the way. Many thanks to the Department of Sociology, the Gender and Sexualities Studies Program, and the Latina/o Studies Program, including the helpful staff in those units. I particularly thank Ken Alder, Ana Aparicio, Frances Aparicio, Gerry Cadava, Chas Camic, Bruce Carruthers, Tony Chen, Nick Davis, Micaela di Leonardo, Mary Dietz, Jillana Enteen, Wendy Espeland, Lane Fenrich, Jon Glassman, Jay Grossman, Carol Heimer, E. Patrick Johnson, Jules Law, Tessie Liu, Jim Mahoney, Joel Martínez, Jeffrey Masten, Aldon Morris, Ann Orloff, Amy Partridge, Mary Pattillo, Jan Radway, Ramón Rivera-Servera, Mónica Russel y Rodríguez, Art Stinchcombe, Mary Weismantel, Wendy Wall, Gregory Ward, and Celeste Watkins-Hayes.

I also benefited enormously from a nine-month residential fellowship in 2012–13 at the Radcliffe Institute for Advanced Study at Harvard. My thanks go to Judy Vichniac, Liz Cohen, and the program staff. Thanks also to all the members of my cohort; I much appreciated their support, feedback, and camaraderie throughout the year. I am especially grateful to academic colleagues at Radcliffe and in the area with whom I had one-on-one conversations about my book project during my year in Cambridge, including Ana Mariella Bacigalupo, Glenn Cohen, Filiz Garip, Lynn Hudson, Katherine Ibbett, Tsitsi Jaji, Michèle Lamont, Peggy Levitt, Ruth Milkman, Feryal Özel, Benjamin Podbilewicz, Jyoti Puri, Jane Rhodes,

Henry Turner, Amanda Klekowski von Koppenfels, Rebecca Walkowitz, and Suzanna Walters. I am also grateful to two Harvard research assistants, Adrián González and Joshua Hernández.

My warmest thanks go to Doug Mitchell, my editor at the University of Chicago Press, who encouraged this project from its earliest stages. I also extend my appreciation to his helpful editorial associate, Kyle Wagner, as well as Erin DeWitt, Sandra Hazel, Ashley Pierce, Kevin Quach, Joseph Claude, and everyone at the Press who aided in the production of this book.

I am very grateful to the readers who commented on the full book manuscript: Elizabeth Armstrong, Richard Parker, and a third anonymous reviewer. I am especially indebted to Steven Epstein for reading and making editorial suggestions on multiple drafts of the manuscript. My thanks go also to Elvira Carrillo and Ulices Pego for their help in creating and formatting the figures.

Many friends provided support over the years in which I worked on this project, and I especially want to thank Jeff Kilmer, who repeatedly opened his home to me and my partner along the way. In addition, over the course of my study and analysis, I engaged in multiple conversations about my project with colleagues and friends, and I thank them for their interest and helpful suggestions. They include Ian Abramson, Barry Adam, Tomás Almaguer, Dennis Altman, Ana Amuchástegui, Enrique Asís, Judy Auerbach, Lucía Avila (1953–2011, whom I miss terribly every single day), George Ayala, Elizabeth Bernstein, Mary Blair-Loy, Tom Boellstorff, Lars Boesen, Patricia Boesen, Yamil Bonduki, Jennifer Brier, Charles Briggs, Carlos Cáceres, Lionel Cantú (1965–2002), Alex Carballo-Diéguez, George Chauncey, Tod Cochran, Jorge Ignacio Cortiñas, Ellyn Daniels, John Daniels, John D'Emilio, Richard Elovich, John Gagnon (1931–2016), Marsha Gale, Carlos Gallo, Jorge González Casanova, Elisa Greenberg, Ned Greenberg, Sarita Groisser, Ramón Gutiérrez, Liz Hoadley, Pierrette Hondagneu-Sotelo, Cymene Howe, Jerry Karabel, Sue Kippax, David Kirp, Rebecca Klatch, George Lipsitz, Mauricio List, Kristin Luker, André Maiorana, Martin Manalansan, Arturo Martínez, Beth Mertz, Stuart Michaels, Natalia Molina, Kelly Moore, Chandra Mukerji, Steve Murray, Don Opitz, Kurt Organista, Pamela Balls Organista, Mark Padilla, Richard Parker, Jonathan Rabinovitz, Gabriel Ramírez, Jesús Ramírez-Valles, Horacio Roque-Ramírez (1969–2015), Leslie Salzinger, Ruth Schwartz, Nayan Shah, Robert Courtney Smith, Arlene Stein, Indi Talwani, Stefan Timmermans, Clay Tschudy, Salvador Vidal-Ortiz, Tom Waidzunas, Chris Waters, and Daniel Wolfe. I truly appreciate their interest in my work.

I am very grateful for the unfaltering love and support of my family: the Carrillos, the Epsteins, and the Merensteins. Finally, I wish to express my most heartfelt thanks to my partner, Steve. The love we have shared over the past thirty years has been a constant source of vital emotional sustenance.

Notes

1. All participants' names are pseudonyms. Participants had the option of speaking in either Spanish or English; all translations from Spanish are my own. Most Mexican participants chose to be interviewed in Spanish.

2. Hermosillo is Sonora's state capital (population 715,000 in 2010). At seventeen years of age, Máximo moved there from his hometown, a smaller town in Sonora (population 42,500 in 2010), to attend college. In Hermosillo he initially lived with a sister. Population figures are from the Instituto Nacional de Estadística y Geografía (INEGI) (National Institute of Statistics and Geography), http://www.inegi.org.mx/. Accessed March 2, 2017.

3. According to Máximo, apart from a cruisy theater, Hermosillo had no other institutional gay life in the 1980s—no gay bars or commercial gathering spaces. However, a gay man whom he met while in college introduced him to that city's extensive informal gay networks. Since that time, like many other Mexican cities, Hermosillo has acquired at least five gay clubs, as indicated by the website Gay Guide Mexico: https://foursquare.com/gomangopuntomx/list/gay-guide-hermosillo. Accessed March 2, 2017. Also, in 2015 the Mexican Supreme Court approved an injunction that allowed same-sex marriages to take place in Hermosillo. See Bastida Aguilar, "Celebrarán primeros matrimonios igualitarios en Hermosillo, Sonora."

4. Instituto Nacional de Estadística y Geografía (INEGI) (National Institute of Statistics and Geography), http://www.inegi.org.mx/. Accessed March 2, 2017.

5. Máximo's stated desire suggests a Mexican version of the "great gay migration" that Weston identified as taking place in the United States around the same time that Máximo was considering a move to a larger location within Mexico. Weston, "Get Thee to a Big City." See also Langarita Adiego and Salguero Velázquez, "Sexiled in Mexico City."

6. Máximo said the italicized words in English. Throughout the book, I italicize the English words that participants interspersed into their Spanish. I also italicize the Spanish words that I retained in text that I translated into English.

7. Before the events of September 11, 2001, and even for a number of years afterward, American citizens routinely traveled back and forth across the US-Mexico border without a passport. As they returned to the United States from Mexico or Canada, they merely had to indicate to the border agents that they were American citizens, and at the border agents' discretion were waved into the country, questioned, or asked for a form of identification. This procedure changed eight years later, in June 2009, when a policy implemented by the Obama administration required Americans to use a US passport for entry at official border-crossing points. See Higgins, "Practical Traveler."

8. Carrillo, "Sexual Migration, Cross-Cultural Encounters, and Sexual Health," 59. See also Parker, "Migration, Sexual Subcultures, and HIV/AIDS in Brazil"; Cantú, "Entre Hombres/Between Men"; Cantú, "A Place Called Home"; Epps, Valens, and González, *Passing Lines*; Cantú, *The Sexuality of Migration*.

9. Carrillo, "Sexual Migration, Cross-Cultural Encounters, and Sexual Health," 59.

10. The various binaries used to distinguish the bloc of wealthier and more powerful countries from the rest of the world—including rich/poor, developed/developing, First World/Third World, West/non-West, and global North/global South—are all imperfect. Following the lead of scholars such as Raewyn Connell, I have chosen the labels *global North* and *global South* because they seem to be most closely aligned with widely accepted understandings of globalization—which depict the countries of the global North as the sources of capital, technologies, ideas, practices, and cultural expressions that disseminate to the global South. I nonetheless challenge those understandings (as does Connell in "The Northern Theory of Globalization"). Moreover, like the other binaries this one is problematic and in some respects confusing, especially since the global North includes countries such as Australia and New Zealand that are geographically located in the Southern Hemisphere, while the global South includes countries such as Mexico, which geographically is part of North America (even when, as a way to distance themselves from their neighbor to the south, many in the United States would probably argue that Mexico is part of Central America or Latin America more generally).

11. Luibhéid, introduction, xxv.

12. See, for instance, Cantú, *The Sexuality of Migration*.

13. Massey, Goldring, and Durand, "Continuities in Transnational Migration," 1500. Although Mexican migration has diversified in recent years, the patterns identified in earlier decades continue to inform the popular imagination about Mexican migrants. For more on those patterns, see Durand and Massey, "Mexican Migration to the United States." See also the interesting analysis provided by Malkin, " 'We Go to Get Ahead.' "

14. See, for instance, Cerruti and Massey, "On the Auspices of Female Migration from Mexico to the United States."

15. One exception is Robert Courtney Smith's limited discussion of sexuality (within a larger discussion of gender). Smith, *Mexican New York*, 100.

16. On the topic of lifestyle migration, see Stone and Stubs, "Enterprising Expatriates"; Benson and O'Reilly, "Migration and the Search for a Better Way of Life"; Benson and O'Reilly, *Lifestyle Migration*; Benson, "The Context and Trajectory of Lifestyle Migration"; von Koppenfels, *Migrants or Expatriates?*

17. See Hondagneu-Sotelo, *Gendered Transitions*; Hirsch, *A Courtship after Marriage*; Gutmann, "Dystopian Travels in Gringolandia"; Malkin, " 'We Go to Get Ahead' "; González-López, *Erotic Journeys*. Among other findings in this literature, Malkin demonstrates that immigrant women must often implement complicated strategies in order to pursue their desires for change while also retaining a reputation of respectability.

18. Gutmann, "Dystopian Travels in Gringolandia," 480. Emphasis in the original.

19. See Garip, "Discovering Diverse Mechanisms of Migration"; Garip and Asad, "Network Effects in Mexico-U.S. Migration."

20. See Altman, *Global Sex*; Altman, "Sexuality and Globalization"; Binnie, *The Globalization of Sexuality*.

21. Cantú, "Entre Hombres/Between Men"; Parker, *Beneath the Equator*; Manalansan, *Global Divas*; Cantú, *The Sexuality of Migration*; Thing, "Gay, Mexican and Immigrant"; Decena, *Tacit Subjects*; Vasquez del Aguila, " 'God Forgives the Sin but Not the Scandal' "; Acosta, *Amigas y Amantes*; Peña, *¡Oye Loca!*; Adam and Rangel, "The Post-migration Sexual Citizenship."

22. Cantú, *The Sexuality of Migration*. Unfortunately, Cantú died unexpectedly at an early age, and his work was brought to publication by Nancy A. Naples and Salvador Vidal-Ortiz.

23. Manalansan, *Global Divas*.

24. Gagnon and Simon, *Sexual Conduct*; Simon and Gagnon, "Sexual Scripts."

25. Blair-Loy, "Cultural Constructions of Family Schemas," 689. As Blair-Loy also notes, schemas contain cognitive, normative, and emotional dimensions, and "are objective in the sense of being shared, publicly available understandings [but also] subjective and partially internalized." Ibid. See also Sewell, "A Theory of Structure."

26. My characterization of sexual schemas as a kind of cultural schema roughly parallels Wendy Roth's depiction of "racial schemas." See Roth, *Race Migrations*.

27. As an alternative to "sexual schemas," one could speak of "sexual repertoires," therefore relying on the concept of cultural repertoires, as developed by Lamont and her collaborators. See Small, Harding, and Lamont, "Reconsidering Culture and Poverty"; Lamont and Small, "How Culture Matters"; Lamont, "Toward a Comparative Sociology of Valuation and Evaluation." However, *sexual repertoires* is usually used more narrowly as a term denoting a range of sexual behaviors (indeed, I sometimes use that term in that way in this book). By contrast, *sexual schemas* refers not only to a repertoire of sexual behaviors and practices but also to a broader, organized framework of sexual meanings, interpretations, and possible courses of action that becomes available in a cultural setting (and which may compete with other sexual schemas present in the same setting).

28. See, for instance, Green, "The Social Organization of Desire"; Green, "Erotic Habitus"; Green, *Sexual Fields*.

29. Foucault, *The History of Sexuality*, vol. 1; Epstein, "A Queer Encounter"; Stein and Plummer, " 'I Can't Even Think Straight' "; Gamson and Moon, "The Sociology of Sexualities."

30. On the political economy of sexuality, see, for example, Bernstein, *Temporarily Yours*; Padilla, *Caribbean Pleasure Industry*; Cantú, *The Sexuality of Migration*. On sexual rights, a few selected references are Adam, Duyvendak, and Krouwel, *The Global Emergence of Gay and Lesbian Politics*; Armstrong, *Forging Gay Identities*; de la Dehesa, *Queering the Public Sphere in Mexico and Brazil*. On sexual citizenship, among others see Evans, *Sexual Citizenship*; Alexander, "Not Just (Any) Body Can Be a Citizen"; Weeks, "The Sexual Citizen"; Bell and Binnie, *The Sexual Citizen*; Seidman, "From Identity to Queer Politics"; Stychin, "Sexual Citizenship in the European Union"; Plummer, *Intimate Citizenship*; Bell and Binnie, "Geographies of Sexual Citizenship"; Langdridge, "Voices from the Margins"; Canaday, *The Straight State*; Payne and Davies, "Introduction." On the topic of sexual regulation, see Stein, *The Stranger Next Door*; Canaday, *The Straight State*; Herdt, *Moral Panics, Sex Panics*; Lancaster, *Sex Panic and the Punitive State*. On the relationship between sexuality and space, see, among others, Bell and Valentine, *Mapping Desire*; Bell and Binnie, "Authenticating Queer Space"; Bell and Binnie, "Geographies of Sexual Citizenship"; Brown, "Counting on Queer Geography"; Ghaziani, *There Goes the Gayborhood?*; Greene, "Gay Neighborhoods"; Saracino, "How Places Shape Identity." On the globalization of sexuality, some key sources are Altman, "Rupture or Continuity?"; Altman, "Global Gays/Global Gaze"; Altman, *Global Sex*; Altman, "Sexuality and Globalization"; Binnie, *The Globalization of Sexuality*. On sexual culture, among others I have been influenced by Herdt and Stoller, *Intimate Communications*; Parker, *Bodies, Pleasures, and Passions*; Herdt, *Sexual Cultures and Migration in the Era of AIDS*; Parker, *Beneath the Equator*. The literatures on sexuality, race, and class include, among many sources, Valocchi, "The Class-Inflected Nature of Gay Identity"; Viveros Vigoya, "Dionysian

Blacks"; Nagel, *Race, Ethnicity, and Sexuality*; McBride, *Why I Hate Abercrombie and Fitch*; Binnie, "Class, Sexuality and Space"; Heaphy, "Gay Identities and the Culture of Class"; Ferguson, *Aberrations in Black*. Finally, on the growing field of gay Latina/o studies, see, for example, the essays collected in Hames-García and Martínez, *Gay Latino Studies*. See also Rodríguez, *Queer Latinidad*; Rivera-Servera, *Performing Queer Latinidad*; Rodríguez, *Sexual Futures*; Quesada, Gomez, and Vidal-Ortiz, *Queer Brown Voices*.

31. On recent sociological approaches to studying the embodiment of sex, see Weitman, "On the Elementary Forms of the Socioerotic Life"; Carrillo, *The Night Is Young*; Fontdevila, "Framing Dilemmas during Sex"; Shilling and Mellor, "Sociology and the Problem of Eroticism."

32. Baumle, "Border Identities," 243.

33. The US General Services Administration has estimated that approximately 50,000 vehicles and 25,000 pedestrians cross daily into the United States through the San Ysidro crossing point, located in the southernmost suburb of the San Diego metropolitan area. See http://www.gsa.gov/portal/content /104872?utm_source=R9&utm_medium=print-radio&utm_term=sanysidro &utm_campaign=shortcuts. Accessed March 2, 2017.

34. See Ponting, "San Diego Cities among State's Most Conservative."

35. Award number R01HD042919. The content of this book is solely my responsibility and does not represent the official views of the National Institutes of Health.

36. Lamont and Swidler, "Methodological Pluralism and the Possibilities and Limits of Interviewing," 154–55.

37. Ibid., 158–59.

38. Three of the eighty men lived on the Mexican side of the border. These men, who were recruited and interviewed in San Diego, technically were not migrants. But they crossed the border routinely for work in San Diego and/or participated extensively in San Diego's gay life. They are included in most of the analysis, except for the sections that refer specifically to those who had lived as adults in the United States.

39. We included five participants of Mexican origin who were born in the United States but brought to Mexico by their parents or caretakers at an early age. These five remained in Mexico during childhood and returned to the United States as young adults.

40. For a study with this specific population in San Diego, see Parrini et al., "Identity, Desire and Truth."

41. Since then, the Distrito Federal has been dissolved as an administrative unit, and Ciudad de México has become an autonomous entity with many of the same characteristics as the rest of the states. See Chávez, "DF no es el estado 32."

42. The core research team created a comprehensive codebook for this purpose, which was refined in sequential iterations in the early stages of the analysis. We used seventy-six codes altogether, which allowed us to mark

passages devoted to such specific topics as childhood sexual labeling, racial/ethnic discrimination, prior knowledge of gay San Diego, HIV/AIDS knowledge, migration networks, and many others important for our analysis. The bulk of the coding was conducted by seven graduate students, under the supervision of the core team, who read through each transcript, assigning relevant codes to specific blocks of text. Throughout the coding process, we achieved a high level of intercoder reliability (81 percent on average, calculated based on the number of times that all coders assigned the same codes to a selection of random pages of interview material previously coded by the researchers). We derived our approach to measuring intercoder reliability from the discussion on this topic by Miles and Huberman, *Qualitative Data Analysis.*

43. This discussion is partially based on analysis conducted for Carrillo and Fontdevila, "Border Crossings and Shifting Sexualities."

CHAPTER ONE

1. Engardio, "You Can't Be Gay—You're Latino."
2. Carrillo, *The Night Is Young,* 112. On the notion of *el ambiente,* literally "the environment" or "the milieu," see also Murray, *Latin American Male Homosexualities;* Monsiváis, *Que se abra esa puerta.*
3. Early works on this topic, published during the period from 1995 to 2000, include Manalansan, "In The Shadows of Stonewall"; Gopinath, "Funny Boys and Girls"; Espín, *Latina Realities;* Herdt, *Sexual Cultures and Migration in the Era of AIDS;* Parker, "Migration, Sexual Subcultures, and HIV/AIDS in Brazil"; Luibhéid, "Looking Like a Lesbian"; Cantú, "Entre Hombres/ Between Men"; Parker, *Beneath the Equator;* Patton and Sánchez-Eppler, *Queer Diasporas.*
4. Sánchez-Eppler and Patton, "Introduction," 3.
5. In addition to the works listed in note 3, other works published between 2001 and 2005 include Cantú, "A Place Called Home"; Fortier, "'Coming Home'"; Cruz-Malavé and Manalansan, *Queer Globalizations;* Fortier, "Queer Diaspora"; Luibhéid, *Entry Denied;* Manalansan, *Global Divas;* Carrillo, "Sexual Migration, Cross-Cultural Encounters, and Sexual Health"; Cantú, Luibhéid, and Stern, "Well-Founded Fear"; Luibhéid and Cantú, *Queer Migrations;* Manalansan, "Race, Violence, and Neoliberal Spatial Politics in the Global City"; Manalansan, "Migrancy, Modernity, Mobility." The most recent wave of work in this area, published over the past decade, includes Manalansan, "Queer Intersections"; Bianchi et al., "The Sexual Experiences of Latino Men"; Howe, "Sexual Borderlands"; Acosta, "Lesbianas in the Borderlands"; Luibhéid, "Sexuality, Migration, and the Shifting Line between Legal and Illegal Status"; Cantú, *The Sexuality of Migration;* Carrillo, "Leaving Loved Ones Behind"; Thomas, Haour-Knipe, and Aggleton, *Mobility, Sexuality and AIDS;* Carrillo, "Immigration and LGBT Rights in the USA"; Thing, "Gay,

Mexican and Immigrant"; Decena, *Tacit Subjects*; Toro-Alfonso, López Ortiz, and Nieves Lugo, "Sexualidades migrantes"; Vasquez del Aguila, "'God Forgives the Sin but Not the Scandal'"; Acosta, *Amigas y Amantes*; Peña, *¡Oye Loca!*; Carrillo and Fontdevila, "Border Crossings and Shifting Sexualities"; Adam and Rangel, "The Post-migration Sexual Citizenship"; Fassin and Salcedo, "Becoming Gay?" In addition, emerging work on transgender migration emphasizes its own distinctive set of concerns; see for instance Padilla et al., "Trans-Migrations."

6. Luibhéid, introduction, ix.
7. Ibid.
8. Canaday, *The Straight State*. See also Puri, *Sexual States*.
9. Luibhéid, *Entry Denied*; Coleman, "US Immigration Law and Its Geographies of Social Control."
10. Cantú, Luibhéid, and Stern, "Well-Founded Fear"; Luibhéid, introduction; Randazzo, "Social and Legal Barriers"; Reddy, "Asian Diasporas, Neoliberalism, and Family"; Canaday, *The Straight State*; Carrillo, "Immigration and LGBT Rights in the USA"; Vogler, "Legally Queer."
11. Luibhéid, introduction, xxvi. See also Manalansan, *Global Divas*; Cantú, *The Sexuality of Migration*; Thing, "Gay, Mexican and Immigrant"; Decena, *Tacit Subjects*; Vasquez del Aguila, "'God Forgives the Sin but Not the Scandal'"; Acosta, *Amigas y Amantes*; Adam and Rangel, "The Post-migration Sexual Citizenship."
12. Cantú, *The Sexuality of Migration*, 23.
13. Ibid.
14. Naples and Vidal-Ortiz, editors' introduction, 15.
15. Included in this list are studies such as those by Manalansan, *Global Divas*; Bianchi et al., "The Sexual Experiences of Latino Men"; Cantú, *The Sexuality of Migration*; Thing, "Gay, Mexican and Immigrant"; Decena, *Tacit Subjects*; Vasquez del Aguila, "'God Forgives the Sin but Not the Scandal'"; Acosta, *Amigas y Amantes*; Adam and Rangel, "The Post-migration Sexual Citizenship."
16. Exceptions are the present study and the study by James Thing, who recruited small samples of Mexican gay men in Mexico and Los Angeles. Like me, Thing explicitly emphasizes the need to recruit a diverse sample of immigrants in terms of their experiences and sexual interpretations. However, his sample involves almost exclusively working-class immigrants, which limits a kind of diversity that proved to be important in my study. Thing, "Gay, Mexican and Immigrant."
17. Manalansan, *Global Divas*, 25.
18. As Cantú was conducting this research, I was in the process of writing *The Night Is Young*. Therefore, Cantú had no access to my own analysis.
19. Cantú, *The Sexuality of Migration*. On the topic of queer migration and the search for home, see also Fortier, "'Coming Home.'"
20. Cantú, *The Sexuality of Migration*, 78.

21. Ibid., 148.
22. Ibid., 161.
23. Ibid., 29. Cantú's concern and proposal are consistent with Dennis Altman's view that sexuality scholars "often ignore questions of material and institutional power," fail to link sexuality to the politics and materiality of everyday life, and depict sexuality instead as simply representing decontextualized, natural, and apolitical "pleasures of the body." Altman, *Global Sex*, 1–2.
24. Cantú, *The Sexuality of Migration*, 148.
25. Manalansan, *Global Divas*. See also my discussion of this aspect of Manalansan's work in Carrillo, "Sexual Migration, Cross-Cultural Encounters, and Sexual Health."
26. On the topics of race, attraction, and sexual objectification among gay men, see Teunis, "Sexual Objectification and the Construction of Whiteness"; Wilson et al., "Race-Based Sexual Stereotyping."
27. McClintock, *Imperial Leather*; Stoller, *Race and the Education of Desire*; Young, *Colonial Desire*; Altman, "Rupture or Continuity?"; Altman, "Global Gays/Global Gaze"; Altman, *Global Sex*; Hawley, *Postcolonial, Queer*; Stoller, *Carnal Knowledge and Imperial Power*; Nagel, *Race, Ethnicity, and Sexuality*, 77; Altman, "Sexuality and Globalization"; Binnie, *The Globalization of Sexuality*.
28. Altman, *Global Sex*, 15.
29. Altman, "Rupture or Continuity?," 77.
30. Ibid.
31. Ibid., 77–78.
32. Evidence of the interactions between "Western" and local sexual schemas emerged at the time in various ethnographic case studies conducted in countries such as Indonesia, Mexico, China, and Brazil. Boellstorff, *The Gay Archipelago*; Carrillo, *The Night Is Young*; Farrer, *Opening Up*; Parker, *Bodies, Pleasures, and Passions*; Rofel, *Desiring China*; Rofel, "Qualities of Desire"; Parker, *Beneath the Equator*.
33. Altman, *Global Sex*, 16.
34. Ibid., 17.
35. Luibhéid, introduction, x.
36. See, for instance, Rofel, "Qualities of Desire"; Jackson, "An Explosion of Thai Identities"; Jackson, "Pre-gay, Post-queer"; Rofel, *Desiring China*.
37. Rofel, *Desiring China*, 88.
38. Ibid.
39. Altman, *Global Sex*, 1.
40. On the emergence of this term, see Povinelli and Chauncey, "Thinking Sexuality Transnationally."
41. This was made clear in a number of scholarly studies conducted in the global South, including, for instance, Parker, *Beneath the Equator*; Carrillo, *The Night Is Young*. See also Binnie, *The Globalization of Sexuality*, 6. That

these adaptations also occur within the countries of the global North is exemplified by research on contrasts between the meaning of *gay* and related notions in the United States and France by Stambolis-Ruhstorfer, "Labels of Love"; Stambolis-Ruhstorfer and Saguy, "How to Describe It?"

42. García-Canclini, *Hybrid Cultures*; Carrillo, *The Night Is Young*. See also Parker, *Bodies, Pleasures, and Passions*; Parker, *Beneath the Equator*; Boellstorff, *The Gay Archipelago*.

43. Boellstorff, *The Gay Archipelago*.

44. Jackson, "Pre-gay, Post-queer," 13.

45. Ibid.

46. Binnie, *The Globalization of Sexuality*, 5, 36.

47. As I mentioned before, an exception is the analysis by Manalansan, *Global Divas*.

48. On this point, see Rofel, *Desiring China*, 90. As part of her critique of Dennis Altman's work, Rofel has argued that when Altman conceives of a spectrum from tradition to modernity, he regards the sexual expressions that seem more consistent with Western styles as being more modern, a link that is taken to be "self-evident." Rofel's critique is based on her reading of Altman, "Global Gays/Global Gaze."

49. On the emergence of glocalized sexual modernity in Mexico, see Carrillo, "Imagining Modernity."

50. Altman, *Global Sex*, 17.

51. Ibid.

52. McClintock, *Imperial Leather*, 12–13.

53. Young, *Colonial Desire*, xi–xii.

54. Ibid., xii.

55. Ibid., 4.

56. McClintock, *Imperial Leather*, xi.

57. Hawley, *Postcolonial, Queer*, 5. Emphasis in the original.

58. Bhabha, "Signs Taken for Wonders." Page 156 cited in Young, *Colonial Desire*, 22.

59. Stoller, *Carnal Knowledge and Imperial Power*, 23.

60. Young, *Colonial Desire*; Boellstorff, "The Perfect Path"; Hawley, *Postcolonial, Queer*.

61. Nagel, Race, *Ethnicity, and Sexuality*, 14.

62. Boellstorff, "The Perfect Path"; Binnie, *The Globalization of Sexuality*.

CHAPTER TWO

1. This reputation of the last car on Metro trains as a gay cruising site has become so commonplace that in 2012, city officials tried to end gay male cruising in the Metro system by shutting down the last car during certain hours. Gay activist groups responded by claiming that the last car of the Metro trains serves as a gay liberated space. They sought to institutionalize

this by baptizing the last car of the Mexico City Metro as the *jotivagón*, or gay Metro car. See Montalvo Fuentes, "Crónica"; Montalvo Fuentes, "Reportaje."

2. Adam, Duyvendak, and Krouwel, *The Global Emergence of Gay and Lesbian Politics*.

3. Carrillo and Fontdevila, "Rethinking Sexual Initiation"; Carrillo and Fontdevila, "Border Crossings and Shifting Sexualities." These forms of homoeroticism have also been identified and discussed by Nuñez Noriega, *Sexo entre varones*; Nuñez Noriega, "Reconociendo los placeres"; Nuñez Noriega, *Just between Us*.

4. The Mexican phrase *el ambiente*, literally "the environment" or "the milieu," is a euphemism for a wide range of homoerotic practices and spaces. In some settings, describing a place as *de ambiente* is meant to be recognized only by those in the know, which historically offered some protections against social stigma. On this topic see Carrillo, *The Night Is Young*; Nuñez Noriega, *Masculinidad e intimidad*.

5. There is a commonplace perception that access to gay culture and gay-inflected understandings is limited to middle-class Mexicans who live in large urban areas—Mexicans who have the cultural capital to participate in global gay culture and communities. Yet such a perception is only partially accurate. I similarly challenge the assumption that it is only working-class or rural men—who may have less access to a global gay discourse—who adopt forms of homoeroticism that are not based on gay subjectivities. On these topics, see also Nuñez Noriega, *Masculinidad e intimidad*; Vasquez del Aguila, " 'God Forgives the Sin but Not the Scandal.' "

6. Carrier, "Urban Mexican Male Encounters"; Carrier, "Family Attitudes"; Carrier, "Cultural Factors"; Taylor, "El Ambiente"; Taylor, "Mexican Male Interaction"; Almaguer, "Chicano Men"; Carrier, *De los Otros*. See also Murray, *Latin American Male Homosexualities*.

7. See my discussion of cultural and sexual schemas in the introduction.

8. Almaguer, "Chicano Men."

9. In this model, passivity is equated with femininity and activity with masculinity. This is empirically questionable, as Nuñez Noriega has noted and my own findings also confirm. Nuñez Noriega, *Masculinidad e intimidad*. Joseph Carrier also identified a third, lesser category, the *internacionales*—men who took both the receptive and the insertive roles during anal sex, which Carrier argued was seen as anomalous and thus foreign (hence its label). Carrier, "Urban Mexican Male Encounters"; Carrier, *De los Otros*.

Equivalent gendered interpretations were identified in other Latin American countries such as Nicaragua (in terms of passive *cochones* and active *hombres-hombres*) and Brazil (in terms of passive *viados* and active *homems*) in the 1980s and 1990s. See Parker, *Bodies, Pleasures, and Passions*; Lancaster, *Life is Hard*; Kulick, *Travesti*. But the view that a highly gendered model of homosexuality is sufficient to describe all Mexican and US Latino male homosexualities has been questioned. See, for instance, Irwin, "La Pedo Embotellado"; Carrillo, *The Night Is Young*; Cantú, *The Sexuality of Migration*; Vidal-Ortiz et al., "Revisiting Activos and Pasivos." More recently, Almaguer clarified that "no one actually believed that this model was anything more than an ideal type construction in the first place. It merely attempted to identify the normative ideals or metanarrative that shaped the way gender and sexuality were giving meaning through the honor and shame system structuring different pan-Latino cultures." Yet its influence in shaping how people in the United States came to view Latino male homosexuality seems undeniable. See Almaguer, "The Material and Cultural Worlds of Latino Gay Men," 169–70.

10. Parrini and Amuchástegui, "Un nombre propio, un lugar común," 185–86.

11. According to Lionel Cantú, overreliance on cultural arguments leads to viewing "Latino culture as static, monolithic, and exotic (if not primitive)." Cantú, *The Sexuality of Migration*, 161. Moreover, as Susan Kippax and Gary Smith note, the binaries of active/passive, dominant/submissive, man/woman, and top/bottom are alive and present in Western societies that have adopted a global gay sexual schema. Kippax and Smith, "Anal Intercourse and Power in Sex between Men." But, as Robert C. Philen observes, the same sexualities in Latino and White men are interpreted differently according to the men's race/ethnicity. For instance, while White non-gay men who have sex with men are seen as closeted ("as men whose sexual orientation was defined by object choice but who could not come to terms with their sexuality"), their Hispanic counterparts are seen as "not gay because of their ethnicity and a sexual role pattern" that is distinctly Hispanic. Philen, "A Social Geography of Sex," 32.

12. Adam, "Age, Structure, and Sexuality"; Murray, "Homosexual Categorization in Cross-Cultural Perspective." Beyond the need to consider gay subjectivities, Guillermo Nuñez Noriega has sought to destabilize both the gay and the *pasivo/activo* sexual schemas in the Mexican context by pointing out that those schemas obscure expressions of homoerotic affection and mutuality. Nuñez Noriega, "Reconociendo los placeres." They include homosocial sexual encounters of the kind that Eliseo described—homoerotic interactions between masculine friends that require no special labels in terms of non-normative identities or sexual roles. In the present study, homosocial sexual interactions were particularly prevalent at the time of my participants' sexual initiation, but were also reported by some adult men. See Carrillo and Fontdevila, "Rethinking Sexual Initiation"; Carrillo and Fontdevila, "Border Crossings and Shifting Sexualities."

13. Besides research conducted in the two largest cities, Mexico City and Guadalajara, social scientists have conducted studies of male same-sex desires in several other locations in the states of Sonora, Tabasco, Puebla, Morelos, Oaxaca, and Chiapas. See Prieur, *Mema's House*; Carrillo, "Cultural Change, Hybridity and Contemporary Male Homosexuality in Mexico";

Nuñez Noriega, *Sexo entre varones*; Carrillo, *The Night Is Young*; Miano Borruso, *Hombre, Mujer y Muxe'*; List, *Jóvenes corazones gay*; Nuñez Noriega, *Masculinidad e intimidad*; Parrini Roses, *Panópticos y laberintos*; Parrini and Amuchástegui, "Un nombre propio, un lugar común"; Nuñez Noriega, *Vidas vulnerables*; Gallego Montes, *Demografía de lo otro*; Laguarda, *Ser gay en la ciudad de México*; Laguarda, "El ambiente"; Thing, "Gay, Mexican and Immigrant"; Carrillo and Fontdevila, "Rethinking Sexual Initiation"; Laguarda, *La calle de Amberes*; Balbuena Bello, *Gays en el desierto*; Carrillo and Fontdevila, "Border Crossings and Shifting Sexualities"; Teutle and List Reyes, *Húmedos placeres*. Some scholarly work has also broached the topic of male homosexuality in Mexican indigenous groups, including Miano Borruso, *Hombre, Mujer y Muxe'*; Stephen, "Sexualities and Genders in Zapotec Oaxaca"; Nuñez Noriega, *Vidas vulnerables*; Mirandé, "Hombres Mujeres." Other scholars have analyzed the history and political strategies of the gay and lesbian movement in Mexico, including de la Dehesa, *Queering the Public Sphere in Mexico and Brazil*; Díez, "La trayectoria política del movimiento Lésbico-Gay en México"; Lumsden, *Homosexualidad, sociedad y estado en México*.

14. Carrillo, *The Night Is Young*.
15. On this topic see also Altman, *Global Sex*.
16. Parker, *Bodies, Pleasures, and Passions*.
17. Boellstorff, *The Gay Archipelago*.
18. Povinelli and Chauncey, "Thinking Sexuality Transnationally." See also Carrillo, "Sexual Migration, Cross-Cultural Encounters, and Sexual Health"; Rofel, "Qualities of Desire." A recent comparison between France and the United States showed that the global gay sexual schema also becomes localized in rich Western democracies such as these, where the tenets of gayness acquire distinct meanings, including in relation to the notion of "coming out" and the importance of making one's sexual identity fully public. See Stambolis-Ruhstorfer, "Labels of Love"; Stambolis-Ruhstorfer and Saguy, "How to Describe It?"
19. See the essays in Irwin, Nasser, and McCaughan, *The Famous 41*.
20. Monsiváis, *Que se abra esa puerta*.
21. Novo, "Memoir"; Novo, *La estatua de sal*. See also Monsiváis, *Salvador Novo*.
22. Such community forms were described to me by the Mexican intellectual Carlos Monsiváis (personal communication, ca. 2003). See also Monsiváis, *Que se abra esa puerta*, 124–28.
23. Chauncey, *Gay New York*; Stein, *City of Sisterly and Brotherly Loves*; Boyd, *Wide-Open Town*; Houlbrook, *Queer London*; Beachy, *Gay Berlin*. In Mexico, perhaps the closest approximation is the lucid cultural analysis contained in essays written by Carlos Monsiváis in *Que se abra esa puerta*. See also the historical, cultural, and literary analyses by American academics, including Buffington, "Los Jotos"; Irwin, "La Pedo Embotellado"; Buffington, "Homophobia and the Mexican Working Class, 1900–1910"; Irwin, Nasser,

and McCaughan, *The Famous 41*; Gollnick, "Silent Idylls, Double Lives"; Macías-González, "The Bathhouse and Male Homosexuality in Porfirian Mexico"; Macías-González, "The Transnational Homophile Movement."

24. Several scholars have explored the relevance of urban/rural and class origins for sexual and gay interpretations, including Howard, *Men Like That*; Valocchi, "The Class-Inflected Nature of Gay Identity"; Brekhus, *Peacocks, Chameleons, Centaurs*; Gray, *Out in the Country*; Binnie, "Class, Sexuality and Space"; Heaphy, "Gay Identities and the Culture of Class"; Kasyak, "Midwest or Lesbian?"; Gray, Gilley, and Johnson, *Queering the Countryside*. In the case of Mexican gay men, an interesting account consistent with my own analysis is provided by Thing, "Gay, Mexican and Immigrant."

25. A few participants acquired gay or bisexual identities only after moving to the United States. Moreover, three participants became exposed to transgender identities after migrating. But in Mexico, these three viewed their primary identities as connected to their sexual orientation as gay or homosexual rather than to trans identities defined primarily in relation to their gender (separately from their sexual orientation).

26. Such practices seem to date back to at least the 1920s. During that decade, as Salvador Novo indicated in his memoir of homosexual life in Mexico City, he discovered "that Mexico City's public transportation system is one of the best places to connect with casual sex partners." Gollnick, "Silent Idylls, Double Lives," 245. See also Novo, "Memoir"; Novo, *La estatua de sal*.

27. The century-long history of Mexico City's bathhouses and steam baths as homoerotic spaces has been documented by Macías-González, "The Bathhouse and Male Homosexuality in Porfirian Mexico."

28. For more on Cálamo and other gay groups that organized around HIV/AIDS in Mexico City in the 1980s, see Díez, "La trayectoria política del movimiento Lésbico-Gay en México"; Peralta, *El clóset de cristal*.

29. My translation. Jordi Díez indicates that a contingent of approximately forty homosexuals "joined a march against the repression of the political regime" and demanded the liberation of homosexual citizens. Díez, "La trayectoria política del movimiento Lésbico-Gay en México," 687. Hernández and other FHAR activists went on to found Colectivo Sol in 1981, which Hernández still directs (FHAR had been a gay men's group). Soon afterward, two other groups formed: the Grupo Lambda de Liberación Homosexual, a mixed organization of gay men and lesbians, and Oikabeth, a lesbian group. On October 2, 1978, FHAR and Lambda joined the march commemorating the tenth anniversary of the Tlatelolco massacre, at which the Mexican army had shot and killed an unknown number of people at a protest, just ten days before the opening ceremonies of the Mexico City Olympic Games. De la Dehesa and Laguarda differ on whether Oikabeth had joined this October 1978 march, which Laguarda notes as the "first homosexual pride march in Mexico City." See de la Dehesa, *Queering the Public Sphere in Mexico and Brazil*, 17; Laguarda, *Ser gay en la ciudad de México*,

78–87. However, the first exclusively gay and lesbian pride march in Mexico City took place in 1979. Braulio Peralta traces the origin of these public expressions of gay activism to earlier in the 1970s—to the private organizing efforts by intellectuals and professionals such as Nancy Cárdenas, Carlos Monsiváis, and Antonio Cué. See Peralta, *El clóset de cristal*.

30. Lumsden, *Homosexualidad, sociedad y estado en México*; de la Dehesa, *Queering the Public Sphere in Mexico and Brazil*; Díez, "La trayectoria política del movimiento Lésbico-Gay en México."

31. Laguarda, *Ser gay en la ciudad de México*, 82.

32. In the early years of the march, some commentators complained that many more gay and lesbian people were watching the march go by from the sidewalks than actually marching. Watching seemed safer, as a person could claim that he or she was just passing by. Marchers often wore masks and other disguises so that they would not be recognized.

33. See Carrillo and Fontdevila, "Rethinking Sexual Initiation."

34. Ciudad Nezahualcóyotl was the site where Annick Prieur conducted her research for her well-known study of gender and sexuality. Prieur, *Mema's House*.

35. Kippax and Smith, "Anal Intercourse and Power in Sex between Men," 416.

36. Spartacus has been described as "one of the most emblematic [working-class] discotheques of the gay *ambiente* in Mexico." Islas Vela, "Zona Rosa," 197. My translation.

37. In Mexican gay lingo, the verb *perrear* (derived from *perra*, "bitch") refers to playfully or nastily criticizing others as a form of entertainment, which Antonio Marquet calls "verbal lapidation." Marquet, *El coloquio de las perras*, 51.

38. Crecencio used the word *hombre* to refer to "real men," men who are not effeminate or gay. In my research in Guadalajara, people sometimes emphasized this idea by saying "hombre hombre," the type of man who is a real and masculine male. Carrillo, *The Night Is Young*.

39. Ibid.

40. On the topic of incest in Mexico, see González-López, *Family Secrets*.

41. See the section "The Corner in the Plaza" in Carrillo, *The Night Is Young*, 52–56.

42. During his interview, Rogelio wondered if these men may have been bisexual, and he asked the interviewer to confirm that bisexuality means having sex with both women and men. His sexual interactions with these men, however, seem more connected to the kind of homoerotic or homosocial sexual interactions that are outside both the strictly gendered *pasivo/activo* sexual schema and the global gay sexual schema. Nuñez Noriega, *Masculinidad e intimidad*; Carrillo and Fontdevila, "Rethinking Sexual Initiation."

43. The term *travesti* refers to men who cross-dress. A Portuguese equivalent is used in Brazil, as reported by Kulick, *Travesti*.

44. Prieur, *Mema's House*.

45. Carrillo, *The Night Is Young*, 52–56.
46. See http://www.gsanborns.com.mx/historia.html. Accessed March 6, 2017.
47. See Sánchez Crispín and López López, "Visión geográfica de los lugares gay de la ciudad de México"; Laguarda, "El ambiente"; Jiménez Marce, "Ser gay en la ciudad de México."
48. In the film, based on a novel by José Donoso, town residents are depicted as positively inclined toward Manuela and her place of business. A fascinating flashback shows Manuela in the brothel performing her signature version of a Spanish flamenco dance before an enthusiastic male crowd of the local cacique's first election as mayor. The cacique dares the brothel's owner, a female sex worker nicknamed "La Japonesa," to prove her sexual prowess by seducing Manuela, which he sees as an impossible feat. But "La Japonesa" succeeds, and from that encounter Manuela becomes a father.
49. Those shifts have been documented as well in relation to the ways in which men and women interact within heterosexual relationships. See, for instance, Hirsch, *A Courtship after Marriage*. In relation to the emergence of gay culture in small-town Mexico, see also Parrini and Amuchástegui, "Un nombre propio, un lugar común."
50. A term used in the Mexican gay world to describe non-gay-identified men who have sex with men. Nuñez Noriega, "Reconociendo los placeres"; Carrillo, *The Night Is Young*, 41. In US Latino cultures, *mayate* also is a derogatory term for Blacks, but that is not the use here.
51. Carrillo and Fontdevila, "Border Crossings and Shifting Sexualities."
52. A man in Guillermo Nuñez Noriega's study in Sonora expressed his concern that being penetrated might eventually effeminize him and turn him physically into a woman. Nuñez Noriega, *Masculinidad e intimidad*.
53. On these behavioral variations within gendered forms of Mexican homoeroticism, see Nuñez Noriega, "Reconociendo los placeres."
54. The notion of networks of same-sex desires in small Mexican towns—networks fully known only to those who participate in them—also emerges in an analysis of a small location in Tabasco. Parrini and Amuchástegui, "Un nombre propio, un lugar común."
55. This situation differs from the cases of homosocial sexual interaction reported by Guillermo Nuñez Noriega involving two masculine non-gay-identified men. What is significant here is that the man who could be seen as a *mayate* wanted to be penetrated by Justo, who in that relationship seemed to incarnate a more feminized role. Nuñez Noriega, *Masculinidad e intimidad*. Justo's partner's request may have been motivated by what Susan Kippax and Gary Smith have called "a rite of reversal" reserved for specially festive occasions (Kippax and Smith mention Carnival, birthdays, and Christmas). Kippax and Smith, "Anal Intercourse and Power in Sex between Men," 419.
56. There is evidence of similar kinds of spaces in larger cities such as Hermosillo. Nuñez Noriega, *Masculinidad e intimidad*.

57. Parrini and Amuchástegui, "Un nombre propio, un lugar común," 181. My translation.
58. Gutmann, "Dystopian Travels in Gringolandia," 479. See also Hirsch, *A Courtship after Marriage.*
59. Guillermo Nuñez Noriega has noted that Carrier was influenced by Octavio Paz's *Labyrinth of Solitude* and by the work of the anthropologist John Ingham. Nuñez Noriega, *Masculinidad e intimidad.*
60. Lionel Cantú noted that when "culture" is used as a factor of analysis only of US minorities or non-Western peoples, "there is a tendency to either directly or indirectly imply that their 'culture,' which is a 'backwards' culture, is to 'blame' for what are represented as pathological traits or what may be called 'cultural pathologization.'" Cantú, *The Sexuality of Migration,* 79. The United States is thus construed as "a bastion of freedom and liberty and a haven for the oppressed, including gays and lesbians," which can easily create the illusion that "it is only in this context, in the United States, that a Mexican man can be his true self, his gay self." Ibid., 63.
61. Carrillo, "Cultural Change, Hybridity and Contemporary Male Homosexuality in Mexico"; Carrillo, *The Night Is Young.* An illustration of the tenacity of the belief that the *pasivo/activo* model uniformly characterizes Mexican male homosexuality is that despite the fact that my research explicitly sought to emphasize a broader diversity of sexual interpretations in urban Mexico, it sometimes has been mistakenly cited in the United States as exclusively highlighting the existence of the *pasivo/activo* model in Mexico— missing my central point that such gendered interpretations had become hybridized in interesting ways with object choice interpretations.
62. Nuñez Noriega, *Sexo entre varones*; Nuñez Noriega, "Reconociendo los placeres."
63. Carrier, *De los otros,* 181. For critiques of Carrier's description of Mexican sexual cultures as static or monolithic, see Nuñez Noriega, "Reconociendo los placeres"; Carrillo, *The Night Is Young.*
64. Carrillo, *The Night Is Young*; Carrillo, "Imagining Modernity"; Díez, "La trayectoria política del movimiento Lésbico-Gay en México."
65. Carrillo and Fontdevila, "Rethinking Sexual Initiation"; Carrillo and Fontdevila, "Border Crossings and Shifting Sexualities." See also the interesting discussion of this topic by Nuñez Noriega, *Sexo entre varones*; Nuñez Noriega, *Masculinidad e intimidad*; Nuñez Noriega, *Just between Us.*
66. See Carrillo and Fontdevila, "Border Crossings and Shifting Sexualities." The homosocial sexual schema was more common at the time of Mexican study participants' sexual initiation, when 38 participated in homosocial homoerotic behaviors. Within this subgroup, 13 exclusively experienced homosocial sexual initiations involving other boys in their age group, 22 had homosocial sexual initiations but also experienced early sexual encounters that were highly gendered, and 3 had homosocial sexual initia-

tions as well as early sexual encounters that could be seen as "gay" or "object choice." See Carrillo and Fontdevila, "Rethinking Sexual Initiation."

67. See also Cantú, *"De Ambiente."*

68. Velázquez, "En México 98 por ciento."

69. By then, a local gay and lesbian movement had been under way, which Jordi Díez has traced back to the formation of the first gay group in Mexico—the Movimiento de Liberación Homosexual—in Mexico City in 1971. Díez, "La trayectoria política del movimiento Lésbico-Gay en México."

70. Díez refers to the period from 1984 to 1997 as having produced a weakening of the gay and lesbian movement, due in part to the distraction and emergency created by AIDS, and in part to ideological differences among groups and leaders. Yet by being forced to articulate a defense of homosexuality and a strong condemnation of homophobia in the mass media, the leaders of gay and lesbian groups may have reached a much larger audience than in the earlier stages of the Mexican gay and lesbian movement. Ibid.

71. On these various points, see also Carrillo, *The Night Is Young*; Carrillo, "Imagining Modernity."

72. According to the organizers' website, the International Day against Homophobia, or IDAHO, is now commemorated by more than 130 countries worldwide. See http://dayagainsthomophobia.org/. Accessed March 6, 2017. In Mexico, this event is covered by the mass media, and has also become widely acknowledged by the Mexican state at the national, state, and local levels. On May 17, Mexican national newscasts now typically discuss and broadcast segments meant to address homophobia as a social problem, and to promote positive attitudes toward homosexuality and the importance of LGBT rights. A few years back, I watched an uninterrupted and quite didactic fifteen-minute segment on one of Televisa's prime-time national channels, which is noteworthy given the high cost of airtime. During this segment, the news anchor characterized homophobia as a social problem affecting everyone—as no family is exempt from having LGBT loved ones—and encouraged everyone to combat homophobia within Mexican society. This was not a minor statement, particularly since Televisa, both admired and reviled by many, is the largest television network in the Spanish-speaking world. And in 2016, Mexican president Enrique Peña Nieto took the opportunity of the IDAHO to invite a group of LGBT activists to Los Pinos, the presidential residence, where he announced his support for a (some say politically opportunistic) federal initiative to legalize same-sex marriage.

73. According to the World Bank, in 2015 57.4% of the Mexican population used the Internet (compared with 74.5% in the United States). Source: http://data.worldbank.org/indicator/IT.NET.USER.P2. Accessed March 6, 2017.

74. For interesting analyses of the history and strategies of the LGBT movement in Mexico, see de la Dehesa, *Queering the Public Sphere in Mexico and Brazil*; Díez, "La trayectoria política del movimiento Lésbico-Gay en México."

75. In 1997, Patria Jiménez was elected to the Chamber of Deputies, becoming the first openly lesbian politician in Mexico to hold public office. Díez, "La trayectoria política del movimiento Lésbico-Gay en México."

76. In 2003, a Federal Law to Prevent and Eliminate Discrimination was instituted that expressly prohibits discrimination, including that due to sexual orientation; this law led to the creation of a new federal agency, the CONAPRED (National Council to Prevent Discrimination, part of the Secretariat of the Interior). Two years later, CONAPRED teamed up with another federal agency, CENSIDA (National Center for AIDS Prevention, part of the Secretariat of Health), and created a federally sponsored national anti-homophobia campaign that was implemented despite opposition from social conservatives. Carrillo, "Imagining Modernity."

77. See Norandi, "Constitucionales, las bodas gay en el Distrito Federal."

78. The community-based organization Letra S, Sida, Cultura y Vida Cotidiana, A.C. recently reported that in Mexico between 1995 and 2015, 1,310 homicides were allegedly motivated by homophobia. See Redacción NotieSe, "Registran 1310 homicidios por homofobia en México."

79. See Laguarda, La calle de Amberes.

80. Redacción NotieSe, "Autoridades capitalinas niegan la existencia de crímenes por odio homofóbico"; Reyes, "Proponen en senado tipificar crímenes por homofobia"; Parrini and Brito, "Ensayo: Crímenes de odio por homofobia."

CHAPTER THREE

1. Massey, Goldring, and Durand, "Continuities in Transnational Migration"; Kandel and Massey, "The Culture of Mexican Migration." See also Wilson, "The Culture of Mexican Migration."

2. Women in Mexico often hold similar imaginaries about the greater freedoms enjoyed by women in the United States as well as the state's protection of women's rights, even when those freedoms, rights, and protections are not always available to undocumented migrants. See Hondagneu-Sotelo, *Gendered Transitions*; Malkin, " 'We Go to Get Ahead.' "

3. Three additional Mexican men in the study lived either in Tijuana or Ensenada and crossed the border regularly, but had never lived on the US side. Therefore, they are not included in this analysis.

4. The inclusion of participants who, like Rodolfo, did not migrate for economic reasons makes my sample more diverse than those of other studies of Mexican and other Latin American gay immigrant men. For instance, Lionel Cantú indicated that all twenty of the Mexican men whom he inter-

viewed "in one form or another, gave financial reasons for migrating to the United States." Cantú, *The Sexuality of Migration*, 132. This led Cantú to conclude that gay men's sexual and economic motivations for migrating are always intrinsically linked, and this point helped him highlight the need to "connect the micro with the macro dimensions of life." Ibid., 131. In this view, however, sexuality seems to represent the "micro," and economic factors the "macro"—an oversimplification that I would question.

I do not dispute the notion that sexual and economic motivations for migration are often intertwined, as my own data in this chapter confirm. But I think it is important to emphasize that sexuality alone can be the motor propelling the transnational relocation of gay men from countries such as Mexico, and also that sexuality should be understood in terms of both its micro- and macro-level dimensions, including macro-level sociocultural factors that may operate independently from economics.

5. See Parker, "Migration, Sexual Subcultures, and HIV/AIDS in Brazil"; Carrillo, "Sexual Migration, Cross-Cultural Encounters, and Sexual Health"; Cantú, *The Sexuality of Migration*.

6. Portes, Mcleod, and Parker, "Immigrant Aspirations," 252.

7. See Carrillo, *The Night Is Young*; Carrillo, "Imagining Modernity."

8. A derogatory Mexican term that is roughly equivalent to *fag*.

9. Acosta, "Lesbianas in the Borderlands," 640. These spaces seem similar to the gay kinship relations described by Weston, *Families We Choose*.

10. On the management of stigma, see Goffman, *Stigma*.

11. See chapter 6 in Carrillo, *The Night Is Young*.

12. Ibid. These same strategies have been detected by scholars conducting research with other Latin American groups, including Carlos Decena, who coined the term *tacit subjects*. See Cáceres and Rosasco, *Secreto a voces*; Decena, *Tacit Subjects*; Peña, *¡Oye Loca!*

13. As Martin Manalansan has noted, "Discourses on coming out are about verbal narratives and confrontations with friends, families, and significant others," and this model is "founded on a kind of individuation that is separate from familial and kin bonds and obligations." Manalansan, *Global Divas*, 23.

14. This idea of starting a new life under different conditions by moving transnationally to leave one's family life behind was also noted by Martin Manalansan in his study of Filipino gay immigrant men. Manalansan observed that "the freedom that comes with distance from the family affords some Filipino gay men a chance to try new experiences and remake themselves." Ibid., 101.

15. However, we must consider that many gay men in Mexico manage to live their sexualities freely or somewhat freely without leaving their hometowns. This group includes men who decide to be discreet in some contexts and open in others (including those who learned to live double lives by carefully managing who knows about their being gay), as well as men who

choose to disclose their sexual orientation to others, including their families. But neither of those strategies seemed attractive to men who decide that distance from familiar places is a better alternative to either the pains of coming out to their families or the enormous amount of labor involved in living a double life in the same location where their families live.

16. This same strategy has been found also among Peruvian gay men and their families. Vasquez del Aguila, " 'God Forgives the Sin but Not the Scandal.' "

17. As Guillermo Nuñez Noriega has noted, this labeling is as much about sexual orientation as it is about the perception of gender nonconformity (a lack of manliness in men). Nuñez Noriega, *Masculinidad e intimidad*. This observation is similar to C. J. Pascoe's conclusions based on her well-known study of an American high school. Pascoe, *Dude, You're a Fag*.

18. The role of homophobia within the family in promoting sexual migration has also been reported by Bianchi et al., "The Sexual Experiences of Latino Men."

19. This association points to a profound perception in Mexico that "unmanliness" or "effeminacy" is the strongest indicator of a boy's potential to become gay or homosexual. Carrillo, *The Night Is Young*; Nuñez Noriega, "Reconociendo los placeres."

20. Humberto's experience resembles Joaquín's, quoted before, whose friends in Michoacán called him *jotito* (little fag) because he did laundry and ironed clothes.

21. Pascoe, *Dude, You're a Fag*.

22. Carrillo, "Leaving Loved Ones Behind."

23. Guzmán, " 'Pa'la escuelita con mucho cuida'o y por la orillita,' " 210, 27.

24. Carlos Decena explains that "keeping the closet door ajar is accomplished only to the extent that the gay subject and his others coproduce the closet when they interact with one another." Decena, *Tacit Subjects*, 32.

25. Patterson, *Freedom*, vol. 1.

26. Leopoldo may have been confusing the situation in San Diego and California with that of the entire United States, or he may have been alluding to the fact that generally speaking, US employers may be wary of asking potential hires about their sexual orientation—even in states where it would not be illegal to ask such a question during a job interview.

27. This literature includes a focus on the "importation" of mail-order brides by men from rich countries. See, for instance, Cheng, *On the Move for Love*; Manalansan, "Queer Intersections."

28. In addition, being a *güero* is often perceived as desirable within the racial and class stratification of Mexico, where the more socially and economically privileged tend to include a higher percentage of people who are part of the minority that can claim primary European ancestry. See Villarreal, "Stratification by Skin Color in Contemporary Mexico."

29. Preston, "Gay Married Man in Florida"; Rosenthal, "The Court's Same-Sex Marriage Rulings."

30. Barnes, "Supreme Court"; Flegenheimer and Yee, "Jubilant Marchers."
31. "José" is a pseudonym I picked for Facundo's partner, who did not participate in my study.
32. The use of this euphemism has also been noted among Latin American lesbian immigrants. Acosta, *Amigas y Amantes*.
33. Throughout the epidemic, AIDS activists often noted that "difficult" patients— those who are willing to take charge of their health and question their doctors when they are not satisfied—may have better chances of survival than those who passively accept their doctors' orders. They resemble the kind of people who became AIDS activists and transformed how medical science is done, as Steven Epstein noted in *Impure Science*.
34. Ibid.
35. Preston, "Obama Lifts a Ban on Entry into U.S. by H.I.V.-Positive People."
36. Manalansan, "Queer Intersections," 243.
37. The "combination of sexual liberation and economic opportunities" was also reported by some participants in the study by Cantú, *The Sexuality of Migration*, 132.
38. On the difference between being an immigrant and being an expatriate, see von Koppenfels, *Migrants or Expatriates?*
39. *Chilango* is the nickname given throughout Mexico, often pejoratively, to the people of Mexico City. However, as Marcelo noted, "previously it was an insult, but it has been . . . turned into a source of pride. . . . It used to be an insult, and now we assume ourselves to be *chilangos*."
40. For information on LLEGÓ, go to http://www.lib.utexas.edu/taro/utlac/00273/lac-00273.html. Accessed March 8, 2017. See also Cantú, *The Sexuality of Migration*, 144.
41. A White Party is a kind of gay circuit party in which everyone dresses in white. See https://en.wikipedia.org/wiki/White_Party. Accessed March 8, 2017.
42. Benson and O'Reilly, "Migration and the Search for a Better Way of Life"; Benson and O'Reilly, *Lifestyle Migration*; von Koppenfels, *Migrants or Expatriates?*
43. Among the 34 non-Latino participants, 8 were originally from California (including 4 who grew up in San Diego), and 26 from other parts of the United States. Among the 36 US Latinos, 9 were originally from outside California, 9 were from San Diego, and 18 were from other California locations (including 15 from locations in Southern California). A number of these men moved around the country before arriving in San Diego, while for others San Diego was the location to which they moved directly from their hometowns. Indeed, for several American participants, San Diego was the "big city" to which they went in search of a gay life. See Weston, "Get Thee to a Big City."
44. Two other points about the definition of sexual migration deserve note. First, it should be clear that sexual migration may be either voluntary or forced, or some combination of the two. Perhaps with the exception of those Mexican

participants whose families asked them to leave Mexico and become sexual exiles, and who could be thought as having been forced to relocate, the rest of my participants engaged in what could be called voluntary migration. However, the degree to which participants who left seeking sexual freedom left voluntarily, or felt the pressure to leave due to external circumstances, is sometimes hard to discern. Second, in addition to the types of migration already described, migration that results in sex work can be considered to be a form of sexual migration (and one in which sexual and economic aspects of migration are especially tightly linked). To be sure, the question of whether migratory sex work—or any sex work—can be seen as voluntary or is always forced has been intensely debated. See, for instance, Bernstein, *Temporarily Yours*; Hoang, *Dealing in Desire*; Mai, "The Fractal Queerness of Non-heteronormative Migrants Working in the UK Sex Industry."

45. Cantú, *The Sexuality of Migration*.
46. Ibid.

CHAPTER FOUR

1. Howe, "Sexual Borderlands," 90.
2. Ibid.
3. Massey, "The Social Organization of Mexican Migration," 104.
4. Massey, Goldring, and Durand, "Continuities in Transnational Migration"; Kandel and Massey, "The Culture of Mexican Migration."
5. In recent years, however, this expectation may be shifting given a considerable slowdown in Mexican migration to the United States after the 2008 financial crisis. Recent reports have suggested that the current net balance of Mexicans' movement between Mexico and the United States is down to zero or has become negative—that possibly more Mexicans are leaving the United States (or are being deported) than entering the country. See the 2012 report by the Pew Hispanic Center: Passel, Cohn, and Gonzalez-Barrera, "Net Migration from Mexico Falls to Zero." See also Sáenz, "A Transformation in Mexican Migration to the United States."
6. See Massey and García-España, "The Social Process of International Migration"; Massey, "Social Structure, Household Strategies, and the Cumulative Causation of Migration"; Massey, "The Social and Economic Origins of Migration."
7. Massey, "The Social Organization of Mexican Migration," 105.
8. This is consistent with Douglas Massey's observation that "male relatives . . . have evolved well-established expectations of mutual aid and cooperation in the United States. The strongest relationship is between migrant fathers and sons." Ibid., 104.
9. As I indicated earlier, my sample included eighty Mexican men. Three, however, had never lived on the US side of the border, although they crossed the border regularly for work-related, educational, or social reasons.

10. Weston, *Families We Choose*.
11. The role of extended family networks in supporting Mexican migration has been noted by Massey, "The Social Organization of Mexican Migration."
12. The *Merriam-Webster Unabridged Dictionary* defines *compadrazgo* as "the reciprocal relationship or the social institution of such relationship existing between a godparent or godparents and the godchild and its parents in the Spanish-speaking world." http://www.merriam-webster.com/dictionary/compadrazgo. Accessed March 8, 2017.
13. When Armando described his parents, he said they had found him abandoned by the side of a road when he was an infant, and had taken him with them and registered him as their own son.
14. Fussell and Massey define "cumulative causation" as a series of mechanisms that produce an "accumulation of social capital, by which members of a community gain migration-related knowledge and resources through family members and friends who have already traveled to the United States." According to these scholars, "each act of migration creates social capital among a migrant's friends and relatives, which encourages some of them to migrate, which creates more social capital, which produces still more migration," therefore perpetuating expectations that community members will migrate. Fussell and Massey, "The Limits to Cumulative Causation," 152.
15. This difficulty is also noted in Ernesto Vasquez del Aguila's research with Peruvian immigrant men in New York. Vasquez del Aguila, " 'God Forgives the Sin but Not the Scandal.' "
16. Decena, *Tacit Subjects*, 10.
17. The historian Víctor Macías-González found that since at least the 1930s, Mexican middle- and upper-class men have participated in a "transnational homophile movement" by traveling abroad as tourists or interacting with foreign tourists visiting Mexico. Macías-González, "The Transnational Homophile Movement," 519.
18. Pierre Bourdieu and Loïc Wacquant defined *social capital* as "the sum of the resources, actual or virtual, that accrue to an individual or a group by virtue of possessing a durable network of more or less institutionalized relationships of mutual acquaintance and recognition." Bourdieu and Wacquant, *An Invitation to Reflexive Sociology*, 119.
19. Jorge Durand, for instance, has referred to heterosexual intermarriages involving Mexican citizens and US citizens as an alternative, noneconomic motivation for Mexican migration. Durand, "Migration and Integration."
20. See Massey, Durand, and Malone, *Beyond Smoke and Mirrors*, 18–19.
21. The help provided by friends has also been observed among Mexican heterosexual immigrants. For instance, Douglas Massey noted in an early analysis that migrants sometimes receive supports outside familial kinship networks. He also highlighted help provided by friends who are roughly the same age as the migrants, especially if they grew up together. Massey, "The Social Organization of Mexican Migration."

22. Toribio chose to be interviewed in English, which may also reflect an effort to assert his middle-class status and education.
23. Interestingly, Toribio switched to speaking Spanish in describing his grandfather's support. I find that language switches among Mexican interviewees who chose to be interviewed in English (or in Spanglish) are significant in that they point to the compartmentalization of their lives in the United States and in Mexico. Such language switching has been extensively studied in analyses of the sociolinguistic concept of code-switching. See Toribio, "Spanish-English Code-Switching among US Latinos"; Auer, "A Postscript."
24. The same could be said of the case of Edwin (born 1974), whose motivations for migrating I discussed in chapter 3. Edwin's gay connections had been crucial for him when moving from Cancún to Spain, then to Germany, and then to the United States.
25. See Ortiz Hernández and Granados Cosme, "Violencia hacia bisexuales, lesbianas y homosexuales de la Ciudad de México." See also Carrillo, *The Night Is Young*.
26. Cantú, *The Sexuality of Migration*, 133.
27. Thing, "Gay, Mexican and Immigrant," 823.
28. Ibid.
29. Fussell and Massey, "The Limits to Cumulative Causation."

CHAPTER FIVE

1. Portes and Rumbaut, *Immigrant America*, 14.
2. Benson and O'Reilly, "Migration and the Search for a Better Way of Life"; Benson and O'Reilly, *Lifestyle Migration*; von Koppenfels, *Migrants or Expatriates?*
3. See Cantú, *The Sexuality of Migration*, 163.
4. See Bae, "Tijuana-San Diego." In 2016, the total number of people (including Mexicans, Americans, and people of other nationalities) who crossed into San Diego from Tijuana at the two border-crossing points of San Ysidro and Otay Mesa numbered almost 49 million. See http://transborder.bts.gov /programs/international/transborder/TBDR_BC/TBDR_BCQ.html. Accessed March 10, 2017.
5. Chang-Hee Christine Bae has reported that "there are about one million shopping trips (mainly to shopping centers close to the border) from border crossers per month, involving about 150,000 individuals and generating about $120 million of sales taxes for California." Bae, "Tijuana-San Diego," 185.
6. According to the website of the US Customs and Border Protection, "The current BCC border zone is within 25 miles of the border in California and Texas; within 55 miles of the border in New Mexico; and within 75 miles of the border in Arizona." https://help.cbp.gov/app/answers/detail/a_id/1635/~/border -crossing-card---who-can-use-it%3F. Accessed March 20, 2017.

7. Bae has noted that "transmigrant workers move north across the border in large numbers for daily work, many of them without any legal rights to work. When they cross the border, they can take the light rail system (called the San Diego Trolley) or other forms of public transit to get to work at points north." Bae, "Tijuana-San Diego," 182. Similarly, some reports have estimated that in the early 2000s, approximately 6 percent to 7½ percent of Tijuana's labor force worked informally in San Diego. See Escala Rabadán and Vega Briones, "Living and Working as Cross-Border Commuters."

8. Kiy, preface, ix.

9. Wayne Cornelius has indicated that by the mid-1990s, immigrants "had replaced U.S.-born workers in nine of the most common types of low-paying jobs in California, statewide." Cornelius, "The Structural Embeddedness of Demand for Mexican Immigrant Labor," 126. Those jobs included gardeners, restaurant cooks, maids, child caretakers, and janitors, among others. Cornelius also noted that employers in San Diego interviewed for his research "reported that U.S.-born persons never apply for the same types of jobs held in their firm by immigrants, or apply only rarely for these jobs." Ibid., 127. See also Escala Rabadán and Vega Briones, "Living and Working as Cross-Border Commuters."

10. See http://travel.state.gov/content/visas/english/visit/visitor.html. Accessed January 3, 2017.

11. See the references in chapter 3, notes 29 and 30.

12. See my discussion of this topic in chapter 4. See also Kandel and Massey, "The Culture of Mexican Migration."

13. These forms of crossing have been described as a " 'game of cat and mouse' where INS border enforcement [now the US Citizenship and Immigration Services (USCIS), Immigration and Customs Enforcement (ICE), and Customs and Border Protection (CBP), all of which are part of the Department of Homeland Security (DHS)] arrested migrants and voluntarily deported them back to Mexico, permitting them to enter again." Donato, Wagner, and Patterson, "The Cat and Mouse Game at the Mexico-U.S. Border," 331. See also Chavez, *Shadowed Lives*; Singer and Massey, "The Social Process of Undocumented Border Crossing."

14. Donato, Wagner, and Patterson, "The Cat and Mouse Game at the Mexico-U.S. Border."

15. On the Minuteman Project, see Chavez, "Spectacle in the Desert."

16. The configuration of the border-crossing point at San Ysidro has changed considerably since these events took place.

17. See Luibhéid, *Entry Denied*, x; Luibhéid, introduction.

18. Luibhéid, *Entry Denied*.

19. Many *tijuanense* youths cross the border daily to attend school in the United States. Observers have indicated that this is "a strategic practice [that has] been going on among Tijuana residents for years, even generations. This

behavior is not based on the assumption that schools are better in California simply because they are U.S. schools. Rather, language training is the main reason that families send their children to school on the other side." Escala Rabadán and Vega Briones, "Living and Working as Cross-Border Commuters," 162.

20. The sociologist Pablo Vila, for instance, has been critical of a popular romantic and one-sided view of the hybridity and liminality of the US-Mexico borderland that emerges in the work of well-known scholars such as Gloria Anzaldúa, Renato Rosaldo, and Guillermo Gómez-Peña. Vila has expressed concern about the US-centeredness of this view, which in his opinion tends to "homogenize the border, as if there were only one border identity, border culture, or process of hybridization." Vila, "Processes of Identification on the U.S.-Mexico Border," 608.

21. Such scrutiny, and the subjectivity associated with it, is conceptually consistent with the view advanced by Luibhéid, *Entry Denied*.

22. Recent debates about executive orders preventing individuals from certain countries from entering the United States, and the reported cases of people with visas detained and deported upon arrival, should call attention to the long history of subjective and discretionary decision making at US entry points.

23. Donald Dobkin has referred to "recent information suggesting that consular officers sometimes rely on racial and economic stereotyping when they deny visas." Dobkin, "Challenging the Doctrine of Consular Nonreviewability," 118. Under those circumstances, "racial discrimination can easily work its way into consular decisions because many of those decisions rely upon subjective factors." Ibid., 119.

24. This issue relates to what Dobkin calls "consular nonreviewability" and "consular absolutism." As this author puts it, "When a consular officer denies a visa, the visa applicant is generally without any recourse." Ibid., 114.

CHAPTER SIX

1. See Ghaziani, "Post-Gay Collective Identity Construction"; Greene, "Gay Neighborhoods"; Ghaziani, *There Goes the Gayborhood?*

2. See Birnholtz et al., "Identity, Identification and Identifiability."

3. This view connects to scholarly critiques of the normalization, conventionality, and commodification of gay life—a kind of normalization that mainly favors people who fit particular molds of middle-class (White) respectability. See Duggan, "The New Homonormativity"; Rushbrook, "Cities, Queer Space, and the Cosmopolitan Tourist"; Manalansan, "Race, Violence, and Neoliberal Spatial Politics in the Global City."

4. The legal drinking age in San Diego, as in the rest of the United States, is twenty-one.

5. In this comment, "blond" stands for White.
6. His description suggests that this group may have been one of the high school organizations associated with the Gay-Straight Alliance (GSA), a network of student-run groups that was founded in San Francisco in 1998, and that had spread to the rest of California by 2001. However, the timing does not quite work. Either the information that he provided in the interview is inaccurate (he may have been slightly younger than he claimed) or this group was a local precursor of the groups that later became part of the GSA network. See https://gsanetwork.org/. Accessed March 10, 2017.
7. See http://www.richssandiego.com/. Accessed March 11, 2017.
8. Over the past decade, Mexican cities and states have increasingly adopted laws to protect nonsmokers from exposure to tobacco. Durango, Heriberto's home state, adopted such a measure in 2008. See http://www.cofepris.gob .mx/Documents/Bibliografias/Tabaco/01ley05nov2008.pdf. Accessed March 11, 2017.
9. A similar sentiment was also reported by participants in a study of cross-border commuters who live in Tijuana, some of whom explained that they would not move to San Diego because they liked the freedoms they had in Tijuana that they felt were restricted in San Diego. Escala Rabadán and Vega Briones, "Living and Working as Cross-Border Commuters."
10. *Buga* is a term for "straight" in Mexican gay slang. See Carrillo, *The Night Is Young*, 41.
11. See my discussion of this issue in chapter 3 and in *The Night Is Young*. See also Decena, *Tacit Subjects*. Marcelo's friend seemed to agree with the idea that it was possible for men to be gay and accept "their gayness as a private matter." Ibid., 22.
12. Club Papi Productions puts on Latino gay parties in LGBT venues in a number of cities around the United States. See http://clubpapi.com/. Accessed March 11, 2017.
13. Marcelo clarified that they did not have sex.
14. Bacchus House closed its doors in 2010. See Cartwright, "North Park Car and Dance Club."
15. See http://www.thebrassrailsd.com/. Accessed March 11, 2017.
16. The best-known version of these cards dates to the late nineteenth century. See Stavans, "¡Lotería!"
17. This is a quotation from an article that appeared in the gay publication the *Update* in November 2001. See http://www.lambdaarchives.us/timelines/lgbt /timeline2000.htm. Accessed March 11, 2017.
18. See https://sdpride.org/announcement/2003–2/. Accessed March 11, 2017.
19. Ibid.
20. Young, "Pride Criticized for Lacking Diversity." As noted in this article, Latino and Black LGBT activists complained about broken promises and a lack of diversity at the San Diego LGBT Pride events.
21. On this concept, see Chavez, *Shadowed Lives*.

22. Cuauhtémoc did not specify who "they" are in this statement.
23. Povinelli and Chauncey, "Thinking Sexuality Transnationally"; Altman, *Global Sex*; Carrillo, *The Night Is Young*; Boellstorff, *The Gay Archipelago*.

CHAPTER SEVEN

1. This chapter was written with Steven Epstein, and it reflects in part the further development of some of the themes we explored in Epstein and Carrillo, "Immigrant Sexual Citizenship." See that article for additional theorization of "immigrant sexual citizenship" as an intersectional construct and for further elaboration of specific citizenship "templates" that gay immigrant men encounter as they negotiate their intersecting social statuses as gay/bisexual and as immigrants—including an "asylum" template, a "rights" template, and a "local attachments" template.
2. Herdt, *Sexual Cultures and Migration in the Era of AIDS*; Manalansan, *Global Divas*; González-López, *Erotic Journeys*; Manalansan, "Queer Intersections." For a partial exception, see Smith, *Mexican New York*, 100.
3. On sexual citizenship see, among others, Evans, *Sexual Citizenship*; Alexander, "Not Just (Any) Body Can Be a Citizen"; Weeks, "The Sexual Citizen"; Bell and Binnie, *The Sexual Citizen*; Seidman, "From Identity to Queer Politics"; Stychin, "Sexual Citizenship in the European Union"; Plummer, *Intimate Citizenship*; Bell and Binnie, "Geographies of Sexual Citizenship"; Langdridge, "Voices from the Margins"; Canaday, *The Straight State*; Payne and Davies, "Introduction." Steven Epstein and I have detected five strands in the sexual citizenship literature: the articulation of sexual rights; the claims to equal treatment of groups such as sexual minorities; the heteronormative presumptions of citizenship more generally; the state's policing of boundaries between "good" and "bad" sexuality; and state-sponsored projects of subject formation via the inculcation of sexual norms. Epstein and Carrillo, "Immigrant Sexual Citizenship."
4. Holston and Appadurai, introduction; Varsanyi, "Interrogating 'Urban Citizenship' vis-à-vis Undocumented Migration"; Isin, "City."
5. Shah, "Policing Privacy," 281. See also Provencher, *Queer French*, 149–91; Hubbard, "Sex Zones."
6. Desforges, Jones, and Woods, "New Geographies of Citizenship," 441.
7. Just as the immigration literature has often ignored sexuality, the literature on sexual citizenship has often ignored the unique circumstances of immigrants. Instead, the term has often described how de jure citizens are rendered "second-class citizens" as a consequence of their sexuality. For further discussion, see Epstein and Carrillo, "Immigrant Sexual Citizenship." And for exceptions see, among others, Manalansan, "Queer Intersections"; Cantú, *The Sexuality of Migration*.
8. Other studies of Latin American gay immigrant men have similarly reported that their participants often encountered sexual contexts, venues,

and practices in the United States that were unfamiliar to them. See Bianchi et al., "The Sexual Experiences of Latino Men."

9. On the notions of sexual fields, erotic capital, and erotic habitus, see Green, "The Social Organization of Desire"; Green, "Erotic Habitus."

10. On the significance of mental maps of gay space in a study of urban sexual citizenship, see Provencher, *Queer French*, 159.

11. Somers, *Genealogies of Citizenship*.

12. On holding hands as a marker of sexual citizenship, see Johnson, "Heteronormative Citizenship."

13. Valverde, "A New Entity in the History of Sexuality."

14. These points relate to the politics of heteronormativity, public space, gay visibility, and passing discussed in Hubbard, "Sex Zones"; Johnson, "Heteronormative Citizenship."

15. See Carrillo, *The Night Is Young*.

16. A common refrain that straight people in Guadalajara used to express their discomfort at public expressions of homosexual intimacy was *"Uno como quiera, ¿pero y los niños?"* This phrase roughly translates as "I can handle that, but what about the children?" The idea is that adults may cope with the spectacle of sexual expressions that they would rather not see, but innocent children would inevitably be very negatively affected.

17. On the Zona Rosa as a space of gay sociability in Mexico City see Laguarda, "El ambiente"; Laguarda, *Ser gay en la ciudad de México*; Laguarda, *La calle de Amberes*.

18. Gutmann, *The Meanings of Macho*.

19. The name of the event is interesting in itself. It suggests the blending of the Latin American traditions of Carnaval with the American tradition of Mardi Gras (both of which have the same Catholic origins). On the topic of sexuality in relation to Carnaval, see Parker, *Bodies, Pleasures, and Passions*. As a public gay event, this parade was joined in 2012 by Vallarta Pride, which is described as a "12-day festival" by its organizers. See http://vallar tapride.com/en/about -vallarta-pride/. Accessed March 13, 2017.

20. See "Puerto Vallarta Carnaval." http://www.carnavalvallarta.com/history/. Accessed March 13, 2017.

21. Ibid.

22. Ibid.

23. Ibid.

24. According to the original parade's website, the ownership of this event has been in flux, suggesting the tensions between gay groups' interests, the city government, and commercial interests in the city, as well as the politics involved in the institutionalization of public events originally created by LGBT people as they come to be seen as catering to a broader audience.

25. Puerto Vallarta has indeed become such an international gay resort that many iconic gay artists from the United States are booked to perform there

every year, turning this Mexican resort into a destination within the American and Canadian gay circuit.

26. Ghaziani, *There Goes the Gayborhood?*
27. As I mentioned before, in recent years there has been considerable debate about whether these gay neighborhoods may now be passé in a post-gay era, as gayness has become more normalized and openly gay and lesbian people are increasingly moving to, and becoming incorporated into, suburbs and non-gay-identified parts of US cities. See ibid.
28. An additional five Mexican participants discussed this topic but did not express an opinion about whether same-sex marriage might ever be approved in Mexico.
29. On this topic see Hirsch, *A Courtship after Marriage*; Carrillo, "Imagining Modernity"; de la Dehesa, *Queering the Public Sphere in Mexico and Brazil*; Díez, "La trayectoria política del movimiento Lésbico-Gay en México."
30. In English in the original.
31. On the implementation of this campaign, see Carrillo, "Imagining Modernity."
32. Carrillo, "How Latin Culture Got More Gay."
33. See Adam and Rangel, "The Post-migration Sexual Citizenship."
34. The waiver policy reinforced their second-class sexual citizenship status: it required proof of a close relative who was a citizen or legal resident, but at the time, in the absence of marriage equality, a same-sex partner did not qualify. Human Rights Watch/Immigration Equality, *Family Unvalued*.
35. Cruikshank, *The Will to Empower*; Decena, "Profiles, Compulsory Disclosure."
36. Similarly to Venustiano, after they moved to San Diego other Mexican participants revealed their sexual orientation to their families, particularly after they had become financially independent. Lionel Cantú found a similar pattern among some of his participants, who became "empowered to 'come out' to their biological families as gay men" due to their newly acquired financial independence. Cantú, *The Sexuality of Migration*, 140. Carlos Decena has noted a similar pattern among Dominican gay men. Decena, *Tacit Subjects*.
37. This flexibility is also represented in Lionel Cantú's work in terms of what he called "fluid and shifting identities that may be context-specific." Cantú, *The Sexuality of Migration*, 36.
38. Fisher, "Immigrant Closets," 171.
39. A similar separation of sexual worlds has been noted among Latin American lesbian migrants. Acosta, *Amigas y Amantes*.

CHAPTER EIGHT

1. Cantú, *The Sexuality of Migration*, 135.
2. Ibid.
3. Bianchi et al., "The Sexual Experiences of Latino Men," 512.

4. Ibid., 516.
5. Thing, "Gay, Mexican and Immigrant."
6. Vasquez del Aguila, " 'God Forgives the Sin but Not the Scandal.' "
7. Decena, *Tacit Subjects*, 180.
8. Ibid.
9. Acosta, "Lesbianas in the Borderlands," 651; see also Acosta, *Amigas y Amantes*.
10. Indeed, the lack of systematic analysis is in part explained by the small samples in most of the studies referenced.
11. Decena, *Tacit Subjects*, 13. For a similar argument in the Canadian context, see Adam and Rangel, "The Post-migration Sexual Citizenship."
12. Decena, *Tacit Subjects*, 14.
13. Roth argues that those complications are typically addressed by treating the Latino category either as an ethnicity within a binary White/Black schema or as a separate race within a "Hispanicized U.S. schema." She concludes that the latter view is "winning out in U.S. culture." Roth, *Race Migrations*, 62, 64.
14. Acosta, "Lesbianas in the Borderlands," 646.
15. Cantú, *The Sexuality of Migration*, 154. On this topic see also Nagel, *Race, Ethnicity, and Sexuality*.
16. Some of the findings I present in this section on my participants' sexuality-related changes draw from a more detailed analysis that my colleague Jorge Fontdevila and I had previously conducted for our article: Carrillo and Fontdevila, "Border Crossings and Shifting Sexualities."
17. Cantú, *The Sexuality of Migration*, 135.
18. Some of these men's migrations to San Diego took place while they were still undergoing the developmental processes that psychologists have typically represented, albeit imperfectly and in overly universalizing terms, in stage models of sexual development. See for instance Cass, "Homosexual Identity."
19. Cantú, *The Sexuality of Migration*, 135.
20. Bianchi et al., "The Sexual Experiences of Latino Men," 516.
21. Ibid.
22. See Carrillo and Fontdevila, "Border Crossings and Shifting Sexualities." Shifts in sexual roles and dynamics of sexual interaction post-migration have also been noted by Bianchi et al., "The Sexual Experiences of Latino Men"; Decena, *Tacit Subjects*; Vasquez del Aguila, " 'God Forgives the Sin but Not the Scandal.' "
23. Notice Prado's use of the feminine pronoun in this statement, which points to the playful use of the feminine form to highlight the transgressions of homosexuality within Mexican "gay speak." On the topic of "gay language" in a global perspective, see the chapters in the edited collection by Leap and Boellstorff, *Speaking in Queer Tongues*.
24. According to the renowned essayist and cultural critic Carlos Monsiváis, "a *chacal*, in the slang of the *entendidos* [meaning 'those who are part of the

gay milieu'], is a proletarian youth of indigenous or mestizo looks, historically described as the Race of Bronze." Monsiváis, *Que se abra esa puerta*,
271. My translation.

25. This corresponds with a common practice in Mexico, where people often
call *güero* or *güerito* anyone who is perceived as White or as having primarily European features (even if they are not blond, the literal meaning of
the word), especially if they are assumed to belong to the middle or upper
class. See Flores and Telles, "Social Stratification in Mexico." An association
between whiteness and social class is also present among the Filipino immigrant men interviewed by Manalansan, *Global Divas*.

26. In the Spanish-speaking world, calling people from the United States
americanos is somewhat controversial. The Royal Spanish Academy accepts
this use, but also clarifies that "the use of *americano* to refer to the inhabitants of the United States must be avoided, because it is an abusive use that
reflects the fact that U.S. people [*estadounidenses*] often utilize the abbrevia-
tion America to refer to their country. We must not forget that America
is the name of the whole continent and that American applies to all who
inhabit said continent." *Diccionario Panhispánico de Dudas*, http://lema.rae
.es/dpd/srv/search?id=4EWtRO1VZD6v7sHSpo. Accessed March 14, 2017.
My translation.

27. This idea was present among both Mexican/Latino and non-Latino men
and is consistent with Wilson et al.'s study of sexual stereotyping among
gay men, in which these authors found that "there were participants who
indicated having no specific preference for sex partners of a particular racial group, and that they enjoyed the possibility of having sex with diverse
men from within and outside their racial group." Wilson et al., "Race-Based
Sexual Stereotyping," 408.

28. Green, "The Social Organization of Desire."

29. McBride, *Why I Hate Abercrombie and Fitch*, 88.

30. Wilson et al., "Race-Based Sexual Stereotyping," 408.

31. Phua and Kaufman, "The Crossroads of Race and Sexuality," 988.

32. Wilson et al., "Race-Based Sexual Stereotyping," 411. See also Han, "I Think
You're the Smartest Race I've Ever Met"; Teunis, "Sexual Objectification and
the Construction of Whiteness."

33. Wilson et al., "Race-Based Sexual Stereotyping," 408.

34. See Han, "I Think You're the Smartest Race I've Ever Met."

35. The dictionary of the Royal Spanish Academy translates *apiñonado* as "the
color of pine nuts." The phrase *"quemaditos por el sol"* relies on the diminutive of the Spanish word for "burned," which suggests a desire for the
phrase to come across as an endearing way of saying "a bit burned by the
sun." See http://dle.rae.es/?id=3AXMvQZ. Accessed March 14, 2017.

36. See Flores and Telles, "Social Stratification in Mexico."

37. Phua and Kaufman, "The Crossroads of Race and Sexuality," 988.

38. For an equivalent sense among Asian men in the Australian context, see Han, "I Think You're the Smartest Race I've Ever Met."
39. Roque Ramírez, " 'That's My Place!,' " 229.
40. Poon and Ho, "Negotiating Social Stigma among Gay Asian Men," 258. See also Han, *Geisha of a Different Kind.*
41. This notion is associated with La Malinche, the Indian lover of the conquistador Hernán Cortéz, who came to be seen as a traitor and is interpreted as a symbol of Mexicans' adoration of the European and the foreign. These images fully entered the Mexican imagination with the publication in 1950 of the famous book-length essay by Octavio Paz, *The Labyrinth of Solitude.*
42. Acosta, "Lesbianas in the Borderlands."
43. *Gabacho* is a Spanish derogatory term for foreigners that in Mexico is often used specifically to refer to Americans.
44. Ezequiel used the feminine version of the word *nosotros,* which positioned him, and other gay Mexicans, as feminine men who seek masculine partners.
45. According to the sociologist Anthony Ocampo, Latino gay men often derive "cultural capital" from particular displays of urban masculinity, including the *cholo* looks favored by some working-class Latino and Mexican American men in large US cities such as Los Angeles. Ocampo, "Making Masculinity," 449, 456.
46. This same notion has been found to be articulated by Asian gay men in justifying their attraction to White men. See Poon and Ho, "Negotiating Social Stigma among Gay Asian Men."
47. This attraction to *cholos* was also present among some Mexican men. For instance, Efraín said that he found "*cholos* very attractive. Like those who wear hair bands, loose pants, and who have tattoos. I'm very attracted to them." For him, part of the allure was the danger posed by *cholos.* As he put it: "But at the same time they scare me, because you don't know what they may do to you."
48. Young, *Colonial Desire.*
49. Cantú, "*De Ambiente.*"
50. The fantasy of Latino men being uncircumcised was also reported by Wilson et al., "Race-Based Sexual Stereotyping."
51. See McClintock, *Imperial Leather;* Stoller, *Race and the Education of Desire;* Young, *Colonial Desire;* Stoller, *Carnal Knowledge and Imperial Power;* Nagel, *Race, Ethnicity, and Sexuality.*
52. Among the remaining eleven, seven were raised in various other Christian denominations, and four were raised with no religion.
53. Nine were raised Protestant.
54. Dignity USA was founded in San Diego in 1969 as a "rap group" for gay and lesbian Catholics, and later expanded to other parts of the United

States and Canada. National Museum and Archive of Lesbian and Gay History, *The Gay Almanac*, 344; Hogan and Hudson, *Completely Queer*, 478.

55. Wilson et al., "Race-Based Sexual Stereotyping," 408.

56. In Mexico, *chino* is often used as a generic term to refer to all Asians.

57. Lucio had never had sex with a Black man. His choice of the Spanish word *negrito*, the diminutive of *negro* (black), suggests the awkwardness that many Mexicans feel when talking about Black people. They consider the word *negro* to be too harsh, even pejorative or racist, so they try to soften it and be polite by saying *negrito* instead. The same happens when people use the word *indito* in referring to Mexican Indians. They seem not to consider that the diminutive also has an infantilizing effect that marks members of those groups as unequal (thus reproducing their unequal status in Mexican society).

58. See Phua and Kaufman, "The Crossroads of Race and Sexuality"; Teunis, "Sexual Objectification and the Construction of Whiteness"; Wilson et al., "Race-Based Sexual Stereotyping."

59. In the study by Phua and Kaufman, Black men were more likely than men of other races to request a partner of the same race, although interestingly, they were also more likely "to write that they have no racial preference." Phua and Kaufman, "The Crossroads of Race and Sexuality," 989.

60. See Han, "I Think You're the Smartest Race I've Ever Met"; Caluya, "'The Rice Steamer'"; Han, "No Fats, Femmes, or Asians."

61. The literature on gay men's cross-racial attractions has noted that the language of "preference" can sometimes mask racial prejudice. See Poon and Ho, "Negotiating Social Stigma among Gay Asian Men"; Han, *Geisha of a Different Kind*. Specifically on the racialization of Asian men and the notion of "rice queens," see also Jackson, "'That's What Rice Queens Study!'"; Nawrocki, "'Rice Queens' and the Men Who Love Them"; Caluya, "'The Rice Steamer.'"

62. Gagnon and Simon, *Sexual Conduct*; Plummer, "Symbolic Interactionism and Sexual Conduct"; Simon and Gagnon, "Sexual Scripts."

63. Sánchez-Eppler and Patton, "Introduction," 3.

64. Green, "The Social Organization of Desire," 25.

65. Ibid.

CHAPTER NINE

1. Green, "The Social Organization of Desire," 45.

2. Ibid.

3. On sexual stereotyping, see McGlone and Pfiester, "The Generality and Consequences of Stereotype Threat." On sexual reputations, see Stombler, "'Buddies' or 'Slutties'"; Kitzinger, "'I'm Sexually Attractive but I'm Powerful'"; Stewart, "'Once You Get a Reputation . . .'" On sexual tropes and discourses, see Foucault, *The History of Sexuality*, vol. 1; McClintock,

Imperial Leather. On sexual scripts, see Gagnon and Simon, *Sexual Conduct*; Simon and Gagnon, "Sexual Scripts."

4. Poon and Ho, "Negotiating Social Stigma among Gay Asian Men"; Han, *Geisha of a Different Kind*. On the role of internalized racism, see Teunis, "Sexual Objectification and the Construction of Whiteness"; Wilson et al., "Race-Based Sexual Stereotyping."

5. Jackson, " 'That's What Rice Queens Study!,' " 183.

6. Participants sometimes referred to Mexican passion and others to Latino passion, but generally treated them as the same. The use of those alternative terms reflects the ambivalence in US society, including among immigrant populations, about whether Latinos are a separate race or an ethnicity, and about whether to invoke national identities (Mexican, Dominican, Salvadoran, etc.) as descriptors or refer to a general sense of Latino ethnicity/race. See Roth, *Race Migrations*. An alternative view is that "a significant segment of the Latino population has been reclassified from a separate race to essentially a White ethnic group." Warren and Twine, "White Americans, the New Minority?," 213. Yet another view is that "we must admit of a system of 'difference' by which one might be both white and racially distinct from other whites." Jacobson, *Whiteness of a Different Color*, 6. Consistent with this range of perspectives, participants in my study seemed to vacillate between thinking of "sexual passion" as a learned cultural characteristic of Mexicans (as a national group) and of Latinos (as an ethnic group). Similarly, they seemed uncertain whether to view it as a racial characteristic (of Latinos as a different race) that is entrenched "in the blood," or whether to discount it altogether as a sexual stereotype. On the topic of Hispanic (and by extension Latina/o) panethnicity, and the institutional creation of the category Hispanic, see also Mora, "Cross-Field Effects and Ethnic Classification."

7. This notion of a "fusion of bodies" is also present in definitions of eroticism offered over the course of the twentieth century by a number of scholars and intellectuals, including the French surrealists. See Bataille, *Eroticism*; Featherstone, "Love and Eroticism"; Shilling and Mellor, "Sociology and the Problem of Eroticism."

8. See chapter 8, "The Sexual Moment," in Carrillo, *The Night Is Young*. The perception that "sexual interactions tended to be more passionate in Latin America" was also reported by participants in the study by Bianchi et al., "The Sexual Experiences of Latino Men," 514. These authors interpreted this as a "view that is in keeping with cultural stereotypes of Latinos."

9. Lionel Cantú reported that in Los Angeles, the notion that Latino men are hot is in itself exploited and co-constructed by the commodified spaces that serve Latino gay men, which "create the fantasy of the insatiable 'hot' Latin sex machine." Cantú, *The Sexuality of Migration*, 144.

10. For an analysis of the "marketization" of casual sex among gay men—of a "market discourse" that lacks "recognition of the potential vulnerability

of the other person, of emotional need, or the dynamics of the search for intimacy"—see Adam, "Neoliberalism, Masculinity, and HIV Risk," 321, 326. Dowsett, in his article "Abjection. Objection. Subjection," also refers to the market logics generated by the "biomedical ascendency" in HIV prevention that followed the advent of pre-exposure prophylaxis, or PrEP.

11. The acronym *BDSM* summarizes a range of structured sexual practices involving bondage, dominance, and sadomasochism. Weiss, "Gay Shame and BDSM Pride."

12. Venustiano, however, was also one of the Mexican participants who disliked US Whites' use of sex toys. As he put it, "Many *güeros* use accessories and all that. And I don't like it. They use accessories on their penises. I don't know what's all that that they use." He also complained that they are "very hygienic" and "shave off their body hair. And I don't like all that."

13. See Carrillo, *The Night Is Young*, 194.

14. Savigliano, Tango and the Political Economy of Passion; Bertellini, "Duce/Divo."

15. Savigliano, *Tango and the Political Economy of Passion*; Bertellini, "Duce/Divo"; Törnqvist, "Troubling Romance Tourism."

16. Green, "The Social Organization of Desire," 34, 36.

17. Ibid., 37.

18. See, for instance, Stombler, " 'Buddies' or 'Slutties.' "

CHAPTER TEN

1. Frankenberg, *White Women, Race Matters*, 1. On whiteness studies, see also Warren and Twine, "White Americans, the New Minority?"; Jacobson, *Whiteness of a Different Color*; Lipsitz, *The Possessive Investment in Whiteness*.

2. On the topics of boundary work and symbolic boundaries, see Lamont and Thévenot, "Introduction"; Lamont and Molnár, "The Study of Boundaries in the Social Sciences." On ethnic boundaries, see also Wimmer, "The Making and Unmaking of Ethnic Boundaries."

3. Roth, *Race Migrations*, 83. Roth's point relates also to George Lipsitz's observation that "white supremacy is usually less a matter of direct, referential, and snarling contempt than a system for protecting the privileges of whites by denying communities of color opportunities for asset accumulation and upward mobility." Lipsitz, *The Possessive Investment in Whiteness*, viii.

4. On the emotional difficulties that some Latin American immigrants experience as they become racialized in the United States, see Roth, *Race Migrations*.

5. Han, "I Think You're the Smartest Race I've Ever Met," 2.

6. Green, "The Social Organization of Desire," 27.

7. Gagnon and Simon, *Sexual Conduct*; Simon and Gagnon, "Sexual Scripts."

8. The practice of paying for others, however, may be shifting in Mexico, at least when people socialize as a group (as opposed to dates between a

man and a woman). See García, "Cuando sales en grupo ¿cómo pagan la cuenta?"

9. It is important to remember that not all Mexican immigrant men disliked the sexual interactions that they had with *mayates*; indeed, some pursued similarly heavily gendered relations after migrating to San Diego. See chapters 6 and 8.

10. Kippax and Smith, "Anal Intercourse and Power in Sex between Men."

11. On the connections between masculinity/femininity and expected degrees of masculine dominance and feminine submission in gay relationships, see Connell, "A Very Straight Gay"; Schippers, "Recovering the Feminine Other."

12. Kippax and Smith, "Anal Intercourse and Power in Sex between Men," 416.

13. Ibid.

14. See Langdridge and Butt, "The Erotic Construction of Power Exchange"; Weiss, "Working at Play"; Yost and Hunter, "BDSM Practitioners' Understandings."

15. Teunis, "Sexual Objectification and the Construction of Whiteness."

16. The connections between sexual roles and power in sex between men have been noted in Latino and Latin American contexts, particularly in relation to the *pasivo/activo* model that I first discuss in chapter 2. Lancaster, *Life is Hard*; Alonso and Koreck, "Silences"; Nuñez Noriega, *Masculinidad e intimidad*.

17. Kippax and Smith, "Anal Intercourse and Power in Sex between Men," 417.

18. Troy later returned to Hillcrest with friends. Like other young men who were not yet twenty-one and so could not enter the gay clubs, he attended Euphoria, one of the cafés where young LGBT people his own age gathered.

19. As I noted before, Tadeo was born in the United States, but was taken to Mexico at a very early age and grew up there. Although he had the right to US citizenship by birth, culturally his subjectivity was in many ways similar to those of other Mexican immigrant men.

20. Green, "The Social Organization of Desire," 43.

21. The reasoning was that because Cuauhtémoc presented himself as both very masculine and bisexual, government lawyers could argue that in Mexico he could easily pass as straight—and lead a heteronormative life— and therefore not be subject to persecution due to his sexual orientation. On this topic see Vogler, "Legally Queer."

22. See Carballo-Diéguez et al., "Looking for a Tall, Dark, Macho Man." However, Carballo-Diéguez's finding does not adequately address the cases in my study in which White partners explicitly sought to penetrate darker Mexican/Latino partners.

23. See Teunis, "Sexual Objectification and the Construction of Whiteness"; Wilson et al., "Race-Based Sexual Stereotyping."

24. This exemplifies a cultural schema of the sort described by Mary Blair-Loy (as I discussed in the introduction). See Sewell, "A Theory of Structure"; Blair-Loy, "Cultural Constructions of Family Schemas."

25. See also Carrillo, "Immigration and LGBT Rights in the USA."
26. Latino sexual passion was thereby deployed as a kind of "queer of color critique" of American capitalist practices, to use the phrase coined by Roderick Ferguson in *Aberrations in Black*.
27. Lorde, "Uses of the Erotic."
28. Ibid., 54.
29. Ibid., 56.
30. Muñoz, "Feeling Brown, Feeling Down," 677.
31. Ibid., 678.
32. Allen, "Black/Queer/Diaspora at the Current Conjuncture," 223.
33. On the connections between emotions and collective action, see Goodwin, Jasper, and Polletta, *Passionate Politics*; Gould, *Moving Politics*.
34. Wilson et al., "Race-Based Sexual Stereotyping," 400.
35. Ibid., 401.
36. Ibid., 411.
37. Ibid., 408.
38. Ibid.

CONCLUSION

1. Chavez, *Shadowed Lives*.
2. In relation to this topic in Mexico, see Carrillo, "Imagining Modernity"; de la Dehesa, *Queering the Public Sphere in Mexico and Brazil*; Díez, "La trayectoria política del movimiento Lésbico-Gay en México"; Díez, "Explaining Policy Outcomes."
3. For a characterization of a global gay schema as "more egalitarian," see Murray, *Latin American Male Homosexualities*, 16.
4. See also Carrillo and Fontdevila, "Rethinking Sexual Initiation"; Nuñez Noriega, *Just between Us*.
5. Carrillo, *The Night Is Young*.
6. Cantú, *The Sexuality of Migration*.
7. Kandel and Massey, "The Culture of Mexican Migration"; Wilson, "The Culture of Mexican Migration."
8. Ghaziani, *There Goes the Gayborhood?*
9. See Murray, *Latin American Male Homosexualities*. As noted by several scholars, sexual role versatility is deemed "foreign" in sexual subcultures where heavily gendered schemas of male same-sex desires are prevalent. This notion of foreignness explains the use of the label *internacional* to refer to sexually versatile men in some settings in Mexico, and the label *moderno* in some settings in Peru. Taylor, "Mexican Male Interaction"; Carrier, *De los Otros*; Peinado et al., "Role Versatility"; Clark et al., "*Moderno* Love."
10. See Kippax and Smith, "Anal Intercourse and Power in Sex between Men."
11. Carrillo, *The Night Is Young*; Carrillo and Fontdevila, "Border Crossings and Shifting Sexualities." This conclusion aligns with the analysis of the sociolo-

gists Eric Fassin and Manuela Salcedo, who, citing my work, noted, "On the one hand, there is no cultural homogeneity, whether pre- or post-migration; on the other, migration does not impose a 'gay' definition of homosexual identity. [Therefore,] thinking in terms of the opposition between 'modern' and 'pre-modern' definitions of gay identity becomes irrelevant—if not counterproductive." Fassin and Salcedo, "Becoming Gay?," 1122.

12. See Carrillo and Hoffman, "From MSM to Heteroflexibilities"; see also Carrillo and Hoffman, " 'Straight with a Pinch of Bi.' "

13. In addition to the Latino Nights in San Diego dance clubs, many American gay men were exposed to Mexican gay culture in the many bars and dance clubs in Tijuana, just on the other side of the border.

14. Green, "The Social Organization of Desire"; Green, "Erotic Habitus."

15. On the topic of immigrant assimilation, see Massey, "Dimensions of the New Immigration to the United States and Prospects for Assimilation"; Portes and Borocz, "Contemporary Immigration"; Portes and Zhou, "The New Second Generation"; Rumbaut, "Assimilation and Its Discontents"; Suárez-Orozco, "Everything You Ever Wanted to Know about Assimilation"; Waters and Jiménez, "Assessing Immigrant Assimilation." On the topic of acculturation, see Hunt, Schneider, and Comer, "Should 'Acculturation' Be a Variable in Health Research?"; Abraído-Lanza et al., "Toward a Theory-Driven Model of Acculturation in Public Health Research"; Viruell-Fuentes, "Beyond Acculturation"; Horevitz and Organista, "The Mexican Health Paradox."

16. Alba and Nee, *Remaking the American Mainstream*, 11.

17. Ibid., 12.

18. See chapter 5 in Manalansan, *Global Divas*.

19. Carrillo, "Imagining Modernity."

20. This line is from Binnie, *The Globalization of Sexuality*, 4. Binnie is paraphrasing the argument in Ong's *Flexible Citizenship*.

21. See, for instance, Stanley, "Russians Find Their Heroes in Mexican TV Soap Operas"; Allen, "As the World Turns"; Sipse.com, "Las telenovelas mexicanas."

22. Chambers, *Migrancy, Culture, Identity*, 3. Quoted in Altman, *Global Sex*, 17.

23. Parker, *Bodies, Pleasures, and Passions*.

24. Padilla, *Caribbean Pleasure Industry*.

25. Bernstein, *Temporarily Yours*; Cantú, *The Sexuality of Migration*; Hoang, *Dealing in Desire*.

26. Catania et al., "The Continuing HIV Epidemic"; Centers for Disease Control and Prevention, "HIV/AIDS among Racial/Ethnic Minority Men."

27. Office of AIDS, AIDS Case Registry.

28. Centers for Disease Control and Prevention, "HIV Surveillance Report, 2014," 26, 69.

29. Nguyen, O'Malley, and Pirkle, "Correspondence," 1435. However, like others who have advocated the importance of social, cultural, and political

issues in HIV prevention, these scholars express concern about what they regard as the remedicalization of the HIV epidemic. Nguyen et al., "Remedicalizing an Epidemic."

30. Race, "Reluctant Objects."

31. Others note that "HIV prevention has not failed—at least not everywhere." Kippax and Stephenson, "Beyond the Distinction," 796.

32. See, for instance, Callen, *How to Have Sex in an Epidemic.*

33. Watney, "Safer Sex as Community Practice."

34. Race, "Reluctant Objects."

35. Kane Race has noted that the uptake of PrEP "has been much slower than expected in countries in which it has become available"; he has described PrEP as a *"reluctant object,* partly because of its putative association with the supposed excesses of unbridled sex." Ibid., 6.

36. Gagnon, "Sex Research and Sexual Conduct in the Era of AIDS"; Kippax and Race, "Sustaining Safe Practice."

37. Parker, Herdt, and Carballo, "Sexual Culture, HIV Transmission and AIDS Research"; Parker, "The Social and Cultural Construction of Sexual Risk"; Dowsett, *Practicing Desire*; Parker, Easton, and Klein, "Structural Barriers and Facilitators in HIV Prevention"; Parker, "Sexuality, Culture, and Power in HIV/AIDS Research"; Carrillo, *The Night Is Young*; Dowsett, "Baring Essentials"; Dowsett, "Abjection. Objection. Subjection."

38. Sobo, *Choosing Unsafe Sex*; Díaz, *Latino Gay Men and HIV*; Parker, Easton, and Klein, "Structural Barriers and Facilitators in HIV Prevention"; Parker, "Sexuality, Culture, and Power in HIV/AIDS Research"; Carrillo, *The Night Is Young*. A recent approach aimed at redefining "structural interventions" in public health and linking them to individual behaviors has been provided by Crammond and Carey, "What Do We Mean by 'Structure.'"

39. See the Mission Neighborhood Health Center website, http://www.mnhc .org/community-prog-group/hermanos-de-luna-y-sol/. Accessed March 17, 2017. See also Díaz, *Latino Gay Men and HIV.*

40. Mission Neighborhood Health Center website, ibid. See also the account of gay Latino HIV/AIDS organizing and activism in Ramirez-Valles, *Compañeros.*

41. My team and I previously analyzed some of these issues in a community-oriented monograph: Carrillo et al., "Risk across Borders."

42. Nguyen et al., "Remedicalizing an Epidemic," 292.

43. Ibid.

44. Kippax and Stephenson, "Beyond the Distinction"; Auerbach and Hoppe, "Beyond 'Getting Drugs into Bodies.'"

45. See Barnes, "Latino HIV/AIDS Service Organization Closes San Diego Center." The importance of community-based HIV organizations for gay Latinos has similarly been emphasized by Ramirez-Valles, *Compañeros.*

46. Gagnon and Simon, *Sexual Conduct*; Plummer, "Symbolic Interactionism and Sexual Conduct"; Simon and Gagnon, "Sexual Scripts"; Gagnon, "Sex Research and Sexual Conduct in the Era of AIDS."

47. Plummer, "Symbolic Interactionism and Sexual Conduct," 228.

48. The sociologist Barry Adam argues that the kind of extreme individualism manifested in Evan's comment is linked to the adoption of a neoliberal ideology that puts the onus on individuals, particularly individual men, to protect their own health. Adam, "Neoliberalism, Masculinity, and HIV Risk."

49. The issue of individual sexual responsibility has become especially charged in light of the adoption of laws that criminalize a person's failure to disclose his or her HIV-positive status to sex partners. In an analysis of felony non-disclosure convictions in Michigan, the sociologist Trevor Hoppe argues that "Michigan's HIV disclosure law was not intended to promote public health; rather, it reflects the perception of the virus as a moral infection requiring regulation and punishment." Hoppe, "From Sickness to Badness," 140. See also Hoppe, "Controlling Sex in the Name of 'Public Health.'"

50. See Newsweek staff, "Transcript."

Bibliography

Abraído-Lanza, Ana F., Adria N. Armbrister, Karen R. Flórez, and Alejandra N. Aguirre. "Toward a Theory-Driven Model of Acculturation in Public Health Research." *American Journal of Public Health* 96, no. 8 (2006): 1342–46.

Acosta, Katie L. "Lesbianas in the Borderlands: Shifting Identities and Imagined Communities." *Gender and Society* 22, no. 5 (2008): 639–59.

———. *Amigas y Amantes: Sexually Nonconforming Latinas Negotiate Family*. New Brunswick, NJ: Rutgers University Press, 2013.

Adam, Barry D. "Age, Structure, and Sexuality: Reflections on the Anthropological Evidence on Homosexual Relations." *Journal of Homosexuality* 11, nos. 3–4 (1986): 19–33.

———. "Neoliberalism, Masculinity, and HIV Risk." *Sexuality Research and Social Policy* 13 (2016): 321–29.

Adam, Barry, Jan Willem Duyvendak, and André Krouwel, eds. *The Global Emergence of Gay and Lesbian Politics: National Imprints of a Worldwide Movement*. Philadelphia: Temple University Press, 1998.

Adam, Barry D., and J. Cristian Rangel. "The Post-migration Sexual Citizenship of Latino Gay Men in Canada." *Citizenship Studies* 19, nos. 6–7 (2015): 682–95.

Alba, Richard D., and Victor Nee. *Remaking the American Mainstream: Assimilation and Contemporary Immigration*. Cambridge, MA: Harvard University Press, 2009.

Alexander, M. Jacqui. "Not Just (Any) Body Can Be a Citizen: The Politics of Law, Sexuality and Postcoloniality in Trinidad and Tobago and the Bahamas." *Feminist Review*, no. 48 (1994): 5–23.

Allen, Jafari S. "Black/Queer/Diaspora at the Current Conjuncture." *GLQ: A Journal of Lesbian and Gay Studies* 18, nos. 2–3 (2012): 211–48.

Allen, Robert C. "As the World Turns: Television Soap Operas and Global Media Culture." In *Mass Media and Free Trade: NAFTA and the Cultural Industries*, edited by Emile G. McAnany and Kenton T. Wilkinson, 110–27. Austin: University of Texas Press, 1996.

Almaguer, Tomás. "Chicano Men: A Cartography of Homosexual Identity and Behavior." *Differences* 3, no. 2 (1991): 75–100.

———. "The Material and Cultural Worlds of Latino Gay Men." In *Gay Latino Studies: A Critical Reader*, edited by Michael Hames-García and Ernesto Javier Martínez, 168–74. Durham, NC: Duke University Press, 2011.

Alonso, Ana Maria, and Maria Teresa Koreck. "Silences: 'Hispanics,' AIDS and Sexual Practices." In *The Lesbian and Gay Studies Reader*, edited by Henry Abelove, Michèle Aina Barale, and David M. Halperin, 110–26. New York: Routledge, 1993.

Altman, Dennis. "Rupture or Continuity? The Internalization of Gay Identities." *Social Text* 14, no. 3 (1996): 78–94.

———. "Global Gays/Global Gaze." *GLQ: A Journal of Lesbian and Gay Studies* 3, no. 4 (1997): 417–37.

———. *Global Sex*. Chicago: University of Chicago Press, 2001.

———. "Sexuality and Globalization." *Sexuality Research and Social Policy* 1, no. 1 (2004): 63–68.

Armstrong, Elizabeth A. *Forging Gay Identities: Organizing Sexuality in San Francisco, 1950–1994*. Chicago: University of Chicago Press, 2002.

Auer, Peter. "A Postscript: Code-Switching and Social Identity." *Journal of Pragmatics* 37 (2005): 403–10.

Auerbach, Judith D., and Trevor Hoppe. "Beyond 'Getting Drugs into Bodies': Social Science Perspectives on Pre-exposure Prophylaxis for HIV." *Journal of the International AIDS Society* 18, suppl. 3 (2015): 1–5.

Bae, Chang-Hee Christine. "Tijuana-San Diego: Globalization and the Transborder Metropolis." In *Globalization and Urban Development*, edited by Harry W. Richardson and Chang-Hee Christine Bae, 181–95. Heidelberg: Springer, 2005.

Balbuena Bello, Raúl. *Gays en el desierto: Paradojas de la manifestación pública en Mexicali* [Gays in the desert: Paradoxes of public expression in Mexicali]. Mexicali: Universidad Autónoma de Baja California, 2014.

Barnes, Megan. "Latino HIV/AIDS Service Organization Closes San Diego Center." *Edge Media Network*, October 10, 2011. Accessed March 17, 2017. http://chicago.edgemedianetwork.com/news/aids/news//125567/latino_hiv_aids_service_organization_closes_san_diego_center.

Barnes, Robert. "Supreme Court Rules Gay Couples Nationwide Have a Right to Marry." *Washington Post*, June 26, 2015. Accessed March 17, 2017. https://www.washingtonpost.com/politics/gay-marriage-and-other-major-rulings-at-the-supreme-court/2015/06/25/ef75a120-1b6d-11e5-bd7f-4611a60dd8e5_story.html.

Bastida Aguilar, Leonardo. "Celebrarán primeros matrimonios igualitarios en Hermosillo, Sonora" [First same-sex marriages to be performed in Hermosillo, Sonora]. Metropolitano, June 23, 2015. Accessed March 17, 2017. http://www

.metropolitanoenlinea.com/2015/06/23/celebraran-primeros-matrimonios
-igualitarios-en-hermosillo-sonora/.

Bataille, Georges. *Eroticism.* London: John Calder, 1962 [1957].

Baumle, Amanda K. "Border Identities: Intersections of Ethnicity and Sexual Orientation in the U.S.-Mexico Borderland." *Social Science Research* 39 (2010): 231–45.

Beachy, Robert. *Gay Berlin: Birthplace of a Modern Identity.* New York: Vintage Books, 2015.

Bell, David, and Jon Binnie. *The Sexual Citizen: Queer Politics and Beyond.* Cambridge: Polity, 2000.

———. "Authenticating Queer Space: Citizenship, Urbanism and Governance." *Urban Studies* 41, no. 9 (2004): 1807–20.

———. "Geographies of Sexual Citizenship." *Political Geography* 25, no. 8 (2006): 869–73.

Bell, David, and Gill Valentine, eds. *Mapping Desire: Geographies of Sexualities.* London: Routledge, 1995.

Benson, Michaela Caroline. "The Context and Trajectory of Lifestyle Migration: The Case of the British Residents of Southwest France." *European Societies* 12, no. 1 (2010): 45–64.

Benson, Michaela, and Karen O'Reilly, eds. *Lifestyle Migration: Expectations, Aspirations and Experiences.* Farnham, England: Ashgate, 2009.

———. "Migration and the Search for a Better Way of Life: A Critical Exploration of Lifestyle Migration." *Sociological Review* 57, no. 4 (2009): 608–25.

Bernstein, Elizabeth. *Temporarily Yours: Intimacy, Authenticity, and the Commerce of Sex.* Chicago: University of Chicago Press, 2007.

Bertellini, Giorgio. "Duce/Divo: Masculinity, Racial Identity, and Politics among Italian Americans in 1920s New York City." *Journal of Urban History* 31, no. 5 (2005): 685–726.

Bhabha, Homi K. "Signs Taken for Wonders: Questions of Ambivalence and Authority under a Tree outside Delhi, May 1817." *Critical Inquiry* 12, no. 1 (1985): 144–65. Page 156 cited in Young, *Colonial Desire*, 22.

Bianchi, Fernanda T., Carol A. Reisen, Maria Cecilia Zea, Paul J. Poppen, Michele G. Shedlin, and Marcelo M. Penha. "The Sexual Experiences of Latino Men Who Have Sex with Men Who Migrated to a Gay Epicentre in the USA." *Culture, Health and Sexuality* 9, no. 5 (2007): 505–18.

Binnie, Jon. *The Globalization of Sexuality.* Thousand Oaks, CA: SAGE Publications, 2004.

———. "Class, Sexuality and Space: A Comment." *Sexualities* 14, no. 1 (2011): 21–26.

Birnholtz, Jeremy, Colin Fitzpatrick, Mark Handel, and Jed R. Brubaker. "Identity, Identification and Identifiability: The Language of Self-Presentation on a Location-Based Mobile Dating App." Paper presented at the Sixteenth International Conference on Human-Computer Interaction with Mobile Devices and Services—Mobile HCI 2014, Toronto, September 23–26, 2014.

Blair-Loy, Mary. "Cultural Constructions of Family Schemas: The Case of Women Finance Executives." *Gender and Society* 15, no. 5 (2001): 687–709.

Boellstorff, Tom. "The Perfect Path: Gay Men, Marriage, Indonesia." *GLQ: A Journal of Lesbian and Gay Studies* 5, no. 4 (1999): 475–509.

———. *The Gay Archipelago: Sexuality and Nation in Indonesia*. Princeton, NJ: Princeton University Press, 2005.

Bourdieu, Pierre, and Loïc J. D. Wacquant. *An Invitation to Reflexive Sociology*. Chicago: University of Chicago Press, 1992.

Boyd, Nan Alamilla. *Wide-Open Town: A History of Queer San Francisco to 1965*. Berkeley: University of California Press, 2003.

Brekhus, Wayne H. *Peacocks, Chameleons, Centaurs: Gay Suburbia and the Grammar of Social Identity*. Chicago: University of Chicago Press, 2003.

Brown, Michael. "Counting on Queer Geography." In *Geographies of Sexualities*, edited by Kath Browne, Jason Lim, and Gavin Brown, 206–14. London: Ashgate, 2007.

Buffington, Rob. "Los Jotos: Contested Visions of Homosexuality in Modern Mexico." In *Sex and Sexuality in Latin America*, edited by Daniel Balderston and Donna J. Guy, 118–32. New York: NYU Press, 1977.

———. "Homophobia and the Mexican Working Class, 1900–1910." In *The Famous 41: Sexuality and Social Control in Mexico, 1901*, edited by Robert McKee Irwin, Edward J. McCaughan, and Michelle Rocío Nasser, 193–225. New York: Palgrave Macmillan, 2003.

Cáceres, Carlos F., and Ana M. Rosasco. *Secreto a voces: Homoerotismo masculino en Lima; Culturas, identidades y salud sexual* [Open secret: Male homoeroticism in Lima; Cultures, identities, and sexual health]. Lima: Universidad Peruana Cayetano Heredia, 2000.

Callen, Michael. *How to Have Sex in an Epidemic*. New York: News from the Front Publications, 1983.

Caluya, Gilbert. "'The Rice Steamer': Race, Desire and Affect in Sydney's Gay Scene." *Australian Geographer* 39, no. 3 (2008): 283–92.

Canaday, Margot. *The Straight State: Sexuality and Citizenship in Twentieth-Century America*. Princeton, NJ: Princeton University Press, 2009.

Cantú, Lionel, Jr. "Entre Hombres/Between Men: Latino Masculinities and Homosexualities." In *Gay Masculinities*, edited by Peter Nardi, 224–46. Thousand Oaks, CA: SAGE Publications, 1999.

———. "A Place Called Home: A Queer Political Economy of Mexican Immigrant Men's Family Experiences." In *Queer Families, Queer Politics: Challenging Culture and the State*, edited by Mary Bernstein and Renate Reimann, 112–36. New York: Columbia University Press, 2001.

———. "*De Ambiente*: Queer Tourism and the Shifting Boundaries of Mexican Male Sexualities." *GLQ: A Journal of Lesbian and Gay Studies* 8, nos. 1–2 (2002): 139–66.

———. *The Sexuality of Migration: Border Crossings and Mexican Immigrant Men*. Edited by Nancy A. Naples and Salvador Vidal-Ortiz. New York: NYU Press, 2009.

Cantú, Lionel, Jr., Eithne Luibhéid, and Alexandra Minna Stern. "Well-Founded Fear: Political Asylum and the Boundaries of Sexual Identity in the U.S.-Mexico Borderlands." In Luibhéid and Cantú Jr., *Queer Migrations*, 61–74.

Carballo-Diéguez, Alex, Curtis Dolezal, Luis Nieves, Francisco Diaz, Carlos Decena, and Ivan Balan. "Looking for a Tall, Dark, Macho Man . . . Sexual-Role Behaviour Variations in Latino Gay and Bisexual Men." *Culture, Health and Sexuality* 6, no. 2 (March–April 2004): 159–71.

Carrier, Joseph M. "Urban Mexican Male Encounters: An Analysis of Participants and Coping Strategies." PhD diss., University of California, Irvine, 1972.

———. "Cultural Factors Affecting Urban Mexican Male Homosexual Behavior." *Archives of Sexual Behavior* 5 (1976): 103–24.

———. "Family Attitudes and Mexican Male Homosexuality." *Urban Life* 5, no. 3 (1976): 359–75.

———. *De los Otros: Intimacy and Homosexuality among Mexican Men*. New York: Columbia University Press, 1995.

———. *De los otros: Intimidad y homosexualidad entre los hombres del occidente y el noroeste de México*. Guadalajara: Editorial Pandora, 2003.

Carrillo, Héctor. "Cultural Change, Hybridity and Contemporary Male Homosexuality in Mexico." *Culture, Health and Sexuality* 1, no. 3 (1999): 223–38.

———. *The Night Is Young: Sexuality in Mexico in the Time of AIDS*. Chicago: University of Chicago Press, 2002.

———. "Sexual Migration, Cross-Cultural Encounters, and Sexual Health." *Sexuality Research and Social Policy* 1, no. 3 (2004): 58–70.

———. "Imagining Modernity: Sexuality, Policy, and Social Change in Mexico." *Sexuality Research and Social Policy* 4, no. 3 (2007): 74–91.

———. "Leaving Loved Ones Behind: Mexican Gay Men's Migration to the USA." In *Mobility, Sexuality and AIDS*, edited by Felicity Thomas, Mary Haour-Knipe, and Peter Aggleton, 24–39. London: Routledge, 2009.

———. "Immigration and LGBT Rights in the USA: Ironies and Constraints in US Asylum Cases." In *Routledge Handbook of Sexuality, Health and Rights*, edited by Peter Aggleton and Richard Parker, 444–52. London: Routledge, 2010.

———. "How Latin Culture Got More Gay." *New York Times*, May 16, 2013. Accessed March 17, 2017. http://www.nytimes.com/2013/05/17/opinion/how-latin-culture-got-more-gay.html?_r=0.

Carrillo, Héctor, and Jorge Fontdevila. "Rethinking Sexual Initiation: Pathways to Identity Formation among Gay and Bisexual Mexican Male Youth." *Archives of Sexual Behavior* 40 (2011): 1241–54.

———. "Border Crossings and Shifting Sexualities among Mexican Gay Immigrant Men: Beyond Monolithic Conceptions." *Sexualities* 17, no. 8 (2014): 919–38.

Carrillo, Héctor, Jorge Fontdevila, Jaweer Brown, and Walter Gómez. "Risk across Borders: Sexual Contexts and HIV Prevention Challenges among Mexican Gay and Bisexual Immigrant Men." August 2008. Accessed March 17, 2017. http://caps.ucsf.edu/uploads/projects/Trayectos/monograph/index.html.

Carrillo, Héctor, and Amanda Hoffman. "From MSM to Heteroflexibilities: Non-Exclusive Straight Male Identities and Their Implications for HIV Prevention and Health Promotion." *Global Public Health* 11, nos. 7–8 (2016): 923–36.

———. "'Straight with a Pinch of Bi': The Construction of Heterosexuality as an Elastic Category among adult U.S. Men." *Sexualities* (2017): 1–19. Accessed March 17, 2017. doi:10.1177/1363460716678561.

Cartwright, Ben. "North Park Bar and Dance Club Bacchus House Closes after Nearly 10 Years." *San Diego Gay and Lesbian News*, December 9, 2010. Accessed March 17, 2017. http://sdgln.com/news/2010/12/09/north-park-bar-and-dance-club-bacchus-house-closes-after-nearly-10-years.

Cass, Vivienne. "Homosexual Identity: A Concept in Need of Definition." *Journal of Homosexuality* 9, no. 2/3 (1983–84): 105–26.

Catania, Joseph A., Dennis Osmond, Ronald D. Stall, Lance Pollack, Jay P. Paul, Sally Blower, Diane Binson, et al. "The Continuing HIV Epidemic among Men Who Have Sex with Men." *American Journal of Public Health* 91, no. 6 (2001): 907–14.

Centers for Disease Control and Prevention. "HIV/AIDS among Racial/Ethnic Minority Men Who Have Sex with Men—United States, 1989–1998." *Morbidity and Mortality Weekly Report* (June 14, 2000): 4–11.

———. *HIV Surveillance Report, 2014* 26 (2015): 1–123. Accessed March 17, 2017. http://www.cdc.gov/hiv/library/reports/surveillance/.

Cerruti, Marcela, and Douglas S. Massey. "On The Auspices of Female Migration from Mexico to the United States." *Demography* 38, no. 2 (2001): 187–200.

Chambers, Iain. *Migrancy, Culture, Identity*. London: Routledge, 1994. Page 3 quoted in Altman, *Global Sex*, 17.

Chauncey, George. *Gay New York: Gender, Urban Culture, and the Making of the Gay Male World*. New York: Basic Books, 1994.

Chavez, Leo R. *Shadowed Lives: Undocumented Immigration in American Society*. New York: Harcourt Brace Jovanovich, 1992.

———. "Spectacle in the Desert: The Minuteman Project on the U.S.-Mexico Border." In *Global Vigilantes: Anthropological Perspectives on Justice and Violence*, edited by David Pratten and Atreyee Sen, 25–46. New York: Columbia University Press, 2008.

Chávez, Víctor. "DF no es el estado 32, aclaran legisladores [DF is not the 32nd state, clarify legislators]." *El Financiero*, January 21, 2016. Accessed March 17, 2017. http://www.elfinanciero.com.mx/nacional/df-no-es-el-estado-32-aclaran-legisladores.html.

Cheng, Sealing. *On the Move for Love: Migrant Entertainers and the U.S. Military in South Korea*. Philadelphia: University of Pennsylvania Press, 2010.

Clark, Jesse, Javier Salvatierra, Eddy Segura, Ximena Salazar, Kelika Konda, Amaya Perez-Brumer, Eric Hall, et al. "*Moderno* Love: Sexual Role-Based Identities and HIV/STI Prevention among Men Who Have Sex with Men in Lima, Peru." *AIDS and Behavior*, no. 17 (2012): 1313–28.

Coleman, Mathew. "US Immigration Law and Its Geographies of Social Control: Lessons from Homosexual Exclusion during the Cold War." *Environment and Planning D: Society and Space* 26 (2008): 1096–114.

Connell, R. W. "A Very Straight Gay: Masculinity, Homosexual Experience, and the Dynamics of Gender." *American Sociological Review* 57, no. 6 (1992): 735–51.

Connell, Raewyn. "The Northern Theory of Globalization." *Sociological Theory* 25, no. 4 (2007): 368–85.

Cornelius, Wayne A. "The Structural Embeddedness of Demand for Mexican Immigrant Labor: New Evidence from California." In Suárez-Orozco, *Crossings*, 115–44.

Crammond, Bradley R., and Gemma Carey. "What Do We Mean by 'Structure' When We Talk about Structural Influences on the Social Determinants of Health Inequalities?" *Social Theory and Health* 15 (2017): 84–98.

Cruikshank, Barbara. *The Will to Empower: Democratic Citizens and Other Subjects*. Ithaca, NY: Cornell University Press, 1999.

Cruz-Malavé, Arnaldo, and Martin F. Manalansan IV, eds. *Queer Globalizations: Citizenship and the Afterlife of Colonialism*. New York: NYU Press, 2002.

Decena, Carlos Ulises. "Profiles, Compulsory Disclosure and Ethical Sexual Citizenship in the Contemporary USA." *Sexualities* 11, no. 4 (2008): 397–413.

———. *Tacit Subjects: Belonging and Same-Sex Desire among Dominican Immigrant Men*. Durham, NC: Duke University Press, 2011.

Dehesa, Rafael de la. *Queering the Public Sphere in Mexico and Brazil: Sexual Rights Movements in Emerging Democracies*. Durham, NC: Duke University Press, 2010.

Desforges, Luke, Rhys Jones, and Mike Woods. "New Geographies of Citizenship." *Citizenship Studies* 9, no. 5 (2005): 439–51.

Díaz, Rafael M. *Latino Gay Men and HIV*. New York: Routledge, 1998.

Díez, Jordi. "La trayectoria política del movimiento Lésbico-Gay en México" [The political trajectory of the lesbian-gay movement in Mexico]. *Estudios Sociológicos* 29, no. 86 (2011): 687–712.

———. "Explaining Policy Outcomes: The Adoption of Same-Sex Unions in Buenos Aires and Mexico City." *Comparative Political Studies* 46, no. 2 (2012): 212–35.

Dobkin, Donald S. "Challenging the Doctrine of Consular Nonreviewability in Immigration Cases." *Georgetown Immigration Law Journal* 24 (2010): 113–46.

Donato, Katharine M., Brandon Wagner, and Evelyn Patterson. "The Cat and Mouse Game at the Mexico-US Border: Gendered Patterns and Recent Shifts." *International Migration Review* 42 no. 2 (2008): 330–59.

Dowsett, Gary W. *Practicing Desire: Homosexual Sex in the Era of AIDS*. Stanford, CA: Stanford University Press, 1996.

———. "Baring Essentials: Science as Desire." *Sexuality Research and Social Policy* 1, no. 1 (2004): 69–82.

———. "Abjection. Objection. Subjection: Rethinking the History of AIDS in Australian Gay Men's Futures." *Culture, Health and Sexuality* (2017): 1–13. Accessed March 23, 2017. doi:10.1080/13691058.2016.1273392.

Duggan, Lisa. "The New Homonormativity: The Sexual Politics of Neoliberalism." In *Materializing Democracy: Toward a Revitalized Cultural Politics*, edited by Russ Castronovo and Dana D. Nelson, 175–94. Durham, NC: Duke University Press, 2002.

Durand, Jorge. "Migration and Integration: Intermarriages among Mexicans and Non-Mexicans in the United States." In Suárez-Orozco, *Crossings*, 209–21.

Durand, Jorge, and Douglas S. Massey. "Mexican Migration to the United States: A Critical Review." *Latin American Research Review* 27, no. 2 (1992): 3–42.

Engardio, Joel P. "You Can't Be Gay—You're Latino: A Gay Latino Identity Struggles to Emerge, Somewhere between the Macho Mission and Caucasian Castro." *SF Weekly*, April 14, 1999. Accessed March 3, 2017. http://archives.sfweekly .com/sanfrancisco/you-cant-be-gay-youre-latino/Content?oid=2136378.

Epps, Brad, Keja Valens, and Bill Johnson González, eds. *Passing Lines: Sexuality and Immigration*. Cambridge, MA: Harvard University Press, 2005.

Epstein, Steven. "A Queer Encounter: Sociology and the Study of Sexuality." *Sociological Theory* 12, no. 2 (1994): 188–202.

———. *Impure Science: AIDS, Activism, and the Politics of Knowledge*. Berkeley: University of California Press, 1996.

Epstein, Steven, and Héctor Carrillo. "Immigrant Sexual Citizenship: Intersectional Templates among Mexican Gay Immigrants to the United States." *Citizenship Studies* 18, nos. 3–4 (2014): 259–76.

Escala Rabadán, Luis, and Germán Vega Briones. "Living and Working as Cross-Border Commuters in the Tijuana-San Diego Region." In *The Ties That Bind Us: Mexican Migrants in San Diego County*, edited by Richard Kiy and Christopher Woodruff, 147–74. La Jolla: Center for U.S.-Mexican Studies, University of California, San Diego, 2005.

Espín, Oliva. *Latina Realities: Essays on Healing, Migration, and Sexuality*. Boulder, CO: Westview Press, 1997.

Evans, David T. *Sexual Citizenship: The Material Construction of Sexualities*. London: Routledge, 1993.

Farrer, James. *Opening Up: Youth Sex Culture and Market Reform in Shanghai*. Chicago: University of Chicago Press, 2002.

Fassin, Eric, and Manuela Salcedo. "Becoming Gay? Immigration Policies and the Truth of Sexual Identity." *Archives of Sexual Behavior* 44 (2015): 1117–25.

Featherstone, Mike. "Love and Eroticism: An Introduction." *Theory, Culture and Society* 15, nos. 3–4 (1998): 1–18.

Ferguson, Roderick A. *Aberrations in Black: Toward a Queer of Color Critique*. Minneapolis: University of Minnesota Press, 2003.

Fisher, Diana. "Immigrant Closets: Tactical-Micro-Practices-in-the-Hyphen." *Queer Theory and Communication* 45, no. 2/3/4 (2003): 171–92.

Flegenheimer, Matt, and Vivian Yee. "Jubilant Marchers at Gay Pride Parades Celebrate Supreme Court Ruling." *New York Times*, June 28, 2015. Accessed March 17, 2017. http://www.nytimes.com/2015/06/29/nyregion/jubilant-marchers-at -new-yorks-gay-pride-parade-celebrate-supreme-court-ruling.html.

Flores, René, and Edward Telles. "Social Stratification in Mexico: Disentangling Color, Ethnicity, and Class." *American Sociological Review* 77, no. 3 (2012): 486–94.

Fontdevila, Jorge. "Framing Dilemmas during Sex: A Micro-sociological Approach to HIV Risk." *Social Theory and Health* 7, no. 3 (2009): 241–63.

Fortier, Anne-Marie. "'Coming Home': Queer Migrations and Multiple Evocations of Home." *European Journal of Cultural Studies* 4, no. 4 (2001): 405–24.

———. "Queer Diaspora." In *Handbook of Lesbian and Gay Studies*, edited by Diane Richardson and Steven Seidman, 183–97. Thousand Oaks, CA: SAGE Publications, 2002.

Foucault, Michel. *The History of Sexuality.* Vol. 1, *An Introduction.* New York: Vintage, 1980.

Frankenberg, Ruth. *White Women, Race Matters: The Social Construction of Whiteness.* Minneapolis: University of Minnesota Press, 1993.

Fussell, Elizabeth, and Douglas S. Massey. "The Limits to Cumulative Causation: International Migration from Mexican Urban Areas." *Demography* 41, no. 1 (2004): 151–71.

Gagnon, John H. "Sex Research and Sexual Conduct in the Era of AIDS." *Journal of Acquired Immune Deficiency Syndromes* 1, no. 6 (1988): 593–601.

Gagnon, John H., and William Simon. *Sexual Conduct: The Social Sources of Human Sexuality.* Chicago: Aldine, 1973.

Gallego Montes, Gabriel. *Demografía de lo otro: Biografías sexuales y trayectorias de emparejamiento entre varones de la Ciudad de México* [Demography of the Other: Sexual biographies and partnering trajectories among men in Mexico City]. Mexico City: El Colegio de México, 2010.

Gamson, Joshua, and Dawne Moon. "The Sociology of Sexualities: Queer and Beyond." *Annual Review of Sociology* 30, no. 1 (2004): 47–64.

García-Canclini, Néstor. *Hybrid Cultures: Strategies for Entering and Leaving Modernity.* Minneapolis: University of Minnesota Press, 1995.

García, Faustino. "Cuando sales en grupo ¿cómo pagan la cuenta?" [When you go out as a group, how do you pay the bill?]. *Brújula de Compra de Profeco*, December 18, 2009. Accessed March 17, 2017. http://www.profeco.gob.mx/encuesta /brujula/bruj_2009/bol154_cuenta.asp.

Garip, Filiz. "Discovering Diverse Mechanisms of Migration: The Mexico–US Stream 1970–2000." *Population and Development Review* 38, no. 3 (2012): 393–433.

Garip, Filiz, and Asad L. Asad. "Network Effects in Mexico-U.S. Migration: Disentangling the Underlying Social Mechanisms." *American Behavioral Scientist* 60, no. 10 (2016): 1168–93.

Ghaziani, Amin. "Post-Gay Collective Identity Construction." *Social Problems* 58, no. 1 (2011): 99–125.

———. *There Goes the Gayborhood?* Princeton, NJ: Princeton University Press, 2014.

Goffman, Erving. *Stigma: Notes on the Management of Spoiled Identity.* Englewood Cliffs, NJ: Prentice-Hall, 1963.

Gollnick, Brian. "Silent Idylls, Double Lives: Sex and the City in Salvador Novo's *La estatua de sal.*" *Mexican Studies/Estudios Mexicanos* 21, no. 1 (2005): 231–50.

González-López, Gloria. *Erotic Journeys: Mexican Immigrants and Their Sex Lives.* Berkeley: University of California Press, 2005.

———. *Family Secrets: Stories of Incest and Sexual Violence in Mexico*. New York: NYU Press, 2015.

Goodwin, Jeff, James M. Jasper, and Francesca Polletta, eds. *Passionate Politics: Emotions and Social Movements*. Chicago: University of Chicago Press, 2001.

Gopinath, Gayatri. "Funny Boys and Girls: Notes on a Queer South Asian Planet." In *Asian American Sexualities: Dimensions of the Gay and Lesbian Experience*, edited by Russell Leong, 119–27. New York: Routledge, 1996.

Gould, Deborah B. *Moving Politics: Emotion and ACT UP's Fight against AIDS*. Chicago: University of Chicago Press, 2009.

Gray, Mary L. *Out in the Country: Youth, Media, and Queer Visibility in Rural America*. New York: NYU Press, 2009.

Gray, Mary L., Brian J. Gilley, and Colin R. Johnson, eds. *Queering the Countryside: New Frontiers in Rural Queer Studies*. New York: NYU Press, 2016.

Green, Adam Isaiah. "Erotic Habitus: Toward a Sociology of Desire." *Theory and Society* 37 (2008): 597–626.

———. "The Social Organization of Desire: The Sexual Fields Approach." *Sociological Theory* 26, no. 1 (2008): 25–50.

———, ed. *Sexual Fields: Toward a Sociology of Collective Sexual Life*. Chicago: University of Chicago Press, 2013.

Greene, Theodore. "Gay Neighborhoods and the Rights of the Vicarious Citizen." *City and Community* 13, no. 2 (2014): 99–118.

Gutmann, Matthew C. *The Meanings of Macho: Being a Man in Mexico City*. Berkeley: University of California Press, 1996.

———. "Dystopian Travels in Gringolandia: Engendering Ethnicity among Mexican Migrants to the United States." *Ethnicities* 4 no. 4 (2004): 477–500.

Guzmán, Manolo. " 'Pa'la escuelita con mucho cuida'o y por la orillita': A Journey through the Contested Terrains of the Nation and Sexual Orientation." In *Puerto Rican Jam: Rethinking Colonialism and Nationalism*, edited by Frances Negrón-Muntaner and Ramón Grosfoguel, 209–28. Minneapolis: University of Minnesota Press, 1997.

Hames-García, Michael, and Ernesto Javier Martínez, eds. *Gay Latino Studies: A Critical Reader*. Durham, NC: Duke University Press, 2011.

Han, Alan. "I Think You're the Smartest Race I've Ever Met: Racialised Economies of Queer Male Desire." *Australian Critical Race and Whiteness Studies Association (ACRAWSA)* 2, no. 2 (2006): 1–14.

Han, C. Winter. *Geisha of a Different Kind: Race and Sexuality in Gaysian America*. New York: NYU Press, 2015.

Han, Chong-suk. "No Fats, Femmes, or Asians: The Utility of Critical Race Theory in Examining the Role of Gay Stock Stories in the Marginalization of Gay Asian Men." *Contemporary Justice Review* 11, no. 1 (2008): 11–22.

Hawley, John, ed. *Postcolonial, Queer: Theoretical Intersections*. Albany: State University of New York Press, 2001.

Heaphy, Brian. "Gay Identities and the Culture of Class." *Sexualities* 14, no. 1 (2011): 42–62.

Herdt, Gilbert, ed. *Sexual Cultures and Migration in the Era of AIDS: Anthropological and Demographic Perspectives*. New York: Oxford University Press, 1997.

———, ed. *Moral Panics, Sex Panics: Fear and the Fight over Sexual Rights*. New York: NYU Press, 2009.

Herdt, Gilbert, and Robert J. Stoller. *Intimate Communications: Erotics and the Study of Culture*. New York: Columbia University Press, 1990.

Higgins, Michelle. "Practical Traveler: New Passport Rules in Effect Today." *New York Times*, June 1, 2009. Accessed March 2, 2017. http://intransit.blogs.nytimes .com/2009/06/01/practical-traveler-new-passport-rules-in-effect-today/.

Hirsch, Jennifer S. *A Courtship after Marriage: Sexuality and Love in Mexican Transnational Families*. Berkeley: University of California Press, 2003.

Hoang, Kimberly Kay. *Dealing in Desire: Asian Ascendancy, Western Decline, and the Hidden Currencies of Global Sex Work*. Oakland: University of California Press, 2015.

Hogan, Steve, and Lee Hudson. *Completely Queer: The Gay and Lesbian Encyclopedia*. New York: Henry Holt, 1998.

Holston, James, and Arjun Appadurai. Introduction to *Cities and Citizenship*, edited by James Holston, 1–18. Durham, NC: Duke University Press, 1999.

Hondagneu-Sotelo, Pierrette. *Gendered Transitions: Mexican Experiences of Immigration*. Berkeley: University of California Press, 1994.

Hoppe, Trevor. "Controlling Sex in the Name of 'Public Health': Social Control and Michigan HIV Law." *Social Problems* 60, no. 1 (2013): 27–49.

———. "From Sickness to Badness: The Criminalization of HIV in Michigan." *Social Science and Medicine* 101 (2014): 139–47.

Horevitz, Elizabeth, and Kurt C. Organista. "The Mexican Health Paradox: Expanding the Explanatory Power of the Acculturation Construct." *Hispanic Journal of Behavioral Sciences* 35, no. 1 (2012): 3–34.

Houlbrook, Matt. *Queer London: Perils and Pleasures in the Sexual Metropolis, 1918–1957*. Chicago: University of Chicago Press, 2005.

Howard, John. *Men like That: A Southern Queer History*. Chicago: University of Chicago Press, 1999.

Howe, Cymene. "Sexual Borderlands: Lesbian and Gay Migration, Human Rights, and the Metropolitan Community Church." *Sexuality Research and Social Policy* 4, no. 2 (2007): 88–106.

Hubbard, Phil. "Sex Zones: Intimacy, Citizenship and Public Space." *Sexualities* 4, no. 1 (2001): 51–71.

Human Rights Watch/Immigration Equality. *Family Unvalued: Discrimination, Denial, and the Fate of Binational Same-Sex Couples under U.S. Law*. New York: Human Rights Watch/Immigration Equality, 2006.

Hunt, Linda M., Suzanne Schneider, and Brendon Comer. "Should 'Acculturation' Be a Variable in Health Research? A Critical Review of Research on US Hispanics." *Social Science and Medicine* 59 (2004): 973–86.

Irwin, Robert McKee. "La Pedo Embotellado: Sexual Roles and Play in Salvador Novo's La Estatua de Sal." *Studies in the Literary Imagination* 33, no. 1 (2000): 125–32.

Irwin, Robert McKee, Michelle Rocío Nasser, and Edward J. McCaughan, eds. *The Famous 41: Sexuality and Social Control in Mexico, 1901*. New York: Palgrave Macmillan, 2003.

Isin, Engin F. "City.State: Critique of Scalar Thought." *Citizenship Studies* 11, no. 2 (2007): 211–28.

Islas Vela, David Román. "Zona Rosa: El territorio queer de la Ciudad de México; El consumo de la disidencia, identidades, cuerpos y habitantes" [Zona Rosa: The queer territory of Mexico City; Consumption by the dissidence, identities, bodies and inhabitants]. *Revista Latino-americana de Geografia e Gênero* 6, no. 2 (2015): 192–212.

Jackson, Peter A. "An Explosion of Thai Identities: Global Queering and Reimagining Queer Theory." *Culture, Health and Sexuality* 2, no. 4 (2000): 405–24.

———. " 'That's What Rice Queens Study!' White Gay Desire and Representing Asian Homosexualities." *Journal of Australian Studies* 24, no. 65 (2000): 181–88.

———. "Pre-gay, Post-queer: Thai Perspectives on Proliferating Gender/Sex Diversity in Asia." *Journal of Homosexuality* 40, no. 3/4 (2001): 1–25.

Jacobson, Matthew Frye. *Whiteness of a Different Color: European Immigrants and the Alchemy of Race*. Cambridge, MA: Harvard University Press, 1998.

Jiménez Marce, Rogelio. "Ser gay en la ciudad de México" [Being gay in Mexico City]. *Letras Históricas*, no. 10 (2014): 259–63.

Johnson, Carol. "Heteronormative Citizenship and the Politics of Passing." *Sexualities* 5, no. 3 (2002): 317–36.

Kandel, William, and Douglas S. Massey. "The Culture of Mexican Migration: A Theoretical and Empirical Analysis." *Social Forces* 80, no. 3 (March 2002): 981–1004.

Kasyak, Emily. "Midwest or Lesbian? Gender, Rurality, and Sexuality." *Gender and Society* 26, no. 6 (2012): 825–48.

Kippax, Susan, and Kane Race. "Sustaining Safe Practice: Twenty Years On." *Social Science and Medicine* 57 (2003): 1–12.

Kippax, Susan, and Gary Smith. "Anal Intercourse and Power in Sex between Men." *Sexualities* 4, no. 4 (2001): 413–34.

Kippax, Susan, and Niamh Stephenson. "Beyond the Distinction between Biomedical and Social Dimensions of HIV: Prevention through the Lens of a Social Public Health." *American Journal of Public Health* 102, no. 5 (2012): 789–99.

Kitzinger, Jenny. " 'I'm Sexually Attractive but I'm Powerful': Young Women Negotiating Sexual Reputation." *Women's Studies International Forum* 18, no. 2 (1995): 187–96.

Kiy, Richard. Preface to Kiy and Woodruff, *The Ties That Bind Us*, vii–xi.

Kiy, Richard, and Christopher Woodruff., eds. *The Ties That Bind Us: Mexican Migrants in San Diego County*. La Jolla: Center for U.S.-Mexican Studies, University of California, San Diego, 2005.

Koppenfels, Amanda Klekowski von. *Migrants or Expatriates?: Americans in Europe*. Basingstoke, UK: Palgrave Macmillan, 2014.

Kulick, Don. *Travesti: Sex, Gender, and Culture among Brazilian Transgendered Prostitutes*. Chicago: University of Chicago Press, 1998.

Laguarda, Rodrigo. "El ambiente: Espacios de sociabilidad gay en la ciudad de México, 1968–1982" [El ambiente: Spaces of gay sociability in Mexico City, 1968–1982]. *Secuencia*, no. 78 (2010): 151–74.

———. *Ser gay en la ciudad de México: Lucha de representaciones y apropiación de una identidad, 1968–1982* [Being gay in Mexico City: Representational struggle and appropriation of an identity, 1968–1982]. Mexico City: CIESAS, Instituto Mora, 2010 [2009].

———. *La calle de Amberes: Gay street de la Ciudad de México* [Amberes Street: Gay street of Mexico City]. Mexico City: Universidad Nacional Autónoma de México, 2011.

Lamont, Michèle. "Toward a Comparative Sociology of Valuation and Evaluation." *Annual Review of Sociology* 38 (2012): 201–21.

Lamont, Michèle, and Virág Molnár. "The Study of Boundaries in the Social Sciences." *Annual Review of Sociology* 28 (2002): 167–95.

Lamont, Michèle, and Mario Small. "How Culture Matters: Enriching Our Understanding of Poverty." In *The Colors of Poverty*, edited by Ann Chih Lin and David R. Harris, 76–102. New York: Russell Sage, 2008.

Lamont, Michèle, and Ann Swidler. "Methodological Pluralism and the Possibilities and Limits of Interviewing." *Qualitative Sociology* 37 (2014): 153–71.

Lamont, Michèle, and Laurent Thévenot. "Introduction: Toward a Renewed Comparative Cultural Sociology." In *Rethinking Comparative Cultural Sociology: Repertoires of Evaluation in France and the United States*, edited by Michèle Lamont and Laurent Thévenot, 1–22. Cambridge: Cambridge University Press, 2000.

Lancaster, Roger N. *Life Is Hard: Machismo, Danger, and the Intimacy of Power in Nicaragua*. Berkeley: University of California Press, 1992.

———. *Sex Panic and the Punitive State*. Berkeley: University of California Press, 2011.

Langarita Adiego, José A., and María Alejandra Salguero Velázquez. "Sexiled in Mexico City: Urban Migrations Motivated by Sexual Orientation." *Bulletin of Latin American Research* 36, no.1 (2017): 68–81.

Langdridge, Darren. "Voices from the Margins: Sadomasochism and Sexual Citizenship." *Citizenship Studies* 10, no. 4 (2006): 373–89.

Langdridge, Darren, and Trevor Butt. "The Erotic Construction of Power Exchange." *Journal of Constructivist Psychology* 18 (2005): 65–73.

Leap, William L., and Tom Boellstorff, eds. *Speaking in Queer Tongues: Globalization and Gay Language*. Urbana: University of Illinois Press, 2004.

Lipsitz, George. *The Possessive Investment in Whiteness: How White People Profit from Identity Politics*. Philadelphia: Temple University Press, 1998.

List, Mauricio. *Jóvenes corazones gay en la Ciudad de México* [Young gay hearts in Mexico City]. Puebla: Benemérita Universidad Autónoma de Puebla, Facultad de Filosofía y Letras, 2005.

Lorde, Audre. "Uses of the Erotic: The Erotic as Power." In *Sister Outsider: Essays and Speeches*, 53–59. New York: Crossing Press, 1984.

Luibhéid, Eithne. "Looking like a Lesbian: The Organization of Sexual Monitoring at the United States-Mexican Border." *Journal of History of Sexuality* 8, no. 3 (1998): 477–506.

———. *Entry Denied: Controlling Sexuality at the Border*. Minneapolis: University of Minnesota Press, 2002.

———. Introduction to Luibhéid and Cantú Jr., *Queer Migrations*, ix–xlvi.

———. "Sexuality, Migration, and the Shifting Line between Legal and Illegal Status." *GLQ: A Journal of Lesbian and Gay Studies* 14, nos. 2–3 (2008): 289–315.

Luibhéid, Eithne, and Lionel Cantú Jr., eds. *Queer Migrations: Sexuality, U.S. Citizenship, and Border Crossings*. Minneapolis: University of Minnesota Press, 2005.

Lumsden, Ian. *Homosexualidad, sociedad y estado en México* [Homosexuality, society, and the state in Mexico]. Mexico City: Solediciones, 1991.

Macías-González, Víctor M. "The Bathhouse and Male Homosexuality in Porfirian Mexico." In *Masculinity and Sexuality in Modern Mexico*, edited by Víctor M. Macías-González and Anne Rubenstein, 25–52. Albuquerque: University of New Mexico Press, 2012.

———. "The Transnational Homophile Movement and the Development of Domesticity in Mexico City's Homosexual Community, 1930–70." *Gender and History* 26, no. 3 (2014): 519–44.

Mai, Nick. "The Fractal Queerness of Non-heteronormative Migrants Working in the UK Sex Industry." *Sexualities* 15, no. 5/6 (2012): 570–85.

Malkin, Victoria. "'We Go to Get Ahead': Gender and Status in Two Mexican Migrant Communities." *Latin American Perspectives* 31, no. 5 (2004): 75–99.

Manalansan, Martin F., IV. "In the Shadows of Stonewall: Examining Gay Transnational Politics and the Diaspora Dilemma." *GLQ: A Journal of Lesbian and Gay Studies* 2, no. 4 (1995): 425–39.

———. *Global Divas: Filipino Gay Men in the Diaspora*. Durham, NC: Duke University Press, 2003.

———. "Migrancy, Modernity, Mobility: Quotidian Struggles and Queer Diasporic Intimacy." In Luibhéid and Cantú Jr., *Queer Migrations*, 146–60.

———. "Race, Violence, and Neoliberal Spatial Politics in the Global City." *Social Text* 23, nos. 3–4 (2005): 141–55.

———. "Queer Intersections: Sexuality and Gender in Migration Studies." *International Migration Review* 40, no. 1 (2006): 224–49.

Marquet, Antonio. *El coloquio de las perras* [The colloquium of the bitches]. Mexico City: Universidad Autónoma Metropolitana, 2010.

Massey, Douglas S. "Dimensions of the New Immigration to the United States and Prospects for Assimilation." *Annual Review of Sociology* 7 (1981): 57–85.

———. "The Social Organization of Mexican Migration to the United States." *Annals of the American Academy of Political and Social Science* 487 (1986): 102–13.

———. "The Social and Economic Origins of Migration." *Annals of the American Academy of Political and Social Science* 510 (1990): 60–72.

———. "Social Structure, Household Strategies, and the Cumulative Causation of Migration." *Population Index* 56 (1990): 3–26.

Massey, Douglas S., Jorge Durand, and Nolan J. Malone. *Beyond Smoke and Mirrors: Mexican Immigration in an Era of Economic Integration.* New York: Russell Sage Foundation, 2002.

Massey, Douglas S., and Felipe García-España. "The Social Process of International Migration." *Science* 237 (1987): 733–38.

Massey, Douglas S., Luin Goldring, and Jorge Durand. "Continuities in Transnational Migration: An Analysis of Nineteen Mexican Communities." *American Journal of Sociology* 99, no. 6 (1994): 1492–533.

McBride, Dwight A. *Why I Hate Abercrombie and Fitch: Essays on Race and Sexuality.* New York: NYU Press, 2005.

McClintock, Anne. *Imperial Leather: Race, Gender, and Sexuality in the Colonial Contest.* New York: Routledge, 1995.

McGlone, Matthew S., and R. Abigail Pfiester. "The Generality and Consequences of Stereotype Threat." *Sociology Compass* 1, no. 1 (2007): 174–90.

Miano Borruso, Marinella. *Hombre, mujer y muxe' en el Istmo de Tehuantepec* [Man, woman, and muxe' in the Isthmus of Tehuantepec]. Mexico City: Instituto Nacional de Antropología e Historia, Plaza y Valdés, 2002.

Miles, M. B., and A. M. Huberman. *Qualitative Data Analysis: An Expanded Sourcebook.* Thousand Oaks, CA: SAGE Publications, 1994.

Mirandé, Alfredo. "Hombres Mujeres: An Indigenous Third Gender." *Men and Masculinities* (2015). Accessed March 17, 2017. doi:10.1177/1097184X15602746.

Monsiváis, Carlos. *Salvador Novo: Lo marginal en el centro* [Salvador Novo: The marginal in the center]. Mexico City: Ediciones Era, 2004 [2000].

———. *Que se abra esa puerta: Crónicas y ensayos sobre la diversidad sexual* [Let that door open: Chronicles and essays about sexual diversity]. Mexico City: Editorial Paidós, 2010.

Montalvo Fuentes, Guillermo. "Crónica: ¡No son las barras bravas, son las metreras doradas!" [Chronicle: It's not the hardcore bars, but the golden Metro riders]. Colores Urbania Blogspot, November 1, 2012. Accessed March 17, 2017. http://coloresurbania.blogspot.com/2012/11/cronica-no-son-las-barras-bravas-son.html.

———. "Reportaje: El último vagón; Historias íntimas en un espacio público" [Report: The last car; Intimate histories in a public space]. Vanguardia, January 21, 2013. Accessed March 17, 2017. http://www.vanguardia.com.mx/elultimovagonhistoriasintimasenunespaciopublico-1466001.html.

Mora, G. Cristina. "Cross-Field Effects and Ethnic Classification: The Institutionalization of Hispanic Panethnicity, 1965 to 1990." *American Sociological Review* 79, no. 2 (2014): 183–210.

Muñoz, José Esteban. "Feeling Brown, Feeling Down: Latina Affect, the Performativity of Race, and the Depressive Position." *Signs: Journal of Women in Culture and Society* 31, no. 3 (2006): 675–88.

Murray, Stephen O. "Homosexual Categorization in Cross-Cultural Perspective." In *Latin American Male Homosexualities*, edited by Stephen O. Murray, 3–31. Albuquerque: University of New Mexico Press, 1995.

———, ed. *Latin American Male Homosexualities*. Albuquerque: University of New Mexico Press, 1995.

Nagel, Joane. *Race, Ethnicity, and Sexuality: Intimate Intersections, Forbidden Frontiers*. New York: Oxford University Press, 2003.

Naples, Nancy A., and Salvador Vidal-Ortiz. Editors' introduction to *The Sexuality of Migration: Border Crossings and Mexican Immigrant Men*, by Lionel Cantú, 1–20. New York: NYU Press, 2009.

National Museum and Archive of Lesbian and Gay History. *The Gay Almanac*. New York: Berkeley Books, 1996.

Nawrocki, Jim. " 'Rice Queens' and the Men Who Love Them." *Gay and Lesbian Review Worldwide* (March–April 2002): 29–30.

Newsweek staff. "Transcript: Barack Obama's Speech at the 2016 Democratic National Convention." *Newsweek*, July 28, 2016. Accessed March 17, 2017. http://www.newsweek.com/barack-obama-full-text-democratic-national -convention-speech-donald-trump-484836.

Nguyen, Vinh-Kim, Nathalie Bajos, Françoise Dubois-Arberd, Jeffrey O'Malley, and Catherine M. Pirkle. "Remedicalizing an Epidemic: From HIV Treatment as Prevention to HIV Treatment Is Prevention." *AIDS* 25 (2011): 291–93.

Nguyen, Vinh-Kim, Jeffrey O'Malley, and Catherine M. Pirkle. "Correspondence: Remedicalizing an Epidemic; From HIV Treatment as Prevention to HIV Treatment Is Prevention." *AIDS* 25 (2011): 1435.

Norandi, Mariana. "Constitucionales, las bodas gay en el Distrito Federal" [Gay weddings are constitutional in the Federal District]. *La Jornada*, Mexico City, August 6, 2010. Accessed March 6, 2017. http://www.jornada.unam.mx/2010 /08/06/politica/002n1pol.

Novo, Salvador. "Memoir." In *Now the Volcano: An Anthology of Latin American Gay Literature*, edited by Winston Leyland, 11–47. San Francisco: Gay Sunshine Press, 1979.

———. *La estatua de sal* [The salt statue]. Mexico City: Consejo Nacional para la Cultura y las Artes, 2002.

Nuñez Noriega, Guillermo. *Sexo entre varones: Poder y resistencia en el campo sexual* [Sex between men: Power and resistance in the sexual field]. Mexico City: Universidad Nacional Autónoma de México, 1999 [1994].

———. "Reconociendo los placeres, deconstruyendo las identidades: Antropología, patriarcado y homoerotismos en México" [Recognizing pleasures, deconstructing identities: Anthropology, patriarchy, and homoeroticisms in Mexico]. *Desacatos* 6 (2001): 15–34.

———. *Masculinidad e intimidad: Identidad, sexualidad y SIDA* [Masculinity and intimacy: Identity, sexuality, and AIDS]. Mexico City: Porrúa, 2007.

———. *Vidas vulnerables: Hombres indígenas, diversidad sexual y VIH-Sida* [Vulnerable lives: Indian men, sexual diversity, and HIV-AIDS]. Mexico City: EDAMEX, 2009.

———. *Just between Us: An Ethnography of Male Identity and Intimacy in Rural Communities of Northern Mexico*. Tucson: University of Arizona Press, 2014.

Ocampo, Anthony C. "Making Masculinity: Negotiations of Gender Presentation among Latino Gay Men." *Latino Studies* 10 no. 4 (2012): 448–72.

Office of AIDS, California Department of Health Services (CDHS). AIDS Case Registry. March 1, 2001.

Ong, Aihwa. *Flexible Citizenship: The Cultural Politics of Transnationality.* Durham, NC: Duke University Press, 1999.

Ortiz Hernández, Luis, and José Arturo Granados Cosme. "Violencia hacia bisexuales, lesbianas y homosexuales de la Ciudad de México" [Violence toward bisexuals, lesbians and homosexuals in Mexico City]. *Revista Mexicana de Sociología* 65, no. 2 (2003): 265–303.

Padilla, Mark. *Caribbean Pleasure Industry: Tourism, Sexuality, and AIDS in the Dominican Republic.* Chicago: University of Chicago Press, 2007.

Padilla, Mark B., Sheilla Rodríguez-Madera, Nelson Varas-Díaz, and Alixida Ramos-Pibernus. "Trans-Migrations: Border-Crossing and the Politics of Body Modification among Puerto Rican Transgender Women." *International Journal of Sexual Health* 28, no. 4 (2016): 261–77.

Parker, Richard, Delia Easton, and Charles H. Klein. "Structural Barriers and Facilitators in HIV Prevention: A Review of International Research." *AIDS* 14, suppl. 1 (2000): S22–S32.

Parker, Richard G. *Bodies, Pleasures, and Passions: Sexual Culture in Contemporary Brazil.* Boston: Beacon Press, 1991.

———. "The Social and Cultural Construction of Sexual Risk, or How to Have (Sex) Research in an Epidemic." In *Culture and Sexual Risk: Anthropological Perspectives on AIDS*, edited by Han ten Brummelhuis and Gilbert Herdt, 257–69. New York: Routledge, 1995.

———. "Migration, Sexual Subcultures, and HIV/AIDS in Brazil." In *Sexual Cultures and Migration in the Era of AIDS*, edited by Gilbert Herdt, 55–69. Oxford: Clarendon Press, 1997.

———. *Beneath the Equator: Cultures of Desire, Male Homosexuality, and Emerging Gay Communities in Brazil.* New York: Routledge, 1999.

———. "Sexuality, Culture, and Power in HIV/AIDS Research." *Annual Review of Anthropology* 30 (2001): 163–79.

Parker, Richard G., Gilbert Herdt, and Manuel Carballo. "Sexual Culture, HIV Transmission and AIDS Research." *Journal of Sex Research* 28, no. 1 (1991): 77–95.

Parrini, Rodrigo, and Ana Amuchástegui. "Un nombre propio, un lugar común: Subjetividad, ciudadanía y sexualidad en México; El Club Gay Amazonas" [A proper name, a common place: Subjectivity, citizenship, and sexuality in Mexico; the Club Gay Amazonas]. *Debate Feminista* 19, no. 37 (2008): 179–96.

Parrini, Rodrigo, and Alejandro Brito. "Ensayo: Crímenes de odio por homofobia; Un concepto en construcción" [Essay: Homophobic hate crimes; A concept under construction]. Crímenes de Odio, May 13, 2013. Accessed March 17, 2017. http://crimenesdeodiodiversummexico.blogspot.com/2013_05_01_archive.html.

Parrini, Rodrigo, Xóchitl Castañeda, Carlos Magis-Rodríguez, Juan Ruiz, and George Lemp. "Identity, Desire and Truth: Homosociality and Homoeroticism in Mexican Migrant Communities in the USA." *Culture, Health and Sexuality* 13, no. 4 (2011): 415–28.

Parrini Roses, Rodrigo. *Panópticos y laberintos: Subjetivación, deseo y corporalidad en una cárcel de hombres* [Panopticons and labyrinths: Subjectivation, desire and embodiment in a male prison]. Mexico City: El Colegio de México, 2007.

Pascoe, C. J. *Dude, You're a Fag: Masculinity and Sexuality in High School.* Berkeley: University of California Press, 2007.

Passel, Jeffrey, D'Vera Cohn, and Ana Gonzalez-Barrera. "Net Migration from Mexico Falls to Zero—and Perhaps Less." 2012. Accessed March 17, 2017. http://www.pewhispanic.org/files/2012/04/PHC-04-23a-Mexican-Migration .pdf.

Patterson, Orlando. *Freedom.* Vol. 1, *Freedom in the Making of Western Culture.* New York: Basic Books, 1991.

Patton, Cindy, and Benigno Sánchez-Eppler, eds. *Queer Diasporas.* Durham, NC: Duke University Press, 2000.

Payne, Robert, and Cristyn Davies. "Introduction to the Special Section: Citizenship and Queer Critique." *Sexualities* 15, no. 3/4 (2012): 251–56.

Paz, Octavio. *The Labyrinth of Solitude.* New York: Grove Press, 1985 [1950].

Peinado, Jesus, Steven M. Goodreau, Pedro Goicochea, Jorge Vergara, Nora Ojeda, Martin Casapia, Abner Ortiz, et al. "Role Versatility among Men Who Have Sex with Men in Urban Peru." *Journal of Sex Research* 44, no. 3 (2007): 233–39.

Peña, Susana. *¡Oye Loca!: From the Mariel Boatlift to Gay Cuban Miami.* Minneapolis: University of Minnesota Press, 2013.

Peralta, Braulio. *El clóset de cristal* [The crystal closet]. Mexico City: Ediciones B México, 2016.

Philen, Robert C. "A Social Geography of Sex: Men Who Have Sex with Men (MSMs) and Gay Bars on the U.S./Mexican Border." *Journal of Homosexuality* 50, no. 4 (2006): 31–48.

Phua, Voon Chin, and Gayle Kaufman. "The Crossroads of Race and Sexuality: Date Selection among Men in Internet 'Personal' Ads." *Journal of Family Issues* 24, no. 8 (2003): 981–94.

Plummer, Ken. "Symbolic Interactionism and Sexual Conduct: An Emergent Perspective." In *Human Sexual Relations*, edited by Mike Brake, 223–41. New York: Pantheon, 1982.

———. *Intimate Citizenship.* Seattle: University of Washington Press, 2003.

Ponting, Bob. "San Diego Cities among State's Most Conservative, Study Finds." Fox 5 San Diego, August 19, 2014. Accessed March 17, 2017. http://fox5sandi ego.com/2014/08/19/san-diego-cities-among-states-most-conservative-study -finds/.

Poon, Maurice Kwong-Lai, and Peter Trung-Thu Ho. "Negotiating Social Stigma among Gay Asian Men." *Sexualities* 11, no. 1/2 (2008): 245–68.

Portes, Alejandro, and József Borocz. "Contemporary Immigration: Theoretical Perspectives on Its Determinants and Models of Incorporation." *International Migration Review* 23, no. 3 (1989): 606–30.

Portes, Alejandro, Samuel A. Mcleod Jr., and Robert N. Parker. "Immigrant Aspirations." *Sociology of Education* 51 (1978): 241–60.

Portes, Alejandro, and Rubén G. Rumbaut. *Immigrant America: A Portrait*. Berkeley: University of California Press, 2006.

Portes, Alejandro, and Min Zhou. "The New Second Generation: Segmented Assimilation and Its Variants." *Annals of the American Academy of Political and Social Science* 530 (1993): 74–96.

Povinelli, Elizabeth A., and George Chauncey. "Thinking Sexuality Transnationally: An Introduction." *GLQ: A Journal of Lesbian and Gay Studies* 5, no. 4 (1999): 439–49.

Preston, Julia. "Obama Lifts a Ban on Entry into U.S. by H.I.V.-Positive People." *New York Times*, October 30, 2009. Accessed March 17, 2017. http://www.nytimes.com/2009/10/31/us/politics/31travel.html?version=meter+at+8&module=meter-Links&pgtype=Blogs&contentId=&mediaId=&referrer=http%3A%2F%2Fquery.nytimes.com%2Fsearch%2Fsitesearch%2F%3Faction%3Dclick%26contentCollection%26region%3DTopBar%26WT.nav%3Dsearch Widget%26module%3DSearchSubmit%26pgtype%3DHomepage&priority=true&action=click&contentCollection=meter-links-click.

———. "Gay Married Man in Florida Is Approved for Green Card." *New York Times*, June 30, 2013. Accessed March 17, 2017. http://www.nytimes.com/2013/07/01/us/gay-married-man-in-florida-is-approved-for-green-card.html.

Prieur, Annick. *Mema's House, Mexico City: On Transvestites, Queens, and Machos*. Chicago: University of Chicago Press, 1998.

Provencher, Denis M. *Queer French: Globalization, Language, and Sexual Citizenship in France*. Hampshire, England: Ashgate, 2007.

Puri, Jyoti. *Sexual States: Governance and the Struggle over the Antisodomy Law in India*. Durham, NC: Duke University Press, 2016.

Quesada, Uriel, Letitia Gomez, and Salvador Vidal-Ortiz, eds. *Queer Brown Voices: Personal Narratives of Latina/o LGBT Activism*. Austin: University of Texas Press, 2015.

Race, Kane. "Reluctant Objects: Sexual Pleasure as a Problem for HIV Biomedical Prevention." *GLQ: A Journal of Lesbian and Gay Studies* 22, no. 1 (2015): 1–31.

Ramirez-Valles, Jesús. *Compañeros: Latino Activists in the Face of AIDS*. Urbana: University of Illinois Press, 2011.

Randazzo, Timothy J. "Social and Legal Barriers: Sexual Orientation and Asylum in the United States." In Luibhéid and Cantú Jr., *Queer Migrations*, 30–60.

Redacción NotieSe. "Autoridades capitalinas niegan la existencia de crímenes por odio homofóbico" [Mexico City authorities deny the existence of crimes motivated by homophobic hate]. Agencia NotieSe, May 11, 2009. Accessed May 11, 2009. http://www.notiese.org/notiese.php?ctn_id=2863 (site discontinued).

———. "Registran 1310 homicidios por homofobia en México" [1310 Homopho-bic homicides reported in Mexico]. DesdePuebla.com, May 17, 2016. Accessed March 17, 2017. http://desdepuebla.com/registran-1310-homicidios-por-homofobia-en-mexico/128168/.

Reddy, Chandan. "Asian Diasporas, Neoliberalism, and Family: Reviewing the Case for Homosexual Asylum in the Context of Family Rights." *Social Text* 23 (2005): 101–19.

Reyes, Mario Alberto. "Proponen en senado tipificar crímenes por homofobia" [Typification of homophobic crimes proposed in Senate]. Crímenes de Odio, October 31, 2012. Accessed March 17, 2017. http://crimenesdeodiodiversum mexico.blogspot.com/2012/11/proponen-en-senado-tipificar-crimenes .html.

Rivera-Servera, Ramón. *Performing Queer Latinidad: Dance, Sexuality, Politics*. Ann Arbor: University of Michigan Press, 2012.

Rodríguez, Juana María. *Queer Latinidad: Identity Practices, Discursive Spaces*. New York: NYU Press, 2003.

———. *Sexual Futures, Queer Gestures, and Other Latina Longings*. New York: NYU Press, 2014.

Rofel, Lisa. "Qualities of Desire: Imagining Gay Identities in China." *Journal of Lesbian and Gay Studies* 5, no. 4 (1999): 451–74.

———. *Desiring China: Experiments in Neoliberalism, Sexuality, and Public Culture*. Durham, NC: Duke University Press, 2007.

Roque Ramírez, Horacio N. "'That's My Place!': Negotiating Racial, Sexual, and Gender Politics in San Francisco's Gay Latino Alliance, 1975–1983." *Journal of the History of Sexuality* 12, no. 2 (2003): 224–58.

Rosenthal, Andrew. "The Court's Same-Sex Marriage Rulings." *New York Times*, June 26, 2013. Accessed March 17, 2017. http://takingnote.blogs.nytimes .com/2013/06/26/the-courts-same-sex-marriage-rulings/.

Roth, Wendy. *Race Migrations: Latinos and the Cultural Transformation of Race*. Stanford, CA: Stanford University Press, 2012.

Rumbaut, Rubén G. "Assimilation and Its Discontents: Between Rhetoric and Reality." *International Migration Review* 31, no. 4 (1997): 923–60.

Rushbrook, Dereka. "Cities, Queer Space, and the Cosmopolitan Tourist." *GLQ: A Journal of Lesbian and Gay Studies* 8, nos. 1–2 (2002): 183–206.

Sáenz, Rogelio. "A Transformation in Mexican Migration to the United States." *Carsey Research, University of New Hampshire*, no. 86 (2015): 1–6. Accessed March 17, 2017. http://scholars.unh.edu/cgi/viewcontent.cgi?article=1246 &context=carsey.

Sánchez Crispín, Álvaro, and Álvaro López López. "Visión geográfica de los lugares gay de la ciudad de México" [Geography of the gay places of Mexico City]. *Cuicuilco, Nueva Época* 7, no. 18 (2000): 1–16.

Sánchez-Eppler, Benigno, and Cindy Patton. "Introduction: With a Passport to Eden." In *Queer Diasporas*, edited by Cindy Patton and Benigno Sánchez-Eppler, 1–14. Durham, NC: Duke University Press, 2000.

Saracino, Japonica Brown. "How Places Shape Identity: The Origins of Distinctive LBQ Identities in Four Small U.S. Cities." *American Journal of Sociology* 121, no. 1 (2015): 1–63.

Savigliano, Marta E. *Tango and the Political Economy of Passion*. Boulder, CO: Westview Press, 1995.

Schippers, Mimi. "Recovering the Feminine Other: Masculinity, Femininity, and Gender Hegemony." *Theory and Society* 36 (2007): 85–102.

Seidman, Steven. "From Identity to Queer Politics: Shifts in Normative Heterosexuality and the Meaning of Citizenship." *Citizenship Studies* 5 (2001): 321–28.

Sewell, William H. "A Theory of Structure: Duality, Agency, and Transformation." *American Journal of Sociology* 98, no. 1 (1992): 1–29.

Shah, Nayan. "Policing Privacy, Migrants, and the Limits of Freedom." *Social Text* 23, nos. 3–4 (2005): 274–84.

Shilling, Chris, and Philip A. Mellor. "Sociology and the Problem of Eroticism." *Sociology* 44 (2010): 435–52.

Simon, William, and John H. Gagnon. "Sexual Scripts: Permanence and Change." *Archives of Sexual Behavior* 15, no. 2 (1986): 97–120.

Singer, Audrey, and Douglas S. Massey. "The Social Process of Undocumented Border Crossing among Mexican Migrants." *International Migration Review* 32, no. 3 (1998): 561–92.

Sipse.com. "Las telenovelas mexicanas, un negocio muy lucrativo" [Mexican telenovelas: A very lucrative business]. Sipse.com, October 14, 2013. Accessed March 17, 2017. http://sipse.com/entretenimiento/las-telenovelas-mexicanas -un-negocio-muy-lucrativo-56158.html.

Small, Mario Luis, David J. Harding, and Michèle Lamont. "Reconsidering Culture and Poverty." *Annals of the American Academy of Political and Social Science* 629, no. 1 (2010): 6–27.

Smith, Robert Courtney. *Mexican New York: Transnational Lives of New Immigrants*. Berkeley: University of California Press, 2006.

Sobo, Elisa J. *Choosing Unsafe Sex: AIDS-Risk Denial among Disadvantaged Women*. Philadelphia: University of Pennsylvania Press, 1995.

Somers, Margaret R. *Genealogies of Citizenship: Markets, Statelessness, and the Right to Have Rights*. Cambridge: Cambridge University Press, 2008.

Stambolis-Ruhstorfer, Michael. "Labels of Love: How Migrants Negotiate (or Not) the Culture of Sexual Identity." *American Journal of Cultural Sociology* 1, no. 3 (2013): 321–45.

Stambolis-Ruhstorfer, Michael, and Abigail C. Saguy. "How to Describe It?: Why the Term Coming Out Means Different Things in the United States and France." *Sociological Forum* 29, no. 4 (2014): 808–29.

Stanley, Alessandra. "Russians Find Their Heroes in Mexican TV Soap Operas." *New York Times*, March 20, 1994. Accessed March 17, 2017. http://www .nytimes.com/1994/03/20/world/russians-find-their-heroes-in-mexican-tv -soap-operas.html.

Stavans, Ilan. "¡Lotería! or, The Ritual of Chance." *Agni* 58 (2003): 30–35.

Stein, Arlene. *The Stranger Next Door: The Story of a Small Community's Battle over Sex, Faith, and Civil Rights*. Boston: Beacon Press, 2001.

Stein, Arlene, and Ken Plummer. "'I Can't Even Think Straight': 'Queer' Theory and the Missing Sexual Revolution in Sociology." *Sociological Theory* 12, no. 2 (1994): 178–87.

Stein, Marc. *City of Sisterly and Brotherly Loves: Lesbian and Gay Philadelphia, 1945–1972*. Chicago: University of Chicago Press, 2000.

Stephen, Lynn. "Sexualities and Genders in Zapotec Oaxaca." *Latin American Perspectives* 29, no. 2 (2002): 41–59.

Stewart, Fiona. "'Once You Get a Reputation, Your Life's Like . . . "Wrecked"': The Implications of Reputation for Young Women's Sexual Health and Well-Being." *Women's Studies International Forum* 22, no. 3 (1999): 373–83.

Stoller, Ann Laura. *Race and the Education of Desire*. Durham, NC: Duke University Press, 1995.

———. *Carnal Knowledge and Imperial Power*. Berkeley: University of California Press, 2002.

Stombler, Mindy. "'Buddies' or 'Slutties': The Collective Sexual Reputation of Fraternity Little Sisters." *Gender and Society* 8, no. 3 (1994): 297–323.

Stone, Ian, and Cherrie Stubs. "Enterprising Expatriates: Lifestyle Migration and Entrepreneurship in Rural Southern Europe." *Entrepreneurship and Regional Development* 19 (2007): 433–50.

Stychin, Carl F. "Sexual Citizenship in the European Union." *Citizenship Studies* 5, no. 3 (2001): 285–301.

Suárez-Orozco, Marcelo M., ed. *Crossings: Mexican Immigration in Interdisciplinary Perspectives*. Cambridge, MA: David Rockefeller Center for Latin American Studies, Harvard University, 1998.

———. "Everything You Ever Wanted to Know about Assimilation but Were Afraid to Ask." *Daedalus* 129, no. 4 (2000): 1–30.

Taylor, Clark L. "El Ambiente: Male Homosexual Social Life in Mexico City." PhD diss., University of California, Berkeley, 1978.

———. "Mexican Male Interaction in Public Context." In *The Many Faces of Homosexuality*, edited by Evelyn Blackwood, 117–36. New York: Harrington Park Press, 1986.

Teunis, Niels. "Sexual Objectification and the Construction of Whiteness in the Gay Male Community." *Culture, Health and Sexuality* 9, no. 3 (2007): 263–75.

Teutle, Alberto, and Mauricio List Reyes. *Húmedos placeres: Sexo entre varones en saunas de la ciudad de Puebla* [Steamy pleasures: Sex between men in the saunas of the city of Puebla]. Mexico City: Universidad Autónoma Metropolitana and La Cifra Editorial, 2015.

Thing, James. "Gay, Mexican and Immigrant: Intersecting Identities among Gay Men in Los Angeles." *Social Identities* 16, no. 6 (2010): 809–31.

Thomas, Felicity, Mary Haour-Knipe, and Peter Aggleton, eds. *Mobility, Sexuality and AIDS*. London: Routledge, 2009.

Toribio, Almeida Jacqueline. "Spanish-English Code-Switching among US Latinos." *International Journal of the Sociology of Language* 158 (2002): 89–119.

Törnqvist, Maria. "Troubling Romance Tourism: Sex, Gender and Class inside the Argentinean Tango Clubs." *Feminist Review* 102 (2012): 21–40.

Toro-Alfonso, José, Mabel López Ortiz, and Karen Nieves Lugo. "Sexualidades migrantes: La emigración de hombres dominicanos gay" [Migrant sexualities: The emigration of Dominican gay men]. *Caribbean Studies* 40, no. 1 (2012): 59–80.

Valocchi, Steve. "The Class-Inflected Nature of Gay Identity." *Social Problems* 46, no. 2 (1999): 207–24.

Valverde, Mariana. "A New Entity in the History of Sexuality: The Respectable Same-Sex Couple." *Feminist Studies* 32, no. 1 (2006): 155–62.

Varsanyi, Monica W. "Interrogating 'Urban Citizenship' vis-à-vis Undocumented Migration." *Citizenship Studies* 10, no. 2 (2006): 229–49.

Vasquez del Aguila, Ernesto. " 'God Forgives the Sin but Not the Scandal': Coming Out in a Transnational Context; Between Sexual Freedom and Cultural Isolation." *Sexualities* 15, no. 2 (2012): 207–24.

Velázquez, Iris. "En México 98 por ciento de las denuncias no se resuelven ni sancionan a los responsables" [In Mexico 98 percent of police cases are unresolved and the perpetrators remain unpunished]. Agencia NotieSe, July 30, 2013. Accessed July 13, 2016. http://www.notiese.org/notiese.php?ctn_id=6820 (site discontinued).

Vidal-Ortiz, Salvador, Carlos Decena, Héctor Carrillo, and Tomás Almaguer. "Revisiting Activos and Pasivos: Toward New Cartographies of Latino/Latin American Male Same-Sex Desire." In *Latina/o Sexualities: Probing Powers, Passions, Practices, and Policies,* edited by Marysol Asencio, 253–73. New Brunswick, NJ: Rutgers University Press, 2010.

Vila, Pablo. "Processes of Identification on the U.S.-Mexico Border." *Social Science Journal* 40 (2003): 607–25.

Villarreal, Andrés. "Stratification by Skin Color in Contemporary Mexico." *American Sociological Review* 75, no. 5 (2010): 652–78.

Viruell-Fuentes, Edna A. "Beyond Acculturation: Immigration, Discrimination, and Health Research among Mexicans in the United States." *Social Science and Medicine* 65 (2007): 1524–35.

Viveros Vigoya, Mara. "Dionysian Blacks: Sexuality, Body, and Racial Order in Colombia." *Latin American Perspectives* 29, no. 2 (2002): 60–77.

Vogler, Stefan. "Legally Queer: The Construction of Sexuality in LGBQ Asylum Claims." *Law and Society Review* 50, no. 4 (2016): 856–89.

Warren, Jonathan W., and France Winddance Twine. "White Americans, the New Minority?: Non-Blacks and the Ever-Expanding Boundaries of Whiteness." *Journal of Black Studies* 28, no. 2 (1997): 200–218.

Waters, Mary C., and Tomás R. Jiménez. "Assessing Immigrant Assimilation: New Empirical and Theoretical Challenges." *Annual Review of Sociology* 31 (2005): 105–25.

Watney, Simon. "Safer Sex as Community Practice." In *AIDS: Individual, Cultural and Policy Dimensions*, edited by Peter Aggleton, Graham Hart, and Peter Davies, 19–33. London: Falmer Press, 1990.

Weeks, Jeffrey. "The Sexual Citizen." *Theory, Culture and Society* 15, nos. 3–4 (1998): 35–52.

Weiss, Margot D. "Working at Play: BDSM Sexuality in the San Francisco Bay Area." *Anthropologica* 48, no. 2 (2006): 229–45.

———. "Gay Shame and BDSM Pride: Neoliberalism, Privacy, and Sexual Politics." *Radical History Review*, no. 100 (2008): 87–101.

Weitman, Sasha. "On the Elementary Forms of the Socioerotic Life." *Theory, Culture and Society* 15, nos. 3–4 (1998): 71–110.

Weston, Kath. *Families We Choose: Lesbians, Gays, Kinship*. New York: Columbia University Press, 1991.

———. "Get Thee to a Big City: Sexual Imaginary and the Great Gay Migration." *GLQ: A Journal of Lesbian and Gay Studies* 2, no. 3 (1998): 253–77.

Wilson, Patrick A., Pamela Valera, Ana Ventuneac, Ivan Balan, Matt Rowe, and Alex Carballo-Diéguez. "Race-Based Sexual Stereotyping and Sexual Partnering among Men Who Use the Internet to Identify Other Men for Bareback Sex." *Journal of Sex Research* 46, no. 5 (2009): 399–413.

Wilson, Tamar Diana. "The Culture of Mexican Migration." *Critique of Anthropology* 30, no. 4 (2010): 399–420.

Wimmer, Andreas. "The Making and Unmaking of Ethnic Boundaries: A Multilevel Process Theory." *American Journal of Sociology* 113, no. 4 (2008): 970–1022.

Yost, Megan R., and L. E. Hunter. "BDSM Practitioners' Understandings of Their Initial Attraction to BDSM Sexuality: Essentialist and Constructionist Narratives." *Psychology and Sexuality* 3, no. 3 (2012): 244–59.

Young, Jonathan. "Pride Criticized for Lacking Diversity: Latin, Ebony, Women's Stages Cut from This Year's Festival." *San Diego LGBT Weekly*, August 25, 2011. Accessed March 17, 2017. http://lgbtweekly.com/2011/08/25/pride-criticized-for-lacking-diversity/.

Young, Robert J. C. *Colonial Desire: Hybridity in Theory, Culture and Race*. London: Routledge, 1995.

Index

Abel (pseud.), 212
acculturation, 182, 265, 323n15
Acosta, Katie L., 72, 180–81
activo. *See* sexual schemas: *pasivo/
    activo*
Adam (pseud.), 140
Adam, Barry D., 320n10, 325n48
Adriana (pseud.), 49–50, 124–25
African Americans, 135, 189,
    208; in gay San Diego, 146,
    148; and power differentials,
    231–32, 233–34; and sexual
    passion, 230; sex with, 249,
    273, 318n57. *See also under*
    attitudes; attraction (Mexican
    immigrants); attraction (US
    non-Latinos); racialization;
    sexual passion
agency, 34; collective, 7, 275; immi-
    grants', 7, 255, 266, 275; indi-
    vidual, 7, 275; in relationships,
    218, 255; sexual, 218, 255
AIDS: 70, 85; activists, 91; epidemic
    in Mexico, 63; groups, 21, 105;
    hospice (Tijuana), 90; patients,
    90, 305n33. *See also* HIV; Latino
    gay: organizations; Latino gay:
    support groups; policy; sexual
    health
Al (pseud.), 211
Alba, Richard D., 265
Aldo (pseud.), 92, 184, 226
Alfaro (pseud.), 138–39, 162–63, 227
aliens, 131, 214. *See also*
    undocumented

Allen, Jafari S., 255
Almaguer, Tomás, 38, 295n9
Alma Latina (AIDS organization,
    San Diego), 150
Altman, Dennis, 28–32, 292n23,
    293n48, 298n23
Alvaro (pseud.), 193, 226
Amberes Street (Mexico City), 65
ambiente, el (Mexico), 21, 37, 45,
    142, 159, 290n2, 294n4
America, 316n26
American: capitalism, 322n26;
    change from exposure to Mexi-
    cans, 267; conservatism, 171;
    as euphemism, 186, 221; lack
    of freedom, 173; mainstream,
    18, 235, 252, 254–55, 265–66,
    276; restrictive culture, 143–
    44. *See also* consulates; sexual
    liberalism
americanos, 138, 188–89, 193,
    316n26
amigo (euphemism for boyfriend),
    87
Amuchástegui, Ana, 39, 60
Andrew (pseud.), 202, 211
Angel (pseud.), 201
Anglos, 192, 196–97, 225. See also
    güeros; US Whites
antigay discrimination: religious,
    76; work-related, 82–84. *See also
    under* gay Mexicans
anti-immigrant sentiment, 160
Anzaldúa, Gloria, 310n20
apiñonados, 190, 316n35

351

materialist approaches. *See* political economy

Matías (pseud.), 85–86, 196, 212

Mauro (pseud.), 212

Máximo (pseud.), 1–5, 22–23, 195, 221, 224, 285nn2–3

"*mayates*," 53–54, 57–58, 241–42, 299n50; *bares de* (San Diego), 149; and dispassion, 227–28; impersonality, 53, 227

Mazatlán (city, Mexico), 111–12

McBride, Dwight A., 189

MCC. *See* Metropolitan Community Church

McClintock, Anne, 33

media: and information on gay issues, 61, 63–64, 140; and social change (Mexico), 63

mejorar la raza, 195

Melchor (pseud.), 22, 171, 186, 224–25

men of color, 212, 233–34; disadvantaged position, 217, 256 (*see also* racism)

mestizo, 316n24

methods, 11–16; triangulation of, 13. *See also* interviews; research

Metro (subway, Mexico City): gay sex and cruising in, 36, 42, 44, 167, 293n1

Metropolitan Community Church (MCC), 142, 149, 153

Mexicali (city, Mexico), 89

Mexican: backwardness, 26–27, 60, 168, 264; conservatism, 21, 38, 63, 170–71, 225; culture, 170, 242; mentality, 168, 171, 192; pride, 216, 256; religiosity, 60, 76–77, 170; respect toward elders, 252; whiteness, 126, 190–91, 200, 214, 316n25. *See also* gay Mexicans; homophobia, Mexican; immigrants (Mexican gay); machismo: Mexican; sexual passion (Mexican/Latino)

Mexican culture of migration, 66, 98, 100–107, 122–23, 260; and attitudes about travel documents, 132; in cities, 102; and failure to achieve sexual autonomy, 104–5, 152; heteronormative expectations, 73–74, 103, 105–6, 113–14, 127, 259

Mexican straight bars (San Diego), 149, 158

Mexico: sexual diversity, 36–65, 258–59; staying to be gay in, 21–22, 97, 128. See also *ambiente, el*; cities (Mexico); closet (Mexico); family (Mexico); gay (Mexico); homosexualities (Mexico); sexual initiation (Mexico); stereotypes: about Mexico; towns (Mexico)

Mexico City, 13, 23, 36–38, 64, 70, 93, 95, 139, 167, 172, 289n41 passim

Mexico-US border. *See* US-Mexico border

Michoacán (state, Mexico), 70, 94, 96

middle class (Mexico), 45, 55–56, 117–18, 122, 130, 294n5, 308n22; expectations, 193

midsized cities (Mexico): *See under* cities (Mexico)

migra, la, 109, 173

migrant, networks, 100–101, 115

migrants: labor, 93, 98, 117 (*see also* motivations for migration: economic); lifestyle, 117 (*see also under* migration; motivations for migration); support by other sexual, 108. *See also* immigrants; undocumented: migrants

migration: and change, 8, 182 (*see also under* post-migration); documents (*see* passports; visas); family supports for, 100; flows, 100; forced, 305n44; gay, 286n5; gay and lesbian supports for, 2, 98, 100–101, 107–10, 109–10; gay culture of, 101, 107–15, 260; justifications for, 73; lifestyle, 6, 286n16; within Mexico, 14, 70, 74, 97, 107, 116–17; and sexuality, 6 (*see also* sexual migration); slowdown in Mexican, 306n5; studies and sexuality, 4–6, 24, 260; trajectories, 26, 116; transgender, 291n5; within the US, 305n43. *See also* arc: of migration; arc: of sexual migration; border crossing; departures from Mexico; deportation; landing pads; Mexican culture of migration; motivations for migration; queer migration; sexual migration; smugglers

Minuteman Project, 124

Mission Neighborhood Health Center (San Francisco), 271

Miss Mexico beauty contest, 151–52

Mitchell (pseud.), 203, 209, 228

modern, 32, 61. *See also* gay (Mexico): modernity

moderno, 322n9

Monsiváis, Carlos, 40, 296nn22–23, 315n24

Montalbán, Ricardo, 229

moreno (referring to Blacks), 210, 212–13